DATE DUE

FE 7 '92			

CHINA'S

UNFINISHED REVOLUTION

JAMES M. ETHRIDGE

CHINA'S

UNFINISHED ✦ REVOLUTION

PROBLEMS
AND PROSPECTS
SINCE MAO

CHINA BOOKS & PERIODICALS, INC.
SAN FRANCISCO

Cover design by Janet Wood
Book design by Janet Wood

Cover photograph by Erica Marcus
Copyright © 1990 by James M. Ethridge. All rights reserved.
Portions of the material in this book originally appeared in
Changing China: The New Revolution's First Decade, 1979–1988,
published by New World Press, Beijing.

Library of Congress Catalog Card Number: 89-60879
ISBN 0-8351-2196-8

Printed in the United States of America by

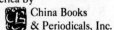 China Books
& Periodicals, Inc.

Contents

Preface

China's Unfinished Revolution is a sequel to, and contains material from, a book on earlier stages of reform which was published in Beijing in 1988 during one of numerous visits and residencies in China since 1979. Because of recent conditions in China it has not been possible in preparing the sequel to have any help from my colleagues on the staff of the original Chinese publisher. It seems appropriate to emphasize here what is usually reserved for last in prefaces: Judgments and errors are entirely my own.

Like its predecessor, *China's Unfinished Revolution* is intended specifically to meet the needs of general readers. It will be of special interest to those who, during the astounding events of the spring of 1989, joined the millions of people already watching the China story with fascinated interest. The book assumes the reader, like most readers, has no specialized knowledge of China or socialism, and wants none.

It gives in clear, nonideological language an overall view of the basics of reform, how things were before reform, what conditions and events made change necessary and possible, and what results and problems have ensued from the implementation of reform.

In particular, the book gives a picture of the last eighteen months or so since the euphoric Thirteenth National Congress, the high point of the reform movement to date. After the congress, reality began even more rapidly to catch up with reform, and inflation, corruption, official profiteering, deteriorating education, and other problems became increasingly unbearable, making the people receptive to the students' call for change and leading to the dramatic marches and protests which preceded the June Fourth Massacre.

China's Unfinished Revolution thus provides a picture of the economic, social, and political conditions of mid-1989 which will be the starting point for the continuing reform China's new leaders have promised.

Among the general readers for whom this book was written there will be some who are critical of modern China because of their own political, religious, social, or moral convictions, and others who lean toward enthusiastic and uncritical admiration. I hope this book will serve both groups equally well.

Regardless of one's attitude toward China and its longstanding attempts to emerge from feudalism, it would seem that the only fair standard for judgment is, "Are the Chinese today better off under their present government than they were before liberation?" This is more open to question than before June 4, but on balance the answer must be "Yes," and the same is true if the question is asked about, say today and 1979, the beginning of the first decade of reform.

To outsiders, the course of Chinese history since 1949 has often seemed to consist of a series of bewildering jolts and struggles and twists and turns (as it has also seemed to the Chinese). It is sometimes hard to keep in mind that the vast social transformation taking place in China dwarfs any such reform ever attempted—including Peter the Great's in Russia, Kemal Ataturk's in Turkey, or the Meiji Restoration period in Japan—and that the process is bound to be convulsive at times. We can only help if asked and wish the Chinese well in their struggle to lead their country into the front rank of nations in the modern world.

James M. Ethridge

One

★

THE RECENT CRISIS

China's Unfinished Revolution is concerned with the history and future of China's reforms, not with its history generally. However, to gain an understanding of new conditions which will profoundly influence the course of reform it is necessary to look first at the historic events of the spring of 1989.

This is being written while the images and sounds of the June Fourth Massacre are still vivid. The governments, journalists, and broadcasters of the world have run through their entire stocks of adjectives of condemnation, trying to put into words the shock of seeing a people's army firing on unarmed compatriots, while the free citizens of the world shake their heads in disbelief and sadness. (The grim individual facts need not be repeated here, but for the record are summarized day-by-day in Appendix Four.)

The dead—soldiers and citizens alike—are to be mourned, and all the more because their deaths were unnecessary.

The student repression may have changed the Chinese people forever, in ways barely felt as yet but that in the long run will be even more significant than the individual lives that were lost. Culminating an ages-long series of historic events that has included such recent infamies as the Great Leap Forward and the Cultural Revolution, it may well be that the June Fourth Massacre was the final evidence needed to destroy their faith in the legitimacy of authority. This would be an epic change in a land with an ancient tradition of reverence for authority, a land which for most of its long history has lived by the commands of emperors and patriarchs.

In any case, however, they have surely lost much of their faith in the legitimacy of the present government, and the degree to which they are able to challenge its authority will determine the pace of reform, especially in the political area, to a far greater degree than any Party program. Although the Party has its roots in a rebellion against authority, it did not eliminate authoritarian attitudes from its own ranks. Indeed, much of the protest at Tiananmen was directed against officials who cling to power and privilege as if it were a hereditary right in a feudal society.

Since the victory of the communists and the founding of the People's Republic in 1949, the legitimacy of their authority has become tarnished sometimes, been buffed up again, become dulled again. But in May 1989 the people of Beijing could still say to soldiers, and believe it was sufficient defense, "You are our army. You are our brothers and sisters. You are Chinese. Our interests are the same as yours. You must not crush the movement." And for days the soldiers, blocked from entering Beijing by massed citizens, seemed to agree, and turned around and drove away.

In the common heritage of the people and the soldiers was a dream their fathers and grandfathers shared when they fought for two generations against a common enemy to establish a genuine people's republic.

The people's republic, when it arrived, endured almost constant travail—hostility and misunderstanding from without, and, within, paranoia, suspicion, intolerance, megalomania, ambition, starvation—a long catalog of evils and excesses. But there was always a hope of better days. Even after the Great Leap Forward and the Cultural Revolution revealed profound defects in Chinese socialism, many people enjoyed a better life than they had ever known. They were hopeful enough to endure hardships and tolerate excesses of authoritarian rule because of the achievements of the Party. They were inspired by the hope that despite the difficult circumstances the Communists had inherited—the pervasive poverty, the wartime devastation, the grim legacy of colonialism and feudalism—their remote and self-perpetuating leadership would pull China through underdevelopment and create an ever-improving society.

Finally, there came a time in mid-May 1989 when it seemed for just a few days that the paternalism, repression, injustice, and intimidation which marred their government might be lifted.

Upon the death in mid-April of Hu Yaobang, a former Party secretary respected by intellectuals, students at Beijing universities demonstrated not only in memory of Hu but for reforms they thought he supported: an end to corruption, freedom of the press, better education, and expanded public involvement in and closer public scrutiny of governmental decisions and actions. Unfortunately, although the students had learned some lessons about organization from their 1986 protests, they suffered from the inexperience of youth and were sometimes discourteous and unnecessarily rigid in their dealings with the government, and their specific demands were changed capriciously several times in the course of the demonstrations. More seriously, they, like everyone else, underestimated the determination of the conservatives to halt reform.

Nevertheless, the Pro-Democracy Movement, as the student movement came to be known, grew, and for several weeks challenged, embarrassed, and humiliated the Party and the government in ways they had never before experienced. (See especially April 17–May 17 in the chronology in Appendix Four.)

As good Chinese officials always do, the leadership attempted for a time to avoid the appearance of any dissension within their ranks, but it was clear from the tone of their public statements that Zhao Ziyang, the rightist (liberal) Party secretary already under stress from leftist (conservative) maneuvers, and Li Peng, the new leftist premier who needed to establish himself, sharply disagreed on how to deal with the students. In retrospect, many observers now maintain that Li Peng actually used the student movement as a means of gaining the upper hand in a power struggle (partly focused on Zhao) that had been underway for years between reformists and conservatives at the highest levels of the Party. (See "Left/Right" in the Mini-Encyclopedia.)

A determined company of 3,000 already skinny students took matters out of the hands of the cliques. They galvanized the nation by going on a hunger strike outside the Great Hall of the People. They demanded, with a little success, to be heard, and their determination began what *In These Times*, a leading US socialist weekly, called "China's fleeting life as a real people's republic."

Correspondent Alisa Joyce described the period this way:

> Imagine an epidemic of manic depression. Imagine a city of 10 million people experiencing mass mood swings from incredulous euphoria and exhilaration to terror, bitter resignation, and furious anger—all within the space of a few days, and sometimes in the course of a single day.
>
> For the last few weeks Beijing has been a city ruled by emotion and dreams. The stereotypically passive Chinese once again have stunned the world with their hidden passions.
>
> While a ferocious power struggle was fought within the ranks of the Chinese Communist Party leadership, the masses took to the streets to create a party of their own. They demanded change and, most importantly, their right to be listened to by their government.
>
> But their mass movement merely pushed forward pre-determined political purgings within the leadership's top echelon. The "Patriotic Democratic Student Movement" that overwhelmed the city and nation in mid-May has, in the short term at least, helped to produce a worst-case-scenario political alignment within the government . . . and those responsible for the housecleaning remain deaf and blind to the people's pleas for progress.

As martial law ended the euphoria on May 20 and indicated that Li Peng and the conservatives were ahead in a no-holds-barred power struggle that had nothing to do with student strikes, a days-long period of unease and uncertainty set in. There were none but the vaguest of clues as to what was happening in a titanic gridlock that had rendered the government immobile in a prolonged internal struggle when public action was sorely needed.

But as Joyce went on to say, "True power in this country is played out on a stage on which the curtains are always drawn. There are no audiences, no public critics, only an after-the-fact press release to explain the final act." Days passed, and there was no press release.

The Final Act

The drawn curtains were stirred occasionally from behind and blind analyses were made as to who might have moved and whether right or left.

Meanwhile, the students, living among squalid and health-threatening conditions in the square, faced with final examinations vital to their futures and recognizing that they could no longer hope for dialogue with the embattled Party, began drifting back to their campuses. The workers, intellectuals, and other citizens who had backed the students and demonstrated with them for weeks knew a climax had passed and began resuming their normal lives.

The most urgent problem facing the Party and the government was solving itself without interference from the cliques behind the curtain.

However, Deng Xiaoping, chairman of the Central Military Commis sion and "paramount leader" of China, decided—out of humiliation, anger, frustration, apprehension, or all of these—that a military crackdown on the students was essential to the safety of the country (although the students had at no time advocated violence, the overthrow of the government, or abandonment of socialism). He obtained backing for his action, out of public view and possibly out of desperation, not from legally constituted bodies authorized to make such decisions but from a miscellany of elderly and mostly retired individuals, former officials who, with only two or three exceptions, have long opposed Deng's and Zhao's reforms.

It was an important determinant of China's future, and a measure of Deng's desperation, that in thus seeking stability he introduced elements of possible serious instability, for he gave the anti-reform faction significantly greater leverage for dictating policy and personnel and gave the army the opportunity it has been seeking for a greater role. One unremarked application of this leverage is that in attacking Zhao (see below) the leftists who attack reform and bourgeois liberalization may well be stalking Deng himself, who supported or even initiated many of Zhao's policies the conservatives are now attacking.

The June Fourth Massacre of unarmed civilians followed Deng's deal with the elders, with the horrifying results that were carried via television to the entire world. (See Appendix Four.) Even the most brutal and repressive of authoritarian regimes understands crowd control and the use of limited force—tear gas, water cannon, specially equipped foot soldiers, other means— and the world is still wondering why in Beijing there was no attempt to clear the already emptying Square and streets with anything but deadly force.

The quickly-fired editor of *Wen Wei Po*, a Hongkong newspaper financed by the Communist Party of China, refused to *biaotai* about the massacre (see *biaotai* in the Mini-Encyclopedia) when he wrote on June 5:

When the Japanese invaded China and eventually Beijing, they did not inflict such a slaughter. After the civil war, Beijing was peacefully liberated by the People's Liberation Army, which entered the city without firing a single shot. Invasion, whether by foreign enemies or by civil war armies, has never brought on a bloodbath to this extent. . . .

The students asked for democracy, adherence to the rule of law, the continued promotion of reform, and the elimination of corruption. Their intentions parallel those of the government. Why [couldn't] we be patient and solve the crisis? The people can never forgive [Premier Li and his clique], for they were given opportunities [to avoid confrontation] but rejected them all. They have completely dishonored the people and entered the course of isolating the people from the truth.

L'Unita, the organ of the Italian Communist Party, said:

Murder has been committed in the Chinese capital. . . . The Beijing regime aimed, shot, and killed. So we deluded ourselves. We thought that to talk of democracy and freedom was no longer a crime to be punished by death. . . . The rationale of arms is the sole policy remaining for those who no longer have anything to say. . . . A power that turns to arms after the experiences of this century . . . cannot last.

And the non-Party press of the world was equally condemnatory. Chinese officials responded flatly that they were not concerned with world opinion.

The government's bloody-fist answer to the peaceful appeals of millions of people unmistakably taught that propaganda phrases—"from the masses, to the masses," "socialist democracy," "the masses must supervise the leaders," "people's democratic dictatorship"—which implied the people had a right to participate in governing were nothing more than slogans peddled by men who consider that they alone are really entitled to rule.

Their leaders' brutal response destroyed forever whatever was left of the people's trust that the Mao Dynasty would someday lead them compassionately and wisely. This dynasty, like bankrupt dynasties of the past before they fell, lost the mandate of heaven. And the students forced out of Tiananmen Square were singing the Chinese national anthem . . .

Arise, ye who refuse to be slaves!
With our flesh and blood let us build our new Great Wall!
The Chinese nation faces its greatest danger.
From each one the urgent call for action:

Come forth; Arise! Arise! Arise!
Millions with but one heart,
Braving the enemy's fire, march on!

Behind the Decisions

It has long been known that elderly Chinese leaders who have left the stage have not necessarily left the theater, but both they and the government have said that their present roles, if any, were minor—and indeed it has appeared so, outwardly.

There had been rumbles for months, however—ever since the Third Plenum in October 1988, in fact, when conservatives gained the economic initiative from Zhao Ziyang—that retired "elderly revolutionary comrades" were becoming increasingly unhappy with him, that they were attempting to oust him, but there were no specific moves known and the threat did not seem lethal. (The elders were responsible for ousting Hu Yaobang, of course, but that was while they were still active in high posts, eight months before many of them were swept from the Politburo and the Central Committee into supposed retirement.)

Apparently, not a single China watcher anywhere in the world saw it coming, but in fact the gerontocracy was grimly serious about getting rid of Zhao, whom they considered too willing to go too far too fast, a disciple of "bourgeois liberalization" who could not be trusted to maintain the supremacy of the type of socialism they believe in. The combination of the students' demands for greater democracy, and Zhao's conciliatory responses to them, provided the perfect opening for a deadly thrust by the conservatives, who after engineering the military crackdown went on to force Zhao Ziyang from the Party secretaryship and began the effort to prove him criminally responsible for encouraging the "counterrevolutionary rebellion." One charge, which says a great deal about both Zhao and his attackers, is that Zhao "put respecting, understanding, and caring for the people in the place of educating, molding, and arming them [with ideological weapons against bourgeois liberalism]. "

On June 9 the elderly power brokers made their first—and, so far, only—public appearance as a group. Following a long period of tension and known struggles among the leadership, Deng Xiaoping appeared with other aging leaders grouped around him at a televised meeting to congratulate military commanders on crushing what the government was by then calling "the counterrevolutionary rebellion" at every opportunity. The circumstances established beyond any doubt who was really in charge in China, even though as a group they had no authority whatever to make government decisions.

The most astonishing thing about the appearance of this group—and something that is ominous for China's stability—was that the ordinarily powerful Party Central Committee, as well as the National People's Congress and its Standing Committee, tolerated without an audible whimper the obvious usurpation of their powers.

The committee of elders includes the three men still in conservative favor who are on the Standing Committee of the Party Politburo, but few of the others are even on the Central Committee. They are mostly long-time Deng associates, but not necessarily allies, and in falling back on these pretenders to power he was forced to negate his own repeated warnings concerning the need to observe a rule of law, not of men.

Their status as "elderly revolutionary comrades" means that they are in fact quite elderly. In returning them to leadership status Deng was also forced to negate his years-long attempts to rid the government of superannuated cadres. Many members of this rump group are men Deng essentially forced to resign from the Central Committee because of age when he himself resigned in 1987. Except for the three now on the Party Standing Committee, their average age is 82. (It should not be thought, however, that there are not many able younger men in the conservative camp whose convictions match their leaders'. Many have worked with the conservatives in positions at various levels, and many, like Li Peng, were trained in socialist rule in Russia and other communist countries.)

As "elderly revolutionary comrades" they are a deceptively benign clique as illegitimate—and, whatever their intentions, as potentially dangerous to China—as the notorious Jiang Qing clique and the "Gang of Four." They are dangerous not because, like the "Gang of Four," they have an insatiable power hunger but because many of them are selfless; would-be autocrats, perhaps, but sincere.

It may seem naively generous at this moment, so close to the barbarities of June 4, to suggest that many Chinese—and not just the elderly conservatives—do in fact feel a moral responsibility for maintaining the Communist Party in power and in perpetuating the present form of socialism as China's political system. But, as suggested in "Are the Chinese Going Capitalist. . . ?"(in chapter 4), there are numerous reasons why older Chinese, in particular, warmly accepted Chinese socialism. This doesn't mean that they necessarily approve of much that the Party and government do, but they prefer the present system to the alternatives—and to the suffering they endured before the Party came to power.

Much comment during the crisis focused on the perquisites and status that go with political power, implying that Chinese politicians are resisting democracy and change merely for reasons of selfishness and greed. Venality is something with which westerners are all too familiar and, with the present level of opportunity for official corruption, it is easy to infer that selfishness is a substantial element in resistance of some Chinese to reform.

However, in this connection an indelible television image comes to mind. It showed Chen Yun, at 84 perhaps the most feeble of elderly comrades and without doubt one of the most prominent, flinty, and persistent of the conservatives. He was pictured entering a meeting with attendants beside him, pitifully, painfully shuffling forward barely an inch at a time. He gave no impression whatever of a man afire to maintain his political position; understandably, he seemed only to want to sit down.

Surely a man at this point in his life, whose every need will be met for the rest of his days, cannot be very much concerned with political power and perquisites. It is hard to see anyone in his condition saying, "I will stay in the Politburo until my last breath!" But it is not hard to imagine a lifetime, dedicated, Party member like Chen and many other conservatives saying, "I will work for socialism until my last breath"—and meaning it literally. When one expert analyzed the reasons China watchers did not foresee the conservative strike, he said simply, "we sold short the resolve of the octogenarian leaders to defend their life's work."

Many conservatives, like zealous fundamentalists of all stripes, see their beliefs as immutable and their faith threatened by change. They are often older, inflexible, poorly educated, out of touch, and relatively untraveled and unsophisticated with respect to the world China lives in today. They have heard all their lives that achieving communism would be the work of more than one lifetime, and they tend to see any attempt to achieve noticeable change as going too fast and any disagreement as a challenge to the fundamental order.

Even more important, probably, is that because they feel threatened they are apprehensive to the point of paranoia, as is apparent in the "evidence" they cite for the existence of a "counterrevolutionary rebellion" fomented by a "very, very few." There is no evidence for this, aside from their own assertions, but to men schooled in Leninism and Stalinism, where iron central control as an article of faith has the same standing as the divinity of Christ in Christianity, the danger of any dissent can be magnified beyond reason.

The leaders' extreme feelings of insecurity show, too, for example, in the way they have from the beginning endowed the students with far more power than they could possibly have had in reality.

A speech attributed to one of the leaders said that to back away from the threatening April 26 *People's Daily* editorial condemning the student demonstrations ("Take a Clear Stand Against the Upheaval!") would be a sign of weakness, that it would lead to "our collapse, the overthrow of the people's republic, and the restoration of capitalism, which," he incredibly went on to add, "was the desire of the American Dulles. " John Foster Dulles was an anti-communist American secretary of state thirty years ago, but invoking him as bogeyman in a crisis today is bizarre. It is, however, not out of line with, and no more bizarre than, claims in the official report by Beijing Mayor Chen Xitong (and repeated endlessly in propaganda materials now being circulated in China) that foreign forces have "always attempted to make the socialist countries, including China, give up the socialist road . . . and put them on the course of capitalism. "

Harrison E. Salisbury, who was in Beijing on June 4, reports in his *Tiananmen Diary* that Deng felt a "plot threatening not only to over-throw the Party but also to take his life and those of other leaders was developing under cover of the student protests. " Li Peng said in a *Le Figaro* interview in September that the leaders felt themselves nearly impotent in dealing with the turmoil and had to behave like a "clandes-tine government. "

(Greater detail on the Party's and government's attempts to defend their brutality—someone has called the defense an effort to "mytholo-gize" the movement and the massacre—is given in Appendix 4 under June 8 and 9 and later, and in the entry in the Mini-Encyclopedia on the World War II phenomenon of the "Big Lie. ")

The many such expressions of apprehension are all the more remark-able because, as the government does not seem to realize, they reveal a severe lack of self-confidence: implicit in all the leaders' claims of overwhelming threats to socialism from shadowy enemies is their fear that the people could be so easily persuaded by the "very few" to turn against them.

From this state of mind, then, it is just a step to a shooting defense of the status quo. As William Safire pointed out following the imposition of martial law,

> Communist leaders brand all serious internal opposition as "counterrevolutionary." They gain, hold, and concentrate their power subtly at first, in the name of democracy, and brutally at the end, in the name of order.

And that is precisely what has happened in China. "We must have stability, stability, stability" became the refrain of Chinese leaders as soon as student demonstrations began, as it has always been at the slightest sign of unrest. But the absolute stability the conservatives demand is by definition incompatible with change, and change is critical to the progress China so desperately needs. Furthermore, stability achieved with bloody repression is not worth much to China or the foreigners it wants to attract. With all their criticism, the conservatives have not shown that they have any new ideas for dealing with the country's problems without change.

It is in their desperate determination to block the attempts of others to achieve progress that the conservative elders are most dangerous to China.

A U-Turn for Reform

China has entered another period of political rigidity that in alarming respects resembles a return to conditions of the Cultural Revolution. It seems certain that reform will be slowed by three factors:

1. By its rejection of the complaints of its people the government lost much—perhaps most—of whatever remained of its support among the people.

    This statement must be qualified, however, because it is easy to forget that the vast, isolated, dispersed peasantry, traditionally unconcerned with politics, were little involved in the tumultuous events of the spring of 1989, nor were their interests threatened in any way that would immediately cause them to be disenchanted with the government. Indeed, given the level of government control of the media, millions of Chinese outside the range of Hongkong and Japanese television may never learn what actually happened in Beijing. Nevertheless, peasants who have had their own problems with the fiscal austerity programs imposed by the conservatives within the last year or so, are more and more having their production essentially requisitioned by the government, which could erode their support.

On the other hand, the factory workers, scientists and other intellectuals, and bureaucrats and clerks who keep the economy running have again been angered by the government refusal to give meaningful attention to their complaints about corruption, bureaucracy, and other problems that affect their daily lives. There is, of course, the appearance of furious activity in combating corruption (see "Offical Corruption Menaces Government's Legitimacy") and constant calls for the Party to improve its work style and to heed the people. But the people have been given none of the powers of participation and effective oversight which they demanded in their marches and which alone can provide the only real safeguard against exploitation and abuse. Official repression may be too great for them to resist openly, and productivity has fallen at a time when greater efficiency and creativity are vital to any improvement.

2. On June 4 the authorities did serious damage—possibly irremediable damage so long as the present leaders remain in power—to China's highly promoted and very important program of "opening." This is discussed further in "Opening to the Outside World" in chapter 5, but it might be noted here that virtually all nations of the world—including the United States, Japan, and the European Community—acted after the June Fourth Massacre to reduce their own technological and financial assistance to China and to block aid from the World Bank and other organizations. A gradual lessening of some restrictions is already apparent because of economic and international political considerations and the quick dulling of memories under stress of other events, but restoration of the genuine good will the Chinese government enjoyed in many quarters will require a considerable time.

3. In remarks on the fortieth anniversary of the founding of the PRC, leaders emphasized their determination to pursue othodox policies in strong terms, some of them reminiscent of periods in which modern China has known its greatest oppression. Jiang Zemin said that the June Fourth Massacre "was not a tragedy" and equated those who seek change with foreign agents who seek overthrow of the government. Other officials served notice in various ways that their government intends to be authoritarian to a degree not seen for years. This means repression, probable stifling of economic prog-

ress and, as the conservatives have already made clear, little likelihood of signifcant political change.

And over it all is the knowledge that whatever exists today is only temporary, pending the death of Deng, when even greater struggles among the leaders are probable, despite Deng's designation of Party General Secretary Jiang Zemin as his successor and Jiang's assuming Deng's chairmanship of the Central Military Commission.

During the peaceful days of early May, after Zhao Ziyang told a distinguished international audience that stability and protest are not incompatible and that he thought the demonstrating students were reasonable people and had a case, *China Daily* ran an editorial called "Reason Grows. " It was not unlike others written around the world at that time which assumed, in ignorance of the government's paralysis, that it was a spirit of conciliation that had averted a clash between Chinese officials and students. It seems a long time ago.

But the editorial made one point that is still valid. Typically concentrating on operational rather than humanistic reform (see "What About Political Reform?" in chapter 4), it said:

> Sooner or later, all Chinese will have to ask: Can the ever-increasing price subsidies ever protect against inflation? Can guaranteed welfare promote labor productivity? Can farmers keep producing when their business is unprofitable and meagerly funded? Can teachers and researchers continue their careers with all their hardships? Can bureaucracy, corruption, and irrational decision-making be controlled without a public supervision mechanism?

At about the same time, prominent Chinese intellectuals at a conference in the United States were asking angry questions about the failure to advance humanistic reform. Wrote Marlowe Hood in the *South China Morning Post*:

> After four decades of suffering, they ask, why must we bribe kindergarten administrators not to mistreat our children, pay the police to return goods stolen from our homes, offer petty officials lavish dinners to maintain a supply of electricity, and beg our superiors for basic necessities of life?. . . It is this moral degeneracy more than material deprivation that has moved intellectuals and students from disillusionment to action.

These, of course, were questions all Chinese were asking before Hu

Yaobang died, before the premature congratulations, before the shooting started. They are still urgent, regardless of which faction is in control.

In the last analysis, the many questions really come down to one: If the old ideologies, the old systems have not served China sufficiently well in the past, is there any reason to think the conservatives' determined revival of them will solve China's problems now?

The following chapters will examine how things were in China before reforms began, what changes have occurred to reach the state of affairs that exists today, and what the problems are that the triumphant conservatives, who have complained about reform for so long, must now show they are able to solve.

Two

THE NEW
CHINESE REVOLUTION, 1979—

Until recent years, much of what the public heard about China was presented in rather simple terms—China, a land of blue-clad ants working on communes, a land of Red Guards rioting in the streets, or a land of heroic, unselfish men and women living in true equality. Unfortunately, the Chinese government and its former leaders have been partly responsible for these stereotypes because of their distrust of the outside world and their unwillingness to communicate freely and honestly with it, which meant that little reliable information was available. Hostile distortions and inaccurate presentations by the foreign press have also contributed to the misunderstanding.

Since 1979, however, a New Chinese Revolution has been going on, and the government is providing much more detail than ever before about most aspects of Chinese life.

To the western mind—and indeed to the Chinese mind—there are still many things about China today that ideally might be changed (although the western observer and the Chinese would not necessarily agree on all of them). Deng Xiaoping himself commented a year or so ago, "People are saying that notable changes have taken place in China. I said to some foreign guests recently that they were only small changes. ... Considering the country as a whole, we must admit that so far the results of our work are not very satisfactory."

Nevertheless, the record to date reveals a fascinating story of a vigorous and imaginative people striving to shape their lives more to their liking in the face of formidable challenges. A Chinese economist in Hongkong has observed that "so swift have been the economic reforms in China that not even the keenest observer could keep pace with what has been going on," and it will be possible to follow only the main thread of the story here.

In reading the story it must be kept in mind that, although China theoretically has a high degree of central control, the control is far from total. Under these circumstances, national policies are seldom carried out in the same way at the same time throughout the country, and there are exceptions to nearly any general statement concerning Chinese actions, conditions, or practices nationally. This is particularly true today, when China is struggling anew with a lack of national consensus as to its reforms under a government which is struggling to restore its legitimacy and gained substantial distrust. (See section below, "Government Power Absolute Only in Theory.") Clearly, more consistent, goal-oriented behavior throughout the government and Party over the long term is essential if China is to achieve the vital conditions that alone will enable it to attain its greatest potential—rule by law and a true democracy, whether a democracy with Chinese characteristics or some other. The social and political controls to direct this behavior, however, can be created only slowly, and will require a change in the entire Chinese ethos, not merely another change in regulations or ruling faction. Some improvement will necessarily be attempted by fiat, but securing more control in this way is basically contrary to the overall attempts (which of course may not continue) to encourage initiative and decision-making at lower levels.

Furthermore, the Chinese government is no different from any other government in the world in that it likes to put the best face possible on events and facts, as its incredible attempts at spin control after the June Fourth Massacre demonstrate. And the Chinese press is no different from the press anywhere else in that it likes to write about the new and the novel; it is not always careful to indicate that a given phenomenon or new fashion is perhaps quite limited, at least for the present.

Even the Chinese press, however, is seldom guilty of the overdramatization and exaggeration displayed by some foreigners, such as a veteran byline western reporter who visited China in 1986 and wrote:

> The great revolution is in the streets. You watch it surging inexorably, irreversibly, overwhelmingly in the savage rush-hour traffic on Shanghai's Huaihai Road, over the construction-filled skyline of Beijing. . . . Clothes worn by men and women show an explosion of color. . . . Successful farmers are moving into new villa-like stone houses. . . .

The reality is not quite so stunning, but until June 4, 1989, few commentators quarreled with this same writer's conclusion that China's people "appear to have been freed, for the first time since the civil wars of the 1930s, from constant political pressures and military tragedies."

BACKGROUND OF THE NEW REVOLUTION

New China was born in December 1978, when the Third Plenary Session of the Eleventh Central Committee of the Communist Party of China met. It was to be the most important session since liberation.

In its essentials, this was the situation the Party urgently needed to deal with:

1. China was only two years away from the death of Mao Zedong and from the end of the Cultural Revolution. Those two years had been a period of marking time, in many respects. Hua Guofeng, Mao's personal choice as his successor, though having played an important role in overthrowing the ultraleft ringleaders of the Cultural Revolution known as the Gang of Four, was himself seen as continuing the ultraleft traditions and menacing slogans that characterized that period, and as creating a new personality cult with himself as the object.

    Furthermore, in the eyes of millions of ordinary Chinese, whether workers, peasants, or government staff members, Mao was still an omnipresent, semidivine figure. On the other hand, there was a strong feeling among others that Mao should be totally negated, particularly because of his egregious mistakes in the latter years of his life. Thus, the leadership was confronted with the delicate task of redressing the malpractices and mistakes of the Cultural Revolution, a step urgently called for by the entire nation but one which could not be taken without dealing objectively with Mao's responsibility for them, while at the same time convincing both sides of the necessity of compromising their differences to avoid ideological chaos and social disorder. Under these circumstances, discussion on the proper criterion for determining truth, mentioned below, assumed a critical importance.

2. Peasants, who make up approximately 80 percent of the total Chinese population, had few work incentives, because their incomes and their lives improved not at all. During the ten-year period of the Cultural Revolution their average per capita income increased a total of only 10.5 yuan, barely 1 yuan per year, and there was a decrease in real income. There was only an insignificant pickup in agricultural production during the two years following.

3. The living standard of the people as a whole was low. Real income of urban workers fell throughout the 1966–76 period. In 1978, the per capita income was only about 10 percent of the Soviet Union's, and about 2 percent of the United States'.

4. The percentage of national income spent for expanding heavy industry and construction was very high (surpassed as of 1978 only by the two most ambitious years of the Great Leap Forward), and there were heavy additional commitments for the future. This left relatively little for investment in agriculture and consumer goods.

These problems were far too complex to be dealt with completely in a single document or at a single point in time, but the Third Plenum made decisions on some points, laid down guidelines on some problems, and called attention to still other matters that required resolution.

Ideological Decisions

Reviewing the Central Committee's 1978 actions four years later, Hu Yaobang (then Party Secretary), said:

> The historic service of the Third Plenary Session . . . was precisely that it thoroughly shattered the heavy chains imposed by the protracted "left" mistakes [and] set right the guiding ideology of the Party. . . . During the two years before the Third Plenary Session . . . the question of rights and

wrongs in the Party's guiding ideology was not clarified as it should have been, and the work of setting things to rights proceeded haltingly....

Much depended upon finally clarifying "the Party's guiding ideology." Essentially, the question came down to this: What is the proper criterion for determining truth (i.e., for determining the correct guiding ideology or the correct policy)? Should the criterion be that a) a certain statement is made in the writings of Mao, Marx or Lenin, or that b) experience teaches and practice proves that a given course or policy is workable and successful?

Prior to the Third Plenum (sparked by a Party paper by Hu which was later widely published), there was widespread discussion in the press and elsewhere of this question, which obviously had implications far beyond just the reliability of Mao Zedong Thought. A decision upholding the absolute infallibility of classic communist writings would have made change difficult.

The finding, however, was for the validity of experience. The Committee defined the guiding principle of investigation to be one of "Seeking truth from facts" (which was not a new concept, being a key theme in Mao's 1940 *On New Democracy*), and stated that "Practice is the sole criterion for judging truth."

Having established that existing principles could be challenged and investigated, it was but a short step for the committee to repudiate the anti-change "two whatevers" policy advocated by dogmatic Party officials and ultraleftists, which stated that "We will resolutely uphold whatever policy decisions Chairman Mao made and unswervingly follow whatever instructions Chairman Mao gave." Together, the decisions on determining truth and rejecting the "two whatevers" gave the Party and government vastly more flexibility for reform and innovation.

Finally, and of perhaps equal importance with the other decisions, the Committee decided to cease using the slogan "Take class struggle as the key link" that had caused so much grief in years gone by, considering it unsuitable for a socialist society. Previously, the urgency of class struggle was taught as the cardinal ideological line to be followed by both the Party and the state during the entire transitional period of socialism leading to communism. In China, this line led to the frequent exaggeration of political and economic differences between people, and generated conflict among different groups by encouraging hostility toward those who were labeled class enemies or who merely happened to be born into a higher caste family, such as urban business people or rural landlords. Even people sympathetic to communism suffered from this stereotyping. Ultimately, this led to the counterproductive political movements and campaigns that caused such turmoil, and that have been abandoned—though comments by the new leadership indicate a possibility of their revival. (See "Class Struggle" in the Mini-Encyclopedia.)

Development Decisions

Other key decisions were:

To speed up agricultural development ("rural reform"). Under large-scale collectivization, arbitrary plans from above were inflexible and often incompetent management in the communes made it a common peasant complaint that "We are being roped together to live a poor life." With the ideological questions resolved, it was possible to work toward basic changes in the countryside by using techniques formerly criticized by many as "capitalist" or "revisionist."

The "ropes" were cut by instituting a "responsibility system" of production, under which management and even some extended planning is greatly decentralized. Individual households or self-formed voluntary groups contract with the state to deliver specified amounts of agricultural products, and can earn additional income as well. They are also responsible for any financial losses. Under this plan, which was enthusiastically received, it is possible to observe the socialist principle of "to each according to his work," with remuneration paid according to the amount and quality of work done. Conversely, the system avoids the incentive-sapping working arrangements formerly used under which everyone "eats from the same big pot" regardless of the work done, a state of affairs into which a great many communes (and industrial enterprises) drifted under the banner of "egalitarianism." (The responsibility system is discussed in detail in chapter 6, "Reform in the Countryside.")

To shift the emphasis of the Party's work to "socialist modernization" (more commonly known as the "Four Modernizations," meaning advancement in industry, agriculture, science and technology, and defense) and *away from enervating, repetitive mass campaigns* promoting class struggle or other abstract ideological objectives. Modernization was not a new idea, but the attention it received at the Third Plenary Session gave it greater importance than before. Modernization as a goal entered public awareness immediately, but concrete targets were not set until 1982, when it was announced that the overall goal was a quadrupling of industrial and agricultural production from 710 billion yuan in 1980 to 2,800 billion in the year 2000. Achieving this goal required a compounded annual increase of 7.2 percent, which was entirely realistic in the light of historic growth and has been exceeded every year since— but with current unbalanced growth, agricultural stagnation, and high inflation, quadrupling may no longer be possible. (See "Progress in Economic Reform" at the end of this chapter.)

To emphasize the strengthening of the legal system. Formal laws and procedures were recognized as being important in enhancing stability, helping discourage arbitrary actions by individuals, and increasing the confidence of foreign investors. Presumably, a rule of law rather than personalities will also put an end to the cynicism engendered by the mystifying and dangerous cycle in which, as one writer put it, "yesterday's orthodoxy all too often becomes tomorrow's heresy, while today's sainted leader becomes tomorrow's tainted villain."

In its Third Plenary Session, then, the Eleventh Central Committee provided for or made possible: a) moving toward decentralization; b) rewarding hard work and discouraging egalitarianism, or "everyone eating from the same big pot"; c) instituting flexibility in management; and d) placing authority in laws and institutions rather than in individuals.

Many Chinese commentators are now saying that it is obvious in retrospect that there was an equally important result that had not been sought at the Third Plenum: The widespread debate over the criterion of truth demonstrated to the people that fruitful discussion of controversial ideas was possible under at least some circumstances, and that dogmatism was dead. As *Guangming Daily* put it, "People have begun to think for themselves about political matters and the path the nation should follow towards its goal of becoming a modernized socialist state."

Historic Background of Decisions

The changes of the 1980s are widely considered to be revolutionary, and of course they are—but only, it appears, in the determination and thoroughness with which they are being carried out.

These changes have an interesting element reminiscent of an observation by a psychologist friend. "You know," he said, "I find that about 90 percent of people who seek counseling already know what their problem is and how to solve it, though they may not be aware that they do. The trouble is that they are so burdened with the expectations of others or other social pressures that they just can't take the right steps unless things get really crucial."

And so it seems to have been with the Chinese.

For example, history since liberation contains frequent hints that the government had recognized extreme centralization was not a workable arrangement in the long run.

Under the influence of Soviet-style socialism, centralization begun during the War of Liberation continued throughout the First Five-Year Plan. Centralization received a strong boost in 1954 when the units known as "greater administrative regions," embracing several provinces, were abolished and all state-owned enterprises were placed under central ministries.

By the time of the Great Leap Forward in 1958 more than 9,000 state-owned enterprises were under central management but all except about 1,000 were transferred to lower echelon control during the next nine months. The severe problems of the Great Leap inspired recentralization starting in 1961.

Decentralization began again in 1964 and became more extensive in 1970, followed by centralization again after the Cultural Revolution. In 1979 the reforms inspired by the Third Plenum set decentralization in motion once more.

Today, a new swing toward centralization is being pushed by the government and the Party, but in this cycle most observers feel that the swing of the pendulum will be damped greatly by the disdain already being shown by the thousands of fiefdoms that have sprung up as the central government has attempted to pass on some of its powers in recent years. (See "Government Authority Absolute Only in Theory," below.)

Similarly, the need for upgrading China's entire economy in relation to the rest of the world is not an idea that surfaced for the first time at the Third Plenum. Mao referred to the idea on several occasions, and in 1957 commented on the need to "make China a socialist country with modern industry, modern agriculture, and modern science and culture." In 1964 Zhou Enlai formally proposed what was essentially the "Four Modernizations," Deng Xiaoping made a similar proposal in 1973, and Zhou brought up the question again in 1975 in what was to be his last appearance before the National People's Congress. It was proposed once more at the Eleventh Congress in 1977.

In the case of both decentralization and modernization, the apparent need for them was not so great as Mao's need to live up to what he thought was demanded by the revolutionary commandments, and they were pushed aside. Similarly, "counterrevolutionary turmoil" appears to have created for the present leaders new imperatives that seem to justify disregarding the great overall progress made since 1979 in a decentralizing mode.

Finally, even the "responsibility system" is not new. Essentially the same concept was tried first as early as 1953–54, was used in varying forms with varying success in many localities until the mid-sixties, and began receiving attention again when the worst of the Cultural Revolution was over. On each occasion it was condemned as a reversal of collectivization and a return to capitalism.

The decisions of the Third Plenum made possible rational re-examination of these and other ideas that are now proving to be valuable in the growth of the nation.

The full significance of the Central Committee's 1978 actions was not immediately realized by most Chinese. However, there was a change in spirit that was no doubt brought about at least in part by the fact that the government had acknowledged "errors" made during the Cultural Revolution and earlier, and was attempting to correct them, and that a return to the excesses of 1966–76 was becoming less likely. The grand national plans of the day and the expectation of a generally brighter future were no doubt other factors.

One writer says of the time that "the totally benumbed quality of much of the population" began to disappear. Others speak of the "heady days of 1979" or "the euphoria of 1979." Personally, it seemed that a good description of the period was "the effervescent days of 1979," for the people were bubbling with life, as though pulling a gigantic cork had released pressure on the entire country. On the whole the years since then have been good ones. There are not as many "10,000 yuan peasants" as some stories made it appear for a while, not everyone has progressed at the same rate, and some simply by not progressing have fallen behind. Nevertheless, most Chinese no doubt agreed when Deng Xiaoping said to a Party conference that the period since reform began "has been a crucial one and one of the best since the founding of the People's Republic." But most people probably also agreed when he added, "It has not been easy to make it so."

THE ILL-MARKED ROAD TO REFORM

As the euphoria generated by early successes passed and the relatively simple changes were made, the pursuit of reform became more challenging to its advocates and more threatening to those who did not agree with or benefit from the policy. The course of reform in specific segments of economic and social life— such as price reform, abandonment of egalitarianism, adoption of the responsibility system in agriculture, etc.—will be discussed in separate sections here. First, however, the broader events of the period since the Third Plenum deserve a look. Since 1978, the key fact in Chinese life has been that it is changing, moving on an unfamiliar road at a speed never known before. Many people are not comfortable with either the direction or the speed. Most people probably have unrealistic expectations of how and how soon reform will benefit them, and perhaps everyone has been surprised, sometimes dismayed, by events along the way.

Who's Wearing the White Hat?

It is not surprising, then, that economic growth brought a swell of uneasiness among those who are nostalgic for the egalitarian practices and the lifestyle of prereform days. Their complaints are expressed as criticism of and resistance to various aspects of reform. (See "Mixed Feelings about Reform," below.) In particular, many facets of reform are not supported by a sizable group—or groups—whose political positions are variously known as "conservative," "leftist," and "ultraleftist," and who favor dogmatic and fundamentalist interpretations of Marx.

Conservatives are usually contrasted with "rightists," who tend to be reformers, whose positions favor less literal interpretations of Marx, and who, in the eyes of leftists, show too much tolerance for capitalism, western lifestyles, free expression: in short, too much tolerance for change. However, it is traditional both in socialism and in Chinese life generally to attempt to achieve unanimity on all matters, so any suggestion of cliques or factions is highly offensive. (For example, one of the "crimes" with which Zhao was charged before his dismissal in 1989 was revealing publicly that there were two schools of thought on some matters within the leadership of the Party.) Trying to avoid recognizing factions leads to a kind of political schizophrenia in which both sides recognize perfectly well what the reality is.

Some Chinese maintain, however, that conservative-rightist distinctions are not meaningful. At a press conference during the Thirteenth National Congress of the CPC, Zhao said, "Some friends abroad think there is a reform faction and a conservative faction. I would say all those who analyze Chinese politics on the assumption of struggle between two factions will make one mistake after another." Harvey Feldman, a veteran US State Department China specialist, accepts the no-factionalism claim, writing that

> In fact, the breakdown of the leadership into "conservatives" (the black hats) and "reformers" (the white hats) has more meaning for foreigners who prefer arguing personalities to examining policies than it does to Chinese. ... Not only is it difficult to tell what color the hats really are, but some in the hierarchy seem to switch them frequently. [If some reforms are in trouble] it is not because they are under attack from mean-spirited conservatives. ... It is because an economy that is neither market nor planned, but a peculiar amalgam of the two, creates strains that are tolerable to some in the ruling group as growing pains but are seen by others as signs of serious trouble.

This may be. The divisions may not always have the importance foreigners assign to them. And certainly disagreements are not necessarily "mean-spirited." Given the turbulent history of China since liberation, however, it is hard to accept the bland assertion of a *Beijing Review* editorialist commenting on the 1987 upheaval that

> In China, there is no social foundation for complicated factional struggles as in the capitalist world, because the fundamental interests of Chinese workers, farmers, and intellectuals are identical.

The interests may be identical but there have been, and are, strong-minded leaders with drastically divergent opinions as to what those interests are and how to achieve them. Their different points of view have been labeled countless times through the years as "leftist" and "rightist" and various in-between degrees of political orientation. Many Chinese, while granting that there may have been factions in the past, argued until the spring of 1989, but probably no more, that differences of opinion within the Communist Party of China were no greater and no more damaging than the wide differences that often appear between the so-called "wings" of political parties in, say, the United States or Great Britain.

They particularly point out that some of the top officials listed by the western press as "conservatives" or "champions of the conservative faction" were leaders in the great theoretical debate before the Third Plenum over the criterion for determining the truth which paved the way for the entire reform program. Some also made decisive contributions to the establishment and improvement of the new legal system which theoretically attempts to move China toward rule by laws, not men. (See "Legal System" in the Mini-Encyclopedia.)

Moreover, they point out that, as in other countries, leaders who wear black hats on one issue may wear white hats on another, or they may change their views or change sides completely on a given issue without being factionalists or villains.

Clearly, there have been divisions on numerous issues, but it is perhaps a matter of one man's faction being another's difference of opinion. In any case, the Chinese (who, it must be remembered, have a traditional preference for achieving consensus wherever possible and are sensitive to anything suggesting dissent) see only normal differences within the leadership concerning the concrete steps to be taken in the process of reform, such as the appropriate speed of reform and priorities in development.

Probably the politics of no country can be said to be like any other, but certainly it sometimes seems that in China the combinations and permutations of personalities, interests, opportunities, loyalties, objectives, and so on are particularly dizzying. Here is what the *Encyclopedia of China Today* says about the phenomenon:

> There are no easy ways to characterize politics in the PRC as "democratic" or "totalitarian" or as a struggle between "revolutionaries" and "pragmatists," or to see the realm of politics as limited only to the institutions, procedures, or personnel of government and Party. Politics as the Chinese experience it is the complex reality of a people with a long tradition and intense revolutionary experience still living through a process characterized by personal and group conflict as well as by sudden swells of mass input. It is a drama that links everyday public life to history, personal values to public behavior, and public behavior to an actively pursued vision of the ideal community.

Student Protests of December 1986 and Their Aftermath

Most of 1986 was one of the infrequent periods in modern Chinese history when political tensions were relatively low and people felt somewhat at ease about speaking their minds—and were encouraged to do so. The press was full of discussions of the need for expression of opinions, and tentatively innovative political and economic points of view abounded.

And then, seemingly inspired by the tolerant atmosphere, university students in a number of cities began staging somewhat unfocused protest marches in December 1986, first in Hefei, capital of Anhui Province, and then over the next four weeks in about twenty cities. *China Reconstructs* later summarized the students' protests this way:

> The immediate causes of the demonstrations were manifold. Some students, for instance, were protesting the quality of the food in their cafeterias; others wanted more student participation in university decision-making; others thought procedures for electing deputies to grassroots people's congresses were not democratic enough. Many did shout slogans calling for "democracy and freedom," but were also calling for a speeding up of the democratization process already being carried out under [Communist Party of China] leadership.

The size of protesting groups reached about 7,000 in Wuhan and Shanghai, and 20,000 in Kunming. Of the roughly two million students nationwide, it is estimated that only about one percent took part, but in individual localities the percentage was far higher and the spirit of the protests in some cases was not as simple and peaceful as the quote above suggested. Apart from a large number of wall posters targeted directly at the "corrupt government" and the Communist Party leadership, students in Xian threatened to seize the provincial radio and television stations, while their counterparts in Shanghai blocked the city's public transportation for a few days. However, unlike what might have happened in the past, authorities reacted with restraint and there were few arrests and fewer jailings, even though their displeasure with the students' behavior was obvious.

In a communist country like China where public rallies and demonstrations used to be either organized by, or in favor and support of, the Party and government, such large-scale protest demonstrations in direct opposition to the authorities were virtually unheard of. The unrest shocked the leadership into re-examination of its policies, and for the antireform forces provided a mobilizing and unifying catalyst, a target on which to vent their pent-up grievances.

In the name of supporting the Party and government, conservative elements vociferously criticized the students and reformers, saying that the protests were evidence of a decay of national and moral values and discipline which they had been predicting would result from the reform. The decay was blamed on loosening of central government controls under the reform; on corruption of Chinese values by foreign ideas to which people have been exposed as a result of the reform policy of "opening to the outside"; on the greater freedom in public discussions and writing that had been allowed; on the unorthodox interpretations of Marxism that had been used to provide theoretical justification for some reforms; and so on.

They called such deviations from prereform beliefs and usages "bourgeois liberalization," and claimed it represented a serious challenge to the Four Cardinal Principles of Socialism (which require upholding the leadership of the Party, etc.) and threatened Chinese society as a whole. (See "Bourgeois Liberalization" and "Four Cardinal Principles" in the Mini-Encyclopedia.)

Under these circumstances, it was not surprising that then Party leader Hu Yaobang, like leaders everywhere when things go wrong, was marked for responsibility by those who had "different opinions" on how to carry out the reform. The leadership's review of the situation concluded that Hu must resign for "having gone against the Party's principle of collective leadership" (i.e., for acting on his own in matters others felt required decisions by leading bodies) and for "serious errors of political principle." (Specifically, he was charged with being over-enthusiastic about, and one-sidedly emphasizing, the aspects of Deng's reform strategy which supported "opening" to the outside world and "reforming" the political and economic structure, to the neglect of upholding the leadership of the Party and the other Four Cardinal Principles.) His post was assumed on an acting basis by Premier Zhao Ziyang in January 1987.

The major fear of observers when Hu was dismissed was that a Mao-style cycle of national conflict and repression was about to begin once more, and that this did not happen says a great deal about the extent of change in China. If Hu had been dismissed under similar circumstances before reform began he might also have been jailed and his family and hundreds or thousands of even distant associates disgraced. Instead, Hu remained a member of the Party's Standing Committee for the remainder of its term and in October 1987 was elected to the Politburo, a position only slightly less prestigious, where he remained until his death in April 1989. (Hua Guofeng, whom Hu replaced as Party secretary in 1982 under less dramatic circumstances, also continues to have a high Party post.) A number of Hu's longtime associates were reported to have been transferred or demoted, but no worse persecution has surfaced.

Nevertheless, antireform or conservative elements took Hu's resignation as a sign of a policy change and did not hesitate to press their advantage. Attempts were made to turn back the clock by urging a return to central planning and by pushing to cancel the most successful of reforms—the responsibility system in the countryside—and to return to essentially commune-style management. For a time, the reform program was nearly brought to a standstill. Reformers and the cause of economic and political reform itself were widely felt (outside China, at least) to have lost stature and power, and serious concern was felt for the effect of still another ideological zigzag on the future of the reform movement.

All in all, however, the handling of the events of 1987 showed a remarkable growth in forbearance and judiciousness compared with the turmoil of past events involving high-level leadership changes. *Asiaweek* wrote that

> Even the most innocent observers of the Chinese scene today would have to admit that there's something qualitatively different about it—something muted, unsure, even tolerant and quite sincere. Nobody is on show in a stadium or getting a bullet in the back of the brain. This is because the reforms are so popular, the appeals to superpatriotism so bankrupt. Even if the hard-liners should win out in Peking, chances are they will not be able to reverse gear. The Chinese want to be in the world.

But that was 1987. China scholars will puzzle for many years over what the critical differences were between 1987 and 1989.

The Big Thirteenth: The Thirteenth National Party Congress 1987

Despite the Chinese denial of a conservative faction within the top Party leadership, many believe that the conservative resurgence was of particular importance because it preceded by less than a year the crucial Thirteenth National Congress of the Communist Party of China in October 1987. Most observers thought it to be part of a strategy to control the congress. If this was the case, not only did the attempt to set in motion a major political campaign fail, but so did the attempt to dominate the congress and thwart reform. Some meticulous observers reported that Zhao used the word *reform* in his political report to the congress more times than in any of his previous speeches, even speeches specifically on reform—a total of 168 times.

Far Eastern Economic Review said of the conservatives' strategy:

> .. the Party recoiled as the antiliberalism campaign broadened and as its style came to resemble the vicious antirightist purges of the past.... [The congress was] a general rejection by nearly 2,000 Party leaders representing

both central organs and local Party organizations throughout China of the conservatives' immediate policy objectives. More particularly, it was a rejection of the use of ideological campaigns as tools of political struggle.

Given the intense secrecy that surrounds Chinese politics, it is not possible to know how Deng and Zhao were able to turn aside the demands of conservative forces in the society in general and those of the leaders with different ideas as to how to carry out the reform. One story is that they reached a mutually acceptable compromise of attaching equal importance to the Four Cardinal Principles of Socialism and the "open and reform" policy of the Party. This balance of policy is expressed in the Party's basic line for the primary stage of socialism laid down in Zhao Ziyang's political report to the congress. Others speculated, however, that the conservatives failed because they offered only negative criticisms of reform, not positive workable alternatives to reform that would deal with the problems the Party and the government are attempting to solve.

Even before the student protests and the events they sparked, however, interest in the congress had been building. Deng Xiaoping had repeatedly stated his intention to step down at the congress from his role as "paramount leader" and to take with him into retirement scores of equally elderly colleagues, many of whom had been strong opponents of reform.

By the time it closed, the Thirteenth National Congress (now nicknamed "The Big Thirteenth") was regarded as having strengthened the reform movement in a number of ways.

1. The congress adopted as the Party's agenda for the next five years Zhao's lengthy report a) strongly affirming the importance of reform; expounding a new ideological basis for reform; b) establishing that whatever is necessary for the development of production (or "productive forces," in Chinese terms) is allowed by socialism; and c) strongly supporting political reform, including the separation of Party and governmental functions that is widely regarded as the crucial change.

2. The congress replaced nearly half the Central Committee, from which the leadership of the Party is largely drawn, with younger and better educated men and women mostly in their fifties and sixties, as compared with those in their sixties and seventies whom they replaced. Deng Xiaoping left all his Party posts except the chairmanship of the Central Military Commission, which gave him

all-important control of the military in the 1989 crackdown on students.

(Deng apparently intended to remove himself from all posts a little later, and in mid-1988 he did confer command of the military on Zhao, first vice-chairman of the commission, in what was considered an attempt to ensure an orderly succession after Deng's death. Deng delayed further action, however, as reform problems multiplied and conservatives gained strength, ousted Zhao, and crushed the student movement. Deng finally resigned his CMC chairmanship, his last formal position, in November 1989, and Party Secretary Jiang assumed the post after earlier being designated Deng's successor. The likelihood of a succession struggle remained, however, since Jiang has a relatively narrow power base in the Party and no military credentials. Following his resignation, Deng made several public statements indicating that he intended to remain "paramount leader.")

Observers felt that the previous ratio of reform-minded to conservative-minded leaders on the Central Committee was approximately maintained, but the leadership as a whole was certainly much younger. People also noticed that none of the few who sought to remain active but failed to achieve election to the 175-member Central Committee were particularly reform-minded.

3. The congress accepted as the Party's new ideological basis for judging various aspects of reform the recent theory declaring that China is now in the primary stage of socialism and will continue to be until about 2050. Because China's socialist revolution occurred in a backward and undeveloped country, rather than in an advanced capitalist country as Marx had theorized would always be the case, China failed to pass through the capitalistic development stage critical to the final success of the revolution. Therefore, the theory states, it is permissible to make use of capitalistic institutions so long as they are needed to achieve an advanced stage of socialism.

It was expected that Marxist conservatives would continue to challenge various reforms as being antithetical to Marxist principles, but that adoption of the primary stage theory by the congress as a whole would help blunt their objections. (For further discussion of the primary stage theory, see "Socialism with Chinese Characteristics" in the Mini-Encyclopedia.)

Mixed Feelings about Reform

The conservative eruption in 1987 was sudden, but it was not a surprise. As mentioned earlier, the relatively liberal atmosphere of the last few years has never been without countercurrents. No aspect of reform has been without its opposition from many people on ideological or personal interest grounds, or both.

Recently, there have been stories in several publications on the complexity of reform, the role of interest groups, etc.

"Lenin once observed," *People's Daily* pointed out, that "interest pushes forward the life of a nation. The recognition and promotion of both the national interest and personal interests is one of the chief driving forces behind reform." This does not necessarily mean, however, that "every specific measure at any specific stage of the reform can count on the unanimous support of the people."

Formerly, under the principle of egalitarianism and central control, people came to accept getting whatever the system uniformly provided, "while being virtually oblivious to interest relationships among themselves and different social groups." Now, circumstances and the awareness of personal and group interests have changed.

In rural areas ancient agricultural lifestyles are being abandoned as peasants become workers with a new outlook. In urban areas some workers still have iron rice bowls, some have no job security beyond a year's contract, and some are entrepreneurs with a fragile "clay rice bowl" who are totally dependent upon their own efforts and the continuation of the government policies that tolerate them. Cadres whose lives used to be stable and whose power was unchallenged are being forced to learn new jobs and give up long-held perquisites. *People's Daily* continued:

> All this is compounded by interest relationships between rural and urban areas, between officials and the masses, between different trades, between central authorities and localities, between coastal areas and the hinterlands, between areas producing raw materials and those processing them, and between manufacturers, consumers, and commercial media.

As well as the widely publicized groups that have benefited, there have been losers in the reforms, too, especially among older cadres and cadres who have suffered loss of prestige through reorganizations and new regulations; they naturally are not among strong supporters of reform.

Neither does reform get a landslide vote from "workers and staff"—

employees of state offices and state-owned enterprises (particularly the former), which are overwhelmingly in the cities. Many surveys have found that workers support reform in the abstract but that there is nevertheless considerable discontent and psychological uncertainty related to reform. Much of the uneasiness comes from the progressive loss of the iron rice bowl (i.e., the guarantee of a job and support from the state), reliance upon which has been for a long time the "right" and "correct" thing to do.

Reform and reformers would get a much stronger vote, however, from urban workers in collective enterprises, who have generally fared better under reform than state workers, as well as from the hundreds of thousands of strikingly successful individual entrepreneurs.

In the countryside, there isn't much question about the support for reform. Some peasants have fallen behind because of personal or family problems, some have overextended themselves in setting up new businesses, and some others may have reason to be disappointed in reform. In the last two or three years inflation and broken government promises have taken the bloom off the rose. Nevertheless, when *Peasant Daily* reported that some leftist cadres were attempting to undo reforms in the countryside it warned that "The great masses of peasants definitely will not agree" to turning back the clock, and predicted a widespread backlash if it were attempted.

Government Power Absolute Only in Theory

These criticisms of reform by interest groups and political conservatives have no doubt brought to many readers' minds the question, "How can there be all this dissension and uncertainty? Doesn't the government have absolute control in a communist country?" The crucial and very significant answer is, simply, "*No, it doesn't.*"

It is true that in many matters a one-party central government can be implacably determined if thwarted, particularly if an individual or relatively small group is involved. In major matters it can force everyone into line and can even control a great many aspects of its citizens' everyday lives with considerable success. (See, for example, the power of workplace managers over employees described in "Unit" in the Mini-Encyclopedia.)

But the government of any sprawling country such as China which is run by an entrenched and unaccountable bureaucracy may have a difficult time indeed in securing day-to-day obedience from its civil servants. (This is also being seen now in the reforms in the Soviet

Union.) Regulations are intentionally misunderstood; a particular rule is conveniently considered not applicable because of supposed special conditions; a friend in higher office will protect against trouble if rules are not followed; and, with no agency outside the jurisdiction of the Party able to blow the whistle in any decisive way, the chances are slim that anyone can object successfully to subversion of official orders for the purpose of gaining personal power or profit.

As willful cadres summarize it, "Those above have their policies; those below have their countermeasures."

The lack of clear and certain punishment for incompetent and corrupt bureaucrats is indicated by a 1987 story in a Shanghai newspaper which reported that "Dereliction of duty is often found to be the cause of damage to property and loss of life but the people responsible are seldom put on trial because of obstruction by their superiors." A 1988 story reported that in three years dereliction had been responsible for 11,700 deaths and losses of 1.4 billion yuan. Deng Xiaoping himself said that "for a long time we have had no strict administrative rules and regulations and no system of personal responsibility from top to bottom"—in other words, no accountability.

Many serious problems have resulted for the government. For example, in the years leading up to the crisis of 1988–89 China has had great difficulty controlling the economy, partly because of excessive investment in unnecessary and unapproved capital construction: hotels, office buildings, etc. Numerous pleas have been made by the government every year to save the money, save the materials, save the energy that goes into these projects, but no one has paid any attention. Said the president of the People's Construction Bank of China recently, "When local governments and enterprises have money, they invest as they like, and you can hardly do anything about them."

Schools are falling apart and teachers have not yet received the small raise promised them two years ago, but some local governments still import automobiles and spend large sums in official banqueting and entertaining in defiance of policies laid down by higher authorities.

Xinhua News Agency reports that price laws are hard to enforce "because of meddling from some officials and institutions who are motivated by their own vested interests." Local cadres claim "each level of government has its own policies and rules. Penalties imposed by the National Price Bureau must be subject to the approval of local governments."

The devolution of authority partly responsible for this administrative anarchy was intended to get operating and decision-making power into the hands of lower-level managers and administrators, with incentives to inspire them to contribute to a true market economy and to rationalize state affairs.

Instead, power relinquished at any given level has tended not to seep very far down or to be abused, or both, but the relinquishing authorities either have not retained or have not used any corrective powers. Consequently, significant control has been lost without the expected commensurate gains.

Power has simply been channeled by unsound economic and political conditions into smaller pools of personal and localized interests and influence. These new power centers range all the way from megacorporations run by children of senior cadres (including Deng) to the little supply co-ops that speculate in fertilizer and diesel fuel. As *Beijing Review* described it:

> With the gradual delegation of power . . . , group and individual interests have multiplied. . . . Chaos has emerged in various economic fields . . . [and] actions against the interests of the state and the public have become increasingly serious. In sum, many orders have been disobeyed and many prohibitions have been ignored. Behind these phenomena are local and group interests—in the final analysis, private interests.

At the same time, it is apparent that national Party discipline and ideological and patriotic beliefs are no longer adequate to prevail over parochial influences, despite pleas from all the major leaders and assertions from Deng, for example, that "it is what the central authorities say that counts" and that the country must return to "the tradition of hard work and plain living."

Such expertise and rationality as central planning formerly contributed to the economy are now diluted or lost, but the disciplining market forces that were supposed to replace central planning have never been allowed to develop. The result is that the authority of the Party and the central government has eroded in many circumstances to the point where control is unpredictable.

Policies from above are now met with such disdainful countermeasures from below that, as *China Economic News* said recently,

> China today is divided into more than twenty independent kingdoms [the provinces] and more than 2,000 fiefdoms [the counties].

Qiao Shi, a member of the Politburo, said that unless the swelling regionalism is counteracted the country "will be in chaos."

It should be remembered that relinquishing some central government authority was a deliberate reform strategy. It was, and is, necessary. However, even those who wish to press reform vigorously and who point to the dangers of strong centralization grant the need for some reapplication of central control in the present circumstances. The current readjustments are ostensibly economic rather than ideological in nature, although conservatives are quick to claim that, as they have maintained all along would happen, the problems have resulted because reform has been both too extensive and too rapid. There is a contrary school of thought, however, now out of favor, which sees many of the problems as resulting from failure to make decisive changes to prevent conflicts between the old and new systems.

China has gone through decentralization-centralization cycles before, as mentioned earlier. The circumstances of the current decentralization phase, however, and the failure to develop alternative controls, have led to conditions which will not be so easily reversed this time. What the government is doing to meet the crisis is discussed in the next section, "Bridling the Runaway Dragon," and in connection with individual problems, particularly in chapter 5, "The Six Big Reforms."

Bridling the Runaway Dragon

The psychological high point of reform thus far undoubtedly has been the previously mentioned Thirteenth National Party Congress in October 1987.

At the Big Thirteenth, reformers got nearly everything they wanted: a younger leadership which included many prominent personalities associated with reform; a broad disavowal of the movement against bourgeois liberalization and several of those who led it; and a new mandate for reform and acceptance of a new ideological basis for the manner in which reform was being conducted.

Even at the time of the congress, however, reality was about to catch up with reform. As preparations were made for the Third Plenum, the following conditions made it clear that China in the fall of 1988 faced a serious predicament:

☐   Government attempts to exert its powers were increasingly ineffective in many directions.

☐   The economy was growing far too fast to be sustained by the country's underdeveloped infrastructure and supply of raw materials.

☐ Inflation was climbing rapidly because of, among other things: wage increases in excess of productivity; new currency issuance and construction growth far in excess of plan; commodity shortages; and widespread speculation. Inflation increased 7.3 percent in 1987 (quite a large rise for China, which until recent years has had little inflation), and was trending toward a staggering 18.5 percent for 1988.

☐ Urban residents in particular were unhappy with rapid inflation, which lowered the living standards of more than 20 percent of them during 1987 (and about 35 percent in 1988). Non-staple foods, a large part of a family budget, were up 40 percent in the fall of 1988. Government efforts to control prices were largely ignored.

☐ Peasants resented high prices for and profiteering in agricultural supplies and the failure of the government to increase official fixed prices to cover the new costs. At harvest time, many were infuriated when, because of bank runs and other problems, there was insufficient currency available in some areas for the government to pay for their crops in cash and they received non-negotiable chits instead.

☐ Price reform, a vital part of economic reform (See "Price Reform: Making Prices Reflect Realities" in chapter 5), was widely blamed for inflation, shortages, speculation, and other problems, and the expectation of still higher prices led to panic buying. Price reform was slowed, but the need for it remained as urgent as ever.

☐ Spending for non-productive purposes such as hotels, automobiles, elaborate government buildings, etc., continued to grow despite government objections. Meanwhile, spending for power generation, mining, roads, agriculture, and other vital needs was neglected, and severe shortages of energy, transport, and materials contributed to inflation, lost production, black markets, and other problems.

☐ Profiteering by officials was rampant, and corruption was a daily topic in both conversations and the press.

In response, the government continued its attempt to exert financial controls and the Party tried to rein in members' blatant misconduct. Meantime, there was a continuing series of high-level meetings to prepare a plan for the third major attempt to enforce a period of austerity

and cutback since reform began. (There were other extended retrench-
ments in 1981–82 and 1986.) The general tension was heightened by
contradictory indications or conclusions coming from some of these
meetings; for example, in mid-August the Politburo announced a vague
plan for "deepening" price reform, and two weeks later the State
Council announced that price reform would be delayed for two years.
(This open contradiction was one of the signs that a mighty tug-of-war
between reformers and conservatives had begun.)

The final plan was announced at the Third Plenary Session of the
Thirteenth Central Committee of the Party which opened in Beijing in
late September, almost exactly ten years after the landmark Third
Plenum of the Eleventh Central Committee that launched reform in
1978.

Unfortunately, 1988's Third Plenum showed no such boldness as
1978's. Its guiding policy for reforms in 1988–89 was formularized as
"Regularization, rectification, readjustment, and reform." The plan
outlined in then Party Secretary Zhao Ziyang's report (which was not
made public for a month after the plenum) did little more than describe
the major problems and the intended solutions in the most innocuous
terms. He not very sagely said, for example, concerning demand
outstripping supply, that "on the one hand, it is necessary to control the
swelling of general demand, and, on the other, to make great efforts to
improve and increase effective supply."

(Premier Li Peng's report to the 1989 National People's Congress six
months later offered nothing any more encouraging. While it stressed
continuation of austerity and recentralization of power even in the face
of unhappy consequences, it was as vague as Zhao's on specifically what
should be done and how it could be achieved in the face of the central
government's obviously diminished authority. It was noted that his
speech made no reference whatever to the market or its role in reform.)

Zhao called for such measures as:

☐ Correcting "the various abnormal economic phenomena" plaguing
China. Correction involves, for example, attempting to "complete
the initial readjustment of prices in five years or more" instead of
the shorter periods previously mentioned, meaning that price
reform was being put aside for the present; improving the productivity
and profitability of state-owned enterprises; separating enterprise
management from governmental administration; and requiring
companies to sever all links with Party and government organizations

and leaders.

☐   Cutting back total demand and checking inflation by reducing investment in fixed assets; curbing unnecessary expenditures by enterprises and institutions; controlling money supply; selling enterprise stocks and bonds and publicly owned housing to soak up excess funds.

China Daily admitted that "none of these policies are new," but added that "they have never been implemented in an effective manner."

A full year into the austerity period, growth of overall gross national product was up only about 6–7 percent (a still very healthy growth rate) and the excessive industrial growth rate was down about a third, both good signs. But there were enough major imbalances to raise some doubt that the policies were being implemented effectively this time, either. For example:

☐   In the first half of 1989, bank credit continued to expand and to be diverted into capital construction, despite a 30 percent tax that is supposed to be imposed on unauthorized projects. There was a long-standing desperate shortage of cash for enterprise operation and agricultural purchases. Non-bank credit had also expanded. Also in the first half of 1989, profits of major state-owned enterprises declined 12 percent, although output value increased 5 percent. Money-losing enterprises were not being disciplined or closed, and instead received increasing subsidies; losses for the first half of 1989 were more than total 1988 losses. Prudence dictated COD delivery ralationships among enterprises, since so many were in shaky condition, but liquid cash was very scarce, slowing or halting commerce in many cases.

☐   Wages in the first quarter of 1989 increased more than 20 percent above the similar period in 1988 but productivity rose only about 3 percent. After the Pro-Democracy Movement began, and especially after the June Fourth Massacre, productivity began dropping because of worker disaffection and the roughly 15 percent of labor time many were forced to spend in ideology classes.

☐   The cost of urban living rose about 30 percent, meaning that workers' real income and living standards fell for the third year.

☐   Workers continued to be paid not only their wages but bonuses as well, even when factories were shut because of energy or material shortages.

☐   The shortage of electricity was so severe that in some areas homes were lighted only by candles for one or two nights a week for months, and factories were often idle for lack of power. Meantime, the production of television sets and refrigerators, which the state had targeted for sharp reduction to save materials and industrial and consumer energy, rose 51 and 60 percent respectively.

By early October 1989, a full-blown crisis loomed with both serious economic and political implications. There were some good signs—inflation was down to about 13 percent instead of the earlier 30 percent, and both summer and fall harvests had been good—but the overall outlook was bleak, starting with the resentments among the government's own cadres whose cash wages had just been abruptly cut 35–65 percent, with the difference being paid in *gongzhai* (non-negotiable bonds). Peasants, too, were angry because many offices buying fall crops were again short of funds and, as in 1988, were paying with IOUs or closing altogether. The booming coastal provinces and other locations with high concentrations of energetic and successful collective and private businesses were becoming bitter about being squeezed by austerity and recentralization.

When the Central Committee's Fifth Plenum finally met in November, it targeted for solution by 1991 five critical conditions—inflation, money oversupply, budgeted deficits, overheated growth, and industrial and agricultural maladjustments. About forty remedial measures were reportedly decided upon but were kept secret. The summary communique was even more vague about solutions than Li Peng's March NCP report, essentially saying only that China should "resolutely oppose decentralism," "gradually establish a macro-economic control system . . . combining planned economy with market regulation," and "continue . . . the struggle against bourgeois liberalization over a long period of time." The only thing really clear was that, despite the official "reform is continuing" line, the kind of reform the government has in mind is a conservative reform of Deng's reform.

One-Track Psyche in a Two-Track World

Implementation of the government's cutback proposals is now more difficult than before, for as changes have occurred the problems have become increasingly complex, and people long accustomed to social, economic and ideological simplicity are increasingly confronted by choices, by wrenching change. China's one-track psyche is confronted by a two-track world.

"Two-track" is a term most often applied to the troublesome mixture of state-fixed and market prices (see "Making Prices Reflect Realities" in chapter 5), but it applies equally to many other changing aspects of Chinese life that are the source of much confusion, misunderstanding, instability, and resentment apparent today.

Said *Outlook Weekly* recently about the "two-track phenomenon":

> A gap has opened up between the old norms and concepts, which have yet to be eradicated, and the new ones, which have yet to really take hold. It has become difficult to judge standards of right and wrong. People have lost their judgment: what's "worth it" has taken on a different meaning to different people. Among these different levels of people, dissatisfaction and conflict are rife.
>
> The myriad abuses of the system have led people to cry out, "Create the conditions for ending the two-track system!"

The nation's whole approach to reform has been marked by cautious experimentation in new programs; even its regulations and laws are issued, as always, in "provisional" form. What someone has called the government's "phobia of discontent" has itself hampered clear, consistent, and decisive action, and has left a society full of ambiguities and what the Chinese call "contradictions" that contribute to a discontented and polarizing nation.

These are but examples:

☐ The most conspicuous contradiction of all is the two tracks exemplified by the Party's condemnation of corruption and profiteering and the failure to put an end to these abuses. (See "Official Profiteers" in the Mini-Encyclopedia.)

☐ While the national government pursues its own concept of mandatory and guidance production plans, Shanghai regulations require allocation of steel, automobiles, and more than twenty other kinds of goods; at the same time, in Guangzhou and Shenzhen there are no controls.

☐ In the same shop, doing the same job side by side, there may be workers whose status is entirely different. One worker is given a position under the state job assignment system and has a job for life.

The other is one of the factory's contract workers, hired under the factory's new right to recruit and select workers and enjoys no job security beyond the end of his one-or two-year contract. The contract worker receives far less in pay and benefits.

☐ Some cadres in government enterprises and offices are appointed under the traditional procedure, usually on the basis of seniority, but others compete for their jobs through competitive examinations. Their status is subtly, but significantly, different.

☐ The same foods, the same industrial products, have two different prices, depending on whether they reach the buyer through state allocation and subsidization or through the above-quota free market.

☐ Students enrolled in universities under the state plan have all their expenses paid, while others must pay their own expenses or rely on their units to pay them.

Outlook Weekly continued:

> ... the not fully eradicated old system and the virtually virgin new system have both had negative effects on society, and these effects are the root cause of many major problems now emerging. If one word can be used to describe the abuse of the two-track system, the word is *chaos*.

In the face of such widespread dissatisfaction, predictions have been made more than once that reform is petering out, losing steam.

Yet, if one looks behind the cutbacks and broad pronouncements on stressful conditions, there are signs that myriad changes have been pressed forward every day in the cities and the countryside, and in virtually all aspects of national life. Undismayed by 1988's Third Plenum and later policy shifts, reform economist Li Yining said shortly before the conservatives took over that "Some people say that delaying price reform is a step backward [but fail to recognize that, for example] encouraging the stock ownership system is a step forward. You can't say that reforms have stopped."

Among other continuing attempts at reform he might have mentioned are increasing refinement and use of the contract responsibility system; the slow but persistent commercialization of housing; further expansion of the coastal development economic strategy; and an Administrative Litigation Law passed by the 1989 National People's Congress which allows citizens to sue the government (but, in the two-track tradition, only in carefully defined cases).

The reform campaign, if it is over, as appears, ran for eleven years, making it the longest sustained campaign in the turbulent history of the People's Republic, including the Cultural Revolution. Unlike the Cultural Revolution, however, the reform campaign appears on the whole to have gained rather than lost strength the longer it went on.

It has already been said, but should be repeated, that what China is attempting has not been tried in any other socialist country until recently, and nowhere on such a scale. There is no historical record to offer guidance to China's leadership and people that might have made reform go more smoothly or made unlikely such events as the explosion of discontent that occurred after the death of Hu Yaobang.

Certainly, more determination in dealing with Party corruption, for example, would have reassured the people. More aggressive work on wage reform and more flexibility on two-track pricing could have helped. Less defensiveness about faster political reform might have prevented many of the present tensions. But this is hindsight. The question now concerns what lessons can be learned from the experience to date—and does the new government want to learn them?

THE RESULTS OF REFORM, 1979–1988

Non-economic Concerns Have Been Increasingly Influential

When reform began in 1979 its primary objectives were economic: increasing national productivity and raising the standard of living. True, successful solutions of the problems confronting the nation required rethinking the Maoist political heritage and implied political reform in the future; it was recognized, for example, that the old centralized governmental structure would not be suitable for the new decentralized economy, but the most urgent problems were economic.

Economic developments precipitated broad national introspection concerning essentially non-economic matters. At the same time (except for the sharp but short-lived criticism of bourgeois liberalization in 1987, the ousting of Hu Yaobang, and some related harassment of intellectuals, closing of individual publications, etc.), authorities until recently had, on the whole, since late 1985 tolerated a noteworthy openness in discussion, some of which involved broad analyses of the national culture, character, and psychology. (Developments in political reform and the new boldness of intellectuals are discussed in "What About Political Reform?" in chapter 4.)

Conservative disapproval was often expressed and was never far from the surface, but intellectual life moved ahead with reform.

Perhaps the best illustration of the national soul searching that occurred, not only in intellectual circles but among thoughtful members of the public, is the sensational broadcast in June 1988 of a six-part TV miniseries called "He Shang." (It is commonly translated "River Elegy" but also as "Premature Death of the Yellow River" or "Death of a River").

Its focus is the historic and modern influence of the ancient culture that developed in the Yellow River Plain beginning about five thousand years ago. Most of the visual content is taken from other documentaries and movies, but its commentary (by three young men who are writers, students, and teachers) bluntly calls into question the modern validity of many of China's oldest and dearest values, symbols, and beliefs. *China Daily* evaluated the series thus:

> All the montage is made to accentuate five points: first, Chinese must stop dwelling on their past glories and face squarely the serious drawbacks in their country's socioeconomic development; second, they must ask themselves what has made their admirable ancient civilization appear underdeveloped now; third, China's self-appointed culture should be held responsible for its decline in dynamism; fourth, Chinese must try sincerely to assimilate the strong points of other nations; and fifth, [they must try] to recreate their culture.

The paper's commentary continued:

> Thanks to reforms and the open policy, a cultural debate has actually been going on for more than two years [with, as mentioned above, some notable exceptions] ... As long as there is free debate, there will always be flashes of inspiration and new ideas.

The contentious history of "He Shang" after its first broadcast tells something about the equivocal state of debate, culture, and intellectual freedom in China even before June 1989, not apparent in the *China Daily* comments. *Far Eastern Economic Review* suggested:

> That it has been screened on Chinese TV is perhaps an indication not of the openness and liberalism of the leadership, but rather of the confusion and paralysis of will from which China's propagandists now suffer.

Prepared and broadcast by government-controlled China Central Television Station (CCTV), the program drew strong criticism from conservatives, who saw rampant bourgeois liberalism in its attitudes toward the past and who succeeded briefly in stopping the immediate rebroadcast demanded by the public. *People's Daily* and other newspapers published complete scripts, but opponents nevertheless were able later to impose limits on discussion of the series and to stall for a time distribution of videos and scripts in book form. In the next round, however, funds were approved late in 1988 for a sequel to "He Shang."

China Youth News commented on the controversy that "it is time for some comrades to break away from the habit of using administrative power to meddle with literary and theoretic works," but the times have clearly changed.

The country's propagandists no longer are constrained and leading comrades have no hesitation in compelling silence concerning anything not in accordance with their own beliefs. "River Elegy" is now banned and at least one of its authors is included in an urgent nationwide list of wanted fugitives, charged with complicity in the Pro-Democracy Movement.

The fate of other thoughtful works and other thoughtful writers is probably signaled by the dismissal in late summer of Minister of Culture Wang Meng, the highest official to have been purged so far. The 1986 appointment of Wang, a distinguished writer persecuted as a rightist for nearly the entire period between 1957 and the beginning of reform, was taken by intellectuals as a hopeful sign that the government would indeed relax its oversight and interference in artistic and intellectual matters.

Wang's succession by He Jinzhi, a poet and high official in the Party's propaganda department, suggests a conservative intention to censor and police on a scale not seen for years. The tone of newspaper and journal articles on cultural, political and economic topics is felt by observers to be increasingly leftist, constituting what *Far Eastern Economic Review* called "the most wide-ranging assault upon China's reform policies to date."

For example, after the campaign by students for a free press, and enthusiastic support for the movement by thousands of journalists, a government-orchestrated surrender by periodicals was suggested by a spate of articles in major publications praising Party control of the press. *China Youth News*, which has been one of the more outspoken reform publications, charged that opponents of Party leadership of the media are opposing socialism and the interests of the masses. By the end of 1989 Jiang was saying "Our country's newspapers, radio, and television are the mouthpiece of the party, the government, and the people. . . . [The 1989 turmoil shows what happens] if the tools of public opinion are not tightly controlled in the hands of true Marxists."

Progress in Economic Reform, 1979–1988

Instituting the responsibility system, increasing the role of the market in determining economic activity, "opening to the world," and other changes pushed growth of the gross national product to an overheated 13 percent by 1984, the highest rate of any country in the world. But continued growth too rapid for the economy to support and assimilate without severe penalties has led to economic conditions often characterized today as "chaos."

Over the nine years 1979–1987 China's state revenue and per capita income approximately doubled. China's gross national product grew an average of 10 percent yearly from 1981–1987, making it the fastest-growing economy in the world—faster than Japan, faster than South Korea, faster than Taiwan or Singapore. China's GNP in 1988 grew by 11.2 percent to 1.385 trillion yuan, far more than double the 1978 GNP, probably maintaining or even improving upon China's 1987 position as the seventh largest GNP in the world. (GNP growth slowed to a still quite respectable 5.7 percent in the first half of 1989 under the austerity program designed to slow growth, and the industrial growth rate fell by about a third to 10.8 percent, but there are numerous and serious economic imbalances within the overall situation. See "Bridling the Runaway Dragon" above.) China now ranks first in the world in agricultural production, first in textiles and cement, second in coal and television sets, third in chemical fertilizer, fourth in steel, and fifth in petroleum and electricity.

It must be remembered, however, that even these impressive figures, divided by China's more than one billion people, yield relatively small shares for each person. For example, the per capita output of electricity is only 4.2 percent of that in the United States. In fact, China, with a GNP in 1987 of US$277.50 per capita, ranked in the bottom 20 percent of nations, and its people have not experienced the even greater growth of affluence found in some other Asian countries.

Nevertheless, the personal consumption level in China is higher than in nearly any other developing country. For example, grain consumption in 1986 was 391 kilograms per capita in China, about 230 in other developing countries; meat, 17.5 kilos versus about 13.5. China used 10.6 kilograms of clothing fibers, other countries about 3.8. As heartwarming as this is to long-deprived Chinese, it is not a desirable development economically, indicating that an insufficient proportion of the GNP is probably being spent on education, health care, and infrastructure for the growing population.

In financial terms, this growth has translated into average per capita income increases, inflation-adjusted, of from 134 yuan in 1978 to 545 yuan in 1988 in rural areas and of from 316 yuan in 1978 to 1,119 yuan in 1988 in urban areas. The government calculates the average annual adjusted 1978–1987 increase at 13.1 percent for farmers and 7.9 for urban residents.

For the last few years, however, price increases have been taking an increasing proportion of additional income. In 1986, for example, urban income rose 21 percent, price-adjusted to 13 percent. In 1987, income was up only 10.6 percent, and with adjustment for price increases amounted to a real gain of only 1.7 percent. In fact, 21 percent of urban families suffered a decline in their standard of living in 1987. In booming 1988, the official inflation rate was 18.5 percent (many feel it was higher), the highest since the 11.2 percent recorded in 1961 at the end of the disastrous Great Leap Forward; income rose 22.2 percent, for

Per Capita Urban Income Since 1981

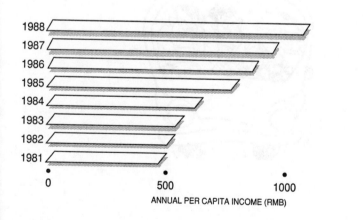

ANNUAL PER CAPITA INCOME (RMB)

Sources: *Statistical Yearbook of China and Bejing Review*

an actual increase of 1.2 percent. Thirty-five percent of urban families suffered a decline.

Average price increases—inflation—in the first half of 1989 were 25.5 percent higher than the previous year, according to the State Statistics Bureau. Premier Li claimed, however, that "18.5 percent of it was caused by the price increases of last year," and the "actual price increase this year has been just 7 percent"—a novel way of interpreting a standard year-to-year statistic, to say the least.

It should not be overlooked that reform has barely begun, has clearly received a serious setback in the accession of the new government, and that the sweeping changes are generating both political and human conflicts. What has been accomplished to date has probably, on the whole, gone more smoothly than anyone would have dared hope. But leftists and reformers, old workers and young, cadres and the masses, and other groups with conflicting interests do not yet work together in full harmony.

Undoubtedly, severe challenges remain—in industry, in population, in political reforms, environmental quality, and in many other areas.

Corruption and profiteering among cadres, especially in the last two or three years, have brought a new term into the language, *guan dao*,

'Who's in charge?

Wei Jiancheng, *China Reconstructs*

"official profiteers." (See this term in the Mini-Encyclopedia). It is hard to escape the conclusion that the Party and the government have not had the will to make and enforce decisions in these and other areas that seem from the outside to be basic to preventing widespread betrayal of trust. (See "Official Corruption Menaces Government's Legitimacy" in chapter 4.)

And over everything is the bureaucracy, a keystone of Chinese life for thousands of years. Reform has hardly made a dent in the power of this ancient institution, which was recently characterized by a consultant to investors in China as consisting, even eleven years into reform, "of many highly autonomous commissions, ministries, bureaus, and other units which guard their jurisdictions and privileges with zeal, and which are reluctant to talk to and deal with each other." Bureaucracy is a source of much of the delay and confusion reform is encountering, combining in itself several elements of possible conflict with the goals of the government, the Party, and society at large.

Despite past and present problems, however, China has already made significant achievements. She has both great opportunities and great challenges ahead. The next chapter examines perhaps the greatest challenge: population control.

Three

ONE BILLION MOUTHS, TWO BILLION HANDS

Writing of China at the turn of the century, [famed missionary] Arthur H. Smith concluded that "The most prominent fact in China is the poverty of its people. There are too many people to the square mile, too many families to the village, too many mouths to the family. Wherever one goes, it is the same weary tale with interminable repetition. Poverty, poverty, poverty, always and evermore poverty."
    That is the specter the Chinese leadership sees.

In the 1950s Ma Yinchu, a distinguished economist, and others warned of the alarming consequences of a continuing surge in population, and called for controls; but they were scoffed at by Mao and subjected to persecution that continued until after the fall of the Four. "One mouth, two hands" was one of the cliches used to defend permissive population policies. "Why didn't we pay attention to Ma Yinchu?" is the cliché now.

—Both quotations from Hugh Deane,
"China's Changing Countryside,"
Far East Reporter, March 1983

Population may seem an odd subject with which to begin a survey of what are essentially political and economic changes, but, because of China's special circumstances, it is really a most appropriate point of departure. Demographic historians now believe that since the seventh century China has had the world's largest population. Considerations of population size, composition, and growth are basic to decisions affecting industry, agriculture, defense, education, health care or any aspect of national life and welfare.

In whatever long-term plans China's leaders make they are burdened with these sobering facts:

☐   China's population has doubled in the 40 years since the People's

Republic was founded in 1949. This increase of 540 million was nearly four times the increase during the entire 129-year period between the Opium War of 1840 which opened China to western trade and 1949. China finds no comfort in the prediction of some demographers that by 2050 India will have taken over the most-populous country record.

☐   China counted 1,008,000,000 people in its 1982 census.

☐   At the beginning of 1989 the population was 1,096,000,000, up 16,000,000 over January 1988. In other words, in a single year China's population grew by a number of people equal to the entire population of Australia—for the third successive year. The 1.1 billion mark was passed in April.

☐   By the year 2000, in only eleven years, the latest estimates are that China will have a population of more than 1,300,000,000, 100 million over the target of 1.2 billion established several years ago and finally abandoned in 1989 (see "The Bottom Line," below).

CAN CHINA COPE?

Will China be able to feed, educate, employ, and otherwise care for the population it will have just over a decade from now? And what will its situation be in the more distant future?

People have to have room to live, and in China inhabitable land is relatively scarce. The forbidding provinces of Tibet, Inner Mongolia, Xinjiang, and Qinghai make up more than 50 percent of the country's area, but contain less than 5 percent of its people. About 85 percent of the people live on 35 percent of the land, making China's population density in significantly populated areas three times the world average; in rich farming areas, the density is 2,000 to 3,500 people per square mile.

And China is not as large as people usually think. True, it is the third largest country in the world, after the Soviet Union and Canada, but it is only a little larger than the United States.

It has about the same north-to-south extent as the continental United States, but greater extremes in climatic conditions.

Hopeful Future, Precarious Present

China is rich in most natural resources *except* agricultural resources. This ˙s a critical lack for a country whose population is expected to grow by

Population Growth Since 1949

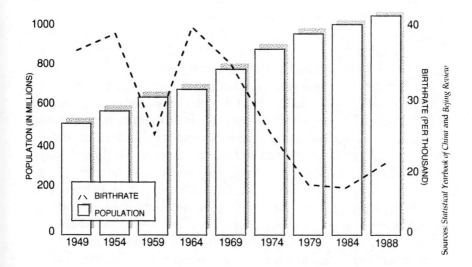

perhaps 250–300 million in the next 20–25 years and whose population must continue to live for at least a few decades as a mostly agricultural society under new social, economic, and ecological conditions which threaten the agricultural base.

Some analysts point out that Chinese agriculture has maintained a fast pace since 1978, making China briefly self-sufficient in food in the mid-eighties, and has had an overall good record since the Great Leap Forward. They maintain agriculture is strong and, under present circumstances, can continue to increase production at a somewhat faster pace than the increase in population (but not, perhaps, faster than the increase in demand, which is not the same thing).

Most government and Party leaders, however, worry both that the present circumstances may not continue and that the advances needed to move Chinese agriculture to a new level of efficiency may not occur smoothly and in time to meet the needs of the present population and those to be born in the beginning baby boom. No emperor, no leader for thousands of years has been able to sleep easy if grain was low. It is not without reason that a solicitous "Have you eaten?" was long a standard morning greeting.

Today's middle-aged adults recall the famine at the end of the Great

Leap Forward when millions starved. The slogan "Take grain as the key link" epitomized national agricultural policy from the 1950s until its errors were recognized in 1979. The dean of conservative Chinese economists, Chen Yun, said after the disappointing grain crop of 1985 that continued grain shortages (though there was not a real shortage) would "lead to social disorder." And in 1988 when then acting premier Li Peng addressed the Seventh National People's Congress he put the growth of grain production at the top of his list of objectives.

No hopeful economic analysis, China's leaders seem to feel, is a substitute for grain in the bin. And they do have legitimate concerns, both current and long-term. At present, for example, many farmers refuse to plant grain because government contract prices are too low and fertilizer and other necessities are too expensive. Further, farmers' income expectations are becoming higher because of the income available through work in rural factories. Meeting those expectations through higher crop prices means the government must either increase subsidies in prices paid to farmers or allow urban living costs to rise still higher, aggravating the already serious discontent in the cities.

(The ferment in farming is discussed in more detail elsewhere. See, for example, "Making Prices Reflect Realities" in chapter 5, and the whole of chapter 6, "Reform in the Countryside.")

In addition to the current economic and political concerns with agriculture there are also long-term anxieties based in China's physical geography and the uncertainties of managing social change in the countryside.

On a per-person basis, China's agricultural land is only *one-third* of the world average, its fresh water is only *one-fourth*, its grassland is only *one-half*, and its forested land only *one-eighth*.

Despite these sparse resources, China manages to feed about 22 percent of the world's population with only 7 percent of the world's cultivated land. Its per capita arable land, less than 0.2 hectares, is half the world average and is becoming ever more limited. It has been estimated that cropland declined from about 270 million acres (about 110 million hectares) in the early fifties to about 245 million acres (99 million hectares) in 1979, with an accelerated loss since. Because of the loss of arable land to nonfarm uses and to desertification, and the growth of population, the amount of available farmland per person has declined in about twenty-five years by a total of 45 percent, and is now disappearing at an annual rate of 0.5 to 1.0 percent a year.

A new Land Administration Law, the first law covering use, conservation, and reclamation of land, became effective in 1987. The report on the first year is encouraging; loss of arable land was down by 26 percent, and illegal use and occupation of arable land down 80–90 percent—but this means there was still a loss of perhaps 400,000 hectares.

Is all possible land being used? No, but the big gains to be made from bringing new land into cultivation have already occurred. In the early eighties, the most optimistic estimates indicated as many as 80 million acres (32.4 million hectares) of potential farm land; other estimates are as low as 32.8 million acres (13.3 million hectares) and the World Bank estimates that only "perhaps another 3 million to 5 million hectares [7.4–12.3 million acres] of 'wasteland' are suitable for development in the medium term."

In addition, it is difficult to bring more than a limited amount of new agricultural land into production each year, for it is arduous, expensive work. The state is now engaged in a number of reclamation projects that will open in four years about as much land as is now being lost in two. Moreover, new land is often of lower quality than land already in use, which is why it has not been farmed before.

What about increases in productivity?

A significant increase in productivity has already come from planting two crops a year in areas that formerly planted only one, or three where there were only two. It is unlikely that a substantial further increase can be obtained from multicropping, and, in fact, some decrease in rice output has occurred since 1978 as farmers have taken advantage of their new autonomy to discontinue unprofitable double cropping of rice in some areas. Improvements have also come from such advances as breeding better varieties of hybrid rice (the modern "miracle" hybrids that produced Asia's Green Revolution in the last twenty years or so probably had as much to do with China's 50 percent production increase since 1978 as did the responsibility system); improving methods of growing seedlings; more careful formulation of chemical fertilizers to overcome soil deficiencies in specific areas; improved insect control; and other measures. No doubt much additional progress remains to be made, but it is dependent upon the availability of agrotechnicians, who are as scarce as other skilled technical personnel, and financial support for them.

Another area of possible stimulation for growth in productivity is increase and improvement in irrigation. Over 50 percent of China's arable land is already irrigated, in some cases by deteriorating systems hundreds of years old. Further irrigation could be a source of both additional arable land and additional production, but this incremental production will also come at a relatively high cost, and total irrigated land has in fact been decreasing for some years. (One reason irrigation has declined is that water control systems are better. As the system improved, the pumps, valves, etc., became larger and more valuable—and the farmers began to steal more of them. Some systems are totally crippled, leaving many towns and cities vulnerable to flooding.)

Finally, there are the gains realizable at some indefinite time in the future from consolidation of small plots, further increases in the use of chemical fertilizers, a greatly increased level of mechanization, and all the other changes that would place Chinese agriculture technologically on a par with more developed countries. These changes too will be relatively slow and expensive.

In summary, improvements in agricultural production are still possible, and likely, but the speed with which they will occur and their overall effectiveness is difficult to predict. But there is no such uncertainty in the specter of uncontrolled population growth, and China cannot afford to gamble.

There was a real possibility that in 1988–89, for the first time since the famine after the Great Leap Forward, a large part of the population—forty million people according to China's own estimates—would suffer severe hunger. In early spring, provincial officials were reported frantically attempting to obtain supplies for five million people "on the verge of starvation." Disaster was averted, but the country will continue to live on the edge.

There is now a critical long-term race for China to maintain a maximum degree of self-sufficiency in food until it can modernize its agriculture and industry and greatly raise its educational and scientific levels. Given these improvements, which will not be broadly effective for decades, the country will gradually be able to increase its exports and earn foreign exchange to increase its food imports. Because of four poor years in a row, China has slipped backwards in the race. It is no longer a grain exporter but in 1989 will become the world's largest wheat importer, at sixteen million tons surpassing the Soviet Union's fourteen million.

But food is not China's only long-term population problem. It cannot afford the large social investment which must be made in educating, housing, and otherwise caring for a greatly enlarged youthful population.

It cannot be certain of achieving solid, sustainable growth sufficient to provide work for a rapidly increasing population. The "one mouth, two hands" cliché used to rebut Ma Yinchu's advice on population control (and still being used by religious and nationalist groups in some developing countries and by some economists) implied that one additional mouth to feed was no problem, because there were also two more hands to grow the food. In a basically agricultural economy with sufficient natural resources, that would be true. But under today's—and tomorrow's—conditions, the two hands are as big a problem as the one mouth.

It has been estimated that the labor force will increase during 1987–90 from 586 million to 673 million, or 22 million new workers each year. Only about 6 million old workers retire each year, leaving China with the formidable task of creating 16 million jobs a year in a market where there is already large "hidden unemployment" in heavily over-staffed government enterprises.

But this counts only new workers. Still other applicants will come from enterprises as they increasingly become responsible for their own finances and have to trim fat (excess staff is estimated as at least 20 million), and from workers made redundant by increased efficiency in their factories (estimated at another 10–20 million). Another 6–7 million persons are expected to lose their jobs in construction as the current cutback of unproductive projects takes hold.

Finally, the government estimates that 20 million peasants will be leaving the land each year for some years to come because of increased efficiency in the countryside and the lure of the larger incomes boasted by peasants now working in rural industries.

THE URGENCY OF POPULATION CONTROL

These facts indicate an ominous problem that threatens the success of everything else the Chinese are trying to achieve. A specialist in Chinese population, Leo A. Orleans, noted in a letter to the *New York Times:*

> In China . . . the size and rate of growth of the population dominate all aspects of national development. A nation whose population is the size of Europe's and Africa's combined, and that annually increases by a number equal to the populations of Austria and Norway, cannot view population control simply as an important priority. It is a necessity for survival.

And this is particularly true today, when China is beginning to face the long-anticipated threat of its second population explosion since liberation, despite all its control efforts have been able to achieve. Wu Canping, a demographer and professor at China People's University, explains that

> Beginning in 1962, a "baby boom" swept through China . . . for more than a dozen years. During that period there was a decade in which more than 25 million babies were born each year. [Over 360 million during 1962–75.] This generation will join the ranks of the childbearing this year [1985] to the end of the century. . . .
>
> Even if all the people of this generation have only an average of 2.2 children per couple, they still would give birth to *another 368 million babies before the end of this century.* Confronted with this enormous childbearing potential, China has every reason to require that this generation lower its birth rate. . . .

Today's baby boom was generated by these historical circumstances:

1. After liberation, improvements in food supply, medical care, working conditions, etc., reduced the death rate by 1978 to only a third of what it was in 1949 (from 2.0 percent to less than 0.7 percent), and approximately doubled the life expectancy by 1981 (from about 35 years for both sexes to 66.4 years for men and 69.6 years for women). Birth rates between the end of the famine after the Great Leap Forward in 1962 and the beginning of the Cultural Revolution in 1966 were in the very high 34–38 per thousand range, and remained relatively high even through those tumultuous years to 1975.

2. Family planning does not seem to have received much attention prior to the seventies, even during the two periods (1954–57 and 1962–66) when there were formal population control campaigns. The Family Planning Office of the State Council has summed up the history of family planning in China this way: "In spite of many explicit directives and correct proposals from the Party and the government for work in family planning, the majority of the people did not understand sufficiently for a long period of time that population growth should be coordinated with the growth of the national economy; instead, most of us clung to the notion that the more people, the better."

The great difficulty of feeding, clothing, educating, and employing vast numbers of new citizens, and the threat of an imminent population explosion, are the twin reasons China embarked after the Third Plenum on an unprecedented population control effort. It is especially notewor-thy because China remains one of the most successful among develop-ing nations in curbing unsustainable population growth.

China and South Korea were the only two large countries whose population control efforts were rated "excellent" in a 1988 survey of 110 countries by the Population Crisis Committee. A population specialist pointed out in the *Washington Post* recently that since the late 1960s population growth worldwide has declined by about 20 percent, and "the credit for practically all of that decline went to China."

For several years, the goal of China's population program has been a net population growth (births minus deaths) averaging 0.95 percent of the total population per year to the year 2000. It has never been that low, however, and in 1988 and 1989 was about 1.4 and 1.5 respectively, for reasons to be discussed later.

By contrast, the population growth rate in developing countries around the world has been more than 3 percent until recently. The average is still 2.5 percent, with Africa growing most rapidly at 3.1 percent.

Barber Conable, president of the World Bank, recently named popu-lation as one of the five major determinants of national poverty or well being. He said:

> I realize that population policy touches upon sensitive cultural and reli-gious values. But the societies in which population is growing very fast must accept the fact that many—perhaps most—of these new lives will be miserable, malnourished, and brief.

The overwhelming birthrate is just one of a growing number of areas—environmental maintenance, drug addiction, organ transplants, geriat-ric medicine, and more—where most societies are being forced to make increasingly painful choices. Unpopular as it is with Chinese who do not understand the problem and some foreigners who are not faced with it, China is trying to choose population control before it is too late.

GOOD RESULTS SINCE FAMILY PLANNING
BEGAN IN EARNEST DURING SEVENTIES

China has made considerable progress in reaching its goal, even though it was not until the early seventies that family planning became a topic of serious and continuing concern to the government and Party and was included in national economic development plans. The new constitution adopted in the spring of 1978 stipulated for the first time that "The state advocates and encourages family planning," and the revised Marriage Law adopted in 1980 provides that "Husband and wife are duty bound to practice family planning." The "one couple, one child" policy, which will be described later, was also adopted in 1980.

Progress is demonstrated by figures for a few key years. In 1970, the birth rate was 33.4 per thousand, and the growth rate was 2.6 percent. By 1979, the birth rate was nearly halved, at 17.8 per thousand, and the growth rate was less than half, at 1.2 percent. By 1984 the birth rate was down a little more, at 17.5 per thousand, as was the growth rate, at 1.1 percent. Both began climbing, however—to 17.8 per thousand and 1.1 percent in 1985, 20.8 per thousand and 1.4 percent in 1986, 21.0 per thousand and about 1.5 percent in 1987, 20.8 per thousand and 1.4 percent in 1988, and over 21.0 per thousand and 1.5 percent in 1989. Control efforts have made a significant difference in the size of China's population, though the full effect of the population control effort has been brought into question by recent reexamination of the statistics.

Behind the 1989 announcement that the goal of a 1.2 billion population by 2000 could not be met are indications that birth figures in recent years are low because of two types of reporting deficiencies.

First, *People's Daily*, *Population Research*, and other sources have recently reported widespread falsification of reports in order to stay within official quotas ("insincere reporting of births," it was called in one publication). A national population seminar concluded that six provinces and cities had reported rates 40 percent below actual births and ten provinces and cities had lowered their real figures by 20 to 30 percent.

Second, the results of a major survey by the State Statistical Bureau show that 17 percent of births between January 1987 and October 1988 were not registered by parents because they incurred additional per capita taxes for each person in the family; because of a lack of personnel trained in statistical compilation in rural areas; and for other reasons.

How Population Control Works

How does China go about reducing the birth rate? In many ways—some of them quite personal and direct. As US Congressman James H. Scheur wrote after a 1987 visit, China "relies on an incessant drumbeat of persuasion and peer pressure, which is undergirded by individuals' sense of responsibility to society and family which supersedes any perception they may have of their own personal rights."

There are the usual speeches, banners, broadcasts, and stories in the press, of course, explaining the need for what the people are being asked to do. There are posters asking people to have only a single child and, interestingly, these posters almost always show a girl rather than a boy, to help erase the prejudice against female infants in some areas.

The primary method, however, is working very closely with women of childbearing age. Husbands are also involved. There are classes on contraception (not coed), and on the importance of holding down the nation's population. Discussions are held with individual couples by the family planning representative of the neighborhood committee, who also records the birth control method each couple is using and provides free contraceptives. Sterilization is widely available, including a new Chinese procedure for blocking the male sperm duct said to be completely effective, cheap, fast, reversible, and approved by the World Health Organization.

Urban couples who wish to have a child request permission from the wife's work unit, which is allotted a portion of the births planned for the year in the locality. The wife later reports the expected time of her delivery to both her workplace and her neighborhood committee, and the committee then arranges for prenatal care, the delivery, and postnatal care.

The work unit is also told how many abortions will be permitted in the unit during the year; the number varies somewhat, depending on the age composition of the work unit, but the allowance has been said by Chinese informants to be small. (This does not square with the acknowledgment by Chinese officials at a "Day of the 5 Billion" [world population] news conference in 1987 that about one in three pregnancies in China—11.58 million in 1986—ended in abortion, about the same proportion as in Singapore, and, according to the Alan Guttmacher Institute, as in the United States.) If the quota of births is exceeded, it is reported that the work unit's bonuses may be affected, and a man's work unit may be penalized for an unauthorized birth.

This obviously puts considerable pressure on birth control units to do their work well, and perhaps an even greater social and psychological pressure on couples to avoid unauthorized conceptions. Clearly, abortion rates are higher than, say, ten years ago, and women also are often pressured into terminating second pregnancies, but there is nothing to indicate that physical force is used if women refuse abortion. Reports are unclear on how late abortions are normally performed. Nor do they indicate whether the pregnancies are deliberate attempts to circumvent the authorities, whether contraceptive failures are up, or if abortion is being increasingly substituted for contraception.

Comparable conditions and procedures prevail in the countryside, although rural families are not under such close surveillance or as easily disciplined. Therefore, rural control measures are both less stringent and, as is obvious from comparative birth rates, less effective. It is clear that, depending on local cadres and local circumstances, enforcement of population policy may vary widely.

Even where an attempt is made to enforce regulations strictly, as one writer put it, "with the wealth that de-collectivization . . . has brought to many peasants the heavy fines for having two, three, or more children are little more than an affordable tax on procreation." It is said that there are rural children called "TV Set," because the fine for their birth was equal to the cost of a television.

THE ONE-CHILD POLICY

The "one couple, one child" program is the symbolic centerpiece of the current population control campaign, and the aspect which almost alone represents Chinese population control to foreigners. Under this policy couples who agree to have only one child receive a certificate as a "one-child couple" and the following benefits (or most of them, depending on the family's location): a monthly subsidy of 5 yuan until the child reaches 14; free child health care; assurance that there will be a place in a nursery school and a further subsidy to cover part of the school fees; and preference in housing or allocation of land for homes. (Some offered benefits simply are not forthcoming in some areas, such as housing.) If a couple has a second child, these benefits are lost for the future.

The official position is that parents "may" be fined for having an additional child; the fine in urban areas is reported to be 15 percent of the annual salary of both parents (though for how many years is not clear) and housing and even jobs may be forfeited. Individual Chinese have said that usually the past benefits must be repaid. The actual amounts involved are not great, but repaying these small amounts from a small income represents a substantial sacrifice. There are administrative punishments, as well, such as a demotion of one grade for each parent or denial of promotion for several years. Additional penalties may include denial of subsidized grain for the new child and other obstacles.

Strangely, no incentive whatever has been offered to couples who may consider not having children at all. As matters stand, the prospect of securing more satisfactory housing as a one-child family than they can expect as a childless couple may tip the scales in favor of a child for those who are undecided.

As is always the case with major Chinese programs, considerable work was done to try out the one-child proposal before it became governmental policy. In fact, in the formal announcement of it, the policy was credited with reducing births by several million in 1979, the year before the plan was officially promulgated. The policy was proposed for the first time at a symposium on marriage early in 1980, and a fuller statement of it was made in September 1980 in an open letter to members of the Communist Youth League.

This short but detailed letter reviewed the reasons for large past population growth, pointed out the threat posed by the coming of age

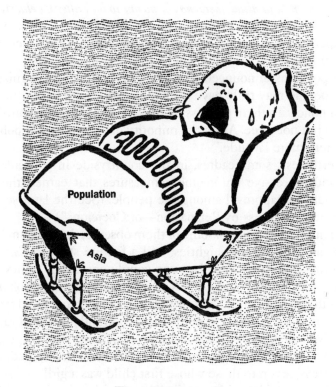

The cradle's too small

Zhu Genua, *Beijing Review*

of the 1962–70 "baby boomers" and summarized the need to control future population growth.

The open letter also analyzed several implications of the policy that were obvious possible problems and gave the Party's conclusions, namely:

Aging of the population—This would not be a problem because the youthfulness of the population, with 65 percent being under 30 in 1980, gave ample time for future precautions.

A shortage of labor—The 1980 labor force of 500 million was expected to swell to 600 million in 20 years, and by 10 million yearly thereafter, and no shortage was expected.

What if a couple's one child is a girl?—"People of new China, especially the young, should discard the outdated idea of men being superior to women. If the only child happens to be a girl, give good care to bring her up just as well [as a boy]."

With such small families, there may be no one to look after the elderly—This is a problem common to many countries, but when production has developed there is bound to be a corresponding steady increase and improvement in social welfare and social security facilities.

The policy as announced had some flexibility. It recognized that "Some people may truly have difficulties which are within the provisions of policy. To them permission may be granted to give birth to two children but not three. As for the minority nationalities, our policy is to allow them more latitude."

Nevertheless, some cadres, in the countryside in particular, used harsh and repressive enforcement measures that earned the policy considerable disapproval among the people. (See the later section of this chapter, "Success by Persuasion—or Coercion?")

For a number of reasons, some of them obscure, the program became more lenient in the mid-eighties, and a feature story in *China Daily* denied that there was actually a one couple-one child "policy" at all, claiming that "the government has never issued any regulation limiting couples to one child only." The population program operated for two or three years under a variety of permissible local and provincial variations that allowed second children to, for example, farmers with "special economic difficulties," couples whose first child was disabled, and in several areas, even to those whose first child was a girl!

Finally, recognizing widespread violation of the government's policy, it was officially declared in the fall of 1988 that farmers whose only child is a girl may have a second child. "Our real problems are with the families that have three, five, and even seven children," said a State Birth Control Commission spokesperson. "We need to concentrate on those now."

Other steps to be taken are, for example: devising ways to detect and control births in the families of transient, government-approved self-managed laborers (about 18 million of them), who now easily evade birth regulations; completing and utilizing a major national survey on fertility and birth control problems and practices which was started in mid–1988; and returning to enforcement of the legal minimum marriage ages (twenty-two for men, twenty for women), limits which are widely disregarded, especially in the countryside.

Even though it has not met with unqualified success, there can be no doubt that the one-child policy has made a major contribution to the future quality of life in China. According to a 1985 State Family Planning Commission survey, China had approximately 35 million one-child families (most of them in urban areas), about one-fifth of the nation's married couples of childbearing age. Since most families traditionally have had two or more children, and still do, it can be assumed that the one-child program has reduced by perhaps 35–50 million the number of births that might have occurred without it.

SUCCESS BY PERSUASION—OR COERCION?

As the Chinese themselves report, the national population policy is not popular with everyone. There is considerable resistance in the countryside, where many still feel with Confucius that "the greatest filial impiety is the failure to have a male offspring," and where the new economic system makes sons especially desirable. Nevertheless, despite problems, dramatic reductions in birth rates are reported for some rural areas, and, as has been shown, national rates have fallen substantially.

There have been charges by some conservative American religious and political groups opposed to family planning, and by members of Congress affiliated with them, that these reductions have been achieved through an official government policy that encourages or condones intimidation, forced abortions, and female infanticide. Regardless of how often the Chinese say that such incidents are not common and not the result of official policy, a few foreign critics continue to make their charges, even though they have no supporting evidence aside from information furnished by the Chinese themselves when abuses are discovered.

On the question of coercion, Congressman Scheur wrote that:

> The delegation not only found that it is condemned by officials but also that the government had severely penalized local officials who violated official policy. Infanticide is illegal, and violators face prison. Chinese officials readily admit that some overzealous local officers went off the deep end and practiced coercion when the one-child policy was first implemented in 1980. But they say, and western observers agree, that such instances are increasingly infrequent and that the uproar in the western media focused government attention on the problem.

Even an investigation by the Agency for International Development, a US agency which has withheld funds from a United Nations population program in China because of coercion charges, found no evidence that the Chinese government or the UN program approved coerced abortions. (AID now withholds funds for any purpose from any group whose services include even voluntary abortions or abortion counseling.) Senator Daniel Inouye, co-sponsor of the law under which the AID acted, called the charge against China "absurd." The agency administrator has continued to withhold funds, nevertheless, refusing to recognize that less help with contraception inevitably leads to more of the abortions the US government was criticizing.

Reflecting displeasure at the lack of US sympathy with China's severe population problem, Foreign Minister Qian Qichen said recently,

> If the United States population were five times its current size [as China's is], it would be fairly easy for members of Congress to agree on China's family planning policy.

Nafis Sadik, executive director of the United Nations Fund for Population Activities, pointed out that

> The fact that all the information [critics] collected was from Chinese sources and newspapers means that the Chinese government was itself concerned about these factors, otherwise they would not have published them. It was clear the government does not have a coercive policy.

Wholesale female infanticide is another charge that has been laid against China. While China acknowledges that as in many other countries women sometimes secure abortions after their unborns are determined to be female, and that cases of female infanticide do occur, it denies that killing of infant girls is condoned or is as widespread as has been charged. A government spokesperson said in *China Daily*:

> Based on China's sex ratio of newborn babies, it was recently suggested in the United States that the country's family planning program and infanticide had led to the loss of more than 230,000 baby girls in 1981. . . . It was claimed in the United States that China intended to control population growth by encouraging the killing of baby girls.
>
> According to a survey conducted by the Chinese government in 1982, the female-male ratio of newborn babies in 1981 was 100:108. Some arbitrarily concluded that, compared with the world's sex ratio pattern of [100:] 106, the high [number of boys] means the loss of 232,000 baby girls in 1981.
>
> Sex ratios differ from one country to another and from one period to another. For example, in 1977 the sex ratio in Malawi was 100:90, while in Iraq it was 100:109. In South Korea, the sex ratio was 100:106 in 1980 and rose to nearly 100:110 in 1982.
>
> Do all the examples point to great losses of babies in these countries? All these data point only to the fact that differences exist. . . . But without making any systematic quantitative analysis, it has been asserted that more than 200,000 baby girls were killed in China in 1981. This is sheer irresponsibility.

Australian population specialist Penny Kane agrees in her book *The Second Billion* that

> There is . . . some evidence that sex ratios do vary a little in different races, and that the Chinese in China and in other Southeast Asian countries have higher than average ones. When [statistics on Chinese children] are compared with model life tables . . . they are quite plausible. This suggests that . . . infanticide has not been on the kind of scale which affects the national ratios.

She saw cause for concern in some provinces, however, such as Shandong, Henan, and Guangdong, where the ratio is 100:110, Guangxi at 100:111, and Anhui at about 100:112.

The Chinese government has gone to great lengths to publicize what it says are isolated instances of the killing of female children by parents and of abortion resulting from coercion and intimidation by cadres. It makes these stories widely public for the very purpose, it says, of emphasizing to its people that both the cadres' and parents' behavior is wrong and illegal.

For the outsider, the nonspecialist, the question quickly comes down to, "Whom can I believe?" A key part of the judgment has to be related to what one believes the motives of the Chinese government are in giving such widespread publicity to unfavorable population control information.

It must be recognized that there was nothing in the situation which required the government to be frank about these problems of coercion. Indeed, the government exposed itself to possible criticism by publicizing the incidents in *People's Daily* and other major Chinese publications (where the world press picked them up). And it was even riskier to permit stories in the English-language *China Daily* and the multilingual editions of *Beijing Review*, since both of these are read by people who are friends of China or have a special interest in the country. While critics may often question the government's credibility in other matters, there seems little reason to challenge its accounts of population control enforcement.

As Leo A. Orleans wrote in his letter mentioned earlier, "To question China's sincerity in this matter is to suggest that since child abuse exists in the United States it is supported by Washington."

If the intimidation and coercion of the parents, and the danger to the child, are as grave and certain as the critics suggest, one wonders why so many couples run the risk.

It is more likely that because brutality is *not* a government policy that four-fifths of married couples of childbearing age still have two or more children, despite 15 years of work on population control.

Lack of government control as much as lack of public cooperation may be the reason that China's population by 2050 will probably rise 200 to 300 million above the target level, according to China's ambassador to the United Nations.

Finally, the government has many times laid its credibility with its people squarely on the line in official statements forbidding coercion in population control.

For example, the open letter on the one-child policy distributed to millions in 1980 said that "Every comrade should actively and patiently persuade the masses around him. Comrades . . . must unhesitatingly refrain from coercion and commandism and from acting against law and discipline, and they should further advise others to refrain from doing so as well." And no less an official than the Party Secretary and then Premier Zhao Ziyang said, in a widely publicized speech to the National People's Congress in 1983, that "The whole society should resolutely condemn the criminal activities of female infanticide and maltreatment of the mothers, and the judicial departments should resolutely punish the offenders according to law."

Those unwilling to credit the reduced birth rate to voluntary cooperation fail to recognize the many historic instances of strong response by the people to other major campaigns. Their attitude denies that fewer children would be in the people's best interests, and denies too that many of the people have the ability to recognize this. It fails to recognize that on the whole birth rates have been falling worldwide, if at varying rates, in both developed and developing nations. On the available evidence, there is no reason to doubt that the progress to date has been made, in the last analysis, because of the people's understanding of their own self-interest.

THE BOTTOM LINE

For a number of years now, the Chinese government has worked toward the goal of holding the country's population at the end of this century to 1.2 billion. To achieve this, it would have been necessary to hold growth to 1.0 percent in 1980 (it was actually 1.2) and 0.5 percent in 1985 (actually 1.1), with an overall average of 0.95 through 2000. Even higher rates have been experienced since the early eighties and are expected to continue. *People's Daily* announced in early 1989 that the goal of 1.2 billion will be missed by about 100 million. Nevertheless, control efforts have been tremendously beneficial, according to China's delegate to the United Nations Population Commission, who told the group in 1989 that China estimated its work had averted about two hundred million additional births between 1971 and 1986.

Four

"IT HARDLY MATTERS WHETHER A CAT IS BLACK OR WHITE"

At least once somewhere in this book there must appear Deng Xiaoping's famous observation from the early sixties, "It hardly matters whether a cat is black or white. As long as it catches mice, it is a good cat." This down-to-earth philosophy underlies virtually all the changes that have occurred in the New Chinese Revolution, but nowhere is the quotation more appropriate than in this chapter on the broader aspects of the Chinese experiment with social, political, and economic change.

Pragmatists is the word most often used to characterize Deng Xiaoping and the other Chinese leaders responsible for the rethinking of old problems and for the innovations and experiments that have been typical of the last decade (and it should not be overlooked, in the disappointment of June 1989's Great Leap Backward, that a vast amount of courageous change has occurred). Frequently, there are implications that Deng, Zhao, and their associates who spearheaded reform for most of its first decade were more concerned with results than with socialist principles. Many of the reforms that have developed out of seeds planted at the Third Plenary Session in 1978 have been criticized by some as socialist heresy bordering on capitalism—and in China, as an American writer has put it, "one man's reform is another man's abandonment of Marxism."

It has recently become commonplace for commentators to say that Marxist ideology is losing its power in China, just as it is, at least in its more doctrinaire forms, throughout the world, and that appears to be true. This is, of course, one thing that so upsets the conservatives. The ideological madness of the Cultural Revolution, the Party's bland toleration of its elitism and the country's smothering corruption, and the general irrelevance of Marxism to the life of the country have reduced interest to a lower level than in many years. The three ideology-based conservative campaigns against reform mounted since 1978 have had short lives. And, until the elderly leaders began successfully to exploit the circumstances to exert an ideological spin on economic and organizational problems, the reform ferment of 1988 and 1989 was much more heavily economic than ideological in content.

Fear of the demise of socialism is seldom expressed as dramatically as in the crackdown on the Pro-Democracy Movement, but it is nevertheless true that, even for many Chinese who would genuinely welcome some reforms, anything that appears to abandon Marxism seems to invite capitalism, and that continues to be a serious matter indeed. There are still many men, aging to be sure but with their own young and influential disciples, who fear capitalism, who have seen with their own eyes and felt in their own hearts the misery and shame capitalism brought to themselves and their families in the old China. The loss of power that would afflict cadres in a thoroughgoing reform is perhaps of less concern to many of them than the real and deeply felt fear of grave social instability if there is a loss of central control. "Abandonment of Marxism" is of grave concern to all of them on several levels. Finally, there are people who, as one Beijing broadcast put it, are simply worried about changes that will create a greater "unevenness of joys and sufferings."

For their own part, however, many of the reform leaders have also known misery and shame from mindless "Marxism" during the Cultural Revolution and the campaigns and purges that went before it. Deng was twice humiliated and removed from power and his family persecuted and injured. So were many other present Party and government leaders. Thus, reform leaders, intellectuals, and millions of other Chinese have as much to fear from the return of this distorted type of "Marxism" as the "Marxists" think they have to fear from capitalism.

Furthermore, the reformers recognize that although the country undoubtedly progressed under Mao's brand of Marxism it also suffered turmoil, famine, persecution, and a failure to achieve what it otherwise might have. By the time Mao died both the Soviet-style economy that inspired the Great Leap Forward and the "Marxist" model that Mao envisioned in his later years had been tried, and both had blighted the country with chaos and stagnation. The living standard of the people remained low. Both peasants' and workers' real incomes had decreased, not grown, during the ten years of the Cultural Revolution, and the relentless "Marxist" class struggle of that period had wounded the country grievously.

Thus, there were many urgent reasons in 1978 for seeking a new way to deal with China's problems, even if the change meant a reinterpretation of its former understanding of Marxism.

Hu Yaobang, then Party secretary, suggested a need for such a reinterpretation when he observed to an interviewer that the Russian Revolution occurred more than 65 years ago, and asked, "How is it that many socialist countries have not been able to overtake capitalist ones in terms of development? What was it that did not work?"

China embarked in 1979 on a bold and risky course of trying to find out what works. It still does not know.

ARE THE CHINESE GOING CAPITALIST?

There has been a lot of commentary, analysis, and speculation in recent years about where the Chinese revolution is headed. Among western writers and diplomats, a lot of what has been expressed demonstrates cultural and political bias as much as anything else.

For example, when the Chinese in December 1984 re-evaluated the applicability of Marxist theory to contemporary conditions, a wire service story in a conservative American newspaper was headlined "China Rejects Marxism as 'Obsolete.'" The early paragraphs of the story itself spoke of the "Repudiation of the philosophy the nation has followed since... 1949." One expected to read in the next sentence that the portraits of Marx and Lenin then still found in China had been replaced by Adam Smith's! There was absolutely nothing in either the

Chinese announcement or the American story to support the use of "rejects" or "obsolete" or "repudiation," but anyone who did not read the story carefully was left with the quite clear message that China had, in fact, abandoned Marxism.

It was not until well into the story that quotations from the Chinese announcement made it plain that, actually, only "some" of Marx's ideas and "certain" Marxist principles were being questioned, for reasons that even the founders of socialism would not challenge.

What exactly did the Chinese say to create such misinterpretation— or misrepresentation?

In its issue of December 7, 1984, *People's Daily*, the official government newspaper, carried a front page article by the "Commentator" headed "Theory Not Enough for Success." It included these passages:

> Marx died 101 years ago. His works were written more than 100 years ago. There have been tremendous changes since his ideas were formed. Some of [Marx's] ideas are no longer suited to today's situation, because Marx never experienced these times, nor did Engels or Lenin. And they never came across the problems we face today. So we cannot use Marxist and Leninist works to solve our present-day problems. [The next day's issue corrected the sentence to read, "... to solve *all* our present-day problems." Emphasis supplied.] In terms of Marxism and Leninism, we cannot be dogmatic. Times are changing. If we continue to use certain Marxist principles ... our historic development will surely be hampered.

In a follow-up commentary a few days later *People's Daily* reassured the people that their government was not abandoning Marx. It emphasized that both Marx and Mao had recognized that Marx's writings were subject to revision in the light of events. It quoted Lenin as saying that Marxism should "Never be taken as unalterable or sacred and inviolable." As an example, *People's Daily* pointed out that classical Marxist doctrine said that successful revolution was dependent on urban workers, but that it was Mao's adjustment of Marx's thinking to fit China's situation that led to successfully basing the Chinese revolution on the peasants. (The commentary might also have mentioned that another major reform as long ago as 1942, the Party Rectification Campaign, had as one of its main targets the eradication of "formalism," i.e., dogmatism.)

Finally, the commentary asked,

> If whatever Marx has not said must not be done, what should we do now? ... This issue concerns the success or failure of socialist construction:

Whether we should stick to the assumptions made by Marx years ago and achieve nothing or promote socialism according to the Party Central Committee's policies and proceed from reality. The answer is self-evident.

This point of view continues to trouble many conservative Chinese, however. Dogmatic Marxism was again an element in the spring 1987 upheaval, and for a time the free and vigorous discussion of economic and political topics which had begun after the 1984 pronouncements was heavily muted.

By midsummer of 1987, however, leading officials—if not still-cautious academics and other intellectuals—were again broadly asserting their views of Marxist malleability. Deng told a visitor, for example, that

> The original essence of Marxism lies in the development of material things. We have since added many superfluous notions. It is now time to make things clear.

And *People's Daily* said that the Party must:

> . . . look upon Marxism as a developing science, and not simply recite dogma. . . . Marxism itself is open and outward-looking. As it develops it must. . . ceaselessly absorb new fruits from the social and natural sciences.

The new concept developed by Zhao at the Thirteenth Congress (that China entered a primary, low-level stage of socialism without first passing through the capitalist stage Marx envisioned and therefore must develop some of the useful capitalist mechanisms), may not be accepted by classical Marxists, but it does provide a new way to think about China's situation. Some officials have indicated a willingness to accept what might be called "socialism with capitalistic Chinese characteristics," but in a country where private enterprise contributes less than one percent of gross national product it is far too early to proclaim, as some foreigners have, that China has succumbed to capitalism.

"Socialist" and "socialism" mean to the Chinese a system in which government owns all the means of producing wealth and is devoted to the common prosperity of all the people. To a capitalist, the same words may mean a system in which central control stifles initiative, damages productivity, and does not reward fairly those who make the greatest contributions to a nation's economy.

"Capitalist" and "capitalism," on the other hand, are usually, in Chinese contexts, merely code words implying exploitation, unbridled individualism, corruption, and class division. In western contexts "capitalist" and "capitalism" often imply freedom of action, opportunity for creativity and initiative, and substantial rewards for risk-taking and entrepreneurship.

China's reforms are essentially an attempt to combine socialism and capitalism—but by taking only the Chinese concept of socialism and the western concept of capitalism! The result, whatever else it may be called, is not capitalism.

Commenting on economic reform following meetings in China with Deng and others, Helmut Schmidt, former chancellor of capitalist West Germany, gave in *Die Zeit* a realistic summary that puts the present reforms into perspective:

> It is not communism that the Chinese are giving up, but the narrow-minded attempt to construct a Utopia on earth. This is not the beginning of a counterrevolution but an attempt to proceed from a period of revolution to pragmatic economic development. The principle of property ownership will remain intact. The Party's supreme leadership role will not change. Deng Xiaoping and Zhao Ziyang are concerned essentially with reform. They are working for innovation and efficiency within communism. To see this reform as aiming for something beyond communism is either an ideological assault from the left or naive Western stupidity.

The Chinese call the new system that is coming into being (and that the new conservative leaders have promised to continue) a "commodity economy," or, in full, "a planned commodity economy based on public ownership." They say the nation is creating "socialism with Chinese characteristics." (See this term in the Mini-Encyclopedia.) It might also be called "market-oriented socialism." ("Commodity economy" is a political rather than an economic term that might more understandably be translated "market-oriented economy," i.e., an economy in which people direct their labor to goods and services others wish to purchase, and purchase their own needs in the same marketplace. In China, however, the market obviously has not been free, as state planning has played a significant role, and will surely continue to do so.)

A current popular joke in socialist countries is that "communism is the longest and most painful route from capitalism to capitalism." As the new "primary stage" theory recognizes, China's reforms are undoubtedly introducing into its socialist life some elements of capitalism. But Deng and other officials have said many times that they see no possibility that China will become a capitalist nation as a result of using capitalist techniques to improve China's economy, nor do they feel that they are deviating from sound socialist principles in their reform plans. The primary stage theory permits such ideological imports and they can be made respectable because Lenin urged:

> Don't hesitate to absorb good things from abroad: Soviet political power + Prussian rail system order + American technology and trust organization + [other beneficial elements] = Socialism.

The major safeguard, as the Central Committee's 1984 decision on economic reforms points out, is that the essential difference between capitalist and socialist economies lies "in the difference in ownership, in whether there is an exploiting class, and whether the working people are masters of the state." In China, state and collective ownership attempt to assure that there is no exploiting class.

As for the existence of new private businesses which own their resources, an aspect of capitalism that is of special concern to some, it has been pointed out that China's circumstances make fear of this development unwarranted. The private economy is subordinate to the socialist economy, makes up only a small proportion of the whole economy, is (in theory) limited to specific products and lines of business, and, finally, is in any case subject to state control. (It is likely to be subject to increased state control under the new conservative government. See "Private Business" in chapter 5.)

Deng Xiaoping and others have often rejected predictions of various reform problems, including a slide into capitalism, polarization (or "the red-eye disease," envy of successful people by those less successful), etc. He gave an early summary of the official position, since repeated many times, in a talk to scientists in early 1985. Pointing out that China is today building socialism with the ultimate purpose of achieving communism, he said that

> The four modernizations we are striving for today are none other than socialist modernizations. All our policies concerning opening to the world, invigorating the domestic economy, and structural reform are directed towards developing a socialist economy.
>
> We allow private businesses, joint ventures with Chinese and foreign investment, and wholly owned foreign enterprises to grow in China, *but we see to it that socialist public ownership always remains the mainstay. The goal of socialism is common prosperity for all the Chinese people, not class polarization.* [Emphasis supplied] If our policy results in polarization, then we have failed. If it produces a new capitalist class, then we have really taken to evil ways.

Today, a transition into pure capitalism is not nearly as likely as a return to a centrally controlled economy relatively closed to the world. Since the beginning of reform, Deng and his fellow reformers have been adamant even during campaigns against bourgeois liberalization that there will be no such change. Whether, as they claim, there will be no change of policies under Li Peng and his allies may turn out to be a matter of definition of what reform was considered to be in the first place.

In the view of the new decision-makers, it may very well be that much of what has happened in the last ten years was merely a bourgeois liberal perversion of the policies adopted at the Third Plenum in 1978, and therefore requires substantial correction. (In fact, this seems to be the line that is being taken. See "Bourgeois Liberalization" in the Mini-Encyclopedia.) It is hard to believe that the leadership took the risks of declaring martial law and using deadly force to control unarmed demonstrators merely to maintain the status quo of which they have been so critical and which has caused them so much fear and anxiety.

There Are No Ideal Solutions to Reform Dilemmas

The problems the Chinese government is attempting to deal with in its reforms are challenging under any circumstances, and the choices and trade-offs to be made are difficult, no matter which faction is in command. Here is an analysis of the essential difficulties written earlier in the reforms. It is by Gao Shangquan, then vice-minister in charge of the State Commission for Restructuring the Economic System, who is still a major economic official and one of those advocating continuation of reforms:

> We should acknowledge in a spirit of seeking truth from facts that the new economic system which is established as a result of reform cannot be a perfect system. We have to make policy decisions about economic life using a system which has imperfections, which is not as good as originally planned; frequently we do not choose between absolutely good or absolutely bad programs, but between all kinds of programs which have both good and bad aspects. We have to choose the one which most closely approximates to our own objective.
>
> Consequently, what is required here is a "choice of the lesser of two evils" . . . [which] have a certain kind of interrelated connection. Or, one might say, the toleration to a certain extent of the existence of the greater evil and the full utilization of the potentials of the [program embodying the] lesser represent precisely the two opposing sides of a coin. . . .

All we can do is to find a suitable "level" between the two and strive to the limits to give full play to the potentials of the one and at the same time to lessen the negative effects of the other as much as possible.

THE SCOPE OF REFORM

Gao Shangquan also wrote later in *Economic Weekly*, "The situation as regards different problems which crop up in the course of reform is a very complex one. . . . A concrete problem of a certain kind is often a product of many different factors."

Conversely, dealing with a problem may require taking parts of the solution from several different areas. A single reform measure such as the responsibility system addresses some aspects of several problems— centralization, insufficient incentive, lack of autonomy, egalitarianism, etc.

With such wide-ranging problems, equally comprehensive changes were needed which reached into the very ideology of the nation (as was seen in chapter 2). The Third Plenum proceeded to build important operational reforms—especially in agriculture—on the newly revised ideological base.

Effects began appearing almost immediately in the countryside, where, in fact, experiments with possible changes had already begun. The entire program for agriculture was shortly formalized in the Fourth Plenum's 1979 "Decision on Some Questions Concerning the Accelera- tion of Agricultural Development." Key points of the agricultural re- form are discussed in chapter 6, "Reform in the Countryside."

Reform in the state industrial-commercial-institutional sector is known as "economic reform" or, just as commonly, "urban reform," because it affects state-owned factories and other enterprises, and, where the principles are applicable, institutions and government offices as well, all of which tend to be in cities. It is among state-owned enterprises that some of the most serious problems with reform have arisen. The major urban reforms are described in chapter 5.

The Role of Experimentation

It is important to understand that the "experiments" in the countryside mentioned above typify a longstanding feature of Chinese government (it is called "working from a point to a plane," using a successful experience as examples to others nearby) that has no real counterpart in American practice, and perhaps no counterpart in other western sys- tems. In the west, there may be occasional "model programs" of one type or another with rather limited objectives, but it would be unheard of, for example, for some Americans to be subject during an experimental period to more taxes or less taxes than persons in similar circumstances in other parts of the country. This is currently happening in China, however, as it begins experimental implementation of compulsory reporting of income and payment of income taxes in only selected areas.

This is typical of what happens in many of China's "experiments,' which usually are delimited geographically and expanded over months or years to additional areas as experience is gained. Thus, when a national regulation is promulgated, the prescribed actions may have already been taken in many places—but not necessarily in a uniform way everywhere, which compounds the confusion of attempting to determine what the new policy really is.

The Chinese call their approach "groping for stones to cross the river." It is necessary, they say, because there are no precedents for what they are doing, no models to copy; they can learn how to reform only by reforming.

Some are now arguing for "using radar to cross the sea," for a more planned and comprehensive approach to dealing with problems which are coming to be understood better. For the present, however, the "groping for stones" approach continues

WHAT ABOUT POLITICAL REFORM?

Let the discussion begin with the understanding that no one in China or abroad expects political reform to go very far very soon, judged by western standards, even if comparative "moderates" are able to regain control or to exert more influence than now seems likely in the post–June 4 circumstances. When official China and dissident Chinese speak of "political reform" they have their own quite different definitions in mind. Dissident Chinese propose a humanistic reform which would make their leaders more responsive to the guidance of the people, which is supposed to be assured under socialism as under democracy, and more sensitive to what the critics regard as human rights. China's leaders, on the other hand, envision an operational reform essentially limited to political matters which impact upon economic concerns, a reform which does not address many concerns of some citizens.

On humanistic political reform—Even Zhao Ziyang, now deposed for his comparative liberalism, told US President George Bush during Bush's 1989 visit that China was opposed to introducing "a multiparty political system and the parliamentary system of western countries," saying that it was not appropriate. He threw up other usual roadblocks, claiming (this was before the Pro-Democracy Movement) that "there are a lot of people not mentally prepared for reform" and then charged that proponents of democracy "do not promote reform; they provide a pretext for retreat from reform, and therefore stir up social disorder."

And even Fang Lizhi, known in the west as China's most vocal dissident, agreed, (though he may not have welcomed Zhao's veiled criticism of dissidents), saying

> We do not yet have good enough conditions for a multiparty democracy. The education level is quite low and we have no independent newspapers.

Fang left no doubt, however, that he did not think waiting for a high level of education and political sophistication was the remedy:

> What we need first are basic human rights: freedom of speech, freedom of the press, freedom of thought.

Despite the lack of progress in political reform officially, however, for most of the time between 1980 (and especially since late 1987) and the declaration of martial law in May, there was a relatively relaxed atmosphere in intellectual and cultural matters reminiscent of the Beijing Spring of 1979, the Democracy Wall period. (See "Bourgeois Liberalization" and "Democracy Wall" in the Mini-Encyclopedia.)

The world may be most aware of the widely reported first-ever exhibit of nude paintings at the end of 1988, but more significant are probably the outspokenness in magazines and newspapers, the daring of some books, and the new assertiveness of intellectuals.

For example, *People's Daily*, the official Party newspaper, not long ago published (under the editor subsequently sacked by the conservatives) the introduction to a new book titled *On Democracy* which calls for democratic participation in government, making the point that centralized decisions by a limited group or a single person divorced from public opinion and accountability produced such disasters as the Cultural Revolution. *People's Daily* added comments that included, " . . . only when democracy is injected into economics, culture, etc., can reform in those fields succeed." *China Daily* recently mentioned stories which have appeared in the Chinese press concerning black markets, abuse of office, etc., and said, correctly, that "A decade ago such negative reports would never have surfaced."

The Party has recently given increased prominence to the so-called "democratic parties" (see "Political Parties" in Mini-Encyclopedia), and has said that it will open one-third of major national and provincial senior administrative posts to noncommunists, but this is not necessarily the same as promising to share power democratically. According to the *South China Morning Post*, a vice-chairman of the largest of the democratic parties is

> pessimistic about the promise and future trend of democratization in China. . . . [He said that] the most important factor of all was whether noncommunist parties could sustain their role and air their opposing views when the situation called for it, . . . [that] there was no point just to put more democrats or people without party affiliation into the government.

(And, in the event, only two seats were filled by non-Party members out of the twelve supposedly to be offered.)

For the first time ever, China's leading intellectuals took a concerted action in the course of the Pro-Democracy Movement to seek redress of grievances when thirty-three persons (later joined by many others) sent an open letter to the government asking release of those they consider political prisoners and whom the government considers "counterrevolutionaries."

Shortly thereafter, in an equally unprecedented action, more than 1,000 reporters and editors employed by official publications and news services presented a petition to the government requesting that officials discuss with them greater independence for the press, more accurate reporting of events such as the student demonstrations following Hu Yaobang's death (which, the petition said, was "extremely distorted"), and other matters. Hundreds of journalists also marched behind identifying banners in the pro-democracy demonstrations.

Liu Binyan, a famous dissident expelled from the Party in the anti-bourgeois liberalization campaign of 1987, pointed out to the *New York Times* in an interview at Harvard University, where the Chinese government had allowed him to accept a fellowship, that

> This is very different from before. In 1957, when Mao attacked me in the anti-rightist campaign [see "Hundred Flowers Policy" in Mini-Encyclopedia] no one would defend me. Everyone believed whatever the Party said. Even I myself felt so disgraced that when I was walking down the street and

saw a friend, I would cross to the other side to avoid embarrassment. Now wherever I go people invite me to lunch or write me letters asking me for help or invite me to give speeches. It is just the opposite. This shows the Chinese people have made progress.

The spring of 1989 was perhaps different from the previous false springs but there were warning signs long before martial law was declared that official toleration was strained. A bookshop used for an informal meeting to discuss jailed dissidents was closed. A large security effort was mounted to prevent Fang Lizhi from attending a dinner given by US President George Bush. The "openness" and "transparency" that were so touted at the 1988 National People's Congress were largely absent at the 1989 sessions. Li Peng promised at those same sessions that the government would delay political reforms (which were decreasing the power of lower cadres). Officials at all levels have increasingly talked about the absolute necessity of "stability" in the present uncertain times, and steps to assure greater state control were only to be expected.

So, as has happened before, the weather changed very rapidly.

However, the weathermakers should remember the analysis of commentator Xiao Qian, who has pointed out that there are two forms of stability:

> The first kind means that nobody dares speak up. The second means that people can speak their minds freely for the consideration of leaders. [This second kind may be disturbing to leaders, but, dialectically] it is stability and unity with a real basis. [Stability from repression] gives tranquility on the surface. Yet if something [unsettling] happens, an explosion may follow.

On operational reform—In the beginning nearly everyone recognized that economic reform inevitably implied political reform. Economic reform is oriented toward decentralization, giving the market a role in the economy, breaking the iron rice bowl, rationalizing prices and production, and so on. These objectives are not compatible over the long term with the existing political structure, characterized by a tight (though bloated) vertical bureaucracy, direction of economic life through central planning, decision-making concentrated at the top, etc. Conventional wisdom holds that China has concentrated on economic change, unlike Russia, where political change had been stressed.

Not so, said Gorbachev while in China in May, according to *China*

Daily. "In fact, the Soviet Union first took on economic reform, but then it found that economic reform could not proceed without political restructuring. . . .The roots of many economic problems were much deeper than expected and they stemmed from politics. Without political restructuring economic reform could not make headway," Gorbachev said.

China's Party leaders have yet to realize this and clearly have not considered real political reform of much importance, despite evidence in Russia and Poland and other communist countries that political reform is an urgent demand of awakened peoples. When Muscovites voted in massive numbers in 1989 to turn out Party officials, one leader is reported to have said in astonishment, "Why, we didn't realize they cared that much!" China's leaders can no longer say they have not had a chance to learn.

In 1980, Deng made a speech titled "On the Reform of the System of Party and State Leadership" in which he called for removing such harmful elements of the present system as "bureaucratism, the over-concentration of power, paternalism, the life tenure of leading cadres, and various forms of special privilege."

The speech did not make its greatest impact until seven years later, and indeed Deng is not regarded as being nearly as concerned about political reform as economic reform. For example, some weeks after the Pro-Democracy Movement was crushed the government finally came up with a draft law—in preparation for *ten years*— covering the "right" to demonstrate, supposedly guaranteed under Article 35 of the constitution. The law so hedges and regulates the "right" as to make it meaningless.

Reform has not, in fact, been attempted in any comprehensive way, although a start was made on three important operational basics: abolishing lifelong tenure, promoting younger cadres and retiring tens of thousands of elderly ones, and beginning to establish a legal system. (See "Legal System" in the Mini-Encyclopedia.)

The most important move to date, however, probably is the experimental beginning in 1986 of administrative reform, a key component of political reform. Administrative reform involves the untangling of inter-relations and overlapping of government and Party interests and personnel.

China Daily explained the present situation this way:

> For a long time in China, the Party's organizations have been directly involved in administrative management. So in addition to the administra-

tive center formed by the State Council there has been another administrative center—the Party.

Under the provincial government, for instance, there exist economic, cultural, and educational departments; there are also similar organizations under the provincial Party committee. There are vice-governors in charge of industry, agriculture, and education, and there are Party committee secretaries with similar duties. Within [governmental] organs, administrative heads such as ministers often take charge in name, while leading Party groups in the ministry actually make the decisions.

This wasteful and distracting duplication exists from national to local levels in the Chinese government, except that the Party Central Committee and the State Council do not overlap in this way. To streamline functions

the Party and the government must be separated from each other, but, first of all, the functions of the two must be clearly defined. The Party should exercise political leadership, while the government should perform admin istrative functions.

Speedy, permanent and meaningful separation of the Party and government will be hard to achieve. It has been a problem from the start but was never attacked with much determination. Shortly after the June Fourth Massacre, various attempts were made to improve Deng's image, including republication of his old papers and speeches. Included was an article in which he criticized confusion of Party and government functions—published in *1941*.

Sixteen medium-sized cities were authorized in 1986 to begin political reform on a trial basis, beginning with administrative reform. In recent months there have been numerous reports on preliminary results, which seem to be good, although, as *China Daily* put it, "One touchy issue that requires utmost prudence in the administrative reform is the proper resettlement of surplus officials."

Despite opposition, management departments in one city were reduced from 78 to 43, and government and Party officials reduced by over 30 percent. Another closed 40 of 81 departments and reduced city government cadres by 40 percent. Other cities reported similar results. To replace government bureaus formerly concerned with distribution of materials, all the experimental cities turned over distribution to outside agencies on a contract basis, and also established rudimentary financial exchanges and trading centers for raw materials and technology.

Deng "On the Reform of the System . . ."

Of course, simple overlapping and confusion of function are not the principal problems to be dealt with in overall political reform, and after hanging fire for years, the broader issues of political reform were placed on the agenda with great publicity on July 1, 1987, the sixty-sixth birthday of the Party, by the republication in major newspapers of Deng's 1980 speech "On the Reform of the System. . . ."

Xinhua, the Chinese news agency, said that the speech "charted the orientation of the upcoming reform of China's political set-up," a process generally considered to be directed toward three main goals:

☐ Separating Party responsibilities and prerogatives from the government's—the critical change mentioned in all discussions.

☐ Strengthening and improving the Party's leadership.

☐ Delegating power to the lower levels and restructuring organizations.

In the speech, Deng talks more about problems than solutions, but what he has to say is very quotable and very pertinent. Some of the conditions and practices he criticizes, which by implication interfere with achieving the three goals of political reform as he sees it, are:

Accountability: " . . . For a long time we have had no strict administrative rules and regulations, and no system of personal responsibility from top to bottom in the leading bodies of our Party and government organizations and of our enterprises and institutions."

Bureaucracy: "Bureaucracy remains a major and widespread problem in the political life of our Party and state." Here he mentions more than twenty-five characteristic behaviors of bureaucrats, from "divorcing oneself from reality and the masses" through "being dilatory, inefficient, and irresponsible and failing to keep one's word" to "vindictively attacking others" and "participating in corrupt practices."

Concentration of power: "Overconcentration of power means inappropriate and indiscriminate concentration of all power in Party committees in the name of strengthening centralized Party leadership. . . . Our leading organs at various levels have taken charge of many matters which they should not and cannot handle, or cannot handle efficiently. Moreover, the power of the Party committees themselves is often in the hands of a few secretaries, especially the first secretaries, who direct and decide everything. Thus 'centralized Party leadership' often turns into leadership by individuals."

Life tenure: "Tenure for life in leading posts is linked both to feudal influences and to the continued absence of proper regulations in the Party for retirement and dismissal of cadres. . . . No leading cadre should hold any office indefinitely."

Special privilege: "At present there are still some cadres who, regarding themselves as masters rather than servants of the people, use their positions to seek personal privileges. . . . To eradicate privilege, we must solve both the ideological problems involved and problems relating to rules and regulations. . . . Everyone has equal rights and duties prescribed by law, and no one may gain advantages at others' expense or violate the law."

Organizational errors: "Stalin gravely damaged socialist legality, doing things which Comrade Mao Zedong once said would have been impossible in western countries. . . . Yet although Comrade Mao was aware of this, he did not in practice solve the problems in our system of leadership. This led to the decade of catastrophe known as the Cultural Revolution. There is a most profound lesson to be learned from this."

Without going into detail as Deng did, the work report adopted by the Thirteenth National Congress endorsed the principles of political reform and some broad changes have already been made at the upper levels. In addition, plans were made for reforming the present cadre system, in which appointments to government posts are now made without examinations and often on the basis of personal connection.

As of 1989, all prospective employees of state administration bureaus must pass written and oral examinations before being hired, and numerous exams have already been given, including one in Guangdong Province where 120,000 applicants took tests for 10,000 openings. It is expected that a Public Servants Law (a civil service law) will be passed in the near future, requiring selection by open examinations and promotion strictly on the basis of merit, and that the system will be effective nationwide in ten years.

These changes do not extend into the areas of human rights that dissidents want safeguarded but, if the Party can somehow be made accountable and if the other problems Deng described in his 1980 speech are substantially solved, there will be significant changes in the political arena in China perhaps even more far-reaching than the economic changes already in motion.

One thing that will not change, however, is the primacy of the Party. On this point, Deng said:

The purpose of reforming the system of Party and state leadership is precisely to maintain and further *strengthen* Party leadership and discipline, and *not to weaken or relax them.* [Emphasis supplied] In a big country like ours, it is inconceivable that unity of thinking could be achieved among our several hundred million people or that their efforts could be pooled to build socialism in the absence of [the Party]. . . .

The core of the four cardinal principles is to uphold leadership by the Party. The point is that the Party must provide good leadership.

And that is indeed the point. The way the Party wields its power, whether it is flexible and receptive to legitimate concerns of the people, will determine whether democracy can grow in China.

In a report on the Thirteenth National Party Congress *Wenhui Daily* quoted a chillingly prescient remark about the Party's cyclic dictatorial behavior. Said Tan Jian, director of the Organization for Research on Reform of the Political System in China:

Over the last thirty-eight years our Party has been guilty of many mistakes and shortcomings. These have caused enormous damage to our country. How can a Party in power be prevented from committing mistakes and shortcomings in the policies it adopts?

Besides requiring that the policies it adopts be scientific and democratic it is also necessary to have some kind of supervision of the ruling Party itself. As long as there is no democracy in government we may scream and struggle as much as we want to but it will all be to no avail.

OFFICIAL CORRUPTION MENACES
GOVERNMENT'S LEGITIMACY

Chinese officials have for nearly ten years been increasingly defying repeated Party and governmental orders which sternly forbid them to participate in commercial businesses. (See "Government Power Absolute Only in Theory," in chapter 2.)

In a fall 1988 story, *Workers' Daily* reported identifying *twenty-four* separate orders issued since 1983 prohibiting business involvements.

Nevertheless, not only were tens of thousands of cadres at all levels continuing to have growing involvement in private business or official profiteering, but ministries and commissions under the State Council itself were operating more than seven hundred companies in violation of the repeated warnings.

An epidemic of profiteering, speculation, market manipulation, bribery, extortion, embezzlement, and other crimes by Party and government cadres has led to a crisis of confidence in the leadership and system of government, and is a major factor in the present economic and political chaos. Elimination of corruption was high on the list of demands of the Pro-Democracy Movement. Cynically, the new leaders are including failure to end corruption among the charges being built up against Zhao Ziyang, as though the whole subject has just come to their attention.

(Corruption is discussed in several other places throughout this book. For example, official profiteering and other misbehaviors are described in "The Big Challenge: Two-Track Prices" in chapter 5; ways in which cadres engage in extortion from workers in their work unit are mentioned in "Unit" in the Mini-Encyclopedia.)

Corruption is not new in China. It had existed for thousands of years before liberation, but as the respected *South China Morning Post* of Hongkong put it a few years ago, "Eliminating overt corruption, always an integral part of Chinese society irrespective of the nature of government (note Taiwan today), has been a major achievement under communist rule." The People's Liberation Army and Party officials had an apparently deserved reputation for almost never exploiting the people in any way. (And, ironically, before liberation the army's slogan was "Chinese must not fight Chinese," while Mao assured everyone in the sixties that the people and the army are like fish and water.)

It was saddening, in these days of official profiteering, to come across in a 1965 issue of *The Political Quarterly* this account of conditions in China after the Russians pulled out in 1960, relating how hardships were shared equitably:

> The secret, it seems, lay in sensible policy and incorruptible administration. The staples—grain, vegetable oil, and cotton cloth—are dealt in exclusively by government agents. This makes it next to impossible for a black market to develop in those commodities, for no authorized person dared be seen moving them.

But there is an old saying from the days of the emperors that "After three years in a position of authority, even an upright official becomes rich," and not even three years were needed for feudal misbehavior to reappear among cadres and officials at all levels after China began its reforms.

At that time, the government began to loosen central controls without substituting other firm administrative restraints, laws, and enforcement capabilities, and thereby opened up to authorities glorious new opportunities for illegally making money.

Since then, tens of thousands of cases of corruption and economic crime have been reported nationwide each year, ranging from businesses illegally operated by government bureaus, and by Party officials and cadres and their families, to large-scale fraud and bribery, abuse of office, embezzlement, theft, profiteering, and numerous other crimes—while, as a foreign writer put it, "cynicism grows with each lapse from the communist ideal of selfless leadership."

And cynicism is fueled by the fact that the Party has failed to devise an impartial, sure, and stern method of supervision and punishment for its members, and particularly for its leading cadres. *People's Daily* in 1988 quoted top Party official Qiao Shi as saying that the central committee "is still in the process of working out specific stipulations concerning orders which are not followed and prohibitions which are ignored," just as though this were a new problem.

A large proportion of offenses by Party members and other cadres are thought to go unpunished—even uninvestigated—and when cadres are found guilty punishment is usually light, even for flagrant offenses. In July 1989, *People's Daily* reported what *China Daily* called "the first publicized case of imposing severe penalties on high-ranking officials involved in corruption." Typically, however, the only "punishment" reported was the loss of jobs and expulsion from the Party; they will, however, face "legal punishment," which is unusual.

The resentment of abuses by the country's elite is compounded by the fact that the people are essentially helpless to redress these problems. (See entry on "Legal System" in the Mini-Encyclopedia.)

The increase in economic crime has at times threatened the entire reform movement. The 1983 Campaign against Spiritual Pollution blamed opening China to the world and economic reform for much corruption, and the 1987 criticism of bourgeois liberalization also had an anti-reform and anti-opening aspect. Much of the criticism has a political bias, with opponents of change claiming that deviation from Marxist and Maoist orthodoxy has brought a deterioration in morality, and implying that the cure is to slow or even reverse reform.

The feeling the Chinese have regarding the failure of the Party to control its offices and members was capsulized in a typically Chinese way in a short contribution to *China Daily*. The writer told of seeing a cartoon based on the old saying,

"When a rat runs across the street, everybody cries, 'Kill it!'" but the rats know nothing will be done. To me, it seems the same kind of inaction applies in the case of fighting against another enemy of our society—the unhealthy tendency toward corruption. In some units and departments this unhealthy tendency has not been killed but has become even more widespread. An important reason is that authorities spend more effort in shouting than doing something about it.

The cynicism is well founded. The twenty-four orders forbidding operation of businesses by officials cited here have not been any more effective than crackdowns on drug dealers in other countries, although ending corruption and bureaucratism has been a constant theme since 1979 (especially since price reform and two-track pricing began in 1985). Citizens are well aware that the rats have not been killed or even bloodied, and the long delay in dealing with this corrosive problem is proving costly to the government and the Party in public confidence.

For a long time, official comments usually referred to corruption and crime as "unhealthy tendencies" or used other euphemisms surprisingly mild in view of the blunt headlines and the nature of the problem. This attitude reflected the view of then Party Secretary Zhao and other officials who maintained (although their reasoning is not explained) that corruption and crime are inevitable accompaniments of the shift to a commodity economy.

By the fall of 1988, however, public indignation had caused the official view of cadre cupidity to change from "unhealthy tendencies" to "whirlpool of corruption." Said Zhao at the Third Plenum of the Thirteenth Party Central Committee, as reported by *People's Daily*:

> Since we want to learn to swim in the sea of a commodity economy, we must also manage to avoid being swallowed up in the whirlpool of corruption. At present the greed, corruption, profiteering on the resale of commodities at exorbitant prices, graft, extortion, embezzling of public funds, lavish waste, and other such economic crimes that have occurred in the course of the work of certain officials of the Party and government are utterly detested and hated by the people. The results of this have already gone beyond affecting the reputations of Party members, cadres, and other individuals. The image of the Party itself and that of the government have also been injured. If this problem is not solved we may lose the hearts of the people.

The pro-democracy demonstrations, in which complaints about corruption played a major part, apparently jolted officials into taking complaints about corruption more seriously than ever before, because the Party and the government have reacted positively and swiftly, if not always significantly. For example, the Party adopted "Seven Tasks" for

Ding Cong, *Beijing Review*

fighting corruption, ranging from "severely punish criminals involved in corruption . . . " to forbidding the very highest officials (not even reaching down to ministers) and their families from engaging in business activities, down to the most unkind blow of all, canceling the "special supply" of foodstuffs unavailable to the public that officials formerly received.

The governor of Hainan Province, the highest official disciplined so far, was removed from office for corruption; it may or may not be coincidental that he was also a close associate of Zhao Ziyang. There are numerous statistical reports from procurators of cities, counties and provinces, and the national government with masses of indigestible—and irreconcilable—figures on complaints made on public corruption hot lines, arrests, "voluntary confessions" (which the government says draw lighter penalties), trials, persons sentenced, etc., which, nevertheless, can leave a reader anything but informed.

There may be some substance to the current effort, or it all may very well be sound and fury, smoke and mirrors. Only time will tell. One journalist specializing in China wrote, "Few Chinese believe this anti-corruption campaign will be any more effective than previous attempts to root out official graft. Entrenched and intricate networks of personal connections are almost impenetrable. . . . As in China's past political campaigns, the latest drive relies mostly on persuasion to achieve its ends."

China's *Financial News* boldly went further, reporting the following response to a nationwide survey asking people what they thought of efforts by the Party and governments at all levels to crack down on corruption: "Sixty-six percent summed up the efforts as 'a loud thunderclap but only a few raindrops.' Another 20 percent said corruption was getting more and more serious. So whenever a new measure is announced, people adopt a wait-and-see attitude."

But what are the chances of seeing anything very much? As a critic of China's new-born legal system has said, "Who has the responsibility to punish unconstitutional acts? No one." It may be that the rats are still safe for awhile yet.

THE GOAL OF REFORM

Though it is understandably impossible to avoid the venting of impatience, frustration, and disappointment, by and large most Chinese soberly recognize that what they are attempting is vast, and they are prepared to pursue reform over the long term (though they may differ concerning the speed and scope of reform at any particular time). To that end they have adopted as their objective the "socialist modernization of China's economy," sometimes summed up as the "Four Modernizations."

The extensive improvement of China's capabilities in the key fields of agriculture, industry, national defense, and science and technology is an idea which has been discussed for a number of years as a desirable achievement, but it has been seriously sought only since 1980.

The goal was formally set in the documents of the Twelfth National Congress of the Communist Party of China in 1982 as:

> The general objective of China's economic construction for the two decades between 1981 and the end of this century is, while steadily working for more and better economic results, to quadruple the gross annual value of industrial and agricultural production—from 710 billion yuan in 1980 to 2,800 billion yuan or so in 2000.
>
> This will place China in the front ranks of the countries of the world in terms of gross national income and the output of major industrial and agricultural products; it will represent an important advance in the modernization of her entire national economy; it will increase the income of her urban and rural population several times over; and the Chinese people will be comparatively well-off both materially and culturally.
>
> Although China's national income per capita will even then be relatively low (about US$800 versus US$300 in 1980), her economic strength and national defense capabilities will have grown considerably, compared with what they are today. Provided that we work hard and in a down-to-earth manner and bring the superiority of the socialist system into fuller play, we can definitely attain our grand strategic objective.(See also another expression of these goals in "Three Step Development Plan" in the Mini-Encyclopedia.)

In 1982 these plans seemed quite realistic; in 1985 they seemed easily achievable; but in 1989, with agriculture stagnant, state-owned enterprises not yet healthy, and a projected population considerably larger than expected—and, above all, with a disgruntled citizenry facing a rigid government which has lost credibility—achieving the goals of modernization on the timetable planned can only be called problematic.

Five

THE SIX BIG REFORMS

Economic matters get most of the attention in reform discussions, but it should not be overlooked that it is "ossified" thinking (as the Chinese say of dogmatic political views) in all fields that reform seeks to change. It is research institutes as well as factories, hospitals as well as mines— state organizations of nearly all kinds—that are being expected to "become responsible for their own profits and losses" instead of relying on the state to pay their bills.

The new revolution has these six critical objectives:

☐ Decentralizing decision-making and administrative authority.
☐ Giving the market a role in planning and substituting general guidelines for mandatory plans in most areas of economic activity.
☐ Reforming prices to reflect true costs and values.

☐   Revamping the economic structure.

☐   Opening to the outside world to stimulate foreign investment and technology exchange and to improve foreign trade.

☐   Ending egalitarianism and substituting an improved system of individual motivation and reward.

The industrial, commercial, and organizational aspects of these changes—known generally as urban reform, because most state units are located in cities—will be discussed in this chapter. These six reform objectives apply, of course, to rural China as well, but their special application to rural reform (which is further advanced than urban reform and is in some ways the basis for it) will be covered in the next chapter "Reform in the Countryside."

Urban reform has moved more slowly than rural reform, as expected—much more slowly. *Far Eastern Economic Review* said early in urban reform that the broad picture "suggests that resistance to reform primarily arises from natural considerations of self-interest on the part of Party officials, workers, and state or Party organizations rather than ideological convictions," and this has proved to be true, but reform difficulties involve more than self-interest.

It is now obvious that the Chinese were not prepared for the full range of difficulties that have appeared, but they knew all along that urban reform would be more complex and difficult than rural reform, involving more interrelated changes, more opposition from cadres and workers, increased inflation, and—if it were successful—more unemployment for a while as well.

These concerns have meant that urban reform proceeded with less surefootedness, coordination, and dispatch; the "Decision on Reform of the Economic Structure" did not appear until the Third Plenum of the Twelfth Central Committee in October 1984, five years after reform began. It was reported by *China Daily* under a headline reading "Revolutionary Reforms to Spur Economy," but, in fact, it was essentially an affirmation of directions already taken.

Chicken-or-Egg Complexity

Necessarily, the discussion here will be limited to major aspects of reform. This review of key topics should be considered, however, against the following glimpse of reform's chicken-or-egg complexity provided by two Chinese economists ir *China's Economic Reform* (1982):

A basic requirement of economic reform is to make each enterprise a relatively independent economic entity [which assumes] full responsibility for the results of its operation.... In the conditions of the present serious economic disproportions, however, the environment of the production and management of the enterprises is quite abnormal, and it is often impossible to establish proper links between production, the procurement of the means of production, and the marketing of products. An enterprise may do better or worse in production and earn more or less in profit, but this is frequently determined by external and not internal factors....

The serious disproportions of China's economy, which have existed for a long time, are due in no small measure to the country's unsound economic setup [but] as long as the economy suffers from serious imbalances it is impossible to carry out a large-scale, all-around reform of the setup...

This does not mean that no reform may be undertaken until the completion of readjustment and the elimination of all disproportions....
They have taken shape over a long period of time and cannot be remedied in a short time. Economic reform, a highly complicated task, cannot be accomplished in a short time either [but] if it has to be delayed until economic readjustment comes to an end, the modernization program will be held up for too long.

After a few more years of experience with reform, recent writers in *The Bulletin of Theoretical Studies* found the dynamics of reform even more intricate, saying, "An important sign of the complicated situation is that the country's ideological and theoretical circles have found themselves lost in one strange bind after another, from which they can hardly extricate themselves."

This is a summary of some of their major points:

☐ One bind is determining which should be given priority, price reform or ownership reform. Those who prefer price reform stress the importance of creating a market environment favorable to fair competition. The state still sets prices for part of the output of some key materials, however, and the other part of the output is sold at higher market prices. Collective and private enterprises must buy materials at market prices and take their chances on making a profit State-owned enterprises buy some materials at one price and some at the other but state-owned enterprises which lose money through these (or other) circumstances have their losses made up by the state. Therefore, only when price reform is completed can enterprises compete with each other under true market conditions.

☐ But those who feel "ownership reform" should come first (partly through issuance of stocks and bonds "with Chinese characteristics"—see "Ownership" in the Mini-Encyclopedia) emphasize the mutually accepted argument that fair prices can exist only in a free and competitive market, and therefore, they say, enterprises must be responsible for their own profits and losses if they are to be forced into true competition.

☐ Unless some way can be guaranteed to have high economic growth without significant inflation, the country must choose between bearing the inflation or the increase in unemployment that comes with slow economic growth in a country with a growing population seeking jobs. (One serious bind here is that one section of the new government is getting set to close millions of private businesses and hundreds of thousands of rural enterprises that have provided tens of millions of new jobs in recent years—but the Labor Minister announced at the same time that collective-run and individual enterprises are being counted on to continue hiring many excess workers.)

☐ Finally, economists point out that many problems impeding reform are not economic problems at all, but social and political problems— permanent job assignments, for example, that prevent workers from moving to the jobs where they are most valuable (and best paid), and the continuing interference of Party and government in industrial and commercial matters which sabotages rational economic decision-making.

DECENTRALIZING CHINA'S BUREAUCRATIC ECONOMY

Decentralization as a political objective has already been discussed in chapter 4 under "What About Political Reform?" The special problems presented by a highly centralized economy are the subject of this section.

China's economic section took shape in the early fifties and expanded in the following years, but expanded in its original highly centralized Soviet form, leading to a huge, complex, and unresponsive system with strong vested interests all the way down the organization chart.

Under the Soviet planning method, and in centralized economies generally, the starting point for planning is establishing desired production. Targets for major products are determined first, then the required materials and energy are determined, and last of all the need for consumer goods is considered. What is not planned simply does not get built and there is no point to shopping around for it. An overlooked need, or a new one—whether can opener or computer chip—may not find its way into the master plan for years, if at all.

Because Chinese economic planning followed the Soviet pattern, the emphasis has nearly always been on substantial growth in heavy industry, with only secondary attention to other parts of the economy. For example, at some periods the machine-building industry produced machine tools, but insufficient equipment for agriculture, food processing, light industry, etc. Steel mills produced semi-finished products that light industry was not equipped to process further, but produced no materials for steel window frames or wire and nails. Heavy industry received large appropriations for new facilities and products while light industry could secure little.

Since it is not the function of the central planners to produce what they plan, specialized ministries deal with each industrial sector (as they are doing under reform, although until now their role has been diminishing). Administrative units at various levels below the ministries control all decision-making power of subordinate units through financial departments, material departments, labor departments, and so on, and each acts only according to instructions from above. There are a minimum of five or six levels of authority over a textile or metal products factory. The bureaucratic interplay and red tape can be almost unbelievable. It was recently reported that one project—admittedly a big one—required the chops (official seals) of 860 offices before final approval could be achieved. The following comes from a discussion of "ownership," but it is very appropriate here as a description of what has just been said about complexities:

> In our country at present all the economic units belong to governments at various levels. They are divided according to their level. For example, there is the central level, the provincial level, the municipal and local level, the county, township and village levels.
>
> Moreover, the people in charge of enterprises have different levels [of authority] on the basis of the administrative office that manages them. For example there is the provincial or military region level, the municipal or local level, the county organization level, the department head or assistant department head level.
>
> In the allocation and exchange of plan quotas, labor, fringe benefits, labor insurance, and the materials of production all these various enterprises enjoy different treatment according to the level they belong to.

At the bottom of the ladder are the individual enterprises, which usually receive insufficient attention because the administrative units above have their own interests, as well as other enterprises, to worry about. Obviously, the individual enterprises have little status, and the director of even a fairly large factory, for example, has often been unable to spend as little as 100 yuan without permission of higher authority.

When centralization is extreme, as in Russia, and as it may be becoming again in China, managers and workers care nothing for market needs, sales potential, or profits and losses. Since they have no influence it is pointless for them to care. Their only concern is meeting state production quotas for their products, which their ministry is obligated to purchase from them and offer to end users, whether the products are actually usable or not.

Therefore, the planned economy lacks vigor and drive. The economist Huan Xiang has summarized the situation this way:

> The consequences of over-centralization are: The more centralized, the more rigid; the more rigid the economy, the lazier the people; the lazier the people, the poorer they are; and the poorer the people are, the greater the need for centralization, forming a vicious circle.

A Mother-in-Law Story

The most critical target of urban reform is the portion of industry comprised of state-owned enterprises, i.e., enterprises owned "by the whole people." In this sector roughly 9,000 large and medium-sized state-owned enterprises and 85,000 small ones (together, less than 20 percent of all industrial firms) pay a large proportion of the nation's taxes and produce about 60 percent of its industrial output (down from about 80 percent of industrial production at the beginning of reform). Collective and private enterprises, mostly small and owned by entities other than the national government and making up about 80 percent of all firms, now produce approximately 40 percent of total output. The share of private enterprises, non-existent a few years ago, is now creeping up to 5 percent.

State industries are in precarious financial health, after several good years in the early days of reform. In 1988 the number of state industrial enterprises losing money decreased by 2 percent but total losses soared by 27 percent, while first-half 1989 deficits equaled all of 1988's. Losses have averaged about 40 billion yuan a year in recent years, but the 1989 budget provides 52 billion yuan for enterprise subsidies, the largest of the state's subsidies. This indicates not only low expectations regarding future enterprise efficiency but signals that the government will subsidize losers at an even higher rate rather than risk antagonizing workers and cadres by enforcing the new Enterprise Bankruptcy Law based on the reform principle of making enterprises responsible for their own losses.

For two or three years the growth rate of the state-owned industrial sector has been only about half that of the more flexible, more entrepreneurial collective sector which operates without the interference of a "supervising" bureaucracy.

State enterprise profits also lag, affected by waste, corruption, lackadaisical management (a recent survey showed that over 60 percent of firms saw no need to offer new or improved products), and often abysmal quality (unsalable inventory in 1987 amounted to several times the reported enterprise losses).

Not only industrial and commercial enterprises but organizations, institutions, and other government bodies as well are affected by straitjacketed decision-making, narrowness of vision, inefficiency, complacency, and all the other ills rigid bureaucracy and ideology generate.

It would seem that the key step in freeing enterprises from overcentralization is simply to give them the authority to operate independently. Officially, at least, several steps have been taken in this direction.

Top-level authorities have theoretically now handed down to their mid-level subordinate units decision-making powers that were in turn supposed to be passed to the operating units themselves. However, since many of these mid-level administrative bureaus (which sometimes operate as "companies" and are known as *popo* or "mothers-in-law") have little to do besides making decisions for enterprises, further devolution of authority would reduce their power and prerogatives significantly. Refusing to pass on the delegated powers, on the other hand, gives the units still more opportunities for commercial and political dealing.

Add to this the fact that many grassroots managers are not yet trained or experienced, are fearful of the rough-and-tumble of a competitive marketplace, and really do not *want* to assume responsibility for their profits and losses or for the managerial decisions, and there is a situation which makes it easy for those who wish to retain authority for themselves to do so.

Decentralization was an objective of the national government from

1978 until the conservatives reversed the policy after their takeover in 1989. In 1983 State Industrial Enterprise Rules were promulgated which were supposed to loosen central authority slightly. In 1984 the government published regulations on further expanding decision-making powers of state enterprises which were the basis for the decision on urban reform in the fall, and published even more-detailed regulations in 1985. Said *China Daily:*

> Theoretically, on the premise that an enterprise follows state plans and subjects itself to state control, it now has the power to adopt flexible and diversified forms of operation; plan its production, supply, and marketing; appoint, remove, employ, or elect its own personnel within certain limits; decide on how to recruit and use its work force, and how to pay and reward it; and set prices of products within prescribed limits.

But notice the qualifying *Theoretically.* In order for enterprises to have in reality the power they have "theoretically," there must be an effective delegation of those powers from upper levels of the hierarchy, where the powers have resided. But, rules and decrees to the contrary, delegation still has not occurred, by and large, four or five years later— a perfect demonstration of the statement in chapter 2 that a country run by an entrenched bureaucracy "may have a difficult time indeed in securing day-to-day obedience from its civil servants."

Ta Kung Pao (Hongkong), a Beijing-financed newspaper, reported in the fall of 1988 on a meeting of enterprise executives in Beijing:

> These business executives are interminably harassed by three "evils": lack of autonomy . . . , the levying of an assortment of tributes [i.e., extortion by authorities under pretext of collecting dozens of "fees" or the solicitation of "gifts"], and the "multiple exploitation by officials engaged in illicit trading and profiteering."
>
> It was pointed out that under the Enterprise Law . . . government departments have no right to interfere in the operation of an enterprise so long as it abides by the law and pays its tax. However, it was found that it was still impossible for the enterprises to find protection under the stipulations in the majority of cases. Government officials don't even blush in their claim that "all socialist enterprises have higher authorities."

The Factory Director Responsibility System

Along with devolution of power from higher authority, the showpiece of industrial decentralization was to be a plan called the "factory director responsibility system" (FDRS), which follows the general principles of the responsibility system which has proven to be so successful in the countryside. It also attempts to deal with the managerial-political conflict in enterprises. FDRS has been much less successful than the agricultural responsibility system, however, in part because of the leaders' generally ambivalent attitude toward it.

The 1988 National People's Congress passed the long-awaited Enterprise Law ("Law of the PRC on Industrial Enterprises Owned by the Whole People"). How it may change the conditions described in the following summary of FDRS development will be commented upon later, as will the now-ruling conservatives' disdain for the law.

Under the system that has existed since 1956, when the Party began taking a larger role in all areas of Chinese life, there is a Party committee at each enterprise—office, store, organization, institution, or factory—to which directors are responsible. All decisions must be approved by the committee, which means that, ultimately, the enterprise Party secretary, not the director, controls the enterprise.

FDRS is based on giving to the factory director whatever final decision-making authority in business matters the factory is allowed to exercise by higher echelons, relegating the Party secretary to a secondary role. As *Beijing Review* put it, "While most Party secretaries... may be professional in politics, they are strikingly clumsy at managing an enterprise."

On these premises, and following discussions initiated by Deng Xiaoping four years earlier, the 1984 decision on economic reform gave unqualified support to a plan having the factory director clearly in command, saying

> It is... necessary to establish a unified, authoritative, and highly efficient system to direct production and conduct operations and management. This calls for a system of the director or manager assuming full responsibility.

FDRS was put into effect on an experimental basis in six cities in the fall of 1984 and was rapidly instituted in numerous other cities. Countless enthusiastic articles have appeared about the success of the plan, reporting that tens of thousands of factories are now formally operating under FDRS but without indicating that most "mothers-in-law" are not observing its spirit, as the *Ta Kung Pao* report cited above points out. (This is reminiscent of the way educational authorities announce that a very high percentage of children have been "enrolled" in school without mentioning that large numbers soon drop out.)

Foreshadowing the Enterprise Law to come, in September 1986 the Party's Central Committee and the government's State Council jointly issued three sets of regulations attempting to define the roles of factory directors, Party committees, and workers' congresses in state-owned industrial enterprises. (The workers' congresses had not previously had a prominent part in the controversy.)

The divisions which since 1984 had dogged attempts to write an enterprise law were apparent in the essentially stop-gap regulations, and the director's position remained uncertain.

True, the new regulations provided that the Party committee can overrule the director only by appeals to higher authority, not by simply saying "No," as formerly. But, as one author noted in *Beijing Review:*

> These reforms do not mean abolishing the Party's leadership. Instead, they help improve it. According to the thirty-seven-article regulation on the responsibility of Party organizations in state-run enterprises, Party committees will *supervise* [emphasis added] and guarantee the implementation of Party and government policies. At the same time, they should aid the directors in exercising decision-making power over operation and production. . . .

Now, Chinese friends say that in their parlance "supervision" does not mean "management, direction, or oversight," as in the common understanding, but, rather, denotes "the right to make suggestions." They point out, in trying to allay skepticism that comments coming from the Party would in fact be regarded as mere suggestions, that the Chinese People's Political Consultative Conference, clearly an honorary advisory body with little influence in the last analysis, is said to "supervise" the Communist Party of China. There is plentiful evidence that Party secretaries are not satisfied with only the right to "make suggestions" which can be disregarded, however.

Furthermore, the workers' congress at each enterprise received a substantial amount of fresh power in the new regulations. Its twenty-article charter, through which the congress "exercises democratic management," gives it the power to

> examine its enterprise's major policy decisions, to supervise the work of its administrative leaders, and to protect the workers' legitimate rights and interests

including the power to adjust wages, intervene in punishments and dismissals, and determine bonuses and other incentives. Already, a number of congresses have enforced their interpretations of the new rules as permitting them to discharge directors.

An Enterprise Law was finally passed in April 1988, after having been in preparation for nine years. It had been submitted to the NPC

Standing Committee five times, turned down by the full congress in 1987, and published for general comment, an unusual step. Obviously, this was regarded as legislation of extreme importance. It is quite broad, containing essentially the same stipulations as the 1986 regulations so far as directors, workers, and Party committee are concerned but covering other matters as well. Abstracted from the *China Daily* summary of the law, the following are the major provisions:

Enterprises generally—A state-owned enterprise shall be an "independent accounting unit," i.e., it is to be responsible for its own profits and losses and not receive state support for operating deficits. To this end, the law provides that an enterprise's "being declared bankrupt in accordance with the law *may* [emphasis supplied] constitute a reason for the termination of an enterprise." (Bankruptcy as a new concept in China is discussed in the following section.)

The state shall observe in relation to an enterprise "the principle of separation of ownership and managerial authority," i.e., the state will not interfere in the usual operation of the enterprise.

Factory Director Responsibility System—"The law affirms the factory director responsibility system. . . . The factory director shall occupy the central position in the enterprise and assume overall responsibility for its material and cultural progress."

It will be interesting to learn of the effect on innovation and entrepreneurial energy of a clause stating that a director is criminally liable if, because of undefined "faults in his work," he "causes the property of the enterprise or the interests of the state and the people to suffer heavy losses." *China Daily* said, "Observers agreed that this accords with the principle of combining responsibility with authority." The directors' opinions were not given.

A factory manager said of the 1986 regulations that directors had been "given the bowl but not the chopsticks." The law seems to do little to change that.

Party organizations in enterprises—"The grassroots organization of the Communist Party of China in an enterprise [i.e., the Party committee] shall guarantee and supervise the implementation of the guiding principles and policies of the Party *and* the state [emphasis supplied] in such an enterprise."

Two comments seem appropriate on this section. First, assigning the Party to "guarantee and supervise" on behalf of both the Party and the state clearly runs counter to a primary objective of political reform, namely, that Party and government affairs shall be separated, and, for that matter, counter to another section of the Enterprise Law which also calls for separation.

Second, the sense may be different in Chinese, but, even keeping in mind the discussion of *supervise* a few pages earlier, it is hard to see how director and Party secretary relationships and responsibilities have been clarified. It would seem, rather, that they have been further obscured; formerly there was no question as to where each was placed in the hierarchy and who had ultimate power, but the new description of the Party representative's duties (or of the director's, for that matter) has no such certainty.

Workers—"An enterprise shall ensure that its staff and workers enjoy the status of the masters [of the enterprise] and shall protect their lawful rights and interests. An enterprise shall practice, through the staff and workers' congresses and other forms, democratic management. The trade union in an enterprise shall represent and safeguard the interests of the staff and workers and conduct its work independently according to law."

Management committee—"The enterprise shall establish a management committee or some other form of organization to assist the factory director in making decisions on important issues of the enterprise. . . . The forms of such bodies may vary. . . . Some may introduce the system of the board of directors, some may institute the workers' congress as their highest organs, and others may set up enterprise management committees." The wording indicates that, unfortunately, there is little or no emphasis on bringing in anyone from outside in order to take advantage of special expertise.

It seems to be a worthwhile advance for Chinese enterprises, like companies and institutions the world over, to have a management committee or a board of directors. In this as in other areas of the FDRS where there may be both mutual and antagonistic goals, however, everything depends on the spirit in which the two sides work and whether they are willing to follow the rules. The central government perhaps cannot do much to guarantee warm cooperation of local board members, but even to follow the ambiguous rules provided by the new law committee members needed further clues as to who is really supposed to be the chairman.

Clarification has now been provided, however. Following the conservative takeover, Premier Li Peng wrote in *Seeking Truth* that the three regulations were included in approved reforms which would be continued. Law or no law, however, he stressed the importance of strengthening the Party's supervisory role in enterprises, a self-defeating return to conditions which over the years have produced an increasing number of failing enterprises requiring more and more subsidies. In October, Beijing Party head Li Ximing advocated reinstituting virtual total Party superiority in all government organizations—institutions, organizations, etc., as well as factories.

Enterprise Bankruptcy

The bankruptcy provision of the Enterprise Law was one of its most controversial features, and, in fact, the idea of bankruptcy is so foreign to Chinese socialist thinking that there was no permanent bankruptcy law on the books when the Enterprise Law was passed.

During the period of several years the Enterprise Law was under consideration, a related Enterprise Bankruptcy Law also encountered strong opposition. Many people, and not conservatives alone, simply felt that socialism and bankruptcy were mutually exclusive. In addition, opponents to allowing bankruptcy said that provisions for worker security were incomplete and that as long as enterprises did not have real authority to manage their own affairs they were too greatly at the mercy of economic conditions and the decisions of the Party and the government.

Those who favored the Enterprise Law, however, claimed bankruptcy has a place in socialism with Chinese characteristics, pointing out that making an enterprise responsible for profits and losses had no real meaning and little impact upon management decisions unless the ultimate penalty for poor management and continuing losses was going out of business.

A provisional Enterprise Bankruptcy Law was put into operation in 1986 and took full effect in November 1988, but has never been enforced in more than a few cases. The Shenyan Anti-explosive Devices Plant made history in August 1986 as the first Chinese enterprise to be declared bankrupt; it was a collectively owned plant, however, not a state-owned enterprise, and in fact no state-owned enterprise has yet been allowed to go bankrupt. Chances are that few will ever feel the effects of the law for, as its opponents contended, the work unit is still too interwoven with worker's lives and the social support system is still too weak.

The preferred method of dealing with insolvent companies seems to be merging losing businesses with profitable ones, even though there are immediately apparent drawbacks to this solution. One drawback that seems not to have been foreseen is becoming serious. If action is ever taken against a losing enterprise it is usually just appended to a money-making enterprise without a determined effort to deal with the problems that made the company bankrupt to begin with, providing no benefit to the failed company and causing losses to the healthy one. What the state formerly lost in subsidies paid to the failed company it now loses in taxes because the host company's profits are reduced by subsidizing the bankrupt.

Can Old Bureaucrats Learn New Tricks?

Why is it so difficult to change the old bureaucratic set-up? Some of the difficulties have already been discussed in chapter 2. These are some of the numerous other reasons advanced:

☐ One of the most common problems is that the old system gets in the way of the new. The conflict causes confusion and gives many opportunities for corrupt officials to make illegal profits. This theme was being increasingly emphasized as the 1989 democracy movement, which had ending corruption as a major goal, peaked in the spring. (See "One-Track Psyche in a Two-Track World" in chapter 2.) It is not clear what new steps, if any, will be taken to deal with the problem now.

☐ Until 1988 there was no law governing the rights of state-owned enterprises and they had no recourse if decision-making powers were denied them. Probably they still have no recourse; the law has no enforcement or arbitration provisions.

☐ Every enterprise presents a unique set of conditions, and it is not feasible for either the central government or lower units to install the new system by fiat. Or, in the universal language of those reluctant to change, "The new system is fine, but it wouldn't work for us."

☐ In some industries, it is claimed that the old set-up is necessary for maintaining planning control, especially for enforcing the mandatory quotas that still remain for some raw materials.

☐ Tax collection is still handled through the old administrative set-up under which enterprises formerly turned over all their profits, which tends to keep the old superior/subordinate relationship in effect.

☐ Provinces, counties, or cities which control enterprises producing or using scarce materials want to continue to control the resources, partly to make sure their industries continue to operate, partly to make sure they are able to continue to reap the profits available to those able to buy at low state prices and sell at the usually much higher market prices.

There are no doubt many factors that possibly contribute to the slow pace of decentralization, but in one way or another the fault usually seems to come back to the bureaucracy and its lack of accountability. As Deng Xiaoping observed in his 1980 speech on reform already quoted, "We have had no strict administrative rules and regulations and no system of personal responsibility from top to bottom. . . . "

It seems clear that many officials are shielding each other, and are accepting as "ordinary errors" (which are politically permissible) behavior that in fact constitutes "stubborn resistance and rejection" (supposedly impermissible). Simon Leys, in his 1986 work *The Burning Forest*, says of these omnipotents that

> The problem is not simply that they do nothing, but that they efficiently prevent any useful activity that more talented subordinates might be tempted to launch. Personal integrity, intellectual creativity, imagination, competence, and expertise appear to them as so many challenges and potential threats to their authority.

As he sums it up, the bureaucracy is guilty of "cretinizing the most intelligent people on earth."

And those people are coming to resent it more and more. The democracy movement was fueled in part by widespread resentment measured in surveys that showed far more than half the people placing abuse of power by bureaucrats at the head of the problems that disturbed them most, even ahead of price increases.

It is understandable that bureaucrats, especially cadres too young to retire and too old to re-orient themselves and compete with rising younger cadres, do not welcome change, and that many older leaders, as the events of May and June demonstrated, prefer power to progress. However, to take the long view, it must be recognized that the mere ten years that have passed since the attempt to decentralize began are but a moment in the history of China's bureaucracy—the longest Chinese dynasty of all.

GIVING THE MARKET A ROLE IN PLANNING

There is a popular play in socialist Hungary called *The Hungarian Cube.* It tells the true story of what happened when a small Hungarian manufacturing cooperative tried to manufacture Rubik's Cube, the puzzle that was a worldwide rage in the early eighties, selling an estimated 100 million. The cooperative was the first manufacturer of the toy, turning out small quantities in the beginning and then trying desperately to make larger quantities faster when the Cube's popularity mushroomed.

The co-op tried to expand its operations by borrowing money for plant and equipment, but lost ten months getting the loan approved by all the bureaus involved, and then another six months or so because the Hungarian economy could not give them the equipment they needed any sooner. While all this was going on, the marketers of the Cube were turning over more and more production to manufacturers outside Hungary—and the craze for the toy was slowing down. About the time no one wanted Cubes any longer, the co-op finally got its new plant ready. They had a large plant and nothing to make in it, and a large debt and no way to pay it off. The Hungarian government finally had to bail them out.

The author of the play has said, "Everyone made money on the Cube except the Hungarians, but it was still a good lesson for us. It has taught people that our way of centrally directing the economy has to change. We can be socialists and still have a market-oriented economy."

That's what the Chinese are saying, too.

Pointing out that China is vast, heavily populated, and suffering from poor communication, an official has said that "It is impossible under such conditions to include all socioeconomic activities in the state plan and to use administrative orders alone to direct production. . . . It is precisely for these reasons that China's planned economic system needs to be improved so as to let the market forces play a role in regulating production."

A centralized economy is by definition a planned economy, with little or no competition or other market forces. That does not necessarily mean, however, that a decentralized economy cannot also make use of planning, or that market forces must reign supreme.

China's plan to have a socialist commodity economy implies both state planning *and* enterprise freedom. It is summed up in the catch phrase widely used, "The state regulates the market and the market guides enterprises." But in order for the state to fully regulate the market it not only has to maintain a strong planning function but it must be able to control inflation, economic growth, the money supply and interest rates, and eliminate irrational prices and subsidies. This is not possible yet.

For enterprises to be fully guided by the market, they must have considerably more freedom and more competition than at present; they must have truly independent management responsible for prices, profits and losses; they must be exposed to certain bankruptcy if they are incompetent and inefficient; and they must be able to draw on specialized markets for materials, labor, financing, etc. This is not possible yet, either.

Meantime, in line with its attempts in recent years to decentralize and free the economy as well as to maintain public ownership and control of all key production, China has relied until now on a strategy which combined two different plans. The new government is clearly attempting to recentralize some functions and to recover economic authority surrendered to lower echelons in recent years, but it maintains that it merely wants to adjust, not reverse, reforms to date which utilized these concepts:

A *mandatory state plan*, under which the state seeks to control essential materials and regulate production while at the same time using economic rather than administrative means to direct production of less critical items under the guidance plan. Agricultural and sideline products are no longer purchased on a mandatory delivery or quota basis (although grain and cotton are purchased at fixed prices).

"The number of industrial products subject to mandatory planning has been cut from 131 in 1980 to 14 now, and agricultural products from 117 to 9," and "around 65 percent of all farm and sideline products, 55 percent of all consumer goods, and 40 percent of all industrial materials have their prices determined by the market to varying degrees. This embraces around half of all commodities on sale in China." *(Beijing Review, 1989)*

In a summary of the present scope of Chinese economic planning, *China Daily* said of mandatory planning that in tandem with the quotas set by the plan "are mandatory prices, fixed allocations of raw materials, and controlled sales of such products. If manufacture of a product is included in the state mandatory plan, the state ensures supply of raw materials . . . and designates which corporations will buy the goods at what prices."

An excess of mandatory plan products may be produced and sold at the manufacturer's discretion, unless specifically prohibited, but for these excess products the manufacturer is on his own with respect to raw materials or parts.

A *guidance plan*, which covers in a general way a vast range of goods and services not considered crucial, and in this area there is some competition between enterprises and some direct contact with the market. "The guidance plan," said *China Daily*, sets "targets for manufacturers, which may or may not be met, based on market conditions." Somewhat contradictorily, it added that "The manufacturers, however, bear the responsibility for failing to attain targets." The state may (or may not) assist by reducing taxes on a manufacturer or a product, by providing raw materials, and "by raising or lowering prices." Though price is a fundamental element of a market, prices have only a secondary regulatory role in the new market-oriented economy. *Guangming Daily* says that "the government and private citizens are both caught in mental contradictions," continuing that the government wants to use market forces but "at the same time . . . harbors misgivings about the growth of the market. This is because in the eye of the government, which has never had the experience of indirect management of the economy, the market is wrapped in mysterious clouds."

Services at the level of daily life (such as repair services) and most agricultural products are not covered by either plan.

To illustrate the intended supremacy of the mandatory plan, discussions often use Chen Yun's analogy involving a bird that is almost as well known as Deng's observation about cats:

> A bird cannot be held tightly in one's hand because that would kill it; it must be allowed to fly. But it must only be allowed to fly within its cage: without the cage it will fly away. If the bird represents economic revitalization, then the cage represents state planning.

There are, of course, two ways to look at this analogy, and there are many who see the cage not as a safeguard but a limitation. Nearly everyone on both sides agrees, however, that the existence side by side—in competition, in a sense—of the old and the new systems is a basic cause of many of the problems of economic reform. (See "One-Track Psyche in Two-Track World" in chapter 2.) Reviewing "The Sweet and Sour Decade" of reform, *Beijing Review* said that with neither system predominating

the defects of both systems have been magnified. Confusion has arisen in production, distribution, and management, creating much leeway for speculation and racketeering. [Making the new system dominant, however, is challenging.] So long as social demand far exceeds social supply and inflationary price hikes remain unchecked, it is difficult to remove the fetters caused by the coexistence of the two systems.

Opening the economy to the influences of market forces has demonstrated numerous contributions of market mechanisms to the overall economy. Key among these are:

☐ The market above all both requires and creates competition, setting one enterprise against another in securing orders, the good will of customers, and their repeat business; in hiring; in buying materials, and in many other ways.

For example, factories which thought themselves in a favorable position because of the scarcity of their products formerly refused to sell replacement parts, forcing customers to buy complete new units; today, they are glad to sell spare parts. Another example on a simpler level is that of the dumpling stand in a market that took many customers away from a nearby snack shop by delivering food to keepers of market stands, so they didn't have to close and lose sales at meal times.

☐ Competition forces management to improve its operating practices in order to improve profits, and to spend more in research and innovation, thereby meeting additional needs and creating growth for their companies.

For example, an electric fan manufacturer had for years been content to coast along simply meeting its quotas rather than upgrade its old facilities, improve its designs, and increase production. When the state ceased buying the factory's entire output, the factory was forced to change its ways; now, the factory even subscribes to a long-range weather forecasting service to help plan production.

☐ Direct contact with customers results in faster turnover of inventories, and gives the producer feedback on his old products and the customers' need for new ones. An early hero of reform was the manager of a shirt factory who stopped relying on the state as a customer and marketer of his shirts. He sent people to sophisticated Shanghai to study tastes, learn what stores wanted, and forecast market trends. Coupled with administrative changes in his factory, these techniques enabled the enterprise to grow from 100 workers to over 600 in a few years.

☐ Customers' direct contact with suppliers enables customers to stay
   up-to-date on new technology, to become familiar with products
   before placing an order for them (which was not possible when
   dealing through the state supply system), to locate new sources
   more easily, etc. A factory often did not even know where its
   supplies and component parts came from, under the previous
   system.

In attempting to give market forces a role in their economy, the
Chinese face another of the chicken-or-egg kinds of problems referred
to before: The new economy urgently needs input from the market to
help provide directions for planning. But the market, if it is to be
helpful, must be a *buyers'* market in which there is a sufficient supply of
a variety of goods for buyers to make a meaningful choice, and thereby
to signal clearly what market demand really is. In China, however, a
sellers' market prevails, and is likely to prevail for quite some time until
the economy becomes more vigorous and until state enterprises have
greater autonomy.

No doubt this situation will gradually work itself out, but, clearly,
giving the market a role in the economy is not as easy as simply deciding
to do so.

PRICE REFORM: MAKING PRICES
REFLECT REALITIES

It is commonly said by both Chinese and foreigners that price reform is
absolutely critical to strengthening enterprises and achieving overall
economic reform. What are the reasons? The "Decision on Reform of
the Economic Structure" expressed them this way:

> The prices of many commodities [in China today] reflect neither their
> value nor the relation of supply to demand. This irrational price system has
> to be reformed. Otherwise it will be impossible to assess correctly the
> performance of enterprises, ensure the smooth circulation of goods be-
> tween urban and rural areas, promote technological advances, or rational-
> ize the production mix and consumption patterns.
>
> This will result in an enormous waste of social labor and seriously
> hamper application of the principle of distribution according to work. As
> the decision-making power of enterprises grows, pricing will be increas-
> ingly important in regulating their production and operation. It is, there-
> fore, all the more urgent to establish a rational system of pricing.

What Is Wrong with Chinese Prices?

Like the otherworldliness of centralization, the concept of "price reform" is something a capitalist needs some time to become accustomed to. Normally, the capitalist expects prices to reform themselves, so to speak, to reflect in constantly changing monetary terms all the considerations of supply, demand, usefulness, quality, etc., that supposedly go into determination of prices under capitalism and that have to be balanced out to enable producers to offer a price that will attract buyers but allow business to operate at a profit.

The Chinese pricing system, by contrast, involves a totally different set of political and social as well as economic considerations. For example, the entire system of prices for Chinese agricultural products was for a long time—and to a certain extent still is—based on the need, first, to provide the state with food and clothing for urban workers at low cost, and, second, to milk from agricultural prices an excess of revenue to be used for industrialization. (This intricate process, usually summed up as the "price scissors," is discussed a little further below in "Price Reform Is a Sensitive Issue.")

In a planned economy there is essentially no competition, no market, and no concern with profits or losses by producers, who are subsidized if state policies or their own mismanagement prevent their balancing revenue and expenses. Therefore, prices in this system cannot work in a competitive commodity market economy.

For a long time there has been an extensive system of fixed prices in China, for everything from a ton of coal to a television set to repairing a flat bicycle tire. Most prices have been controlled for more than thirty years (some industrial prices have not been *changed* for that long!). Because they are fixed (and by definition are unaffected by extraneous influences), and because of the sociopolitical rather than economic basis used in fixing them, these prices cannot serve as market indicators and regulators.

In recent years (as will be discussed under "Price Reform Today") floating prices with ceilings and other types of prices not rigidly fixed have appeared. However, the changeover from irrational and fixed prices has been far from complete—hence the continuing need for price reform—and the following discussion of four major shortcomings of the Chinese price system is still quite pertinent.

Chinese pricing policies and practices have led to problems such as these:

1. *Large governmental subsidies are required*—Many consumer prices are kept low by government subsidies to producers, or allowances are paid to individual consumers to offset prices, to such an extent that subsidies in China absorb a share of government revenues higher than in any other socialist nation. Deng Xiaoping has said that subsidies are one of two crippling burdens on the back of the country. (The other is lack of enterprise autonomy.) The burden has since risen, and in the 1989 budget alone there was a 30 percent increase in the amount set aside for consumer subsidies.

    For example, the Chinese government has been in the vegetable business since 1955, when it established special companies which had a monopoly over the market. The companies controlled what and how much was planted, purchased crops at fixed prices, and distributed vegetables to state stores where they were sold at prices set by the vegetable companies. This made sense at the time, because it helped to stabilize erratic food supplies.

    After a few years, however, peasants became dissatisfied with the price levels, and the vegetable companies kept increasing prices paid to them—but the companies absorbed most or all of the costs. There were reasons for this, too, but the companies nevertheless began losing money in the sixties and have been losing money ever since.

    Subsidized housing has presented a different problem. Since liberation China has provided housing to urban workers through work units as part of the iron rice bowl at rents far too low even to cover maintenance, to say nothing of replacement, resulting in large subsidies by the government.

    As with most other products, there is little or no variance in cost according to desirability— size, condition, or location—of apartments. As a result, units are not well maintained, no funds are generated for new housing, and the extremely low rents have meant that people with connections or luck have been able to afford far more room than they need while most others are unable to find sufficient space.

    Rents are now being raised about sevenfold, however, with the hope that some of the present problems will start to solve themselves. Low- and average-income occupants will receive direct subsidies to help pay the new rents (many object that the subsidy, up to 25 percent of wages, does not cover the full increase), but those with higher salaries or larger apartments will be on their own. Space-per-person standards are being adopted, and those occupying larger living units will have to pay a premium for the excess or vacate it.

Commercialization, or privatization, of housing was introduced first in 1982 and again with some hoopla in 1987. A little housing is now being sold to individuals, and payment of housing subsidies direct to occupants will help make it more feasible for people to someday begin choosing their own housing.

It will be a slow process, however. Chinese economists calculate that consumers have tens of billions of yuan in unbanked savings, and have hoped the opportunity to buy apartments would sop up much of this tremendous spending power and cool inflation. This has not happened to any great extent, however, apparently because people are shocked by prices. Free-market, unsubsidized housing is offered in Beijing, for example, at prices that would require an average college graduate to save half his income for a hundred years to buy a two-room apartment.

Prices on existing government-built apartments for sale to people now occupying them are considerably lower, but even with various kinds of assistance schemes most prices are still formidable. So, housing will for some time continue to be very scarce, often poor quality, cheap—and subsidized.

Food subsidies are thought to cost the state about 10 percent of the budget, and housing another 10 percent. There are various other subsidies, such as for transportation, bathhouse fees, shoes, water, funerals, hair cuts, medical treatment, and staple foods (for example, the government pays seven different subsidies on grain, at various points along the production-distribution chain). Medical care is partly subsidized (though China is far from having universal free medical care, as is often thought). *Economic Daily* has estimated that 30 percent of the national budget goes for consumer subsidies, one reason wages can be as low as they are. Because major subsidies are usually paid directly to producers and suppliers, however, the price assistance is often invisible, and, curiously, the government does little to help people understand the extent of their nonwage income. *Economic Daily* reported one survey in a large city where over 90 percent of people did not know how much a kilo of grain was subsidized.

Increasing subsidies is the pragmatic way to deal with the public concern caused by inflation. Under Zhao, the government felt that only price reform, despite its problems, could eliminate or greatly reduce the need for subsidies and make a basic contribution toward eventually rationalizing the nation's economy. Li Peng and the conservatives continue to lean on subsidies; in fact, the 1989 budget (which became their responsibility after Zhao was downgraded in October 1988) provides for an increase in subsidies.

2. *Prices do not reflect value of products or supply and demand*—Prices for minerals, particularly coal, and for other raw materials, are often cited as being too low. In fact, China's state-set prices for raw materials and energy are among the lowest in the world. If the country's foreign trade were developed, many materials whose price is now state-set could not be economically used in production of goods now sold at low prices, but would be more profitable if sold abroad in unprocessed form.

Even with cheap raw materials, however, as Vice-premier Tian Jiyun has pointed out, "Many products turned out by China's processing industries with such cheap raw materials and energy cost far more than products of the same category sold on the international market." The reason appears to be simply that with the advantage of cheap resources the industries do not worry about improving their processes or management, or reducing waste (of energy, for example, of which five times more is used to produce a dollar's worth of GNP than in France, and one and a half times more than in India).

"If we do not resolutely change the irrational price differentials between commodities," he continued, "it will be difficult to fully arouse enthusiasm in the raw material and energy-producing industries to increase production, because there will be no incentive for them to do so."

3. *Prices do not reflect quality*—This story is supposed to have appeared not long ago in a Chinese newspaper:

> When a peasant in Zhejiang Province sold a 100-kilo pig to a state purchasing station, he tied a mouse to the tail of the pig. When asked why he did this, the peasant answered, "I am not the first to do it. The state supply and marketing cooperatives have done it for some time. When we buy something from them, we are often forced to buy things we do not want. So when I sell to the state a 100-kilo pig together with a little mouse, can you say I have overdone it?"

Because local and provincial price departments usually do not set high prices for goods of fine quality and lower prices for poor quality ones, sellers often attempt the kind of tie-in sale the peasant did, in order to move the lower quality items sellers themselves have to buy from wholesalers in order to get the better goods.

As it happens, the market has established two levels of prices for pork, one price for lean and one price for fatty (and it is not uncommon for sellers to "tie a mouse" onto lean pork and make sellers buy an equal amount of fatty pork at the same time). But there is only a single price for most products. There are no grades of fruit or vegetables, chicken or fish, for example. All light bulbs are the same price, whether they are a brand that has a long life or short one. A television set with a good reputation for durability will sell (officially) for no more than an off brand.

Since quality is not rewarded, and fixed prices do not allow enough margin to improve mediocre products, it is the mediocre that is most often found. (Price is not the only factor in mediocrity, however. High demand for many products makes it difficult for consumers to refuse low quality goods, and this in turn gives manufacturers no incentive to upgrade products.)

4. *Low profits kill enthusiasm*—Closely related to the failure to reward quality are the low profits that often accompany fixed prices. Without some economic incentive to produce a given product, it may not be produced, even in a socialist economy, and China has any number of examples of this.

The most famous example involves pigs, again. In the late seventies, conditions inspired great enthusiasm among the peasants for raising pigs, and pork became plentiful, after many years of rationing. Rationing ended as supplies grew, but purchase and sale of pork remained a state monopoly, and prices were fixed. As time passed, the government raised prices for grain, essential to producing lean pork, but did not adjust prices for pork. Finally, the relative prices became such that the price the state paid for pork was actually less than the cost of the pig's grain.

So, peasants lost their enthusiasm for pork raising, and pork rationing had to be resumed in February 1985.

In the following July, however, the state lifted its monopoly over pork purchases and control of its price, "triggering," said *China Daily*, "the biggest shift in pork sales in more than 30 years." When fixed prices ended, so did price subsidies. Prices increased about 30 percent, but pork became readily available.

Now, history is repeating itself, and high grain prices versus low pig prices are again putting pork in short supply. Pork prices haven't kept pace with rising feed prices, and farmers now prefer to raise cattle, sheep, chickens, and fish. It was necessary to reinstate pork rationing in many cities in the fall of 1987.

Price Reform Is a Sensitive Issue

The greatest activity in price reform has occurred since the decision on urban reform in 1984, but price reform had, in fact, begun simultaneously with other reforms in 1979.

At that time, the government increased agricultural prices by more than 20 percent, in order to stimulate rural reform and to begin to close the "price scissors"—the economic legerdemain chosen by China and some other socialist countries to finance industrialization. (Essentially, in this process the state pays peasants less than their products are "worth" in order to keep food prices, and therefore wages, low, and agricultural raw materials cheap. The state then prices products purchased by peasants excessively high. The excess profit derived from "the tributes made by the peasants" has been estimated at over 600 billion yuan from liberation through 1978 and was used to finance industrialization.)

Consumers were sheltered for a time from the consequences of the 1979 and later increases in government payments to farmers, though prices of nonstaple foods did increase, but by 1985 a general 10 percent wage supplement was necessary. However, it was inadequate to keep consumers even with costs because food prices alone, which constitute a large part of household expenses, had risen more than the supplement.

From 1978 to 1987 the average annual price-adjusted increase in per capita income for workers was 7.9 percent—but that is an average. The 1987 inflation rate of 7.2 percent was actually about the same as the year before, but wages did not keep pace so the price-adjusted increase was only 1.7 percent, translating into little more money in the pockets of people who had expected to see their incomes continue to grow. About 20 percent of urban families suffered an actual decline in their living standards in 1987.

During 1986 and 1987 the government slacked off its price reform efforts of the previous two years and attempted instead to stabilize prices, which, nevertheless, continued to rise. After vegetable prices increased 50 percent in the first quarter of 1988, hopes for simple stabilization were seen to be obviously unrealistic, and new goals were announced—control of inflation and stimulation of agricultural production.

To this end the government decontrolled prices of vegetables, eggs, pork, and sugar, and gave a new (but insufficient) ten-yuan subsidy directly to workers. Decontrol was expected to increase supplies and soon stabilize prices; coupling it with the direct subsidy to workers—in effect, increasing their wages with funds already marked for hidden wholesale subsidies, as with the new direct housing subsidies—gave them more flexible buying power than would an equal subsidy to peasants under the old system.

Inflation continued, however, and price controls were reimposed on a wide range of foods and consumer goods in Beijing and some other large cities in the fall of 1988. Price-adjusted income again rose only very slightly and 35 percent of families suffered a decline in living standards.

The situation with price reform at that time was chaotic, and at one point the Politburo announced a plan to go full speed ahead with it and two weeks later the State Council announced it would be halted for two years. In an interview with Chen Yizi, Zhao's top economic aide who is now a refugee in Paris, *Asiaweek* asked, "Aren't [1988's] price reforms the main reason for the present economic difficulties in China? Who is responsible?" Chen replied that Deng "mentioned [price reform] several times," presumably rather urgently, and then Zhao carried it out, although Zhao and Chen had decided that

> China was not in a position to remove price controls because there were no independent enterprises, no market environment, and no regulations regarding market competition. Under such circumstances, uncontrolled prices would only bring about price confusion. Therefore, we wrote seven reports, pointing out that effective price reforms meant far more fundamental adjustments in our economic system. Finally, the price reform program was mapped out by the State Planning Commission, headed by Yao Yilin [now the leading conservative economist]. Of course, we didn't agree with what they proposed. Between price reform and reform of enterprises we had put emphasis on the latter. Therefore, when we heard people say we had advocated price reform and had held that "inflation does no harm" we didn't know whether to laugh or cry.

Further efforts to control prices were made in the spring of 1989, when the government attempted to centralize most pricing authority in the State Council, from which provincial and local governments would have to secure approval to allow higher local prices. The rate of inflation has increased rather than decreased since that time, however.

To reassure wage earners that they would not be abandoned to the unpredictable results of price reform, Premier Li Peng announced that the government would coordinate price reforms with wage and other reforms to protect the standard of living. Wage reform has not yet been attempted in any comprehensive way, however. Price reform, on the other hand, has not been halted in the absolute way people were led to expect by government announcements. A number of approved price increases have been announced, the most spectacular, perhaps, being a September 1989 decision to approximately double railroad, airline, and water transportation passenger fares, the largest jump in the history of the country (and the first significant increase since 1955).

Industry was having its problems also, during the same period. Floating prices began to be used for a few industrial products in 1979 and were applied to most products by 1983, but the allowable range often did not give factories much flexibility. After urban reform began in 1984 the government increased prices to state-owned enterprises for various industrial materials, transport, and energy, but, in order to keep consumer prices down, refused to increase the state-set market prices of manufacturers' products.

Enterprises were expected to make up for increased costs by increasing efficiency, but quick improvements sufficient to cover the new costs were sometimes impossible, since material prices went up 100 percent or more. Many enterprises sharply reduced their production of some items, or stopped making them altogether.

There have been severe shortages of products which have been caught in this bind. For example, school textbooks were in short supply in the 1988–89 school year because school book publishers, whose products are price-controlled while other publications are not, cannot afford the uncontrolled market prices of scarce paper and bribes paid by publishers of comic books, *kung fu* fiction, and other popular materials. In another typical case, the famous Daqing Oil Field, which produces about half of China's oil, lost over twenty-five million yuan in 1988 (its first losing year ever) because, said an official, "the oil field had to buy raw materials at market prices while selling its oil at a state-set price."

When state enterprises such as the school book publishers and Daqing "lose" money, of course the state picks up their losses, but seldom to an extent that adequately recognizes the costs of doing business or provides sufficient incentive, so needed products are not produced and businesses stagnate and deteriorate.

Industry is now trying to get over another hurdle created by loosened controls over raw material supplies. Formerly, the state supplied about

70 percent of factories' needs on a guaranteed basis and at a fixed—though possibly increased—price. As controls are loosened, guaranteed supplies are decreasing to about 20 percent of needs. Factories must buy the remainder of their needs on the open market, where prices may be double the old state prices, driven up not only by legitimate market forces but also by private speculators and officials operating as profiteers. (See "The Big Challenge," below.)

Price changes since 1984 have increased supplies and have begun redressing imbalances, but, on the whole, are considered to have been only partly successful. The head of the State Administration of Commodity Prices has admitted that the government originally underestimated the problems related to price reform and had not done enough groundwork nor taken sufficient remedial measures to minimize the problems.

The consequences of the present price structure have been summed up this way by the State Economic Commission:

> With such irrational pricing, some enterprises make more profit than others simply because the prices of their raw materials are artificially low [and state-set prices for products are excessive in relation to production costs], rather than because they are more efficient. At the same time, some well-run factories barely break even because of the high cost of materials and the low state-set prices of the finished products. Such a situation does not provide [any incentive] to raise quality and lower production costs.
>
> With such shortcomings, prices cannot play the role of economic levers to regulate the economy and promote production.... For instance, many enterprises have not wanted to make low-priced products ... and supply of these goods fell short of demand. On the other hand, there was overstocking of high-priced items....
>
> Enterprises adopting new technology and making new products were not rewarded. Those who kept making the same old thing did not suffer. ... All these show that China's price system must be reformed now.

Price Reform Today

Since price reform began, and especially since economic reform began in earnest in 1984, there has been a move away from the fixed prices which have prevailed since liberation toward a more flexible—and intricate—price system.

China Legality has identified five types of current prices, delimited according to sale circumstances and administrative powers:

☐   State-fixed prices, also called "planned prices," applied to products governed by the mandatory state plan.

- ☐ Floating prices with limits, another form of planned price.

- ☐ Negotiated prices, for sideline commodities and similar products under the guiding state plan, with some state input on price level.

- ☐ Producer-set prices, primarily applicable to small commodities not under state planning.

- ☐ Market prices, or free prices, "that can be freely arrived at by both the buying and selling parties at a rural market or an urban trading market."

The official attitude toward price reform has vacillated somewhat since it became a major objective in 1984, but the line has mostly been that price reform was of the utmost urgency, basic to all other economic reforms. Since the fall of 1988, however, the line has been that the Chinese people have "reached the limit of their tolerance" for price increases—now synonymous with price reform—and that reform must be virtually halted for perhaps two years or more.

During the hiatus, the government will attempt to improve supply; reduce inflation; strengthen state enterprises and make them more profitable; end official profiteering; and, in general, provide more of the conditions which will make it possible for a market economy to operate more effectively than it has in the development period so far. There is general agreement between radical and moderate reformers, and Chinese and foreign economists, that some period of readjustment and stock taking is needed.

Certainly, as expected, price reform has been a difficult, upsetting, contentious process, and, which was not foreseen, it has also been a source of corruption and public condemnation.

It should be pointed out, however, that price reform has not been an unmitigated disaster by any means.

It is true, for example, that there has been considerable "inflation" in prices of daily necessities and agricultural products no longer state controlled—but who is to say that real inflation has occurred when many of these products were seldom available under the state-fixed price and are now available everywhere every day at a market price, even though that price is higher than the old state price? A case could certainly be made that the "inflation" was present all along in the need of the people for the product and their willingness to pay more to have it—they just didn't have a means of expressing their willingness to have prices rise in exchange for the opportunity to buy.

There have been advantages, too (as well as distinct disadvantages) in the partial decontrol of prices of agricultural and industrial products that have remained under, or partly under, state control. The state began early in reform to allow unallocated sales at market prices of a portion of these materials while maintaining fixed prices on the portion required to fill state quotas, a system that came to be known as "two-track prices."

Like floating prices and market prices, two-track prices opened many opportunities for private entrepreneurs and collectives to secure needed supplies they could not get otherwise, because they were out of the allocation mechanism. With these supplies, they could go into competition even with state firms which got supplies cheaper, could prosper and contribute significantly to economic growth. It is in the state's failure to control the two-track system as it was originally planned that criminal abuses of it arose.

The Big Challenge: Two-Track Prices

Two-track prices, however, have presented special and serious problems, despite their benefits. The idea behind two-track prices, as *China Briefing ,1985* put it, was

> to simply let the market play a more and more important role in production decisions until it gradually usurped many of the functions of the planners . . .; in time, planned prices would be adjusted with reference to market prices, and the economy would be guided towards a socialist market economy as planned and market prices came together.

For a variety of reasons—such as unexpected demand, inability to increase supply, and unwillingness to make planned prices flexible—things did not work out as planned, and exactly the reverse happened. For example, at one point

> the market price [for concrete reinforcing bars] was 1,375 yuan per ton, nearly twice the state-set price of 700 yuan . . . [and later rose to] between 1,700 and 2,000 yuan. . . . Thus, instead of being gradually unified, the planned and market sectors gradually grew further apart.

The same spread has developed between the prices of agricultural products sold at fixed prices to the state within its plan quota and those sold above the quota by peasants at market prices.

Price reform is feared because it has led to price increases. It is also linked very closely in the public mind with corruption, however. Some of the most negative, damaging, and challenging problems in the entire reform movement stem primarily from exploitation by some people—mostly Party and government officials—of the speculative potential provided by the big gaps between state and market prices in the two-track system.

The two most commonly exploited opportunities are:

1. The opportunity to acquire scarce goods at low state prices for resale at much higher market prices, or, in other words, the opportunity to profiteer.

It can hardly be called "the opportunity to speculate," because buying low and selling high in the two-track price system is like buying stock while being absolutely sure it will rise the moment it is bought.

Public outrage has been increasingly focused on *guan dao* or "official profiteers," i.e., enterprise officials and Party members who abuse their positions and affiliations to secure scarce goods for trading. Over the years, they have been repeatedly forbidden to engage in commerce but the prohibition has been little enforced. (See "Official Corruption Menaces Government's Legitimacy" in chapter 4.)

Cheap state-priced goods are obtained in numerous ways. They may be withdrawn from a factory's inventory of goods manufactured under the state plan and diverted to dummy trading companies owned by factory, Party, and government officials. They may be simply stolen for trading companies or sold at high prices to individual buyers unable to get supplies at state prices. Goods imported by the state wind up in private warehouses. A legitimate customer may buy at the state price materials intended for further processing but resell them immediately at the market price, rather than bother with manufacturing; he then defaults (with little or no penalty) on the contract with the government for the manufactured product that entitled him to the raw materials originally. And so on. Whatever the mechanism, the *guan dao* make large profits and the final consumer pays a heavy premium.

This sure-fire "buy low-sell high" process results in cases like these, similar to numerous instances known to all Chinese because of wide publicity:

☐ Automobiles imported by a local government changed hands three times merely through paper transactions, rising in price from 36,900 yuan to 75,000 yuan in the process.

☐ The same thing happened with a consignment of rubber originally destined for a state enterprise, the papers for which also changed hands three times and increased in price from 3,900 to 5,730 yuan a ton.

☐ In one county, 150 tons of state-supplied fertilizer were resold 26 times before delivery to the fields, and rose from 446 yuan to 765 yuan per ton in the process. The government estimated that profiteers made 42 million yuan on illegal fertilizer deals in 15 counties in 1988.

2. The opportunity to sell at above-quota prices products originally classified and priced low as within-quota goods.

Taking advantage of this situation requires defiance of the government and/or refusal to honor contracts, as in the case of peasants and agricultural products (see "Static Grain Production" in chapter 6), or, in the case of state-owned enterprises, requires superior negotiating skills, influence, bribery of superior officials, etc., or combinations of all of these.

New Observer Fortnightly described this bargaining scene, which occurs everywhere every year under the two-track system:

> At a steel rolling mill that this reporter visited, the May quota . . . had not been hammered out. The factory manager was bargaining back and forth with the [government] departments concerned and negotiators were having a hard time making any progress. The departments concerned wanted the mill to produce a lot under the [state] plan while the factory wanted to produce a lot outside the plan.

The situation was very clear. If the factory could remove ten thousand tons of its productive capacity from its quota under the plan and use it to produce steel products that fell outside the plan and its quota, it would be able to earn more than seven million yuan.

After surveying other aspects of the two-track system, the magazine summed up the situation thus:

> The inevitable result of the conflict and the friction between the two tracks is that they pull against each other and tend to cancel each other out. With two different price systems in operation, neither one can function effectively. The plan fails and the market mechanism is also ineffective. This is what has caused the chaos in our economy.

China is no different from other countries in its difficulties with prices, and China's problems arise from the same problems as elsewhere—essentially, decisions that seemed correct at one time were not satisfactory over the long term. Making adjustments now is a daunting prospect, but at least China has the nerve to try, which many China watchers denied it would do. Zhao Ziyang wrote in *Red Flag* in January 1985 that "Price reform is a problem which no socialist country has yet properly resolved." It apparently will require a prodigious effort for China to achieve another first.

READJUSTING, RESTRUCTURING, CONSOLIDATING AND IMPROVING CHINA'S ECONOMY

For many years, China's economic development, like its political development, had a tortuous and zigzag course, operating under the slogans "Take grain as the key link" at some times and "Take steel as the key link" at others, and under philosophies that were different still at other times. China's economists began taking a more realistic look at the makeup of the economy in 1978 when ideological restraints on original thought began to be loosened somewhat.

The communique of the Third Plenum in 1978 touched upon the question of major changes in the national economy, using the terms "readjustment, reform, reorganization, and improvement." The Central Committee Work Conference, in April 1979, more fully formulated

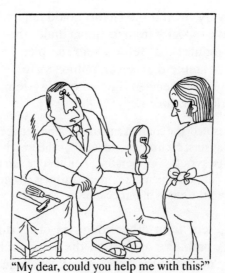

"My dear, could you help me with this?"

Zhu Senlin, *China Daily*

the slogan of "readjusting, restructuring, consolidating, and improving" the country's economy, "with the emphasis on readjustment."

This slogan occurs often in discussions of government actions or analyses of the economy, but it is seldom clear what the four key but general words mean. In the paragraphs below, quoted definitions are from *Almanac of China's Economy 1981*. The concepts overlap somewhat, but associating each term with concrete examples helps make meanings clearer.

Readjustment. "Readjustment means to consciously readjust proportional relations in the economy that had for so long been dislocated; thus, all branches of the national economy can develop in a relatively coordinated manner and a rational ratio can be maintained between accumulation and consumption."

Essentially, readjustment refers to changing the *mix* of economic activity. Too much emphasis had been laid on rapid growth of heavy industry, for example, under the influence of ultraleftist Chinese thinking and the economic plan copied from the Soviet Union. Readjustment reduces the stress on heavy industry and gives more emphasis to agriculture and light industry. In addition, as a result of stress on heavy industry and growth, too much money has been spent on production and capital construction and not enough on raising the standard of living, and this situation is also being adjusted.

Achieving and maintaining the desired mix of investment and consumption has been a problem for years, originally because of deficiencies in planning and control. As the country gained experience, these factors had less weight, but as the collective and private sectors of the economy increased in vitality, so did their investment— which was not included in the central government's plans or control. Since 1982, investment in these sectors has amounted to nearly a third of all investment in fixed assets. From 1986, investment spending in these sectors is being incorporated into the state plan.

Restructuring. "Restructuring means to restructure, both systematically and comprehensively, aspects of the existing economic management system that hamper the development of productive forces, with the result that the superiority of the socialist system can be fully brought out."

"Restructuring" replaced "reform" in the original phrasing quoted above, but it means about the same thing "reform" seems to have meant— changing the *rules* under which economic activity is carried on. Decentralization and price reform are two examples.

Consolidation. "Consolidation means to consolidate [i.e., strengthen, not merge] and better run existing enterprises, especially those whose management was once disrupted, so that they will advance along the correct road and play a full part in China's modernization."

Running existing enterprises better covers a wide range of possible actions. Some moves that have been cited by the Chinese as coming under the heading of "consolidation" are: promoting younger and better-trained cadres to leading positions in enterprises; replacing aging and poorly trained managers; establishing cadres' and workers' training schools; establishing the "Thorough Quality Control" system; and improving accounting practices.

Improvement. "Improvement means to significantly raise production levels, technical levels, and management levels."

These goals are classified as coming under the general objective of improving economic performance, but they clearly overlap with the goals of "consolidation."

OPENING TO THE OUTSIDE WORLD

"Opening" is one of China's two main reform objectives expressed in a slogan which has been current for several years: "Opening to the outside world and invigorating the domestic economy."

This new outlook was a basic change from China's former suspicious rejection of the outside world, and it was not without its opponents. Old fears and humiliations die hard. For example, some Chinese felt that the special economic zones established in 1980 and the granting of special conditions to investors in the newly opened coastal cities in 1984 were too reminiscent of the special privileges foreign powers forced China to grant them in many of the same cities during the 1800s. Deng Xiaoping, who continues to be the most visible proponent of the "opening" policy, agreed that the memory was bitter, saying, "We suffered from this, and so did our forefathers." But he went on to point out that "Isolation landed China in poverty, backwardness, and ignorance. No country can now develop by closing its door."

The abandonment of economic and (to some extent) psychological isolationism has had numerous effects—in business, education, science, culture, entertainment, dress, etc. Western influence in many of these areas has been viewed nervously and criticized vigorously. Including Li Peng's current one, there have been no less than four political campaigns since 1978 aimed at reducing or eliminating the "spiritual pollution" and "bourgeois liberalization" generated by foreign life-styles and political and moral concepts.

Such constant outbreaks of hostility indicate a chronic, fundamental distrust that anyone considering a long-term relationship will want to evaluate carefully. Another vast anti-foreign movement like the Boxer Rebellion seems impossible—but so did the June Fourth Massacre.

Asiaweek made a pungent analysis of the role of xenophobia in Chinese economic and political life:

> Why is liberalism so pernicious? Because it's "Western"—in short, foreign. That it also happens to be communism's worst enemy—when circumstances require it to be, at least—is almost beside the point, because for the last century and a half Chinese politics has been dominated by the obsession to purify the homeland of alien influences, the better for China to reassert its immemorial pre-eminence. . . . Anti-foreign sentiment remains the sterling of political worth.

But, the editorial continued, unwillingness to come to terms with the outside world is an increasingly dangerous attitude:

> One early and prominent victim of the recent [1987] political troubles, in truth, has been the campaign to establish an independent rule of law, which turns out to be easily suspended when exigencies warrant it. This fact in commercial contracts and dealings is precisely why so many Japanese [and other] firms invited into China have soured on doing business there.
>
> Now that the Soviet Union has approved its new foreign-investment law . . . the big push for Japanese capital and know-how is coming: it's just around the corner. . . . Xenophobia is a luxury China's internal politics can no longer afford.

There has been no serious suggestion in the political campaigns against western influence that China should again be closed to the outside world. There are, however, indications from time to time of a lingering determination to open no wider than absolutely necessary, ranging from the protracted difficulties foreign investors have had in setting up businesses to such matters as a requirement that Chinese wishing to do even minor tasks for foreigners in Beijing must first obtain "an introduction" from a government department. Talking blackly about "foreign influence" behind the Pro-Democracy Movement has not really helped, either.

All along, however, and especially since the June Fourth Massacre, the highest Chinese officials have tried to reassure possible investors that the policies of economic reform and opening to the outside are really fundamental and permanent, not subject to harm from political turmoil. One of the few specific comments in the Fifth Plenum communique emphasized continuation of the open policy.

China needs not only investment but foreign trade, and Deng has used this point to demonstrate that the open policy must continue. He said to the Central Advisory Commission in 1984:

> We want to quadruple our gross national product and, once we've done that, aim for a new target, which cannot be attained without an open policy. ... Our foreign trade volume is now at US$40 billion. Can we quadruple production from such a meager base if we pursue a closed-door policy? .. . What do we do with our products when our GNP reaches US$1,000 billion? Will we sell them all in the domestic market? Shall we produce all we need? If we don't open up to the outside world, it will be difficult to quadruple production, and even more difficult to make progress after that.

China Courts Foreign Investors

Overall, the courting of foreign investors (primarily for joint ventures) has had satisfactory if not, until recently, spectacular results, as the statistics cited later indicate. However, the process has presented two well-publicized problems to both the Chinese and investors.

The Chinese objective in opening to foreign investment was to attract industries that 1) would be advanced technologically, in order to improve the level of China's own technology and the skills of its workers, and 2) would produce exportable goods earning badly needed foreign exchange.

So far, however, progress has been spotty. The Chinese have willingly accepted many projects whose very nature obviously depended more on China's cheap (if, as some feel, poorly trained and disciplined) labor than on molding a hi-tech labor force, and other projects whose supporters were clearly more interested in the enormous consumer market China represents than in producing for export.

A 1987 report from the Ministry of Foreign Economic Relations and Trade said that foreign investment in China has been mostly absorbed by what are called "nonproductive projects"—i.e., projects without a salable, and more important, an exportable, product. Hotels, restaurants, exhibition centers, and services such as photofinishing businesses, fall within this category. Only 57 percent of foreign investment has gone into productive projects. (As part of the austerity program beginning in fall 1988, Beijing attempted to reimpose central authority over certain kinds of investments, including manufacture and assembly of cars, buses, and motorcycles; assembly lines for electronic products; alcoholic and carbonated beverages not for export; and others.)

On the other hand, the investors' objective in coming to China has been to make money, but many feel the Chinese are indifferent to the need for profit. A vice-minister of the State Economic Commission acknowledged that "Some are taking a bite out of the joint ventures and even sucking them dry," and Deng Xiaoping said, "We cannot ask foreign investors to come and then not let them make money."

Investors cite a host of problems, such as difficulties in securing foreign exchange; bureaucracy; interminable negotiations (the United States recently advised businessmen to spend no more than three months in negotiations); being forced to accept unsatisfactory employees from Chinese labor bureaus; gouging on fees and other unexpected charges; disregarding laws and contracts when doing so is beneficial to the Chinese side; and lack of recourse when investors are exploited.

Complaints built to such a volume that China was forced to pay attention after 1986 investment volume fell to half that of 1985. Comprehensive new regulations were issued late in 1986 and a new joint venture law was passed by the 1988 National People's Congress. Both leave unsolved several basic problems, such as the lack of ironclad assurance of foreign investors' ability to secure foreign exchange to send profits home, but they do emphasize the national government's strong desire to make investment conditions as attractive as possible.

As observers like *Far Eastern Economic Review* have pointed out, however, "Many foreign investors have found to their cost that Beijing's good intentions take a long time to filter down to the local level. Often, national guidelines are just that, with interpretation of these laws left to local authorities."

There are still so many significant problems, in fact, that a high-level United States Commerce Department official was preparing, just before the June crackdown, to take a delegation of businessmen to China with a set of problems—many of them involving Chinese interference in joint ventures— that they had been unable to resolve with the Chinese bureaucracy.

Investment since 1979 has not been as great as hoped for, some observers believe, but it has grown fairly steadily, soared in 1988, and was up about 65 percent over 1988 in the five months before the June crackdown, according to *China Daily*. By the end of 1988 contracted foreign investment totaled US$25 billion, with US$9 billion actually paid in.

The total number of ventures signed up was a little over 10,000 at the end of 1987, 2,200 of them finalized in that year alone, but 1988 added a startling 5,890 for a total of 15,900. Most are small or medium-sized, with an average investment of about US$1.6 million. Hongkong and Macao are by far the largest investors, followed by Japan, the United States, and about forty other countries. About 4,000 of the 10,000 ventures approved by 1987 were actually in operation, although Ministry of Foreign Economic Relations and Trade figures showed that only 1,300 were profitable.

A new aspect of foreign investment is that, whereas China formerly preferred to be a 51 percent owner in joint ventures, it is now encouraging (partly as an element of the "coastal strategy" mentioned below) the establishment of enterprises wholly owned by foreigners. Wholly foreign-owned ventures increased eight times in 1988 (though the total is still only 410).

Following the June Fourth Massacre, and with a government in power that has long opposed reforms, the question now is: Can China continue to attract foreign money? The answer seems to be: Probably.

Immediately after June 4 there were dozens of statements by business people with joint ventures in China already, some who were planning them, some who represented trade groups, and so on. Most reported receiving assurances of normalcy from the Chinese and encouragement to continue business as before. Some also reported being reminded that if other countries left a vacuum it would be filled by the Japanese, and, in fact, a Japanese official criticized Japanese firms for rushing in to make money "like a thief at a fire." But it was an American firm that made the largest post-crackdown deal reported so far—a deal with a possible value of two billion dollars for industrial park land leases in Tianjin, signed by MGM (M. G. Malekpour Development Company).

The behavior of the Chinese government toward the students entered little into investors' thinking, but they did weigh stability and reliability carefully. The outlook, while not very bullish, was not very negative, either, except for the Taiwanese, who are said to be holding back on finalizing deals to express their shock at the massacre. Investors already operating in China, or committed to do so, intended to continue, but the point was made often that the leadership is going to continue infighting and that new investors will want to be more cautious than they might have been previously. It was widely expected that foreign investors, especially new investors, would demand and could get more favorable terms.

Tourism, however— another important source of foreign dollars and foreign good will—was simply devastated. China has gone to great pains to emphasize that its opening policy is continuing—but few are coming in. The government claimed, for example, that by the first week in July tourism in Sichuan was back to normal, but unless Sichuan was somehow exceptional it is hard to see how this could have been possible. US airlines flying into China lost 75 to 85 percent of their passengers, and tour operators in the states and around the world canceled China trips for months or for 1989. In response, China so reduced its internal charges that by October its tour operators were offering a 10-day trip for $1,399, including first class hotels and air fare from San Francisco; this is approximately the price charged in the seventies when China first opened up and is about half the former 1989 price. Business travel fell sharply and there was apparently an almost total boycott of the many international scientific and technical conferences China was still attempting to hold. Russia was reportedly the only country represented at a major conference on superconductivity.

An estimated one million tourism employees will be out of work or seriously underemployed at a time when unemployment is increasingly worrisome. There seems to be no question that China has damaged for some time to come what it worked so long to build.

Special Investment Areas Offered

China has created the following types of investment areas authorized to provide special incentives to investors (although businessmen report that there is hardly any area in China whose officials do not offer similar benefits under the table):

Special Economic Zones—China's five SEZs have no counterparts in other socialist countries, or, for that matter, in any developing country. They are quite different from the "processing zones" and "free zones" found in some countries, although all three kinds of areas offer favorable tax and other conditions to investors and are export-oriented.

In China's SEZs, the objective is not only to create jobs and generate foreign exchange but to build, from the ground up, completely modern cities that are also comprehensive economic development areas, with a high proportion of technology-intensive, knowledge-intensive, and capital-intensive enterprises. From these, skills and technology are expected to flow to the rest of China. Production for export is the primary objective of SEZs, but they are also seen as an important, if limited, source of advanced products for the Chinese market.

For investors, the attractions are numerous, starting with low wage rates and geographical location. In addition, however, SEZs offer many economic pluses such as these: Enterprise income tax and other taxes may be waived or reduced for several years after profits begin; export taxes are waived; import duties and some business taxes are waived on a wide variety of imports needed to establish or operate an enterprise; land is available on favorable terms and foreign investors may now compete with Chinese in the purchase of long-term land use rights; after-tax profits can be repatriated without penalty (if the investor can get foreign exchange); and under some circumstances special zone products can be sold in the Chinese market.

Four zones were established in 1980 in the coastal areas of south China near the Hongkong and Macao borders, and all have temperate climates, excellent water transportation, and passenger airline and helicopter service. Shenzhen, undoubtedly the best-known zone, is also the largest, about 200 square miles. It spends about a third of its budget on cultural, education, sports, and health facilities, and has its own newspapers, periodicals, television stations, many secondary technical schools, and a university. Zhuhai is about 9 square miles, Shantou about 30 square miles, and Xiamen about 80 square miles (and is noted for its tourist facilities).

Hainan Island, with a tropical climate and rich agricultural and natural resources, became China's thirty-first province in 1988 with considerable hype, and the entire island was designated as the fifth and largest special economic zone. It will be able, but only after a longer-than-expected period of infrastructure development, to offer investors a variety of special privileges and conditions available nowhere else in China.

The zones are regarded as successful, even though until recently they have been less attractive to foreign investors than expected and have not become concentrations of high technology. The zones have a bright future, however, if foreign investors return and if the zones' motivation and flexibility are not sapped by policies of the new government, which sees freewheeling coastal areas as a particular threat to socialist ideology and morality.

Economic Development Zones (Also, "Coastal Cities" or "Open Coastal Cities")—Some of the advantages to foreign investors of operating in SEZs have been extended to sixteen coastal cities— including Dalian,

Shanghai, Tientsin, and Guangzhou—chosen for the same reason some of them had been treaty ports in the 1800s: their strategic locations. In addition, they all have fairly high levels of economic development.

The EDZs, with a population of over 70 million, are fundamentally different from SEZs, in that they are among China's most economically and culturally developed areas, and therefore the business and investment environments are quite different. Since EDZs have more—or, at least, different—advantages, the investment incentives offered are more limited. Not all the incentives found in SEZs are offered in EDZs, and, to those which are offered, more restrictions apply.

Nevertheless, the EDZs attracted in the first half-year after the program was announced in 1984 more foreign capital than had been invested in the original fourteen cities during the preceding five years, and it appears that they have continued to attract more than their share of investment. A larger percentage of contracted enterprises have gone into operation in the EDZs than in the nation at large, and most are said to be prospering.

New Investment Areas—Apparently pleased with their other special areas, the Chinese are engaging in what the west would call "product line extension" and opening still more areas for investment that offer special economic inducements.

Three "coastal open economic zones" were set up in 1985: Yangtze Delta Economic Zone (about 50,000 square kilometers with Shanghai as its center); the fantastically thriving Pearl River Delta Economic Zone (11,000 square kilometers, in which the major city is Guangzhou, or Canton) which may be in line for restrictions from the new national government; and South Fujian Economic Zone (a triangle with its apex at Xiamen).

There were two other less well-defined investment areas created in the fall of 1987 and winter of 1988.

Most important, then Party Secretary Zhao Ziyang announced a broad plan which became known as his "coastal strategy," affecting the three coastal economic zones mentioned above, plus the Shangdong and Liaodong peninsulas.

In these areas, the objectives are almost the reverse of objectives in the SEZs. Zhao pointed out that the shift of labor-intensive jobs from developed countries to low-wage areas continues to grow, and urged that China exploit its labor resources to develop low-wage (and apparently low-tech) export industries in China. It is estimated that Hongkong's labor shortage and rising wage rates has led to moving two million jobs to South China. Also, more emphasis will be placed upon attracting new enterprises funded entirely by foreign investment, rather than upon joint ventures, and upon importing materials needed for processing and export, rather than upon processing domestic materials.

Second, in the spring of 1988 the Chinese seem to have said to themselves, "Oh, well! In for a penny, in for a pound," declaring virtually the entire coastal area from Liaoning Province to Hainan Island to be an economic development region. At one stroke this expanded to 320,000 square kilometers the area open to foreign investment (not that any part of China seems really closed to investment) and increased the affected population from 90 to 160 million people. (All previous coastal special areas retain their identities within the new region, however.)

To miss no market niche, authorities are establishing "Overseas Chinese Cities" to attract investment strictly from returned overseas Chinese or from those still abroad. The first venture will be in a portion of the Shenzhen Economic Zone and will include ten major industrial and residential projects plus Mini-China Park, a sort of Chinese Disneyland featuring miniatures of the Great Wall and many other famous spots.

Chinese Investment Abroad

The Chinese are not only inviting foreigners in through their new open door but they are themselves going out. The nation now has over 500 joint ventures and other investments with Chinese equity of about US$2 billion, about a quarter of them established in 1988 alone. About half the investment is in Hongkong, where it has built a towering seventy-story office building of ultramodern design. Short of funds at home and with scarce foreign exchange, China has borrowed much of its investment stake from foreign banks. "We've been using foreign money to earn foreign money," one official said, although foreign economists claim most of the money comes from a large capital flight from China rather than government money.

Remaining investments are scattered among nearly seventy countries, including the United States (the $27,000,000 Lantana Lakes subdivision outside Jacksonville and other housing developments, in addition to industrial and commercial projects), Britain, and Australia, but are concentrated in the less-developed countries where China's relatively low level of technology will nevertheless be competitive and welcome. Profit and experience are said to be two objectives, but China is also concerned with protecting and increasing secure supplies of raw materials, such as ores and petrochemicals, which are in short supply worldwide.

SMASHING EGALITARIANISM'S "BIG POT"

The idea of the equality of man is basic to communism's classless society. In *Critique of the Gotha Programme,* Marx wrote that under communism the distribution of goods would be "From each according to his abilities, to each according to his needs," and this has become one of the most widely known slogans of the movement.

It comes as a surprise, then, to many people to learn that the Chinese in fact oppose distribution according to need. Instead, China has been trying hard to achieve distribution according to the less well-known principle, "From each according to his abilities, to each according to his *work,*" which Marx also proposed in the *Critique* as the principle governing distribution under *socialism,* the preliminary stage of communism.

A letter to the *Beijing Review* asked, "Aren't you self-contradictory when you practice the system of distribution according to work done, and at the same time advocate the communist attitude which regards labor as worthwhile regardless of rewards?" The reply was:

> The [socialist] principle "to each according to his work" and the communist attitude toward labor are two different things. The former refers to the system of distribution during the socialist period, and the latter represents human consciousness and an ideological response to work. They supplement, rather than contradict, each other.
> The socialist system of distribution according to one's work is formulated, not according to anyone's subjective decision, but according to objective laws. In the period of socialism, the productive forces have not grown to the level of supplying an abundance of products to fully meet the many-sided needs of all the members of society. During this period labor remains by and large a means of making a living, and the system of distribution according to work corresponds with the level of the productive forces and the ideological level of the great majority of the people.

There has been much earnest discussion of the principle of "to each according to his work," and it is common to have the question asked, as *China Youth News* did, "Isn't it socialism, featuring the principle of 'more work, more pay,' for a person . . . to earn more than those who enjoy the 'iron rice bowl?'" The predictable answer, of course, is that yes, it is socialism—but outsiders may question whether that is the ultimate answer. With more experience, it seems likely that the Chinese, who already agree that capitalist institutions like bankruptcy and competition have no class features, may recognize that "more work, more pay" has long been an international phenomenon. Whether or not, it is a better basis on which to build a vigorous modern society than the iron rice bowl.

But, it should be realized, not all Chinese by any means really object to some reasonable form of egalitarianism. "It is a paradox of modern Chinese history," said *Ta Kung Pao* (Hongkong), "that this egalitarian outlook goes quite well with the despicable ultraleftism," an attitude springing from "the so-called peasant mentality, a characteristic trait of which is the dreading of inequality of wealth but never poverty itself." Someone else expressed it with equal pithiness: "Instead of trying to enlarge the economic cake, Chinese are only concerned with distributing it evenly." For more and more people, "more work, more pay" is coming to make a great deal of sense, even as others still comfortably aspire to egalitarianism. However, as one writer put it, "labor has not yet become the prime want of the people in their lives," and until this selfless communistic point is reached "it will not be practical to abolish the commodity economy and money."

China's current problem with reward for labor is partly that since liberation there have been several periods when people *were* rewarded without regard to their work, the egalitarian practice informally called "all eating from the same big pot."

During the Great Leap Forward it was said that the era of pure communism was at hand, and that the principle of "to each according to his need" should be followed. And it was followed, for a time. During the Cultural Revolution egalitarianism was as approved as capitalist thinking was condemned, and distribution "to each according to his work" was abandoned.

Bonuses of some kind have been an element of Chinese wages since the early fifties, and usually they are not based on performance. Still given mostly without regard to performance, bonuses and other payments (such as free goods) on top of salary were reported in 1988 to make up 15 percent of total salary—and the figure is thought to be 20 to 30 percent in Shanghai and Guangdong Province. Promotions have for a long time been based on nothing more than seniority. And egalitarianism on an even grander scale is represented, of course, by using taxes generated by competent firms to keep money-losing and poorly managed companies in business.

Since it is clear that "labor has not yet become the prime want of the people in their lives," it is not surprising that competent people have tended to rest on their oars when they receive no more than incompetents or layabouts, and this has had doleful consequences for the country. As *Beijing Review* expressed it when widespread changes were beginning in 1983, the "big pot" system

> serves only backward enterprises and lazy individuals, and induces people to blindly follow the beaten track without seeking progress. Thus, for years, Chinese enterprises lacked vitality and incentive, and workers' enthusiasm for work was smothered and their sense of responsibility dulled.

It is critical, therefore, to introduce management systems that reduce the importance of seniority in determining status and pay, that deliberately utilize the principle of "to each according to his work," and that reward individual employees or small groups of employees who are relatively more productive and creative, work harder, waste less, and so on.

Until the leftists returned to power, reformers had made considerable progress in rewarding individual effort through two major steps: *wage reform*, i.e., basic changes in the determination of wage scales, and introduction of the *responsibility system*, which links pay to production and has been extremely successful in the countryside. Now, one of the major criticisms conservatives make of reform is that it tries to cover up its departure from the socialist principle of equity in distribution with its condemnation of egalitarianism. Until, or unless, the reforms are reversed, however, the country will continue to live with the results of these two reforms.

Wage Reform

First, some background information on existing wage practices is necessary.

Discussions of the "scaled wage system" for foreign readers have tended to give the impression of a uniform, integrated structure, but this is inaccurate and disguises the true complexity—and the difficulty of reform. For example, most discussions refer only to national wage scales for the two broad occupational categories—workers and cadres. (*Workers* are line personnel in state-owned industrial and commercial enterprises and in collective and private enterprises. *Cadres* are officials and executives—sometimes called "leading cadres"—and staff workers at any level in government enterprises, offices, institutions, and organizations.) In fact, there are many wage scales. Workers, for example, are described as all being covered by a single 8-grade scale, but there are separate scales for light industry, heavy industry, and many individual industries. The distribution of employees in all scales is heavily skewed toward the lower end, however, which is to say that most people do not rise very high.

When the discouraging regulations under which they have worked are considered, it is not at all strange that urban workers have lacked enthusiasm, as the Chinese express it (or have lacked motivation, as foreigners would put it). During the early years, a system of regular promotions was developed, and workers could also apply for promotion at any time and be evaluated on their skills. For a variety of reasons, however, regular promotion of workers was discontinued in 1956; thereafter, promotions were permitted in only three years out of the next twenty-one, and when promotions were made they were based almost entirely on seniority. Further, by 1977 there was a cumulative decline in annual industrial real wages of about 20 percent, compared to a peak reached in 1964.

There were a number of wage increases after 1977, and the average annual wage in state enterprises rose from 632 yuan in 1977 to 1,143 yuan in 1985. These were adjustments, however, rather than reforms, except for the 1985 changes, and provided none of the elements necessary to overcome inertia and egalitarianism.

Moreover, for reasons not entirely clear, cadres did not benefit from any of the post-Mao increases until their 1985 increase, and they did not realize spectacular gains even then. This group is frequently criticized for lack of initiative and susceptibility to corruption, but it has hardly been treated in such a manner as to strengthen its motivation or its integrity. In the past, it has been expected that Party members would be "the first to bear hardships and the last to enjoy comforts"; now, some people believe, past impositions and slights are contributing to the prevalence of abuse of office that is shaking the nation.

The 1985 increases for cadres were the occasion for the most significant comprehensive action thus far in the field of wage reform, creation of a new "structured wage system" with new elements in an attempt to recognize levels of responsibility and individual contributions.

(It should be noted, however, that since this system was unveiled such innovations as the contract worker system, the plans described under "Other Wage Plans" below, and plans to be introduced to help workers cope with inflation have made all wage plans of the old rigid

No losers, no winners.

Wu Zongmin, *China Reconstructs*

type highly problematical.)

Formerly, the major element of the wage was the *standard wage*, which, of course varied according to an employee's position in the set wage scale. The other elements were *awards* (bonuses) and *subsidies* (small cash amounts for adjusting wages to local conditions or for personal expenses such as bathhouse fees and haircuts).

The new system establishes for the first time the concept of a *basic wage*, a low fixed wage intended to provide a minimum livelihood for everyone, of 40 yuan a month, subject to regional variations. The key change is the *post wage*, reflecting the responsibility and demands of the job held. The post wage is set according to a new cadre wage scale containing only six grades but with five or six ranks within each grade, an arrangement that is somehow felt to be more adaptable than the former system with twenty-six grades but no ranks. (Standings in the scale are closely watched. Differences in pay between adjacent levels are relatively small but significant differences in housing and perquisites become available at certain points.)

The other elements are the *floating wage*, or bonus, based on profits, personal contribution, and so on (how this works in nonprofit enterprises is not clear), and the *merit and accomplishment wage*, purely a synonym for seniority pay. The same components, called by somewhat different names, are also to be included in wage scales for workers.

Other Proposed Wage Plans

Two more proposals for new wage systems were made in 1987.

Management alone sets compensation. The State Council proposed as an "outright reform of the country's wage system" that "the management of an enterprise should have a free hand in distributing the wages to their employees—so long as the total amount of such wages does not exceed the quota set for them by the state."

The commission suggested these four systems as among those that may be adopted, depending on circumstances: *floating wages*, based on the employee's ability; *piece-rate wages; contract wages*, based on satisfactory completion of assigned tasks; and *fixed-job-salary plus bonus wages*, primarily for managers, with a different wage for each position and with bonus to float according to performance.

Compensation floats totally on the enterprise's overall productivity. This plan ties productivity to group rather than individual performance, and since it provides for no basic wage at all it probably cannot be widely applied just as announced.

Responsibility Systems

This new management method, or this new attitude toward production, is of crucial importance in China's economic reforms. It will be discussed at length in the chapter on "Reform in the Countryside," since its first great success was in agriculture, but it can be said briefly that the essence of its effectiveness lies in giving an individual or unit full responsibility for carrying out a particular assignment and rewarding them for overfulfillment.

The principle is applicable to both the management of a crop, project, or enterprise, and to management of individual workers.

Management Responsibility Systems

The most prominent responsibility system for management, the factory director responsibility system (FDRS), has already been discussed earlier in "Decentralizing China's Bureaucratic Economy." Among a number of other plans for preventing enterprises from "eating from the public pot" and for judging and rewarding their performance, two presently receive considerable attention: contract responsibility systems and leasing.

The following descriptions based on research by the Institute of Economics of the Chinese Academy of Social Sciences and summarized in *China Daily*, give an overview of the contract system.

Contract responsibility systems, widely used only since mid–1987, require specific economic commitments. Some agreements may be "based on increasing profits, some on decreasing deficits (for the money-losing factories), and some on cost and output value indexes." Almost always however, the agreement requires payment of a specified amount to the state, rather than a percentage of profits, value, etc. Either a factory as such, an individual factory director, or a group of individuals who manage the factory may be contractors, with the state in all cases being the opposite party. A contract is drafted through negotiations.

Most references to contract systems have a tone suggesting that contracts are nearly always favorable to the contractors. The commentary, for example, says "Every contractor strives for the best terms possible" and "Once better terms are achieved, a contractor can earn much more profit than he is required by the contract to hand over to the state . . . and spend it in ways that run counter to the state's interest."

Contract systems "fail to promote an enterprise's concern over its long-term growth, which means the growth of state properties," because managers' and, to some extent, workers' compensation is usually based on short-term profits. They can, however, produce spectacular short-term results; the forty-two iron and steel enterprises under a contract system produced in the first half of 1987 3.8 times as much profit as the sixty-eight that were not.

A supplement to the foregoing system is the *collective contract responsibility system,* under which a common agreement is signed by the factory director, for management, and by the president of the factory's trade union, for the workers. These agreements are said to go beyond western labor-management contracts to "combine the interests of both managers and workers" and to make of management and labor "a united group which shares responsibilities, risks, and interests," according to *Worker's Daily.*

Leasing is becoming an increasingly common way for provincial and local governments to withdraw from involvement with tens of thousands of small enterprises. Lease terms generally have these standard features: first, the lessee is required to turn over to the state an agreed-on amount or proportion of earnings; second, the lessee must make a substantial personal investment in the enterprise, which usually means mortgaging family possessions, to ensure a commitment to success. Leasing is generally used only in connection with smaller enterprises, but, nevertheless, it can be relatively quite profitable. A recent matter of public interest was what was called the "Guan Guangmei phenomenon," referring to a young woman who leased three failing shops and turned them into moneymakers, and now leases several more. She earns a high income that is entirely legal but public attention dwells on the question of whether it is proper for her, or any manager, to make what most people consider a very large amount of money relative to the wages of the enterprises' workers.

Private Business

Private business, a kind of "management responsibility system" that is at the same time also a form of ownership new to socialist China, has created even more interest than leasing, because there are so many people involved and so many stories of wealthy private businessmen.

Common slogans until recently were "To get rich is glorious" and "Some get rich first to lead all to riches," but conservatives have always looked upon such philosophy as bourgeois and they wasted no time in expressing intolerance for it. Jiang Zemin asserted that private entrepreneurs were "ruining the atmosphere of society" because of their freewheeling style and because of incomes that are huge compared to the incomes of workers and cadres—large numbers of whom are envious. One newspaper claimed that permitting private businesses "laid the ideological foundation for the recent counterroevolutionary revolution."

The new leaders have not forbidden getting rich but the official line espoused recently by the State Council is far less exuberant than before: a "certain proportion of the people are allowed to become prosperous first through honest labor and lawful dealings." And, as described below, becoming prosperous will probably be much more difficult in the future; certainly it will be more tightly regulated.

Starting from almost no private businesses at all in 1976 there are now millions. They are divided by the government into two groups: 1) *individual businesses*, which employ seven or fewer workers and whose numbers were quoted in spring 1988 at, variously, 13.7 million (Xinhua News Agency), 22 million (State Administration for Industry and Commerce), and other numbers in between; and 2) *private enterprises*, which employ eight or more workers and (per the Administration) number around 115,000 and hire 1.85 million people. (The number of private businesses is actually higher. Many businesses which are private in reality manage to have themselves classified as collectives: they "wear a red hat," as it's called, to avoid being too conspicuous and to ward off some of the harassment to which private businesses are subject.)

This private sector has been by far the most rapidly growing sector of the national economy. The State Administration of Industry and Commerce reported, however, that more than a million privately owned businesses closed in the first quarter of 1989, about as many as closed in all of 1988. Long-standing problems of indiscriminate local levies and poor management contributed, but the primary cause was the program of economic cutbacks, which led to fewer bank loans and shortages of raw materials, fuel, and other resources. Although its portion of the gross national product is quite small, private business' share of total retail volume exceeds 15 percent.

Most of the *individual businesses* are one-person or family operations—retail stalls or small shops, restaurants, repair or transport services, etc., while *private businesses* may be larger versions of the same kinds of businesses or may be in light industry or other fields. Both forms of private business have been encouraged, and private entrepreneurs have benefited from reform perhaps more than any other group.

A constitutional amendment giving private businesses the right to exist was passed at the 1988 National People's Congress, and a few months later the State Council issued new rules "to provide legal protection" for them (but neither of these supposed protections is likely to provide much protection against conservative ideology). The legal safeguards are weaker than similar rules for state and collective enterprises, and tax income from private business at almost double the rate on other personal income (an apparent attempt to defuse widespread resentment of the affluence of many entrepreneurs). A new 10 percent tax on both private and collective enterprises was introduced in 1989, apparently as an attempt to slow the growth of this sector of the runaway economy.

Questions are raised from time to time as to whether private businesses (particularly the large private businesses now emerging, which employ hundreds) should be permitted under socialism, which sees work for hire as a form of capitalist exploitation. The official position on private businesses has been that they are appropriate in a country such as China that is still in the primary stage of socialism, and where they constitute only a small percentage of total investment and business volume.

Officially, this position is being maintained, but unofficially it is quickly changing under the new conservative regime. No one has yet said "We will not allow private businesses," but private business would

be made unattractive and unprofitable by adapting such recent proposals as these: limits should be placed on the number of private businesses
and what they do because too many will cause economic imbalance;
only the unemployed should be allowed to open businesses; private
entrepreneurs should be required to reinvest at least half their profits in
their businesses to reduce the owners' wasteful consumption; profits
allowed in the private economy should be only a little higher than state
enterprises earn (and the basis of this determination was not explained);
and allowable personal incomes of entrepreneurs should be only a little
higher than top payments for state enterprise employees.

In addition, tight restrictions on credit continued (in fact, the Industrial and Commercial Bank of China has said that it is raising funds for
large and medium state-owned enterprises by calling loans from small
businesses it claims are a drag on the economy); major campaigns are
being launched to collect taxes the government claims (probably
correctly) that small businesses evade, and to examine the management
and social usefulness of private businesses; and other steps are being
taken which by November 1989 had forced about 15 percent of private
enterprises to close, sharply trimming a sector that has provided millions of jobs and valuable minor products and services to the society in
recent years.

The Workers' Role

Just as enterprises are being asked to make drastic changes in the way
they think and operate, so workers are being challenged.

Because of historic economic and political conditions, workers have
become unmotivated, unproductive, and immobilized in a system built
around the work unit (see "Unit" in the Mini-Encyclopedia) that until
now has been self-perpetuating and virtually inescapable. Also, urban
workers generally have fared less well in economic reform than peasants
and workers in rural enterprises. As one commentator in *Far Eastern
Economic Review* put it:

> Workers want more money but do not want to work harder to get it.... This
> unmotivated urban labor force is seriously hampering the restructuring of
> industries.... The bulk of the urban population remains largely unmoved
> by [reform]. Concepts such as job satisfaction, initiative, competition,
> dismissal, and unemployment remain irrelevant to them.

At the same time,

The lack of a comprehensive social welfare system outside the workplace, fear of widespread unemployment, and a host of habits and values bred over four decades make labor reform probably the most difficult of all reforms to implement.

While the government tackles some of the conditions affecting the attitudes of urban workers it is also instituting plans which are intended to improve worker productivity and performance.

During the long decline in real wages during the Cultural Revolution there also occurred a general deterioration in labor discipline. As time went on, lack of incentive and motivation fed on lack of control, and vice versa, until slovenly, lackadaisical work, low quality, widespread absenteeism, and other work force deficiencies had placed Chinese industry in a serious situation that could be dealt with only after the ideological debris of the Cultural Revolution had been cleared away.

Even then, following an increase of 20 percent in workers' real wages from 1977 to 1981, labor productivity increased only slightly, and contention replaced malaise as workers were confronted with attempts to re-establish standards and discipline. The situation at the end of 1983 was described this way by a *China Business Review* writer:

> China's workers have become accustomed over the years to a relaxed pace of work, and the long absence of clear work rules and norms for earning quotas have made it hard for people to agree on what constitutes a fair day's work. China now faces the enormous task of reestablishing work standards almost from scratch.

A 1986 story in *People's Daily* said that even front-line factory workers in China work only 240 minutes a day, compared to at least 370 minutes a day for workers in developed countries. It also made the points that "if quality of work were taken into consideration, the discrepancy would be even more shocking," and that "management and discipline in some units are outrageously slack." It has been reported that in Chinese and American automobile engine plants, each with 10,000 workers, the Chinese plant produced only 10 percent as many engines. The Party publication *Red Flag* reported in 1986 that, compared to Japan, China's productivity is only 9 percent in engineering, 4 percent in steel products, and 6 percent in electronics.

No doubt a number of factors contribute to such low productivity, but one of the most critical is the pervasive overstaffing. It has been said that the Chinese, who boast of negligible unemployment, "have moved unemployment from the street to the factories and offices," a graphic way of saying that at least 20 million urban workers (some say 30 million) are so underemployed as to be superfluous.

Productivity is also poor because longtime workers and staff in state-owned enterprises, institutions, offices, etc. (sometimes now identified as *permanent workers*) still have their iron rice bowls, which means not only that they are immune to discharge but that their impregnable status dulls their incentive. Having a secure job is not the only factor, but it is interesting that a major study by the Chinese Academy of Sciences in 1988 showed that only 5 percent of these protected workers said they did their best to do their jobs well; 35 percent said they gave an 80 percent effort, and things went downhill from there.

Many enterprises received permission in 1988 to discharge surplus workers under a program that translated into "optimum deployment" (sometimes, "optimum reorganization") of workers—a euphemism for using labor to best advantage, i.e., keeping them fully occupied—which led to layoffs of surplus workers from overstaffed enterprises. The plan is on hold, however, having angered both workers who were laid off and some who were not, and having been resisted by local authorities, who wish to avoid discontent of any kind.

Two plans making the worker responsible for quality and productivity have been instituted in the last few years, however:

Some state enterprise workers are under a *contract responsibility system*, which gives them bonuses for production above an agreed-on level and gives the enterprise a standard against which to measure poor work.

A *contract worker* (short term) relationship with enterprises is now mandatory for all new workers hired after new regulations went into effect in 1986. (Apparently, however, university graduates, secondary school graduates, and retired soldiers are exempt from the new regulations in most places.)

The essential difference between the *contract worker* and the worker participating in the contract responsibility *system* is in the job security of the two. The permanent worker's job is totally secure, for all practical purposes, but the jobs of contract workers are *not* secure.

This class of worker has been created to attempt to gain more control over worker productivity and behavior and to avoid adding to the burden of permanent workers. The presumably more highly motivated contract worker can hardly be the salvation of state enterprises in the near future, however, since among 99.2 million staff and workers in state-run enterprises of all kinds only 10.4 million are contract workers as of mid-1989, including an increase of over 360,000 since year-end

1988 and an annual growth rate well over the 500,000 average of recent years.

The contract worker's employment lasts for a year, two at the most, after which neither worker nor employer has any further obligations. If the worker is dissatisfied he is free to look for a job elsewhere, a frightening prospect to some. To many people trapped by the lifetime job assignment system discussed below, however, this would be a shining opportunity. (See "Contract System of Employment" in the Mini-Encyclopedia for the rather simplistic Chinese view of differences between socialist contract system employment and capitalistic employment.)

Set for Life? Or Sentenced to Life?

The most obvious implication of "iron rice bowl" is a steady source of income, but the meaning goes far beyond that to guaranteed jobs for life to employees in state-owned enterprises.

The flip side is that the state has the right to tell workers what jobs they may have, whether and when they may change jobs, and, if they are allowed to change, what their next jobs will be. The security of the iron rice bowl appeals to many, but the restriction of the job assignment system on their lives is coming to be a major concern to many younger people.

As part of the job system that has prevailed since liberation, a young person leaving school at whatever level is normally assigned a job by the local labor office with almost total disregard for skill or personal preference. In the great majority of cases the job, or at least the unit to which the worker is assigned, will be an assignment for life. (The special, and equally harsh and inefficient, system for college graduates is discussed in chapter 7 under "The Revival of Higher Education.")

Such rigidity appears to be so constricting and self-defeating as to defy rationalization. It even defies belief by most foreigners when they first hear of China's job practices. The system has defenders who grant that it might have some disadvantages but who maintain it is necessary for the state to have sufficient control over the work force to assure that necessary skills are always available where needed. They disregard the clear evidence that the actual result is that the state does *not* have control over the labor force—individual managers and bureaucrats do.

According to stories in the press, there are almost as many instances of square pegs in round holes as workers who have been assigned to jobs in accordance with their abilities and interests. Skilled human beings who may have once been needed but are no longer, or who were assigned willy-nilly to units that had no use for them to begin with, are "stored" by bureaucratic managers like so many oddments a housewife keeps because they might come in handy someday.

There has been considerable agitation on this subject, but it was not until mid–1989 that the Personnel Ministry got around to having what one official newspaper called "the nation's first meeting on personnel mobility."

So-called talent exchange fairs and other mechanisms intended to enable enterprises and workers to get together have been tried, but the results have been very poor, partly because some of the rules for using the exchanges were, obviously, self-defeating. For example, there were usually requirements that registrants had to have a letter of permission from their units and that in all cases transfers had to be approved, some of them at the provincial level.

Between 1983 and mid–1987, some 1.1 million applicants with professional knowledge are reported to have registered with such exchanges; only 14 percent managed to make a change.

In October 1986 the government announced sweeping personnel changes that included measures to free labor to seek optimal uses for its talents. About nine months later *China Daily* was still reporting that the willful and intransigent bureaucracy was blocking personnel changes to such an extent that of 14,000 people who attended a Beijing talent fair in the spring "only a few" had been able to make changes. An official of the fair said, "The difficulty lies with the units who control these people. They would rather keep them unused than let them go."

An article by a college teacher in *China Daily* recently capsulizes the situation in a way that is emotional but, given the circumstances, restrained:

> This job security of ours has degenerated into a protective umbrella of the lazy and incompetent and an insurmountable obstacle to the capable and diligent. Either way it has become seriously detrimental to our social progress. I used to wonder how much longer we must bear this heavy cross. ...A friend who has been applying for a job transfer unsuccessfully for over ten years was once told by his boss : "There is no point arranging it for you since you are here on orders from above. Why should we go out of our way to find another person when we have you here? You are ours and you stay where you are." The implied "To hell with what you think and what you like" remained unspoken.

One thing is clear: where personnel transfers are concerned, there is no law guaranteeing the rights of applicants. . . . For all the talk in the media, little has been done. . . .

A drastic reform nothing short of revolution is overdue for the old personnel system. In a truly democratic socialist society everyone should have his or her rights and responsibilities clearly outlined and guaranteed. Only then, not before, can the people be masters of themselves—and of society as well.

Broad Changes in Labor System Proclaimed

The drastic reform called for by the writer quoted above may be on the horizon. The example of the failure of talent centers to improve labor supply and mobility suggests that the new practices are not off to a fast start, but then many of the reforms which moved slowly at first have had an enormous cumulative effect. Nationwide labor reform in state-owned enterprises was warranted in provisional regulations promulgated in October, 1986. The regulations:

☐ Made it mandatory that all newly hired workers in state-owned enterprises be hired as contract workers, ending lifetime hiring and the iron rice bowl for new workers.

☐ Made it clear that it is permissible to discharge unproductive, uncooperative, corrupt, dishonest, and disruptive employees, and specified the grounds for dismissal.

☐ Began to attempt to create a somewhat freer labor market by giving enterprises the right to bypass local labor departments and advertise for and otherwise recruit employees on their own, rather than simply accepting what the labor office sends, and to hire on the basis of examinations. In most cases, the "replacement system" (see Mini-Encyclopedia) in which children take parents' jobs will be ended, and other relatives of managers and workers will be hired only on the basis of examination results.

☐ Established a new nationwide pension and unemployment insurance system now being tested in many cities that will help relieve the pension burden on enterprises (see "Aging" in the Mini-Encyclopedia) and make the consequences of dismissal less harsh for unsuitable employees, who are often retained because dismissal is seen as a drastic punishment in a society with limited "safety nets." Contract workers whose contracts are not renewed will also have something to fall back on, making contract work more attractive.

The results of reform have indeed been slow to build in many areas, but the cumulative effects have been great. Given the influence work units, occupations, and superiors have on the quality of workers' lives, genuine enforcement of these regulations could produce profound changes in social organization, just as they will have a basic effect on economic life.

Six

REFORM IN THE COUNTRYSIDE

Of the six major reforms, there is no doubt that putting an end to egalitarianism by introducing the responsibility system has been the major stimulus for the spectacular changes in China's countryside.

Luo Hanxian, the well-known student of China's rural economy, put it even more strongly in his *Economic Changes in Rural China*, saying:

> Experience has shown that this major transformation in the rural management system is of such far-reaching significance and has such a profound impact on the peasants' interests that its social and economic importance is rivaled only by land reform and the movement for agricultural collectivization.

THE RESPONSIBILITY SYSTEM IS NOT NEW

It is often not realized that the responsibility system developed in the fifties along with collectivization, and is really not new at all. Oddly, the Chinese do not refer to these historic connections in most discussions, although in other matters great care is usually taken to relate current actions to precedents, if they exist. Usual Chinese discussions of the history of the responsibility system leave the impression that it dates from the end of the Cultural Revolution in 1976.

The Short History of the Responsibility System

The story commonly told goes like this: In the old commune system and the advanced cooperative period which preceded it, peasants worked as part of production teams of two or three dozen families. They were, in the phrase already quoted, "roped together to live a poor life." Just as they shared work to be done, they also shared the harvest, through a system many did not like, based on "work points" earned during the year. Some members of the group did not work as hard as others, and some did not work at all, if unwatched. Management of the group by the team leader—often appointed for political reasons—was sometimes poor.

The day-to-day work of the team might be interfered with by higher authorities who had no knowledge of local situations but who issued detailed directives on such matters as crop varieties to be planted, output expected, planting schedules, and methods of sowing, manuring, irrigating, and harvesting. (It was found that as recently as the late seventies a third of cadres in rural areas had little knowledge of management, and another third had no working experience in rural areas nor any knowledge of agriculture.)

Naturally, peasant enthusiasm was often low, and production suffered. Peasants lacked motivation to work hard because they felt the principle of "to each according to his work" was being disregarded, and they would receive no more reward than those who loafed through the day. They had no incentive to think much about what they were doing, because they had no say in how things were done.

In summary, then, under the commune system: 1) The responsible *unit* (also called "the basic accounting unit") was the *production team* of two or three dozen households; responsibility was diffused, making it difficult to hold anyone accountable if anything went wrong. 2) If quotas were exceeded, peasants who had made the greatest contributions were not proportionately rewarded; all the group "ate from the same big pot." 3) Members of production teams were directed from above, often incompetently, with respect to even small details of their work.

That is the way things stood around the time of the Third Plenum.

A series on the rural responsibility system in *Beijing Review* says, however, that even before the Third Plenum some changes from the old commune management system had already begun, with the approval of the government.

One instance is reported in which production teams in one location increased their grain production in the 1978 growing season by 50 percent over the previous year, despite a severe drought. Wondering how this improvement could occur under such difficult conditions, officials discovered that in the teams with high yields the responsibility for meeting the quota had been divided between *small groups of just a few households each* who worked independently and knew they would share directly in the income from a good crop. Therefore, they were willing to tend their fields more carefully and to water their crops by hand.

The provincial Party secretary directed that the *small group* system be tried in several counties in 1979. This is *Beijing Review's* account of what happened in one village:

> In Xiaogang village, a production team of 20 households was so poor that they couldn't grow enough to feed themselves. Between 1966 and 1978 the peasants on the team had to buy grain every year with relief funds.... The team was among those chosen to introduce the [new] system.
>
> Because nobody wanted to be the team leader, they *secretly* assigned quotas to *individual households*, and land collectively owned was distributed to these households for their own use. The team decided farm products could be owned by individual households, provided they delivered their quota of grain to the state, paid off their loans, and allocated sufficient accumulation funds and public welfare funds to the team. This went beyond the scope of merely fixing output quotas for a *group*. It completely abolished the practice of "everybody eating from the same public pot." [Emphasis supplied]

When the commune Party secretary learned what had happened, and that contracting with household units was much more successful than contracting with larger groups, he ordered the arrangement stopped at once. Because the households were working for themselves and not as part of a socialist group, he was afraid he would be accused of "restoring capitalism."

Later, however, the provincial Party secretary, Wan Li (now chairman of the National People's Congress), visited the area and found that everyone supported the reforms adopted by Xiaogang, and he approved them, also. "No matter what methods they adopt," he said, "as long as they help the team increase agricultural production, make more contributions to the state, accumulate more funds for the collective, and gain more income for the peasants, they are good methods."

The Real Story of the Responsibility System

In reality, the coming of the production responsibility system was not quite that simple. The quoted example touches only upon the essential features of the system, and thus gives only a superficial understanding of its importance.

The usual version gives no insight into the overall dynamics of making the system work—no feeling for the vitality of the idea, the wealth of creativity that went into trying to find workable applications of it, nor the importance that peasants obviously attached to assuming responsibility for their lives. A new study by young economists who formerly worked in the countryside catches some of the feeling when it speaks of how the new reforms "gave peasants and village officials many an exciting and sleepless night." Some information on how the system grew may be of interest.

The system has existed, in various forms in various areas at various times, since it was improvised in the agricultural producers' cooperatives of the early 1950s. (The "various" aspects of the development and use of the system should be kept in mind. Many different plans have been tried, and no single practice has ever been developed or applied uniformly at the same time throughout the country.)

In the mutual aid teams from which the cooperatives grew, it was customary for teams to meet each morning to plan the day's work. The practice carried over into the cooperatives, but because larger groups were involved much time was lost. As their management experience increased, some cooperatives began "contracting" to teams or groups jobs which would require longer than a day. The practice seems to have been little more than multiday job assignment in the beginning, but grew to become a system for assigning a wider range of work on a seasonal basis.

It then became a method under which teams or groups contracted to perform a regular task permanently, and were held responsible for all the work involved in, say, planting a particular piece of land. The cooperative (and later the production team) gave credit to workers for their labor in the form of work points, which were used as a basis for distribution of grain and income at the end of the year.

The Chinese study titled *Smashing the Communal Pot* mentions two critical problems which now arose: there was no control over the quality of the work and, because contracts covered a relatively large group, it was hard to create incentive and initiative in all of the households and individuals of which the group consisted.

Quality control—Some way of establishing and maintaining the quality of work was essential. The quality of farm work is often difficult to determine before it is too late to correct sloppiness, and some workers rushed jobs merely to accumulate work points and thereby jeopardized the crop.

> To overcome this shortcoming, some cooperatives, while setting [other] targets for a contracted job, also specified output targets, rewarding those who overfulfilled production targets and penalizing those who did not meet the targets for output by adding or subtracting work points.

This was a critical step, since it not only helped ensure quality but added to the plan the principle of *linking payment with output*, one of two principles that have come to be recognized as being essential. (*Creating incentive* is, of course, the other element.)

At this point cooperatives had developed a generally workable operating method that came to be called the system of "three contracts, one reward"—three contracts covering the job, the output quota, and the production cost; and one reward, extra work points for overfulfillment. (The contract also involved penalties for failing to fulfill the contract.) It was widely used by many successful agricultural cooperatives in the mid-fifties.

Smashing the Communal Pot says that peasants enthusiastically received the unofficial experiments using the contract system, because the changes overcame idleness and waste and raised labor efficiency substantially. The government officially approved the system as a legitimate method of management for a short time in the mid-fifties.

Creating incentive—The contract systems of the mid-fifties continued to be mostly *collective* responsibility systems, under which the contractors were production teams or groups. The contracts helped deal with shirkers and waste in production, but the incentive provided did not stimulate all members equally. Therefore, there were some members who benefited from the enthusiasm and hard work of others without making much of a contribution themselves. This, of course, reduced the enthusiasm of the entire group.

Here began the crucial attempts to inject into responsibility systems the second vital element, *incentive and initiative in the smallest practical work unit.* During 1956–57–58, cooperatives attacked the problem by reducing the size of the contractor unit; many made contracts for certain kinds of work with individuals and single households, or production teams subcontracted work to them. Jobs small units were able to contract for varied, but usually they would be things like weeding, hoeing, and intertilling, although in some cases households might contract for summer management of portions of major crops. Larger jobs, such as manuring, plowing and harrowing the fields, sowing, harvesting, small scale construction, etc., were still managed by the production team.

In the fall of 1957, the legitimacy of contracts with households and individuals was recognized by the Central Committee. Thereafter, individuals and households received contracts for entire projects, such as raising animals or managing vegetable gardens. Small unit contracts came to be fairly common— but were never universal and were not tolerated by ultraleftists for very long. Says *Smashing the Communal Pot.*

> As the Great Leap Forward movement swept across the country, the practice of "large-scale communist cooperation" spread to all areas, and . . . the original forms of labor organization were replaced by military forms of organization into squads, platoons, companies, battalions, and regiments, and agricultural production was carried out in the form of "large formation warfare". . . . As a result, the system of management of . . cooperatives, including the production responsibility system, was almost entirely disrupted.

The system was completely dismantled during the Cultural Revolution, when all the basics of the production responsibility system—fixing quotas, contracting to households and individuals, calculating work points in accordance with output, etc.—were banned as "revisionist," "capitalistic," etc., very serious labels indeed during those days.

Thus, for nearly twenty years, from the beginning of the Great Leap Forward through the Cultural Revolution, the responsibility system and the stimulus it provided were essentially negated or banned. It was not until after the Third Plenum that efforts could be made to restore and develop it.

THE RESPONSIBILITY SYSTEM
AFTER THE THIRD PLENUM

Development of the responsibility system proceeded after 1978 from the base established by the mid-fifties' "three contracts, one reward" operating method already mentioned, but this type of contract was with production teams or work groups and did not achieve the individual motivation other forms of contracts did.

Various other types of contracts emerged, sanctioned by the Party's injunction that contract arrangements should suit conditions, and more and different factors were covered in contracts. A typical agreement of the time was one described as "four fixed, one reward," meaning there were four contracts or fixed agreements concerning the responsibilities of the parties (the collective to supply means of production and pay agreed-on expenses, the peasant to deliver a certain output and receive a certain number of work points), and that there was to be a reward for overfulfillment (there was also a penalty for shortfalls). More complex plans are "five fixed, one reward," "five unifications, five fixed, and one reward," and so on. Today's contracts are nominally simple agreements between a seller and a buyer and include a purchase price rather than work point awards, though they may also include commitments by the buyer—the state—to provide materials or services.

The long-standing disapproval of giving responsibility to units too small to bring social cooperation into play continued for a time, and the 1979 "Decision on Acceleration of Agricultural Development" said quite specifically, "No output quotas shall be fixed on a household basis, except in certain cases. . . . " In another year, however, even this restriction disappeared, and in October 1980 the Central Committee gave direct approval to use of the household contract system, thus moving responsibility and incentive to the lowest, smallest, and most personal unit of the production system.

The appeal of the responsibility system was spectacular. "There was never a detailed rural reform plan from the top which was imposed on the farmers," points out Wang Xiaoqiang of the China Economic System Reform Institute. "The reforms were spontaneous and spread rapidly like an epidemic."

By the winter of 1979 the number of production teams adopting some form of responsibility system involving fixed production quotas was skyrocketing, and by 1985 virtually all of China's production teams (now properly called "villages") had adopted some form of what had come to be called the "contract responsibility system." (Essentially similar plans were earlier called the "household contract system" and the "production responsibility system.")

Under this system contracting families have the right to all net income from their crops—the ultimate incentive.

The Land Question

It is at least partly the system of contracting to households that has led to a dramatic basic change in the nation's land policy which began in the countryside and is now significantly affecting urban areas as well.

Rigid restrictions, amounting to confiscation, have existed on land transactions by individuals since shortly after liberation, when there remained widespread ownership of individual residential plots. Then, the 1982 constitution claimed even those holdings for the state (although private ownership of residential structures continued).

When contracting to small units began, land assignments were made for a relatively short term. Because peasants had no assurance they would receive long-term benefit from trying to improve or even maintain the land, they attempted to get a few good crops out of their plots with as little work or expense as possible before turning the land back at the end of their short contracts.

This problem was dealt with by giving use rights to a family for a minimum of five years, then ten and fifteen years, and currently for as long as fifty. Moreover, rights can be handed down to children or even traded under some circumstances. Theoretically, no profit was to be made on the transfer of the peasants' rights, but apparently peasants usually found a way to benefit.

Such transferability of rights gives the peasant control and effective ownership of the land, and a slowly growing number take advantage of this. So far most peasants, even if they want to work in factories, also want to hold on to their several small strips of land for security, family food, and the feeling of power and status that still surrounds land ownership.

But some would-be workers or those peasants anxious to work in factories or not wishing to farm for other reasons are selling their rights with increasing openness, and peasants who are successful farmers are assembling large plots partly through acquisition of rights, inspired by government model farms and encouraged by government assistance. (See "Farm Size is Growing," below.)

A lucrative market in land has developed, not just in rural areas (which are becoming suburbs subject to development in many areas) but in urban areas as well. Everywhere, *China Daily* reported,

. . . prices are not cheap because everyone in the trade understands the value of land. In a real estate transaction [which includes structures], generally about half the price is [tacitly recognized as being] for the right to use the land.

Under the old rules, however, the state collected nothing and "sellers," having paid nothing for the land, made large profits.

The journal *Problems of Agricultural Economy* described the situation this way in a 1987 series on land ownership:

Since in real economic life the collective-ownership-of-land system has already lost control of land management activity, the peasant, with regard to management of land, is taking the requirements of the market and himself as goals, and the collective-ownership-of-land system has already become an abstract concept.

Originally, lacking the land assignment arrangements of the countryside, private urban land transfers were not so easily accomplished—but they were managed, and flourished. Said *Problems of Agricultural Economy*:

Land used by cities and collectives, which was originally handled by simple requisition formalities that get nowhere, has now become bought and sold in disguised form, with the corresponding creation of a number of get-rich-quick types [being] nothing more than a public secret.

The government recognized that radical action was required to rein in private exploitation of a public resource and to collect a reasonable share of profits. It recognized also the advantages of a real estate market in which each parcel would tend to be used for its most valuable purpose. Rather quickly, considering that ownership and control of land by the state is fundamental to socialism, the government began experimental, regulated—and unconstitutional—sales of rights to land use for twenty to fifty years in the fall of 1987. The constitution was amended after the fact in March 1988 to permit the practice, and today there is a thriving real estate industry and rights sales are common and eagerly watched events, especially in the special economic zones.

The State Land Administration announced late in 1988 that the sales begun barely a year before had already brought in 361 million yuan. Both the national and lower governments are anticipating the stream of revenues which will result from leasing of the huge remaining areas.

HOW THE RESPONSIBILITY SYSTEM WORKS

As will be seen later, a number of kinks have appeared in the contract responsibility system but, ideally, this is the way the system works: The village, township, etc., provides overall facilities and conditions for farming, animal husbandry, etc., by taking responsibility for water conservation facilities, pest prevention and control, and other services. The household is responsible for selecting crops (a single household may contract for grain and pigs, for example), and for planning and carrying out cultivation and field management.

Because of the responsibility system, agricultural products were in such good supply in 1985 that the state was able to substitute nominal contract purchasing for purchasing on the old quota or mandatory delivery basis under which the state required the peasant to deliver an amount set solely by the state. (On occasion, there is still some element of coercion by the state.) More than forty major products were shifted to contract purchasing, including grain, pigs, cotton, and eggs, ending a system established in 1953 to assure adequate supplies and fair distribution to consumers.

In the case of grain, about 20 percent or so of the agreed-on amount, depending upon the grain, is purchased at a base price and the remainder at a somewhat higher price. Peasants keep all income from their production after paying various taxes and contributing to funds for capital construction, operating expenses, welfare, education, etc.

The state purchases large quantities of all kinds of food products for sale in state-owned shops, and, for the most part, the system works very well. Grain purchasing, however, suffers from a number of serious problems described later under "Static Grain Production."

OTHER REFORMS

Important as the responsibility system has been, other changes resulting from new government policies and new circumstances have also had a substantial effect on the picture in the countryside in the last few years. These are probably the major influences:

Higher farm prices—At the time of the Third Plenum nearly all prices, including agricultural prices, were controlled, and agricultural prices had not been adjusted since before the Cultural Revolution. Peasants lagged behind workers in income and in standard of living.

To insure continued agricultural productivity, prices paid to farmers were boosted about 20 percent on average in 1979 (with the government further increasing already high subsidies to avoid price increases to consumers). For the next six years, price increases averaged about 5 percent per year. There has been a substantial increase in agricultural output, but the effect of price increases should be kept in mind in considering peasant income figures, which often are not analyzed to indicate the relative effects of price increases versus increased production.

Overall, after adjustment for price increases, per capita rural income in 1988 was more than three times the 1978 figure. A substantial part of the increase came, however, from higher nonfarming income.

Increased use of chemical fertilizers—Peasants' enthusiasm for the responsibility system was matched only by their enthusiasm for the use of chemical fertilizers after they became available in quantity following the Cultural Revolution. Manure and night soil (human excrement) are still widely used and no doubt will continue to be for a long time to come, but their nutrient content is not comparable to phosphate fertilizer and they require vastly more labor. Farmers in suburbs of large cities, particularly, tend to disdain night soil in favor of chemical fertilizer, thereby creating a serious waste disposal problem. Shanghai, for example, generates about 7,500 tons of night soil every twenty-four hours. Much of it formerly found its way to suburban farms via individual "honey" wagons; now it winds up, untreated, in the badly polluted Huangpu River.

Not only are more acres being fertilized but amounts applied are now nearly three times the world average. This is reflected in improved yields, but it is also reflected in a decline of soil quality. In Heilongjiang Province, China's largest black soil region, organic matter in the soil has decreased from 9 percent in the 1940s to 3 percent. The State Statistical Bureau says that China's farmland in 1988 contained only 1.5 percent organic matter, compared with 2.5 to 4 percent in developed countries.

Fertilizer prices have multiplied in recent years and supply has become uncertain. Fertilizer is a favorite commodity for profiteering speculation.

Specialization—A logical outcome of responsibility systems is that peasants will contract to do the things they do best, leading to a greater division of labor, greater efficiency, and greater production. With the end of mandatory sales to the state, peasants are now free to choose for themselves what they will grow and to concentrate on a single crop or line of work if they wish to do so.

One outgrowth of this new freedom was the "specialized household," defined as a household that devotes its ablest workers and at least 60 percent of its work time to a single crop, product, or service (such as vegetables, poultry, or transport); sells at least 80 percent of its products (60 percent for grain producers); and has an income from sales of its products or services at least double the average of other local families.

According to *Beijing Review*, specialized households reached their peak numerically in 1984, when there were 4.3 million; in 1985 there were only 3.2 million, but, said *Beijing Review*, by 1986 the number had climbed to 3.7 million "because the leaders helped." The proportion of specialized households in agricultural pursuits in 1986 was down significantly, and the new growth was occurring in light industry, construction (especially house construction), transport, commerce, and restaurant and other service trades. (Nonagricultural specialized households are considered private businesses of the "individual business" type. See "Private Business" in chapter 5.)

In 1986 *Guangming Daily* reported that "the riches earned by some specialized households are fast waning. In the face of the challenges of the rural commodity economy, many are deeply in debt or have gone bankrupt."

The paper reported on a survey which found these major reasons for their problems: Lack of experience outside farming; "rash plans that stretched beyond all possibility of realization"; and, as will be discussed later in "Peasants Become Workers," excessive local levies. Less than 5 percent of the households studied had actually become insolvent, but more realism and better planning were clearly needed.

As economic life in the countryside has become more complex and demanding, a new economic form similar to the specialized household has appeared, namely "cooperation units" consisting of several households (perhaps formerly specialized households) which have joined together to produce a product or provide a service. In one busy area, there were twice as many such units in 1986 as in 1984.

Growth of sidelines—Early in rural reform the old fear of being branded a "capitalist roader" for keeping even a single chicken went by the boards, resulting in a boost in sideline production of all kinds. Current rules permit "private plots" (areas set aside for peasants' personal use) even for those whose principal occupation is no longer farming; the plots may occupy as much of 15 percent of the arable land in a village. Raising of small crops of vegetables for personal use and free market sale is practiced everywhere in the countryside, and handicrafts, raising of chickens and pigs, and other work to generate additional income have all increased substantially.

Free markets—A stimulus to the growth of sidelines has been the reestablishment of free markets, which were among the features of rural life prohibited by ultraleftists during the Cultural Revolution. Markets are more numerous than ever—over 70,000 in 1987 in both rural and urban areas—and are a source not only of local goods but of a wide variety of other merchandise as well. (Also see "Free Market" entry in the Mini-Encyclopedia.)

Improved technical education—There are now over 3,500 technical schools for peasants at the county level, and about 17,000 schools offering general knowledge and technical training which are run by township governments. It has been reported that between 1981–85 about 100 million farmers received training of some type from these schools.

REFORM STILL HAS ROUGH EDGES

"Since 1985, the rural economy has not, as many had hoped, kept up its long development trend," said the journal *Agro-Economic Questions* in 1986. "Reform has slowed down, and economic growth has lost momentum. . . . If rural China underwent a 'quiet revolution' in the 1980s, it is now in a 'silent crisis.'"

This outlook would seem to be overly pessimistic; yet agriculture's growth rate in 1987 was one-third of industry's rate but only one-seventh in 1988. There continues to be growth (3 percent in 1988) and, in part, it is unsatisfactory only by comparison with the booming years following the start of the responsibility system and with industry's rapid growth. Also, some growth is dictated by farmers' responses to market considerations, not by irremediable conditions. Still, there are a number of causes for concern.

Static Grain Production

Maintaining a good supply of grain is a serious matter in China. (*Grain* includes rice, wheat, corn [maize], sorghum, millet, and other miscellaneous grains; soybeans; and potatoes and tubers such as taro and cassava. Five kilos of fresh potatoes are considered equal to one kilo of grain.)

It has been more than disappointing, then, that despite urgent measures the harvest hit the record 407 million tons in 1984; 379 million tons were harvested in 1985, 392 in 1986, 402 in 1987, 394 in 1988 (a year of severe drought and widespread natural disasters), and about 400 in

1989—less than a 1 percent per capita increase in available grain after adjusting for population growth. The 1989 increase resulted from an increase in acreage sown, increased subsidies, and similar factors, not from changes in conditions depressing grain production.

Equally disappointing and alarming is that after achieving the status of a grain exporter in 1985 China was forced to import more than 16 million tons of grain in 1987–88. Even so, in 1989 grain available for all consumer and industrial uses was only 393 kilos per person, down 34 kilos from 1984.

The grain problem is essentially a political and economic one rather than an agricultural one or a failure of reform. With farmers no longer forced to grow a minimum amount of grain, they are reluctant to contract for as much grain as the government must buy in order to supply the cities, because the government's nationwide controlled price often does not cover the cost of peasants' supplies bought at uncontrolled prices. Nor does it reflect the different economic conditions in various regions. (See "Other Problems," below.) Further, the government price is infuriatingly unfair when compared with market prices, touched on below.

Mandatory purchasing supposedly ended in 1985, but if the critical quotas for urban grain are not met the state takes its own measures to secure the grain. Often peasants are forced to deliver part of the quota from grain reserved for their own families so it is easy to understand that, as *Agricultural Economic Problems Monthly* expressed it, "Relations with the farmers have become very tense." The magazine continued:

> And yet a number of our comrades are of the opinion that there is no problem. They say that in the last couple of years we've been able to get grain and this proves the farmers have grain. But what means did we use to get it? In order to get grain, administrative cadres have resorted to a wide variety of tricks and pressure. Throughout the entire Party, if one does not have a certificate that one has met one's quota of bringing in grain, if you want to get married you can't get a marriage license; you cannot get approval for a land deed to build a house; you will not be issued supplies.

In more extreme cases grain markets in the uncooperative area are closed and the government secures its supplies by what is euphemistically known as "purchase by requisition." A side effect of this is that with grain unavailable in free markets, persons without urban grain purchase coupons—travelers, transient laborers, farmers who have left the farm but do not have urban registrations, etc.—are unable to purchase their staples; normally they would be able to buy in free markets, though at much higher prices than in their home locations.

Selling grain to the state has some advantages, including a guaranteed market at a known price and promises (too frequently unfulfilled) of cheap fertilizer and diesel fuel for producing the contracted portion of the crop. On the other hand, although the state price for grain was increased 18 percent in 1989, it is still only about one-third of what the peasants can get in free markets, so they may prefer to grow other commodities if they are to be forced to sell to the government. For example, where soil and climate are favorable, they may earn two or three times as much from mulberry leaves for silk production, and three or four times as much from rapeseed or other oil-bearing crops as they could from grain.

Farmers sometimes refuse to deliver products called for in their contracts if they consider the spread between state and free market prices at harvest time to be excessive. In these cases, the government has been known to increase prices paid to the holdouts without compensating those who sold earlier at lower prices.

All in all, the quota system presents many problems, but no one has so far offered any alternative. As long as the grain market is forced to operate on an unjust two-track price system—controlled prices for grain and uncontrolled prices for agricultural supplies and many other esentials—snarls will remain.

The obvious solution is to further increase the contract price to the market price, but this would mean either also raising the state subsidy to consumers (though food subsidies already take about 10 percent of the national budget) or letting prices rise, which would increase consumer discontent.

The government announced in the summer of 1989 that it was establishing the country's first wholesale grain market in Zhengzhou, which *China Daily* described as

> the beginning of the end for state control of marketable grain prices, *except for the subsidized portion of the ration for urban residents*. . . . [emphasis supplied] It is planned that eventually half of marketable grain will be traded in such wholesale markets. Only authorized grain purchasing enterprises will be permitted to engage in buying and selling.

This will be helpful in establishing a broader free market price, but it seems to offer no help in dealing with the most serious problems.

Other Problems

☐ The state's investment in agriculture has, as an economist put it recently, "taken a U-turn" in the last thirty years. After rising to a peak of nearly 18 percent of total capital construction spending in 1963–65, state investment dropped to 10 percent during 1966–80 and continued falling to last year's bare 3 percent, the lowest in the history of the People's Republic. (This has occurred partly because provincial and local governments since 1980 have been alloted increasing tax revenues Beijing formerly received; however, they have not assumed commensurate responsibilities.) The decrease in investment affects basics such as utilization of technicians, maintenance of water conservation facilities, and upgrading farm equipment. And it affects hiring of the technicians that are available. China's sixty-seven agricultural universities graduated about 30,000 students in 1989, but the prospect was that only about 30 percent could be assigned to jobs.

The state had intended to increase its agricultural investment by 17 billion yuan in 1989, a 61 percent increase, but the Agricultural Bank of China announced in the spring that this had turned into a 39 percent decrease because of a continuing shortage of funds and restrictions on credit to rural industries.

☐ One reason farming is becoming unattractive is that prices of family needs and farming supplies continue to climb faster than prices for crops. The government price for grain did not rise in 1987 or 1988, but in 1988 alone a popular fertilizer increased over 25 percent and insecticide prices more than doubled, due partly to speculation and profiteering. Pesticides, water, and electricity needed for irrigation pumps have also soared. And the bicycle the peasant used to buy with 1,000 catties of grain now takes over 1,500. The government resumed its monopoly marketing of agricultural supplies in 1989 and promised to keep prices steady.

☐ Widespread adoption of the responsibility system resulted in division of land into small family-sized plots that many feel are uneconomical and inefficient. (See "Farm Size Is Growing," below.)

☐ At the same time, the loss of arable land to nonagricultural uses (discussed in chapter 3) continues to shrink the total amount of available land.

☐ Scarce fuel, fertilizer, and other necessities are often not distributed efficiently and fairly. New distribution channels are not yet adequate in some places to replace those that existed under the communes. The supply cooperatives that should help solve the problem are themselves part of the problem; some have been found to be selling their allotments of diesel fuel, for example, to industry, transport services, etc., at higher prices than they can charge farmers.

☐ New technology and information does not reach farmers reliably and quickly for lack of suitable networks. However, to help erase technological backwardness in both the industrial and agricultural sectors of the rural economy, the Seventh Five-Year Plan (1986–90) includes a project known as the "Spark Plan" (after the Chinese saying, "A single spark can start a prairie fire"). A million farmers are being given intensive training, urban scientists and technicians are working in the countryside on pilot projects, and hundreds of universities and research institutes have established special units and projects devoted to solving specific problems.

☐ Despite being given longer leases on their land, many farmers are still reluctant to undertake maintenance and make improvements. Policy lurches like the campaigns against bourgeois liberalization and spiritual pollution cause many to fear changes that would void their leases and deprive them of their effort and investment.

☐ Pest and erosion control and maintenance of public facilities, such as irrigation systems and roads, were formerly the responsibility of the communes, which either financed such projects or mustered the cooperative labor to accomplish them. However, the townships which replaced the communes, although expected to do so, have failed to assume these responsibilities, and under the contract responsibility system individual farmers find it difficult to get together for such work. There is growing concern over deterioration of the rural infrastructure.

Unheralded, apparently, increasing numbers of peasants in twenty-four provinces have joined voluntary co-ops in the last two or three years which show promise of providing a way of dealing with many of the problems of agriculture under the responsibility system. According to a mid–1989 issue of *Economic Information*, the co-ops have established standards for responsibility contracts; provided a mechanism for accumulating funds for public use and arranged for contracting maintenance of public facilities and similar jobs to individual contractors; set up administrative systems to ensure performance under contracts among group members; begun to consolidate and commercialize small-scale farming; and taken other steps to supply the needs of peasants and to expand agriculture as it has come to exist under the practices of reform.

NEW ECONOMIC RELATIONSHIPS
IN THE COUNTRYSIDE

Since the early eighties, the people's commune for which China is famous has been undergoing drastic changes described briefly here. (The historical organization of communes is described in the Mini-Encyclopedia under "People's Communes.")

There have been many statements such as one by Deng Xiaoping saying "we put an end to the communes," or a municipal official proclaiming that "communes are no longer suited to further development of the rural economy," or a newspaper stating that "the country's 54,000 communes have been gradually phased out."

But such statements are often contradicted. Consider the following quote from a history of modern China brought out by a respected publisher: "The people's communes are being changed to purely economic units, rather than also serving as the local units of government." An article by a distinguished economist comments that "the relationship between the commune and the production team . . . is no longer an administrative superior/subordinate one." The current (1982) national constitution mentions communes as still existing and belonging to the people.

Why is there a contradiction? The answer is surprisingly hard to pin down. Even interviews with specialists in rural affairs fail to produce clear-cut answers concerning present economic organizational structure in the countryside. It is only safe to conclude that at this stage of the new rural economy it is not fruitful to look for any neat hierarchical relationships resembling the old team-brigade-commune structure.

The current organization in the countryside, however it may be described, has developed from the following two major changes since 1978.

Townships Assume Governmental Functions

Governmental organization in the countryside has reverted during rural reform to the precommune structure, with townships taking over the governmental functions formerly exercised by communes, and economic functions have been decentralized, as described below. Because it significantly strengthened both the economic and governmental organization of the countryside, this separation of powers is considered by some people to be the most important change in rural life since land reform, except for the responsibility system.

Prior to the creation of communes in 1958 the township was the basic level of both state and Party power in rural areas. When communes were formed, they assumed not only economic power over former township areas, but governmental and Party power as well. This meant that leading cadres in a new commune suddenly had many different responsibilities, but had no training or experience in any of them except farming and no time or opportunity to learn.

Altogether, in the Chinese phrase, "a lot of work was neglected or done badly. . . ." Because the leading cadres were repositories of not only economic but political power, they were able to deal with situations through "commandism," the use of administrative orders to handle problems by fiat. And because the system led to the centralization of power in one node of authority, it also led to what one publication called "spectacular abuses of power."

The shortcomings of the commune system as it existed under Mao were a concern of the Third Plenum in 1978. Experiments with separating some of the functions of communes began in Sichuan

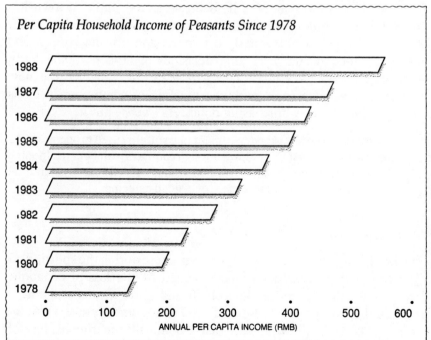

Per Capita Household Income of Peasants Since 1978

Sources: *Statistical Yearbook of China* and *Beijing Review*

Province in 1979, and were later tried elsewhere. During 1981–85, townships were restored throughout the country, and became once again the grassroots units of state power, responsible for education, welfare, culture, public health, and other broad community functions.

(Just as communes did not originally replace townships on a one-for-one basis, so townships did not replace the 56,000 communes identically. There are now about 92,000 township governments. Production teams or brigades under the commune system have essentially become villages. The relatively large shops and other enterprises formerly run by brigades are now simply collective enterprises within the township.)

Townships are responsible for all-around planning of the local economy, but they do not—or are not supposed to—directly control the production, management, or other operational aspects of local collective economic organizations. The township Party committee is likewise supposed to attend to its own responsibilities and not interfere in governmental or economic matters.

Unfortunately, the reluctance to give operating units decision-making powers already discussed in connection with the larger state-owned enterprises extends also into the countryside. It has become increasingly evident that local Party committees have continued to involve themselves in day-to-day administrative matters of the economic units from which they have supposedly been separated, and that township governments interfere in both the business management of township and village enterprises (formerly commune and brigade enterprises) and in production and marketing decisions of farmers. Some Party committees and cadres go so far as to refuse to recognize the new conditions that have come with the breakup of communes, such as ending the mandatory purchasing policy. As *Outlook* put it,

> In many areas, the relevant departments are still only used to operating the compulsory sales system, and will not sign contracts with farmers. In some places, contracts are little more than mandatory sales orders, and are popularly referred to by farmers as 'one-sided agreements.'

Economic Responsibility Decentralized

The loss of power by the old commune structure during the splitting off of government functions was accompanied by the loss of economic power upon the advent of household and enterprise management responsibility systems, which transferred management powers to individual peasant families, and, at least nominally, to the leaders of individual rural enterprises. Today, roughly within the framework of township and town governments, but not in their names or in the names of communes, commercial and industrial enterprises are developing alongside agriculture, frequently across county and provincial lines with related organizations that formerly would have been in another world economically because of rigid vertical commune-county-provincial organization.

Red Flag reported as follows on conditions in a prefecture of seven counties that adopted responsibility systems in 1982 and began taking advantage of new opportunities:

> Local market economies have taken shape, along with 18 production centers for such commodities as grain, cotton, watermelons, vegetables, and building materials. There are now 495 companies mining or processing minerals and 272 other enterprises. More than 10,000 rural people work in transport, either privately or in collectives. The growing commodity market has offered local people more contacts outside their own villages by selling local produce.

A Chinese commentator observed that once the separation of functions of communes was completed, the forms and titles of economic organizations might vary, as they are indeed coming to do. "If," he said, "the masses still prefer to use the name *people's commune*, the commune may remain, but only as a [formless] collective economic organization," i.e., in name only. So, it may indeed be the lingering of an old habit that is responsible for the continuing, confusing references to communes. Apparently they no longer exist, although they have never been officially abolished. They were simply overtaken by events.

WHAT ARE THE RESULTS OF RURAL REFORM?

Standard of Living Improves

The most visible and spectacular result of rural reform is the greatly improved conditions in most areas.

There was a strong 10.8 percent annual growth in agricultural output value during the Sixth Five-Year Plan (1981–85), culminating in a 370 billion yuan output in 1985. Growth continued to 395 billion yuan in 1986 and 445 billion in 1987.

Agricultural productivity showed significant growth. The State Statistical Bureau reports that from 1978 through 1987 the per hectare yield for grain grew 43 percent, for cotton 93 percent, and for oil crops 63 percent.

Peasants' per capita income was 397 yuan in 1985, approximately double the 1980 figure. In 1984 and 1985, in particular, there were considerable increases in income from rural industry, transport, construction, service trades, and food processing that contributed to overall income growth. There was a further 6.7 percent growth in 1986 to 424 yuan per capita; 5.3 percent growth in 1987 to 463; and 6.3 percent in 1988 to 545.

Finally, people in rural areas and small towns built 4.2 billion square meters of housing from 1979 to 1985, 60 percent of all the rural housing built since liberation in 1949. Another estimated 1.56 billion square meters were added in 1986–87.

The improvement is not as spectacular, it is true, as the Chinese press and some officials seemed to feel it was in mid–1984. The economic euphoria in the country as a whole was such that several provincial associations (of which nothing has been heard since) were formed to help stodgy, conservative older people learn how to spend their money instead of saving it! At that time successful farmers and rural entrepreneurs received considerable publicity, and there was widespread interest in the large numbers of "10,000–yuan households" that had supposedly appeared in rural areas.

In a few months, however, reality began to assert itself, and stories on spectacular economic successes, sophisticated lifestyles, etc., no longer appeared. *People's Daily* ran a story detailing how prosperity had eluded most peasants and decrying "premature consumerism." *China Daily* reported a survey by the Institute of Sociology indicating that "the lavish publicity about farmers becoming prosperous has created the wrong impression—that all farmers in China have become wealthy." It was announced that "10,000–yuan" families were less than one percent of all families in 1984. (But, incredibly, the State Statistics Bureau reported the number of families in this rarefied atmosphere climbed to 2 percent in 1985 and to 3.4 percent in 1986.)

A particularly sensitive point was that city people usually had little opportunity for increasing their own incomes, and they were becoming resentful of the opportunities and successes of the peasants. The *China Daily* story attempted to put the situation of peasants in a more accurate light:

> A misunderstanding prevailing among urban people is that farmers are now the richest groups, and that industrial and office workers are, compared with them, a low-income group. Actually, the money that a farmer earns

each year, as published in the media, does not take account of what the farmer has to pay out in production and other costs. And it is not made clear that in making money farmers face many challenges and need great enterprise. When city workers compare themselves with the farmers, they incorrectly take only their basic salary into account, and do not consider the amount of social welfare, bonuses, and various insurance services that they enjoy.

But even if the improvement has not continued at the pace of the earlier years and millions of peasants are still living "a poor life," there has been broad improvement and the percentage of households below the poverty line has declined significantly. According to the State Statistical Bureau, the proportion of rural households with an annual per capita income below 200 yuan was 33 percent in 1978 and 8.2 percent in 1987, while those with 500 yuan or over went from 0.6 percent in 1979 to 28.6 in 1986.

Peasants Become Workers

Partly as a result of the responsibility system, tens of millions of people in the countryside have become so greatly underemployed in recent years as to be without occupations at all, and the effects of this labor surplus have been almost as extensive and revolutionary as the responsibility system itself.

Surplus labor began to be a problem in the 1960s and became more serious in the 1970s. Since the late 1970s, increases in agricultural productivity, the cumulative growth of the rural population, and continued loss of arable land have emphasized the problem of underemployment or unemployment.

Just since 1980 the proportion of the rural work force engaged in farming has decreased from about 89 percent to about 80 percent in 1987. Given current and expected conditions, estimates are that by the end of the century only about 30 percent of the rural population will need to be engaged in cultivation, and only another 30 percent will work in animal husbandry, forestry, fisheries, etc. In times gone by, the prospect of the remaining 40 percent of the peasants being unemployed would have been serious indeed, but recent changes in the countryside and increasing prosperity there will make it possible for the labor surplus to be turned into an asset. The process will be hindered, however—even reversed—by slower growth of rural enterprises due to the government's economic restraints as well as its desire to clamp down on private businesses and to eliminate enterprises that use excessive power and materials or cause serious pollution. The government has announced that for the next three years new rural enterprises will not be permitted, except for those producing exportable goods or in a few other special categories.

One reason China's huge population has been such a burden is that its productivity is so low. Even before 1978 there were a few changes taking place aimed at dealing with rural labor, but lingering political and bureaucratic conditions prevented a vigorous attack. It was only the wind of national change blowing after the Third Plenum that made possible a sufficient range and depth of new thinking to generate the phenomena now occurring.

These phenomena, while quite complex, can be generally discussed in relation to two continuing developments—the growth of rural enterprises and the growth of small towns.

The growth of rural enterprises. As have other developing countries, China has found that a more prosperous countryside has generated demands for products and services never needed before, or that could not be afforded under the old conditions. Christine Wong has written:

> To serve these growing demands, many new enterprises have been set up in recent years under a variety of ownership forms. Aside from collectively owned commune and brigade enterprises (now renamed township and village enterprises), there are private enterprises owned by individuals or groups, and shareholder-owned enterprises.... In the post-Mao period, the rural sector has been turned over to private management to an extent that is unprecedented in socialist countries.

There were about fifteen million rural enterprises employing about 85 million people in 1988, but about ten million enterprises consisted of only one person engaged mostly in sideline activities. The remaining five million enterprises thus averaged fourteen employees each and constituted a significant economic force.

Hundreds of thousands of small rural enterprises were forced to close during the economic cutbacks of 1988–89 because of credit restrictions, materials shortages, etc., and their workers returned to their rural homes and occupations. Large numbers of enterprises were beginning to fail even before the cutbacks, because of increasing competition from better-managed firms with stronger financing and better-quality products. Those that remained, however, grew in the first half of 1989 at an annual rate above 25 percent, several times faster than state-owned enterprises.

The majority of rural enterprises are collectives which have their roots in former commune- or brigade-run shops, although some were founded during the Great Leap Forward. They receive no assistance from the national government nor are they part of the larger bureaucracy of state enterprises. They have special problems because of their nonstate status, such as not benefiting from cheap state-allocated materials, but their flexibility allows them to grow about twice as fast as state-owned enterprises.

These township enterprises, as they are often called, produce a wide range of products, including machinery, textiles, paper, processed foods in great variety, animal feed, chemicals, etc., and provide services such as retail shops, restaurants, construction, and transport. In recent years they have produced about 30 percent of the nation's paper products and coal and over 50 percent of its clothing and building materials. Total output grew from 7 percent of the nation's total industrial output value in 1978 to about 33 percent in 1987 (making rural industrial output value more than half the total rural output value for the first time).

Even though the value of rural industrial output is low in relation to resources and materials used, with especially high wastes of energy, it is considerably higher than the value of agricultural output. The farmer's yearly production is worth an average of about 1,230 yuan, while that of a rural industrial or commercial worker is about 4,400.

Such a disparity makes farming less attractive. One of the reasons for the decrease in grain production since the record 1984 crop has been that some peasants who found they could earn more in factories or other nonfarm work did not plant their contracted land.

The state is anxious to have farming be competitive with industry, but is trying to avoid additional agricultural subsidies or further price increases to consumers for agricultural products. Instead, it is requiring some local governments, especially in well-developed areas, to boost farmers' incomes by giving them incentive awards out of taxes paid by industries that attract farmers from the land. Local enterprises may also be called upon to pay certain taxes for farmers, and experiments have been undertaken in some areas to guarantee farm workers the same income as factory workers by making up the shortfall from enterprise profits.

Subsidizing farmers is not the only demand made on rural industry, however. At least as onerous is the load of additional levies; a 1986 survey in two provinces found that more than 90 types of local taxes, fees, and assessments were imposed in one or more of the townships and counties studied, in addition to state-imposed income and commercial taxes. The local governments see township enterprises as easy sources of revenue but many enterprises and outside government officials say the levies are of questionable validity.

Regulatory restrictions are equally oppressive. For something as simple as providing transport using a small tractor, one province requires eleven different certificates in addition to fees for licenses, management, highway maintenance, etc., that exceed 600 yuan a year.

The state has urged local governments to treat rural enterprises as "hens being nurtured to lay eggs" and not to be guilty of "killing the hen and snatching the eggs." A central government circular banning extortionate practices was issued in 1986, the latest of several since 1982, but it was apparently as ineffective as the earlier ones.

Less manageable, however, and even more serious are these problems:

☐ Such management experience as exists among enterprise staffs has usually been gained in agricultural rather than industrial or commercial undertakings.

☐ Since the staffs have been recruited from the rural population, there were until recently few qualified technicians (an average of one technically trained person for each two enterprises in 1987, which means most of the smaller enterprises probably had none) and the situation will improve only slowly as newly established training schools send out those who have completed their courses (although, as already pointed out, there were insufficient funds in 1989 to hire many of the new technicians).

☐ Many enterprises are suffering from a lack of funds, fuel, and raw materials. An increasing number are losing money.

☐ Rural enterprises are at a price disadvantage in competition with state-run industries, since they pay higher prices for raw materials and energy.

☐ Quality of rural industrial products is generally low, for several reasons: lack of technical skill; emphasis on high productivity and growth rather than quality (a failing not unknown in urban enterprises, also); and if rural factories can afford to upgrade facilities at all they often must buy older machinery being replaced by their state-run competitors.

The "Spark Plan" mentioned above is tackling some of these problems. A hundred kinds of factory equipment especially suitable for rural use are being designed and mass produced; 500 model enterprises are being established with up-to-date facilities, equipment, and management, for both production and training; and groups of better-educated youths and enterprise managers are being given special further training in technology and management.

The growth of small towns. It is predicted that more than 300 million rural residents no longer needed on the land will leave farming in China by the end of this century, and tens of millions have already done so.

Historically, rural people in all countries who have left the land for whatever reason have either emigrated or poured into cities, creating slums and shanty towns in Europe, Asia, Africa, Latin America and even the United States. Such a development is unthinkable to the Chinese. It is equally unthinkable that life would be possible in a Shanghai or other major city already paralyzed by crowding if it had to more than double its size to accommodate rural migrants, which is what would be required if surplus peasants resettled themselves within China's present urban areas.

In early years, Mao and others expected that the necessary industrialization in China's future would follow the same course as industrialization elsewhere, and there are numerous references in early Chinese communist literature to urban industrialization utilizing migrated peasants. Certainly, urban growth has occurred to some extent, and beyond question it has picked up in recent years.

Some students believe that China's rate of urban migration during the 1968–78 period was as great as that of many other developing countries, though net growth was held down because during the same period some 17 million urban youths were sent to the countryside. The urban youth returned to the cities, but many of the migrants did not go back to the land.

A recent source of some growth is "seepage" into major cities by supposed transients who are lured by city life and supposed opportunities and are able to get along without official residence papers and without registering with the police. The seepage became an extraordinary flood during the weeks after 1989 Spring Festival, when hundreds of thousands—many out of work because of newly failed rural industries and apparently enticed by stories told by visiting friends during the holidays— descended on large cities in search of jobs. They camped in railroad stations and wherever else they could find shelter, much to the distress of authorities who were essentially overwhelmed by the torrent. Most shortly became discouraged and left, but there was no doubt a net influx.

In 1989 the Ministry of Labor estimated there were more than 13 million peasants in cities, three million of them unemployed, a figure many considered low. One effect of the 1988–89 cutbacks in construction was that roughly seven million peasants who had gone to cities as building laborers lost their jobs. Most had to return to the countryside, as did many factory workers and others also affected by the economic problems.

The Chinese system of residence registration (see entry in the Mini-Encyclopedia) helped prevent movement into cities on an even larger scale, but, nevertheless, from an estimated 50 to 70 million in the 1950s "China's urban population (not including that of suburban counties...) has reached 108 million" (according to *Beijing Review* in August 1986) *or* "About 20 percent of China's 1.046 billion people [211 million] now live in cities..., not including those living in suburban counties" (according to *China Daily* in June 1986). (Tracing the trend of China's urban population is complicated by a drastic 1984 change in how *town* is defined. The change reclassified thousands of rural villages into towns although their size had not changed at all.)

In any case, the historically predictable mass movement to cities has not occurred in China on a scale comparable to migrations elsewhere. Instead, there began to appear a few years ago, as political and economic change began making the labor of millions of peasants redundant, the phenomenon that has come to be called "peasants leaving the land but not their homes," and going to work in factories and other enterprises not in cities but near their homes.

Fei Xiaotong, a sociologist famous for his work on China's small towns, points out that "This road of industrialization was not planned in advance by theoreticians. Rather, it has been created by the peasants on the basis of their experience in real life."

In his view, it was because of historic forces that the base for development of rural industry happened to be in place when it was needed. The sequence of events went like this:

Before liberation, conditions in the countryside pushed many peasants into bankruptcy, forcing them to urban centers to work in factories. There they learned new skills and became familiar with new technologies.

Luckily, points out Fei, "unlike workers in western countries, most

Chinese workers went to the cities alone to make money, while continuing to support their families in the countryside." When conditions improved, they returned to their families, bringing with them new skills and information. Most returned to farming, but many used their new skills to help their collectives begin small businesses and workshops.

Then, in the early 1970s when the emphasis on "taking grain as the key link" forced many peasants to sow unsuitable land that could not support them, there was a modest rural industrial economy to which they could turn for employment, or which could assist collectives in establishing industries. Today, many retirees from urban factories are also contributing skills. Fei says that in a survey trip made in 1984 he found that "almost all the twenty-eight rural factories we visited got started with the help of retired workers or cadres with factory experience who served as 'go-betweens' or provided technical advice."

The success of rural enterprises, particularly since 1978, has already been described. The rapid growth of the rural economy has generated a strong demand for market, information, distribution, and transportation facilities, all of which require a certain centralization. In turn, enterprises that might once have been established in the countryside have set up in small towns. These developments have meant that villages have become small towns and small towns have become larger towns throughout the country.

According to *Economic Digest*, it is now projected that the growth of major urban centers will be severely checked, and that the number of medium-sized cities and small towns will grow as follows, by the year 2000:

Very large cities, with population of over 1 million—27 versus 20 at present.

Large cities, with populations of 500,000 to 1 million— 32 versus 28 at present.

Medium-sized cities, with populations of 200,000 to 500,000—283 versus 126 at present.

Organizational towns—3,200 averaging 40,000 population versus 2,800 averaging 20,000 at present. (A town normally has "more than" 3,000 nonagricultural residents.)

Market towns—53,000 averaging 1,500 versus 53,000 averaging 500 at present.

According to these projections, some 140–150 million people, about two-thirds of the expected population increase, will be added to the population of organizational and market towns, avoiding extreme growth in the larger cities. Hundreds of millions of peasants will continue to live in the countryside. Many of them will usually not be needed as farm workers, and will provide a valuable element of flexibility in the labor force of the small towns and rural economies. As an article in *Outlook Weekly* put it,

> Since their villages are near the towns, they can easily go to work in town during the day and return to the village in the evening. Another advantage is that some people can simultaneously work the land under contract and do a factory job in town. Family members can do different jobs in farming, industry, and sideline occupations. This can be arranged to assure better economic returns both for the family and the collective, since farming is always seasonal. For people with less than enough contracted land, farming can even be turned into a sideline.

Farm Size Is Growing

There is a clear implication of another change in the countryside resulting from peasants becoming commuter farmer-workers or leaving the land altogether, although the change is not significant in scale, as yet.

The coming change is this: At present, in order to make limited land available to as many households as possible, the amount of land contracted to a single household is relatively small. It may be less land than is needed to keep the peasant and his family busy. Furthermore, as land formerly worked collectively has been divided among contracting households, fairness has made it necessary to give each family a portion of the collective's less productive land along with a share of its better land, with resulting severe fragmentation of acreage.

As a result, it is estimated that an average family has about nine mu scattered in at least three different directions from their home and divided among nine plots chopped up into narrow strips too small for using anything more than simple mechanized equipment, or none at all. (And land must be reallocated each year to account for births and deaths.)

Because mechanization can give needed boosts to productivity, this return to small-scale farming has been a matter of concern.

As changes continue to occur, however, they appear to be supporting one another in a way not clearly foreseen that will lead back to larger tracts suitable for mechanical cultivation. Rural reform first brought the responsibility system, which led to the breaking up of large communal holdings into small contracted shares, and, at the same time, encouraged the growth of specialized households and rural enterprises. As these developments have increased productivity, created an even larger pool of surplus labor, and at the same time encouraged farmers to enter nonfarming occupations, more land has become available for those who want to continue to farm. In a Jiangsu Province county, for example, the agricultural work force has decreased from 75 to 51 percent of total population, and land per farmer has increased from 0.23 to 0.33 hectare. In Shunyi County near Beijing, farmers are only 20 percent of the population, and farms are now 1.3–2.0 hectares.

Through this circuitous route, the rural economy is diversifying, and cropland is becoming concentrated in the hands of specialized farmers who in recent years have gradually begun to take advantage of long-needed mechanization. Larger incomes no doubt had more influence on mechanization than larger plots for part of the period. Nevertheless, it is encouraging that for whatever reason total agricultural machinery horsepower grew by 140 million to about 300 million between 1979 and 1986, or about 17.5 million horsepower per year, and continues to grow. This compares with growth of about 145 million during 1965–78, or about 11 million horsepower per year.

Since the responsibility system was introduced in 1979, the first year peasants were allowed to own agricultural machinery, peasants have spent more than 40 billion yuan of personal funds on agricultural mechanization. In 1987 there were 5.56 million privately owned tractors, 90 percent of the total, and 360,000 private trucks, 66 percent of the total.

Strangely, despite the increase in total power, the tractor-plowed area in 1986 was 7 percent less than in 1979, but this is not necessarily attributable to small plots. The total sown area has declined about 7 percent, it would appear. Also, power is now applied to more than just tillage and harvesting; the figures for increased mechanical power include devices from fodder choppers to wool washers, whereas previous mechanized equipment was largely for field work and processing. Finally, the human meaning of increased mechanization is brought home most sharply by the increased small truck traffic and the noticeably fewer humans with heavy loads on shoulder poles or carts.

DOES RURAL REFORM NEGATE THE REVOLUTION?

Rural reform, and dismantling of the collectives that for some people symbolized the socialist revolution, have brought sadness and disappointment to some Chinese and friends of China. The problems of Mao-style collectivization—the stagnation, the inefficiency, the numbing egalitarianism, the commandism, and all the rest—are seen by many as the fault of the people who failed to make the system work. They do not consider the difficulties as perhaps inherent in a system conceived in a theoretical vacuum, a system never successfully applied anywhere.

William Hinton, a man who has devoted his life to China and to helping the outside world understand China, has made significant and legitimate criticisms of rural reform, and he continues to have a strong belief in the collective way of life. In an interview in *US-China Review*, however, he said:

> The crux of the matter is, I think, a cooperative system has much greater potential than an individual system, but it has to be well run, it has to be well led, it has to have people who believe in it, and it has to have people who are willing to sacrifice for it. If you don't have good leadership, if you don't have cooperative consciousness, then the cooperative can be a hell on earth because you can have a little feudal kingdom where somebody is bossing other people around and taking advantage of them and they lose incentive to produce and it becomes stagnant and unjust and intolerable.

That is probably as good a summary of the need for reform as could be written. The conditions and qualities Hinton describes as necessary for successful collective life are really no different from what is required for the success of any large-scale group effort.

Upon reflection, it can be seen that the problems of the Chinese communes are essentially no different from those faced in numerous experiments with communal living over the past two centuries in other nations. Successful communal living requires enormous educational efforts and/or a strongly held set of common beliefs. The religious orders in the East and West, or the kibbutzim in Israel are examples of such success. Many other efforts at building communes—of whatever ideology—have failed because they have been too utopian. The founders, highly idealistic themselves, have generally failed to recognize the amount of consciousness-raising necessary to bring others to a level of understanding, social responsibility, and altruism necessary to make a commune function properly.

Certainly, there were many genuine success stories due to inspired leadership and group enthusiasm during the commune period in China, but for every example of strong, fair, and imaginative leadership, and selfless and inspired workers, there were all too many mediocre performances and outright failures. After twenty-five years of attempting to make the collective way work, the country found itself in a political and economic bind that fully justified trying some other way.

Nor are the reforms a betrayal of the revolution, as some people feel, unless the aims of the revolution are described very narrowly in political terms alone. If the basic objective was to free the Chinese people from a feudal and colonial culture and to enable them to manage and improve their own lives, then the reforms are but another step in that direction.

Building for the dead...

...but not for the living.

(Reprinted from the ongoing cartoon exhibition Farewell to Superstition)

Ding Cong, *China Daily*

Seven

EDUCATION:
THE VITAL FIFTH MODERNIZATION

Education is one area of Chinese life where progress on reforms is coming relatively late. Raising educational levels is critical to achieving the Four Modernizations, but it is a lengthy, slow process not immediately stimulated by changes in rules and regulations, as farms or factories are.

China now recognizes the long-term importance of education, but recognition has not been accompanied by an all-out effort toward improvement. The centuries-old respect for the scholar has been replaced by years of leftist contempt for education typified by Mao's consigning intellectuals (anyone with middle school or middle school vocational education or above) to a "stinking ninth category" of opponents, along with criminals and traitors.

It is symbolic that China's minister of education came forty-second in an official ranking of forty-five ministers before a 1985 change which removed education from the State Council ministerial lineup and created the State Education Commission. The education minister fell below the ministers of public security and state security, the minister of the textile industry, and the forestry minister, among others; now, the education minister is the head of the State Education Commission, a top-ranking body, and a State Councilor. In a survey of major changes in education during 1985, *Beijing Review* commented that "Education in China has never before received such widespread attention." The progress that has since been made, however, has been slow.

The Chinese education journal *Study and Research* reported in 1985 that

> According to UNESCO statistics, out of 149 countries our country came 130th in terms of the proportion of the gross national product allotted to education. Not only can there be no comparison with countries of the First and Second Worlds, but we are also very backward within the Third World. This type of situation does not accord at all with our status as a socialist nation and is not suited to the building of the Four Modernizations.

It is true that expenditure on education has increased in China in recent years in absolute terms, aided by such steps as a 1 percent tax on businesses imposed by the State Council for the benefit of local schools (expected to rise to 2 percent soon) and by increased funds allotted in the Seventh Five-Year Plan (1986–90). In actuality, however, expenditure has probably not grown at all (it was 9.7 percent of total national expenditure in 1983 and 9.6 percent in both 1987 and 1988) and in other respects it has actually decreased. *China Human Skills Daily* analyzed the question this way:

> The real situation is this: amounts actually spent in the field of education have gradually diminished from year to year . . . because year after year the number of schools has increased. . .; the numbers of teachers, students, and retired personnel [who must be paid pensions from current funds] has increased. . . ; [and] because of . . . promotions, attainment of higher rank, etc., the great bulk of expenditure . . . has had to be channeled into payments to individuals. Both the proportion of the total expenditure and the absolute amounts spent on books, installations, and other costs of education have actually been decreasing. Then too, we must add on the increased costs due to inflation.

A 15 percent increase in funding is included in the 1989 budget, but this is not quite sufficient even to keep up with inflation.

The official contempt for learning has undoubtedly damaged national progress. Nevertheless, over the forty years since liberation China has made enormous progress in education, compared to the educational levels and opportunities of the people before liberation. In the 1964 national census, for example, a little over 50 percent of the people were classed as illiterate; in the next census (1982) a little over 24 percent were. Since liberation, college enrollment has increased more than ten times and middle school enrollment more than fifty times. The statistics on graduates, teachers and faculty, and so on, are staggering.

But the increased demands on education are also staggering. China's high proportion of young people in its population is putting a heavy burden on funds, teachers, and facilities. The section "Primary and Middle School Problems" below describes the critical problems faced at these levels. Colleges are hard-pressed to maintain the current level of something over 500,000 graduates yearly. At the same time, a 1989 survey by the State Education Commission found that 50 million specialized workers—12 million of them with at least undergraduate training—will be needed by the year 2000.

In a country which now has only five or six million university graduates and about two million university students (including 113,000 in graduate programs), these requirements represent a major challenge.

THE 1985 DECISION ON EDUCATIONAL REFORM

After an intensive study during late 1984 and early 1985, said to have involved more than 10,000 persons nationwide, the Central Committee of the Communist Party of China issued in May 1985 its "Decision on the Reform of the Educational System," which is still as close to a national guideline as exists.

The decision could have been as significant in its field as have been the previous major declarations concerning economic and agricultural reform, but it apparently did not receive wide approval. Consensus on education policy seems to be difficult to achieve and the 1985 statement is far from full implementation. (Readers will notice considerable similarity between the major points of the decision listed below and today's problems discussed in more detail in this chapter.) A broad education policy statement is said to be in its eighth round of discussions, and the Politburo recently requested still further discussions.

The 1985 document pointed out serious shortcomings, including:

☐   Lack of compulsory and universal nine-year education.

□ Overstrict control by government departments over schools at all levels, particularly at the college level.

□ Weak elementary education, as exemplified by shortages of schools and qualified teachers.

□ Poorly developed vocational and technical education, unable supply the millions of urgently needed middle-level technicians. (This is an area where considerable progress appears to have been made.)

□ Overspecialization in certain subject areas.

□ Outdated textbooks.

LEVELS OF CHINESE EDUCATION

Because descriptions of schools in China use some terms not familiar outside of China, an explanation here will be helpful. The details pertain to the educational structure as it has existed since about 1978; from the beginning of the Cultural Revolution through the couple of years after the death of Mao Zedong, both the structure and content of Chinese education were highly fluid.

Preschool Education

There are perhaps 175,000 nurseries (nursery schools) and kindergartens with about 18.1 million children in their care. Nurseries are attended by children under three and are run by a variety of groups, including neighborhood committees or private families in the cities or the larger production units in rural areas.

Kindergartens are also run by a variety of organizations. About 30 to 40 percent of them are state-run. The remaining 60 to 70 percent are locally run by factories or other work units, villages, neighborhoods, etc., and are not the responsibility of the government. Kindergartens have junior, middle, and senior grades, one for each year; the junior grade accepts children at the age of three.

Primary Education

Covering six years, grades one to six, primary schools are attended by children of about six and a half through twelve years. Under the constitution, primary education is to be "compulsory and universal," but this has not yet been achieved throughout the country. (See further information under "Primary and Secondary School Problems" and "Compulsory Education," below.)

In 1987 there were about 830,000 primary schools and 128.4 million primary school students. The primary school year is nine and a half months, with vacations in urban areas of one and a half months in the summer and one month in the winter. Two rural vacations coincide with harvest seasons; the real rural vacation comes in winter, at the time of the lunar New Year. The school day is about six hours long, six days a week, with instruction in Chinese, mathematics, politics, common knowledge (such as simple biology, physics, chemistry, etc.), a foreign language (almost always English), music, and fine art. There is also about a hour of physical exercise and play.

Primary school students are taught the importance of work. Urban schools have a two-week labor session, in which grades four and five plant trees, clean classrooms, etc. Rural students take part in light labor in farming or household chores on a planned basis.

Middle School (or Secondary) Education

Middle schools are divided into junior middle school and senior middle school, discussed separately below. (See other material under "Primary and Secondary School Problems" in this chapter.)

In 1988 there were about 53.2 million secondary school students— about 13.0 million senior middle school students and 40.2 million junior middle schoolers (less than half the total middle school age group)—in more than 90,000 schools. Senior middle school enrollment included about 5.6 million students enrolled in the specialized agricultural, technical, and vocational schools that fall somewhere between junior middle schools and the university level.

Middle schools in rural areas allow students to take time off for farm work. Urban students generally have two months of vacation a year, and rural students at least one.

Junior middle school—Formerly, students were required to pass an examination for admission to junior middle school, the first of three major exams in a student's academic career. (The second and third are for admission to senior middle school and to university.) All three exams focus on recall of memorized material rather than intellectual understanding, and have been heavily criticized inside and outside China for continuing a tradition of rote learning that produces only passive and incurious students.

The entrance exam requirement was dropped in 1986 in areas where compulsory nine-year education is now in effect because it conflicted with the goal of having all students receive a junior middle-school education. It is also hoped this change, and others, will de-emphasize rote learning; relieve pressure on primary teachers, who are judged by the number of students who pass; and reduce stress on the youngsters, who often complain about strong pressure from their parents.

Junior middle school, consisting of three years, is attended by children thirteen to sixteen. There are twenty-eight hours of class in each six-day week, devoted to thirteen courses: Chinese, mathematics, foreign language, politics, history, geography, biology, physics, chemistry, physiology, physical culture, music, and fine art. They must also pass physical education. (Many rural schools, in particular, lack qualified teachers in most of these subjects, although the situation is improving.) Increasing concern is being shown for providing some kind of post-primary-school vocational or technical training for students who do not wish to pursue, or are unable to benefit from, the normal junior middle school curriculum.

Senior middle school—There continues to be an entrance exam for admission to senior middle school, which is attended for three years by students about sixteen to eighteen years of age, again for about twenty-eight hours per six-day week. Essentially the same subjects are studied as in junior middle school.

Senior middle school is the final step before entrance into a college or university. (Chinese parents who have experience with American schools say that at the upper level the Chinese curriculum is one to three years ahead of the American high school, particularly in science and math. This view is supported by several studies, including a standard math test taken by gifted Chinese and US seventh graders; 7 percent of the Chinese scored 700 or higher, against only 0.2 percent of the Americans.)

Besides having to worry about passing college entrance exams, senior middle-school students now have to face the possibility they may not even have a chance to sit for the exam. Beginning in 1988, political, ideological, and moral qualities were given major weight in permitting students to take college entrance exams, and toeing the ideological line has now, of course, assumed even greater importance.

Under the new regulations, exams may be taken only by those who "support the four basic principles, cherish the motherland, observe discipline, and express determination to study hard for the development of the socialist modernization program." In addition, approved students must take part satisfactorily in a new program of "experience in society," also called "social practice." The program involves participation in "social investigation," meaning field work in neighboring small towns, and in "learning from workers and peasants" through volunteer work on farms or in factories.

Some observers feel that the new emphasis on ideology was pushed through by conservatives under the campaign against bourgeois liberalization, but exactly how strong their influence was may never be known. Concern with ideology is not exclusive to conservatives.

China's socialist leaders, left and right, have always placed high value upon political education. It has not been given major emphasis in the last few years (as conservatives bitterly complained during the Pro-Democracy Movement), but, even so, it was not during a conservative ascendancy that *Education and Research*, a major journal, said in early 1985:

> The new, modernized generation of people should be patriots and revolutionaries armed and politically strengthened with Marxist theory. They should be protectors of China's state power and nothing else.

Since at least 1982 a high-level National Committee on Education under the State Council has been working to set up revised and strengthened courses in ideology and politics in schools from the primary level through university, and has established courses in many individual cities.

Several months ago, Deng Xiaoping caused a stir among those concerned about the perilous state of education when he told some foreign visitors that the "worst omission of the past ten years was in education." It turns out, however, that he was not speaking of the failure to train and reward teachers or of the shacks used for schools in too many places but, as he explained in his famous June 9 speech following the June Fourth Massacre, "What I meant was *political* education, and this doesn't apply to schools and students alone but to the masses as a whole."

The new leadership is already moving to remedy this omission with requirements for study of political and ideological topics with an intensity not experienced by Chinese citizens since the Cultural Revolution. Workers everywhere have been required to study Deng's June 9 speech at meetings in their work units, with other topics to follow, and *People's Daily* recently reported that Party Secretary Jiang Zemin has ordered invigoration of political study units at all universities.

Specialized senior middle schools—These schools appear to be very flexible in concept and operation, and embrace a great many technical, agricultural, and vocational areas. Some offer curriculums that require one or two years beyond the usual three years of senior middle school for completion. They may be called variously polytechnic colleges, secondary specialized schools, vocational and technical schools, secondary professional schools, etc. (Technical schools offer practical training and polytechnics stress theoretical studies; vocational schools try to combine the two.)

The proportion of vocational and technical school students in senior middle schools rose from 5 percent in 1978 to 40 percent in 1987, and the goal is to have equal enrollment in vocational and technical schools and in liberal arts senior middle schools by 1990.

Their importance to the future of the Chinese economy is being emphasized more and more, and the reason is simple. With Chinese education relatively undeveloped for many years, specialization was not possible to any great extent, especially at the lower levels. Shortly before the Cultural Revolution, the practice of "two educational systems" or a "two-tiered educational system" was begun, which provided educational options.

On one tier were schools concerned exclusively with academic subjects. On the other were schools that divided their curriculum between academic instruction and supervised work experience in farm or factory production. But this plan was later denounced as capitalist, elitist, and designed to exploit those who received less academic instruction (never mind that academic knowledge was also roundly condemned), and the vocational schools were closed.

The incongruous result has been that in Beijing's textile industry there are about four graduate engineers for every trained technician, and about seven engineers for each technician in Shanghai's metallurgical industry. In these circumstances, it is easy to see the importance of specialized technical education in China's future.

Outsiders have urged China, however, not to attempt to recover from the shortage of technicians at the expense of a generally improved level of education. The World Bank has pointed out that "international experience strongly suggests that [sound general education] could contribute not only to faster economic growth, but also to a less unequal distribution of its benefits."

Adult Education

This category of educational offerings has had explosive, almost frantic growth since 1978. For example, *Beijing Review* recently reported that

500,000 part-time students in Guangzhou have created a third traffic peak in addition to the morning and late afternoon rush hours. This is in the evening when they hit the streets to attend night schools, colleges, and workers' universities.

A special category of adult education is literacy training. Anyone unable to read at least 500 characters is considered illiterate. Workers are expected to read 2,000 characters and peasants 1,500. According to the national census in 1982, about 24 percent of the population over twelve was illiterate (about 235 million people). About three million people are brought to literate levels each year but because of the low levels of primary education about two million new illiterates are added. During 1988–92, the goal is to bring 85 percent of rural people and 90 percent of the urban population to literate levels.

There are now four types of spare-time education in China:

Adult universities—Also called evening, worker, or spare time universities, with nearly two million students in about 1,200 schools, these schools are usually run by groups independent of regular universities, such as very large enterprises, or by workers' congresses (similar to unions), cities, or groups organized for the purpose. Regular universities are increasingly entering the field. The State Education Commission began conducting unified (standard) entrance exams for adult universities and checking on the quality of the schools in 1986. A two-year certificate can be earned in three years, a regular college diploma in five.

Commercial "universities," called *wuxing* (formless) universities, have proliferated in the last two or three years to such an extent that the Chinese, fond as they are of statistics, acknowledge they have lost count. There are thought to be about 250 in Beijing alone. They are called "formless" because they lack the ordinary operating structure of a university, and, in fact, teach whatever courses are in demand and do not offer degrees. Courses are usually taught by qualified teachers or practitioners, however, and may cost as much as one to three months' wages.

Correspondence colleges—These programs, run by about ten universities, have over 200,000 students. Academic recognition and length of time required for graduation are the same as for evening universities.

Television and radio colleges—By far the largest undertaking of this kind is the Central TV Broadcasting University, (known as "TV University") which manages a nationwide system involving a communications satellite and about 1,200 TV education stations at the county level. TV

University has graduated nearly 900,000 students since 1979. More than a million students are enrolled, and probably another 750,000 or more participate as students of single subjects. People who wish to enroll officially must take an entrance examination, and, to remain enrolled, complete seventeen or eighteen courses in three years. They may take college equivalency examinations to secure diplomas; those who do not enroll but simply follow a single program can obtain certificates for single courses by passing exams.

Employer-paid educational assistance is common in many countries, but there is an unusually innovative arrangement in China for TV education. Employees who have the permission of their work units can enroll in the TV University as full-time TV students (taking four courses) and be released from work while receiving their regular wages; half-time arrangements are also made. Courses available at present include general courses in science and technology as well as courses in advanced mathematics, physics, chemistry, engineering, computer science, etc.

College equivalency examinations—This method of certifying competency achieved by self-study is becoming established on a national basis. Begun experimentally several years ago in Beijing, local forms of exams were used by provinces and cities throughout the country. The State Council in 1988 announced national regulations for the program.

Exams are held twice a year in about 225 subjects by local branches of the commission. Recently, about two million people a year have taken the exam.

Students pay a fee for each exam and receive a certificate in each subject passed. About ten to fifteen certificates, depending on the subject major, are required for a college diploma. The diploma entitles the student to the same kinds of jobs and pay as graduates of regular two-year colleges.

Higher Education

In 1988 there were 1,063 colleges, universities, and other institutions of higher education in China (a little less than one per one million people). Probably all are underfunded, and many are small and overstaffed by inadequately trained and often elderly faculty; on average, in the US one teacher has 14 students, but in China he has only 3. Only about 100 institutions are considered to be of national or provincial importance.

About 65 percent of all institutions are governed by provincial and municipal authorities, 30 percent by ministries and commissions under the State Council, and 5 percent by the State Education Commission. There is a small but growing number of private colleges.

Total enrollment for the 1988–89 school year was 2,066,000, up about 5.5 percent, of which 640,000 were entering students; new enrollment will be the same in 1989–90. There were 554,000 graduates in 1988, and 527,000 (including 40,000 postgraduates) are expected in 1989.

Total enrollment of graduate students in 1988 was 113,000, down 5 percent, which is the first decline since graduate study was reinstated, and is attributed to growing disillusionment with the pay, career, and quality of life of educated persons in China. (For example, *Guangming Daily*, a newspaper devoted to the interests of intellectuals, recently reported studies indicating that a manual worker who leaves school after primary school earns an average of 25 yuan a month more than a senior middle school graduate, who in turn earns 34 yuan more than a college graduate.)

A further decline can probably be expected; the new government announced very shortly after taking over that most students who wish to go on to graduate studies would in the future be required to spend at least one year, perhaps two, as workers or peasants before being admitted to graduate school. This applies particularly to social science students. The move, similar to the rustication of the Cultural Revolution, is intended to erase bourgeois liberalization and familiarize students with the daily rigors most Chinese experience.

The 1987–88 enrollment marked the end of a period dating from 1979 during which enrollment increased about 17 percent per year. The government announced in the spring of 1988 that, in order to help improve teaching quality and school facilities, enrollment growth would be held to 2 to 5 percent (no growth was shown in 1989–90 estimates, however, and a pre-opening announcement reduced admissions by 30,000 or about 5 percent), and the number of postgraduate students would not increase at all. (Enrollment outside the state plan by students who pay tuition or are sponsored by work units is discussed later under "The Revival of Higher Education.")

China ranks 113th among 114 countries with respect to percentage of university students, according to UNESCO statistics. Less than 5 percent of the college-age population is enrolled in higher education in all forms, compared to about 40 percent in developed nations. In the 1989 national college entrance examinations (exams are annual, always July 7–9), some 2,660,000 senior middle school graduates (about 60 percent men, 40 percent women) competed but only 610,000—less than one out of four—were enrolled.

Until recently, college entrance exams were prepared and administered by local education bureaus, and hence neither the content nor the way the exams were given were standardized; the entire process is now managed by the State Education Commission. The examination subjects are set: Chinese, mathematics, geography, history, a foreign language, political science, physics, chemistry, and biology.

Currently, the state provides students both tuition and housing, at a cost of about 2,500 to 3,000 yuan (US$675–810) per student, but since 1985 has experimented with charging a partial tuition fee. The initial fee was foolishly high, beyond the reach of nearly everyone, and widely resented. Lower fees have since been tried but there is widespread disagreement with the government's contention that an "average" family can afford tuition of 1,000–2,000 yuan a year. It was originally planned that by the 1989–90 school year more than thirty of the principal universities would begin charging tuition of 50–150 yuan per semester, and that tuition will be charged nationwide by 1990–91, except for courses in critical fields. Probably because of a general lack of funds, however, the plan was begun in the fall of 1989.

Under a "grant-in-aid system" a stipend of 23 yuan a month was formerly provided to everyone, although expenses for food and books are estimated at about 45 yuan. Since 1986, however, grants-in-aid have been slowly discontinued school-by-school, and by 1993 students nationwide will be expected to provide their own living expenses.

Scholarships for excellence and for specialization in needed fields are available to students in the upper 10 percent of their classes, and a third type is available to students, apparently regardless of class rank, who volunteer for work in hardship posts.

Loans are available to students in the upper 30 percent of their classes. Students' future employers will pay off the loans in a lump sum when the student is hired, and recover the cost by deductions from pay. Loans and scholarships together may not amount to more than 400 yuan yearly.

The cut in aid would appear to be self-defeating, given China's need for trained people, but experience gained in its gradual application may lead to modification by the government and necessity may inspire self-support efforts similar to those already being made by cash tuition students who receive no subsidies at all. Meantime, however, the new arrangement is a source of anxiety and resentment to many students.

More detail on major changes is given under "The Revival of Higher

Education" later in this chapter.

COMPULSORY EDUCATION

One of the most important recent developments in education was the adoption by the 1986 National People's Congress of a draft law creating a compulsory nine-year education program, as proposed in the educational reform decision. The program will be free, and it will be illegal for any organization or individual to employ children before they have completed their nine years of schooling.

It is not clear exactly what the actual meaning of "compulsory" will be; the present program does not envision that a set number of years of schooling will ever be universally enforced.

The 1982 constitution says in Article 19 that the state "makes *primary education* [emphasis supplied] compulsory and universal," but the goal established in 1980 for meeting the constitutional requirement is 1990 and as of 1987 only a majority of cities and about 1,000 of 2,100 counties have universal primary (six-year) education available. (The general schedule for nine-year schooling is described below.) Some clue as to the dimensions of the problem of further guaranteeing education for all is shown by reports that there were only 120,000 places in Shanghai kindergartens in the fall of 1986 for a total of more than 300,000 eligible children.

An education official pointed out recently that the idea of education for all has been promoted since 1951 without success because, among other reasons, until 1986 there was no law which in fact made it possible to enforce such a program.

It is also difficult to force attendance even with a law, a problem certainly not unique to China, as can be seen by dropout rates in the United States. According to the State Education Commission, there were 7.15 million dropouts in 1988: 6.9 percent of junior middle school pupils and 3.3 percent of primary school pupils, reflecting the increasing feeling among students at all levels, including university, that "education is useless" when compared with the benefits of early employment and private entrepreneurship. As a result, there is a growing child labor problem.

(From time to time, a statement appears in print implying that more than 95 percent of Chinese children attend school. For example, *Beijing Review* quoted an official of the State Education Commission as saying that "the nationwide enrollment rate reached as high as 95.9 percent among children of primary school age." Obviously, that rate is out of line with the attendance rates mentioned above. When these contradictions were pointed out, the commission explained that the 95.9 figure refers to *initial* enrollments only, and acknowledged that unfortunately many children do not remain in school very long.)

It appears that in addition to making education *available* more has to be done to make it *desirable*, or at least acceptable, for in China as elsewhere, the glamour of quick money versus spending additional time in school has been hard to resist. The previously mentioned article in *Study and Research* makes this point:

> Of course, the conditions for the institution of completely free compulsory education in China are rather difficult. But if we go on [not requiring a reasonable level of education] for a long time the consequences will be very serious. . . . In the past few years the villages and rural towns have been very lively, there have been many means of making money, and employment as a laborer means that one can earn a lot of money quickly. If one goes to school for several years, not only is it not possible to increase one's income, but quite the opposite: you have to spend money. So, thinking along these lines some people believe that it is better to find a job than to go to school.

At present, students in major cities have available to them five years of primary school education and three years of lower middle school, but in the countryside only four to six years of schooling may be available. Worldwide, according to UNESCO figures, about 45 percent of countries which have compulsory education provide seven to nine years of schooling, and another 25 percent provide 10–12 years.

Plans for introducing the nine-year compulsory program recognize that the new level cannot be attained throughout the country for a number of years, because of differences in social and economic development among the major areas. The general plan, however, provides three different timetables for three principal types of geographical areas.

First are inland and coastal cities where the economy is already comparatively well developed and the educational level is relatively high. It is expected that nine-year education can be achieved in such areas within about five years, and that within about fifteen years it should be possible for many places in this type of area to give all their children senior middle-level (eleven-year) schooling. Such areas have a total population of about 250 million, and are counted on to provide a solid intellectual base for the country.

Second are areas consisting largely of rural towns and villages, which will concentrate on making junior middle schooling—i.e., schooling through grade nine—universal, with further improvement to come later. Eight to ten years are expected to be required for these areas. It is estimated that about half of the total population of China lives in such areas.

Third are remote and sparsely populated areas, which are as yet under-developed and have comparatively low living standards. Since the educational level in such areas is presently rather low, the first emphasis will be on literacy.

By the first or second quarter of the next century, China expects to be able to provide senior middle school education for about 25 percent of its population, junior middle-schooling for about 50 percent, and basic education for the remaining 25 percent.

PRIMARY AND MIDDLE SCHOOL PROBLEMS

Pointing out that China spends less on education, as a percentage of its gross national product, than nearly any other country, one writer has wondered how it is that "China has done so much better than other developing countries in providing education for its citizens." (China spent 2.7 percent of its GNP on education in 1983, 2.5 percent in 1987; other developing countries at the same level spend about 4.0 percent.) The answer, he concluded, was that "on the one hand, there has been greater political commitment and control than elsewhere, and, on the other, very little has been spent on teacher's salaries and on facilities, especially in rural areas."

The level of funding and teacher quality, status, and remuneration are probably the two most serious problems in primary and secondary education.

Teachers—Teachers are the lowest paid professionals in China, which means, as in many other countries, that competent, talented people tend to avoid the profession or to escape from it as quickly as possible, public regard for those remaining is therefore very low, and a self-sustaining cycle leading to a corps of poorly qualified teachers with low morale is set up.

The funding of education and its effect on teachers will be discussed later but, first, it is worth looking at teachers just in terms of their present ability to do their jobs. A few sentences from *China Daily* sum up the problem:

☐　310,000, or 61 percent, of the 510,000 senior middle school teachers do not have a BA or BS degree.

☐ 1.63 million, or 73 percent of 2.23 million junior middle school teachers have not gone through full-time training in a three-year professional school.

☐ 2 million or 37 percent of 5.4 million primary school teachers do not have the diplomas required by the state.

Moreover,

> Teachers in normal institutes and schools are in demand [but] many of them are unqualified. Statistics from the State Education Commission show that of the 49,800 teachers in these institutes and schools, only 48 percent received four years of higher education and only 34.6 percent had studied in colleges for three years.
>
> ... During the Seventh Five-Year Plan (1986–90) the country will need 900,000 new middle-school teachers. However, the teachers' colleges can only supply 500,000.

The problem is being tackled by insisting that local governments assume greater responsibility for teacher training and retraining, and by enrolling nearly 300,000 teachers for retraining at some 11,000 TV centers, while about 500,000 are studying by TV independently. Fall 1988 examinations of 900,000 uncertified teachers in primary and

Zhang Yaoning, *China Daily*

middle schools showed that 34.7 and 43 percent, respectively were not qualified, and testing is continuing. Those who fail will be given five years to bring their skills up to par by TV retraining programs or whatever means they can manage. Those who do not make steady progress and achieve competence certificates in five years will be assigned to other work.

Funding—The educational funding problem is no different in China from most other places in the world—only bigger. There is only so much money. How is it to be allocated?

In China, some say the state should simply guarantee enough money to do the job, since education is so important to the future. Others say that there must be a balance kept between the needs of education and the needs of development in other sectors of the society.

The reality appears to be that, even though the government has increased funding to local education, national resources are simply insufficient, and authorities are increasingly attempting to make that point. At the 1989 annual working conference of the State Education Commission the education minister again bluntly warned that schools must look for other resources.

Since 1983 schools have been allowed to solicit funds from local enterprises and institutions to solve the shortage of central government funds for education. Many schools, however, took this as a license to impose fees on local work units beyond those permitted by the government, and to double or triple the normal schooling charges paid by parents. Also *China Education Journal* reported that officials were being deluged with letters from parents complaining that they were being asked to pay large unauthorized fees for various purposes, such as for office management, furniture repair, snacks at breaks, and so on.

A committee of the National People's Congress proposed in 1989 a 1 percent tax on income for those with incomes over 100 yuan a month, 2 percent on 200, and 3 percent on 300 or over as a means of localizing educational taxes and relieving the burden on the state. The proposal has a long way to go before approval, however.

People's Daily reported two years ago that 350 schools in Beijing itself had been discovered to be leasing out school buildings, or parts of them, to rent-paying occupants, in some cases on ten-year leases! This resulted in shortages of space for teaching, libraries, laboratories, etc. In reporting this story, Xinhua News Agency said that this practice had also become common in other parts of the country. The schools use this means to finance benefits for teachers and staff that are commonly provided in other work units but are not covered in education budgets.

US citizens may be somewhat puzzled to hear that work-study programs are being used in China to shore up school finances, because the usual programs in the United States involve alternate periods of study and vocationally related work, and students' wages are their own.

In China, "work-study" has other meanings. For a number of years, especially during and since the Cultural Revolution, work-study has been used in some upper schools so that students may become accustomed to and develop respect for manual labor, as well as contribute to national production. Enlarging the old concept of work-study to permit school-run enterprises to support individual schools has been encouraged in an article in *People's Education*. While recognizing that "Some comrades and family heads worry that doing this will disperse the school spirit, increase the burden already shouldered by teachers and pupils, and affect teaching work," the article argued that this was not so. It pointed out that some schools which run businesses "merely" transfer a small number of cadres and teachers to manage them, allow the pupils to work during the times they would have worked anyway under the previous curriculum, and have other labor performed "by organizing retired teachers, family members of teachers, young graduates of the school who are awaiting work, and other unutilized labor."

To an outsider, this sounds like a most ambitious plan. The article grants that "certain particular conditions" are necessary for such programs to succeed, but, it comments, "this is an area for creativity and striving."

As an example of what creativity and striving can accomplish, the article cites the case of "an ordinary school in Qingdao [which] turned its classroom into a specialized television and telephone repair shop outside of school hours, and offered short-term training courses in fine arts, sewing, and other such classes, and realized an income of almost 10,000 yuan." This was then used as capital for "setting up paper box processing, limestone processing, wireless switches, processing of television parts, and the cultivation of flowers and plants," which activities yielded profits of over 300,000 yuan in three years.

More than 650,000 primary and middle schools now have school-run enterprises, the State Council has approved special tax breaks for them, and local and county governments are now required to include school-run businesses in their development plans. The gross output of school businesses in 1988 was more than nine billion yuan, with profits over two billion.

Results like these speak volumes for the skill and industry of the Chinese people, but the necessity for supplemental fund-raising on such a scale by the teachers themselves suggests a shocking lack of regard for the profession.

Teachers in the countryside often have another special problem, not unlike teachers involved in a work-study project. In the rural areas, 60 to 70 percent of primary school teachers are appointed by their local communities, which are also responsible for their wages. (The other 30 to 40 percent are assigned and paid by the state.) While the commune system was in operation, locally appointed teachers received work points each day equal to those of an average commune worker, and at the end of the year shared in the distribution of commune profits according to work points accumulated. They also received an annual government allowance of 250 yuan. Their income from the commune, plus the government allowance for locally appointed teachers, gave them a higher than average income, which was in line with governmental directives.

Under the responsibility system, however, the work point system is no longer in use, and there is no mechanism for teachers to share in production. They receive the 250 yuan per year allowance—but, in most places, in order to receive anything more they have to farm a plot of land. They therefore have to do two jobs to earn one living wage, just as teachers with work-study projects do.

The Chinese press has been lamenting since 1979 the unfavorable situation of teachers, particularly in comparison to other workers who are benefiting in numerous ways from economic and agricultural reforms. Teachers have no opportunities for bonuses, and it has been reported that teachers in publicly run (state-run) schools earn in the range of 40 to 50 yuan per month, while teachers in locally run schools earn 30 to 40 yuan per month. In both cases, these wages are less than the teachers' pupils could earn immediately after leaving junior middle school, and the income of an experienced worker is often three times that of a teacher.

Teachers in publicly run schools did receive, or at least received promises of, small salary increases in 1985 and 1987, but the increases seem only to have raised the salary level to a low average rate, and no attempt was made to deal with other pressing needs, such as bringing their housing up to at least average standards. It is telling that as of early 1989 the education minister was still calling on the state to pay teachers the ten percent increase promised them two years before.

Indicating the seriousness of the problem, *People's Daily* gave it both a front-page story and front-page commentary in May of 1985, treatment reserved for major concerns of the government. The story emphasized the damage being done to the country's educational system by the increasingly widespread practice of recruiting teachers into the higher-paid, higher-status work forces of industrial enterprises, government organizations, and research institutes. Other reports document wholesale resignations by teachers to work in nonteaching positions. In one case, recruiters from the Shenzhen Special Economic Zone went to Shanghai to recruit cadres with special skills, and more than 800 secondary school teachers applied. (Why teachers are seemingly able to change jobs so much more easily than other workers is unclear. See the discussion of job transfer difficulties under "Set for Life?" in chapter 5.)

Other unattractive aspects aggravate the problem of inadequate salaries. The social status of the teacher is low. How low is shown by statistics for the 1988–89 year in which in one province alone three teachers were killed by disgruntled relatives of failed or disciplined students, and another twenty-six were permanently disabled and thirteen seriously injured. Physical assault of teachers is a holdover from the Cultural Revolution, when, as intellectuals, they were thought to be bourgeois and to favor old ideas.

Teaching materials and equipment are outmoded or lacking, school buildings tend to be poorly constructed and poorly furnished, and living quarters are often not much better. Experimental instruments and equipment are either seriously lacking or do not exist at all in 80 percent of secondary schools and 90 percent of primary schools. Until the most serious of the problems are alleviated if not eliminated, the country will continue to suffer a huge loss of both time and talent.

THE REVIVAL OF HIGHER EDUCATION

To a much greater extent than primary and middle school levels, higher education suffered serious damage during the Cultural Revolution. The first highly dramatic and public incident of those "ten lost years" occurred at Beijing University in May of 1966, and universities throughout the country were the scenes of many bitter battles and persecutions throughout the period. The value of knowledge and schooling was generally downgraded or denied, and faculty members, like nearly all other educated people, were subjected to harsh criticisms, deprivations, and, in many cases, physical abuse, torture, and murder.

In June of that year, the government announced the abolition of entrance examinations for universities and ordered the closing of senior middle schools, colleges, and universities for six months to enable the schools to make various adjustments to the new conditions. The chaos of the period was such, however, that nearly all schools at all levels had closed by the end of the year. Lower schools began reopening after a few months, but colleges and universities were closed for about three years, and only in 1970 did they gradually begin operating again, under radically changed conditions.

Admissions were based upon political attitudes and work background. Graduates of senior middle schools could be considered for admission only after they had proved their socialist fervor by completing at least two years of military service or work in factories or the countryside, while veteran workers or peasants were admitted, with the right political credentials, regardless of previous schooling. Management of universities and of many other intellectual endeavors was taken over by revolutionary committees and propaganda teams. Curriculums were purged of the "four olds" (old culture, ideas, customs, and habits) and the strictly ideological and practical were emphasized in teaching and in teaching materials. It was not until after Mao's death and the arrest of the Gang of Four that universities were able to begin the long process of recovery.

The ravages of the Cultural Revolution have been repaired to some extent by:

☐ Restoring the university entrance examination system. (See "Higher Education" in this chapter.)

☐ Enrolling more students in alternative forms of higher education such as specialized technical schools, which had been discontinued as discriminatory and capitalist. (See "Specialized senior middle schools" in "Middle School Education" in this chapter.)

☐ Restoring faculty titles and promotion procedures, which were eliminated in the interests of egalitarianism. In Beijing, the average faculty member's monthly salary had gone to 165 yuan by the end of 1985, up 135 percent from 1978 (although the top salary had actually decreased).

For many older faculty members, however, the increases mean only that they are barely above their incomes of the 1950s, and professors earn less than a busy barber. Like academics in other countries, faculty members take second jobs, do consulting, or otherwise try to supplement their incomes, but the financial situation of academics and other Chinese intellectuals is much more precarious than that of their western counterparts.

☐ Reestablishing foreign study programs discontinued during the xenophobia of the Cultural Revolution. Both government-supported and self-supported students are now studying in many foreign countries. About 80 percent of the students are doing graduate work, and about 90 percent are in technical or scientific fields.

Studying abroad is an opportunity and distinction most eagerly sought and worked for with energy and determination. *Outlook Weekly* reported in 1988 that more than 50,000 students have gone abroad since 1978, of whom about 30,000, or 60 percent, have not returned, and that almost none of the over 10,000 self-funded or scholarship students have returned. Overall, some 65 percent of students have remained abroad, and this during relatively good times in China.

Previously, the government has sent 7,000–12,000 graduate students abroad each year and a large number have also gone on their own, on scholarships, or with other support. The recent protests revived the old fear that foreign experiences were contaminating students and caused the conservative government to announce that henceforth the number of graduate students going abroad with government support would be reduced. (The effect on privately funded students is not known.) Opening to the outside world is all very well, indicated an education commission official quoted in *China Daily*, but a " 'wire screen' must be put in the 'window' . . . to prevent 'flies and worms' from entering through it freely." China expects to improve its own educational facilities to provide more graduate education.

Students who do not return are said to be discouraged by having to face the government's dictatorial employment system (see discussion of job assignment below); by fears that recurrent ideological campaigns, which hit intellectuals hardest, will turn into another Cultural Revolution; and by poor facilities and poor status and rewards for intellectuals in China. (A Chinese scientist told the American Association for the Advancement of Science at a 1989 meeting that one-third of Chinese scientists are idle for lack of suitable work or facilities.) The president of Beijing University told the 1988 Chinese People's Political Consultative Conference the country should not "blame the students abroad for not returning. The real problem is whether or not they are respected in their work." A distinguished professor who himself returned to China in 1937 said that

> Neither housing problems nor poor working conditions is the major impedi-
> ment to many students' returns. A number of intellectuals came back [for
> patriotic reasons] in the 1920s, 1930s, and 1950s when living and working
> conditions were poorer than those of today.

Now, of course, the June Fourth Massacre has made students even
more reluctant to return and foreign governments more willing to have
them stay. All major countries have given extensions of a year or more
on expiring visas held by Chinese students.

In March 1988 the government said "minor changes" were being
made in the foreign study program but that the general policy "was not
changed." Other sources, however, gave specifics indicating that
numerous restrictions had in fact been applied, including a sharp
reduction in the number of government-supported students allowed to
go to the United States (where about 70 percent have gone in recent
years) and a requirement that students sign contracts which carry heavy
fines for themselves or their families if they fail to return as agreed.

OTHER CHANGES

Over-strict control of higher education relaxed—The decision on
educational reform stated that excessive restraints on the powers and
discretion of universities and colleges had stunted their growth and
vigor. It attempted to give local administrations greater authority in
dealing with curriculums, teaching materials, cooperation with other
establishments in research and other matters, proposing personnel
changes, budgeting and use of funds, etc. However, as in the case of
decentralization in the economy, the new authority has not reached
those for whom it was intended, in many cases.

The apparent reassertion of conservative central control over higher
education began in the fall of 1989 when the State Education Commission and the State Planning Commission ordered "suspension" of
teaching of unspecified subjects in the social sciences, students of
which are considered "not qualified for socialist construction."

Enrolling students only according to state plan abolished—A large portion
of each year's new enrollment will continue to be in accordance with the
state plan, which specifies the number of students to be enrolled at each
school. Beginning in fall, 1989, the state plan will be refined by means
of "oriented enrollment," under which a fixed quota of students will be
enrolled from specific areas and they will be required to return to those

areas after graduation; the same principle will be used in oriented occupational enrollment, where mandatory assignment will be made to specialties where enrollment has not met state needs.

However, two other enrollment plans have recently appeared on the higher education scene. (In both cases, students must pass entrance exams.)

Education by contract—Schools may contract to train employees of factories, offices, and other enterprises for fees. (This has a special importance because at present the state makes job assignments for students enrolled under the state plan, and enterprises cannot be sure of getting graduates with needed skills; see discussion of job assignment below.) For example, a college recently announced a plan to charge 10,000 yuan a year each for forty students it expected to enroll in a three-year course in computer science; 30,000 yuan is what the school felt a company would have to pay to recruit such a specialist, if one could be found.

The "buy-a-graduate" plan, as it has been called, thus makes it possible for small and medium-sized enterprises eventually to add well-trained graduates to their staffs, which would have been impossible under the system of state assignment. That this method of staffing is well received is shown by the figures: 3,200 students were enrolled under this plan during the first year, 1983; 60,000 were enrolled in 1985, and 81,000 in 1987.

Private payment—Schools may admit self-paying students who passed entrance exams but did not place high enough to secure admission under the state plan. They do not receive stipends and pay tuition that is required to be at least two-thirds of the cost of educating them. The cost varies from place to place, but in Shanghai, for example, liberal arts study costs 800 yuan a year, and science, engineering, medicine, and physical education cost 1,200. Such students are eligible for scholarships and loans, but, as with other students, they cannot receive more than 400 yuan a year. Lodging is available for a further fee.

Like the "buy-a-grad" program, the self-pay plan is growing rapidly. There were about 2,000 self-paying students in 1985 and 1986 combined; there were 14,000 in 1987, and, according to a national *Outlook Weekly* survey, 30,000 in 1988.

A number of colleges and universities have been founded in recent years which enroll qualified students unable to secure admission to traditional universities under the state plan. These schools are for commuters only, who pay all their own expenses. Expenses are kept low, however, because the institutions also receive payment from work units which hire graduates.

THE JOB ASSIGNMENT SYSTEM

The long-standing system of assigning college graduates to jobs by the state is being modified. (The job assignment system as it affects all workers is discussed in "Set for Life?" in chapter 5.) Since liberation, it has been the practice for college students completing their courses to be assigned to jobs by the state, whether or not the students liked the jobs or were suited to them or not, and regardless of whether the new employers thought them unqualified or even wanted a new employee at all.

Employee and employer are in the position of brides and bridegrooms in old China—they never even see each other before the match is made. This method has had a number of unhappy and disadvantageous results. For example, the possibility that anyone can change jobs is still very slight, occasional positive-example news stories notwithstanding, and blind assignment to an unsuitable job can mean a lifetime of frustration for the employee and numerous problems for the manager who has to deal with him.

In the spring of 1985 the State Education Commission began permitting preassignment consultations between some colleges (not individual students) and employers to whom the state proposed to assign graduates, but it was not considered successful. According to *China Daily*, "the system did not ensure that key industries and government units, especially those in remote and backward regions, receive muchneeded graduates," but some attempts toward change continued on an experimental basis.

Informants say that although, officially, only four national universities are participating in the experiment, graduating students in most of the major universities in Beijing and Shanghai were permitted to find jobs for themselves in 1988. In the experiment, personal canvassing and interviews are allowed, and employers may select from among the applicants by examinations. Only those who fail to find jobs on their own come under the conventional job-assignment program.

It is clear, however, that progress has been slow, difficult, and meager. "Interviews on paper" are the norm if there is any consultation at all. As one student put it, even at schools participating in the job assignment experiment "the power of recommending [assignments] is held tightly in the hands of the teachers. [And, some have said elsewhere, in the hands of the school's Party apparatus.] The meetings between those seeking workers and those seeking work never get down to the level of the student."

From the employer's side come comments like the following in *China Youth:*

> We are only able to meet with the teachers. We are not allowed to meet with the students. It is as if there were a huge wall separating them from us. It is not enough to have the teachers tell us whether the student is a male or a female and whether he or she is a good student or a bad student. Even when you go shopping for commodities you have to have a look. How much more necessary it is when you are shopping for human beings.

The schools, on the other hand, appear to be taking unnecessarily large burdens upon themselves, continuing to tell enterprises what talent they can have rather than letting them discover for themselves what is available. Administrators all say, according to the article,

> that the amount of work schools have to do has been increased. Originally . . . there was just one plan for [job assignment]. Once this plan had been carried out the work of allocation was over. Now . . . they have to make a plan that takes each special enterprise into account one by one. They need to work with a number of plans. The teachers . . . take the initiative and negotiate back and forth with the enterprises a number of times. Finally they have to take all the separate plans and unite them into one . . . report to those above and contact those below, make adjustments, and make everything fit.

As the schools see it, if they allow face to face meetings they will have even more work, although the reasoning is unclear unless they expect to continue to control who hires whom.

And apparently that desire enters in, probably in more ways than one. Curiously and sadly, schools say that "It is also necessary to take into consideration the quality and abilities of the student"—not to fit the right person to the right job but to prevent what teachers consider unseemly success. "Some students have an excessively high estimate of their own abilities. If they get assigned to some especially desirable placement, that will just confirm their notion that they are cock of the walk."

All the experiments and objections may have suddenly become moot, however. In the spring of 1988 the State Education Commission announced that students enrolling in 1989 and thereafter, who will begin graduating in 1993, will have to find their own jobs after graduation, and the state will have no responsibility for those who fail to find work.

The effective date appears to have been set back, however (see below), because students are beginning to see drawbacks to the plan. For example, many fear that under it personal connections will be even more influential than now in determining who gets the best jobs. That concern should dwindle, however, as enterprises and institutions become responsible for their own profits and losses and are forced to find the people most qualified for a given position.

Another problem is that employers have been increasingly reluctant to accept female graduates even under the assignment system. Women feel that few employers will hire them willingly, and the validity of this is borne out by reports that in current assignments employers in many locations are being forced to accept one female graduate for every male assigned to them. Officials fear that, with job prospects diminished, most women may stop competing for university admission.

The students' problems are further complicated by the fact that those who live in one province and attend school in other provinces may not be allowed to work there after graduation, because many cities are attempting to reduce the number of new residents.

And, of course, there are students who wish to keep the secure "iron rice bowl" job assignment gives them and are fearful of competing for jobs on their own.

Whether because of student opposition or for other reasons, in 1989 there was once more a "State Plan to Give All Grads Jobs," according to *China Daily*. There was a single national "job assignment information conference" in the spring which "provides the country's more than 1,000 universities and colleges with an opportunity to exchange job information with employing units," but nothing else of an experimental nature was mentioned.

However, another *China Daily* story a month or two later on a different aspect of job assignment contained several significant contradictions. It said, for example, that "all" colleges and universities had adopted a system for 1989 "under which students are given more freedom to choose the jobs they prefer and employers may choose the best candidates by means of interviews and tests." As often happens, the truth may lie somewhere between these two official pronouncements.

In fact, the reality may be that all students are going to receive job assignments—assignments to jobs as farmers and factory workers. The previously mentioned plan to require candidates for graduate school to work for a year or two before graduate school was reportedly only one part of a larger proposal which requires *all* who have graduated since 1985 or who graduate in the future to work in ordinary jobs before beginning the more skilled employment for which graduates qualify.

Like other reforms, changes in the job assignment system will not be easy. The important element in the situation, however, is that in one way or another demands of economic development as expressed through the needs of employers and students are slowly coming to have greater influence on the planning and operation of the entire educational system, and to extinguish the paternalistic, stifling job assignment system.

Appendix One

A Word About Chinese Statistics

Are Preform Statistics Reliable?

In the politically supercharged atmosphere of most years from liberation through the Cultural Revolution, statistical data could be used as ideological ammunition, and in many periods and places was compiled and published with an eye to political advantage. Also, the Chinese attitude toward information of all kinds—not only statistical data but even things like official biographies of leaders—is much more cautious than in most other countries.

Material which would be publicly distributed elsewhere might be highly classified in China, and only two or three years ago a high official said of data on the progress of special economic zones that "The figures aren't secret, but there is no imperative need for the people to know them." This means not only that the information would be withheld from the public but that it also might not be available for use even by statisticians or responsible managers in related bureaus or areas of interest, or even in the same bureau.

China announced with some pride in 1989 that it was inviting foreign scientists to head some research projects, and added that China has now established nearly sixty "open" research institutes which are able to exchange information with foreign researchers. The converse of this is that China has several thousand other institutes which are not "open."

Also, in many subjects there simply isn't much data (a condition not limited to China among developing countries). A public health researcher working in China has said that "The limited information demands a near-addiction to making estimates and interpretations based on a sense of context, general principles, and incomplete data."

When the Great Leap got underway, such little statistical information as had been coming from the People's Republic quickly became useless, as everyone from units in the countryside to ministries in Beijing vied for the most impressive production records and reported statistics which would have been unbelievable in any other milieu, and were not credited among foreigners.

William Hinton reports in *Shenfan* this recollection by a peasant who resisted making false reports:

> "Our total production for 1958 was 150,000 catties above that of 1957. Each person had produced 500 catties more grain than the year before. . . . [But] the wind of exaggeration was blowing very hard. Anyone who had actually harvested 100 catties would report 1,000. I had no idea that things like this were going on. As a result of the all-out effort we made, we had harvested 540 catties per mu. Yet all the others reported more than that. . . .One 'sputnik' brigade reported 33,000 catties per mu. Reports came in from a 1,000–catty county and a 10,000-catty commune. . . .
>
> "At that time I thought, if I lie, if I make an empty boast, what will the landlords get out of it? They know we only harvested 540 catties. . . . I also thought, Communists can't tell lies. I can't do that.
>
> "The members of the Party committee spoke with anger. . . . They demanded that I go and learn from 'advanced' units [i.e., units which claimed high production]. I said, 'Fine. I'd love to learn from them.' These leaders believed that those 'advanced units' had really produced such yields. They said we must learn from others, but actually they were just trying to make people change their figures to please the upper leadership."

Clearly, raw statistics from such an era mean nothing, although very careful analysis, correlation, and reconstruction by scholars both inside and outside China have yielded some numbers that they seem to feel comfortable with.

Reviewing two compilations of post-1980 statistics from China, Thomas G. Rawski described in the *Journal of Economic History* some of the problems of distortion, definition, technique, etc., that plague the statistician using historical Chinese data.

He commented, "Careful attention to these and other difficulties is essential to meaningful quantitative research on China's economy. . . . Despite their drawbacks, Chinese data can be deployed to quantify the impressive achievements and the equally substantial obstacles facing China's economy."

In the interests of achieving greater understanding of China, even flawed data must be used, if nothing else is available. The layperson can no doubt be excused for being relieved at not having to deal with the data, however, when the results can be as variable as the following three different conclusions on the severity of famine in the late fifties and early sixties.

It has been known for some time that during the Great Leap Forward there were years of serious crop failures. In *China: The People's Republic, 1949–1976*, published in 1977, the distinguished French authors wrote that by 1960 "scarcity (though probably not famine) was now widespread." However, "China's Food" in the December 1985 *Scientific American* referred to a much different conclusion by two American demographers, who found that "a famine lasting from 1959 to 1961 had caused at least 16.5 million excess deaths." Or, if *Time* magazine's figures in its 1986 "Man of the Year" story on Deng Xiaoping are accepted, the famine "starved some 27 million people during the years 1958 to 1962."

Postreform Developments

Since the late seventies, large quantities of good-quality statistical materials have been coming out of China. They are not without problems, but they are also apparently without the blatant distortion that characterized prereform statistics. The State Statistical Bureau began approaching normal operations in the early eighties, and started publishing in 1982 the *Statistical Yearbook of China*, a compilation of statistics from all areas of Chinese life. (As might be expected, there are few retrospective tables.) It was the first such volume since *Ten Great Years* was published in China in 1960. Another important advance was made in July 1988 when the bureau established a weekly newspaper of official statistics, *China Statistical Information* (in Chinese), and there is now *China Statistics Monthly* in English published by the Bureau and the University of Illinois at Chicago.

The most encouraging sign of the improving health of Chinese statistics, however, was the way the State Statistical Bureau conducted the third national census, which took place on July 1, 1982, and the results that were widely reported and published. (The second [1964] census results were withheld from the public until 1982 when preparations were being made for the 1982 census; the first [1953] were published in two pages.)

More than two and a half years were spent in preparing for this census, the most thorough in Chinese history. Twenty-eight computer centers and thousands of local offices were established throughout the country, and training had to be provided for 5,000 computer technicians and data entry personnel, 130,000 coding workers, and 5 million census staff and instructors. The total cost was over US$200 million, not including contributions of computers and advisory personnel by the UN Fund for Population Activities amounting to about US$16 million.

The enumeration covered nineteen items related to characteristics such as age, sex, education, occupations and trades (with a total of over 600 categories), plus several items pertaining to household composition, etc. The first results of tabulations (by hand) of major items were released in October 1983; additional results are being published over a period of several years and in great detail, even down to the township level in some areas.

The results have been criticized by some outside analysts, particularly because (among other reasons) there was a close linkage between enumeration planning and already existing household registration records, which are maintained in each locality on a day-to-day basis. The census takers were given a list taken from the household registrations showing households to be covered. They even knew how many people were supposed to be enumerated in each household.

This procedure assumed, of course, that the household registrations themselves were accurate. There was some doubt of that in the minds of outside observers, since even the Chinese had previously complained that people failed to report births to avoid running afoul of population control rules, failed to report deaths so they could keep the deceased's ration coupons, etc. The Chinese and their UN advisers felt the records were sufficiently accurate for the purpose, however, and that it would not have been possible to conduct the census without using the registrations and already-experienced registration personnel.

Despite relatively minor shortcomings, the 1982 census was widely hailed. John S. Aird, a US Census Bureau analyst, wrote in *China Business Review* that "Methodologically, this census represents an enormous advance in technical sophistication over all previous national censuses and surveys taken in the country. . . . All things considered, China's 1982 census is a credit to the statisticians who planned and directed it and to the political leaders who supported their efforts."

There is no regular schedule for censuses, but it was recently announced that the fourth national census would be made some time in 1990.

The Situation Today

In 1984 and 1985, as economic reform successes became widely discussed, many glowing, ecstatic stories appeared in the Chinese press. They inspired an article by a high Party official who recalled, with examples, the Great Leap period as a time when exaggeration ruled Chinese official life. "By repeating so many old stories, I don't mean to say that things are still the same now," he pointed out. "But can we say that we have not been influenced by those events at all?"

Apparently not, for in 1986 when other top officials were emphasizing the need to follow the principle of "seeking truth from facts" and to avoid exaggeration, *People's Daily* pointed out that the false reports, exaggerated achievements, and hidden shortcomings of some cadres "leave accurate reporting of developments to letters from the public, Chinese journalists, and even foreign journalists, in too many instances . . . leaving people to rightly wonder what Party organizations are doing."

There is now a law on statistics that includes protection for statisticians, and the Chinese journal *Statistics* recently urged them to take advantage of it:

> Statisticians should play their part in checking exaggeration. Unless they are sure mistakes have been made, they should refuse any demand to change the figures. For important figures, especially those which indicate developments in a certain locality or trade, and those used for policy-making, no check can be too careful.

Recently, as it has become apparent that population control has not gone as well as was believed, allegations of both deliberate and accidental underreporting of births have been made. (See "Good Results since

Family Planning Began in Earnest" in chapter 3.) And under the headline "A Little More Realism at Trade Fair, Please" the *South China Morning Post* pointed out that the exaggerated reports on the 1989 Guangzhou Trade Fairs coming from all sources were so extreme that "If [they] were true the two Guangzhou trade fairs a year would account for more than a quarter of China's total foreign trade" projected for the entire year. "But the 'information' machine of the fair keeps on churning out 'record' after 'record' with every fair."

It looked as though the fair had taken the *Post's* comment to heart when *China Daily* announced on May 1 that the US$5.2 billion sales at the spring fair failed for the first time ever to exceed the previous session, but along came another story a week later announcing that sales totaled "US$5.3 billion, $84 million more than that of the 1988 spring fair."

At least as important as factual accuracy, however, is the need for statistical workers and users at all levels to be concerned with the basic problems of sampling, definition, comparability, and clarity.

A typical problem users of statistics encounter is the widely varying figures available for China's foreign trade. For example, the Ministry of Foreign Economic Relations and Trade reports one set of figures, the Customs Bureau another; they are different because the Ministry's figures do not include some categories included by Customs, such as materials which are imported and then processed and exported, but each body's figures are cited freely without explanation and sometimes without even any indication as to which set of figures is being used. To complicate matters, the State Statistical Bureau issues a third set of trade figures.

Statistics May Lose Something in the Translation

At a recent lecture in English on renewable forms of energy given to a Chinese audience, there was an excellent translator. Even the lecturer's little jokes in English seemed to get across in Chinese. The translator used a large blackboard to make notes for himself on the rather technical material as the lecturer spoke, and he sometimes checked a fact or a number with the lecturer before translating for the audience.

The thing that gave the translator the most trouble was large numbers. The reason is that Chinese numeration is less flexible than decimal numeration. For example, the unit *wan* stands for 10,000 and there is no convenient expression for larger quantities before *100 million*, called *yi*. One million, for example, for example, must be expressed as 100 *wan*. It is understandable that decimal points may float bewilderingly.

Sometimes the problem is clearly with decimal points, but the source of the difficulty is usually not so obvious. Chinese informants say the problems may exist in the original Chinese version, too, not because statisticians have erred but because many editors and writers do not yet have a very wide range of knowledge. Hence, they misplace decimal points, confuse sugar and sugar cane, kilowatts and kilowatt hours, number of stock shares and value of stock shares, etc.

Often, material that is translated into English from Chinese shows such a good command of English (even if it retains a distinctive character) that readers or listeners may not be alert for significant mistakes. Where numbers are involved, however, it is well to apply a critical eye or ear.

For example:

☐ A story in a trade magazine says that "Last year Shandong Province exported more than 4,000 square feet of carpets in Chinese traditional and Persian designs, totalling more than US$30 million." Innocent enough, until the mind recognizes that those carpets would have had to be priced at US$7,500 per square foot! So, one— or more—of those numbers must be wrong.

☐ A story about a hotel that had been open for 18 months says "the 1,200-room hotel has played host to nearly 4.5 million guests for total business volume of 120 million yuan." Foreign guests who are stunned by rapacious charges at some hotels could easily believe that the hotel could take in over 220,000 yuan a day, but it seems unlikely a 1,200-room hotel could handle 8,400 guests a day.

☐ The report says that low stocks of insulin were becoming a worry to the 2.5 million Chinese diabetics who require regular daily injections. Only 1.02 million doses were produced in 1985, the story says, whereas the country needed 1.3 million doses a year.

☐ A story in a Chinese national magazine says, "Average annual income for urban people rose from 762 yuan per person in 1980 to 1,176 yuan in 1985." This seems to be saying that the average urban annual per capita income increased as stated, but "urban people" actually refers only to "urban workers." The statistics are for average wages for employed persons.

☐ A survey of 1985 statistics reported by the State Statistical Bureau says, "Living standards in both the cities and the countryside improved in 1985. A sample survey showed an average annual per capita net income of 397 yuan . . . , 42 yuan, or 11.8 percent, more than in the preceding year." The context implies that this is the national per capita income for "both the cities and the countryside." In fact, it is the rural figure.

☐   In a story on economic crimes, it is stated that China prosecuted about 225,000 offenders between 1982 and 1985; 44,000 cases were handled in 1983, 85,000 in 1984, and the number "then jumped by 160 percent" to approach 225,000 in 1985—making the three-year total 354,000. The story comments, however, that "more than 90 percent of these cases were related to business contracts," and, if so, most of these 225,000 (or 354,000) cases concerned civil disputes, not economic crimes. This interpretation is strengthened by a statement by the national procurator-general that 28,000 cases of economic crime were investigated in 1985.

The Public Opinion Poll Comes to China

China took another step toward modernization, for better or for worse, when it enthusiastically adopted in the last year or so another feature of contemporary life abroad: the opinion poll. Polls have been reported from time to time for a number of years, but polling has now increased significantly, with government agencies, newspapers, organizations, and institutions all asking questions.

Unfortunately, it is still common to see reports of surveys biased by poorly planned questions and poor sampling technique. Many surveys still rely on responses to mailed questionnaires, for example, ignoring the well-known distortion that results because only people with a strong interest in a subject, and possibly on only one side of a question, bother to respond.

And how can pollsters deal with the biggest source of possible distortion, the longtime government attempt to secure acceptance of a single point of view, plus the traditional inclination of the Chinese toward conformity and consensus? To what extent can a researcher count on getting a spontaneous and candid opinion to any question from even the best sample?

There is increasing recognition of the possible benefits from accurate surveys and improved techniques, however, and at the same time a demand for polling services is developing among both state agencies and enterprises and nonstate enterprises.

Appendix Two

The Mini-Encyclopedia: Quick Explanations of Important Terms, Events, Slogans and Features of Chinese Life

Note on Use of the Mini-Encyclopedia: The index (which covers both the text and the Mini-Encyclopedia) is the key to locating topics anywhere in the book. Topics are not included in the Mini-Encyclopedia, even though important, if they are covered in detail in the text.

The Mini-Encyclopedia is intended to provide information on concepts, events, catchwords, slogans, features of Chinese life, and odd bits of information which are often not found in a handy form anywhere else. The brief entries are not intended to be exhaustive (some of the terms, such as "May Fourth Movement" and "Cultural Revolution," have had entire books written about them), but only to provide sufficient information to enable a reader to understand the meaning of a term or the significance of a slogan when it is encountered in reading or conversation.

Suggestions for terms to be included in the next edition are welcome.

ACCUMULATION FUNDS   The portion of national net assets used for construction of physical facilities. The accumulation may be divided into *productive accumulation* (or capital construction, as for factories, etc.) and *nonproductive accumulation* (or noncapital construction, as for housing, water supply facilities, etc.). Too much accumulation reduces the supply of everyday necessities, depresses living standards, and slows economic growth. One of China's basic readjustments during the eighties has been aimed at decreasing accumulation, particularly for productive purposes, relative to consumption. Consumption in the years since 1978 has increased at about 7 percent a year, compared to the average 2 percent a year earlier.

ADVANCED AGRICULTURAL PRODUCERS' COOPERATIVES See AGRICULTURAL COOPERATIVES.

AGING China's population is aging rapidly because of the dramatic increase in life expectancy since liberation on the one hand, and the dramatic fall in the birth rate on the other. China now has more than ninety million people above sixty, and the number will more than double by the end of the century. Life expectancy is now 66.4 years for men, 69.3 for women—nearly double the average 35 years in 1949.

Caring for this increasingly large number of elderly people is no easier for China than for other countries. The government emphasizes collaborative efforts by the individual, the family, and society as a whole, with substantial responsibility being accepted by the family (much more than in the west) as has historically been the case. Family care will be increasingly difficult, however, since with a drastically reduced birth rate there will be fewer younger persons in the family to support the older. In society at large, considering only non-agricultural workers who are formally retired (as from government factories, offices, etc.) there were in 1989 21.2 million drawing pensions, according to the State Statistical Bureau, and they have increased in the past ten years at the rate of 1.8 million a year; the number of employed has not increased as rapidly, however, so again there are fewer and fewer younger workers to support the retired.

Furthermore, modernization is working against the old extended family structure, as in other countries. For those without families to care for them, there were in 1989 more than 35,000 homes for the elderly run by the government serving about 400,000 residents; there were another roughly 35,000 privately run homes serving another 400,000. Obviously, the homes are small, with an average of about eleven residents.

A slightly longer working life is probably in the cards. Men usually retire at sixty, women at fifty-five; women doing manual labor, of whom there are many, may retire at fifty. Delaying retirement would help reduce the number of dependent persons but it would also mean China would have to create even more new jobs annually than at present.

The need for greater governmental participation in the care of the elderly was recognized at the 1986 National People's Congress, when "a socialist social security system with Chinese characteristics" was included in the 1986–1990 five-year plan. It was emphasized that the government would not take over full responsibility for welfare benefits.

A few months later, provisional national regulations went into effect under which state enterprises pay "a certain percentage" of their payrolls to newly established local labor insurance departments, to be used eventually to meet pension obligations of all retirees from local state-owned businesses. The new system, being phased in gradually city-by-city, will supersede the current practice described below. There are no known plans for covering workers who are increasingly employed outside state enterprises, such as those in collectively run enterprises and by private entrepreneurs. The majority of contract workers are reported to be covered by individual pension plans partly paid for by employers. Also, no plans have been announced for dealing with related problems, such as funding health care.

Farmers and other rural workers are to be provided for in a separate system not yet operative in which the township will be the basic unit and individuals will finance their own coverage on a voluntary basis.

At present, social security is provided in two general ways: Former government employees, primarily urban people, receive pensions and other benefits from their old government workplaces—benefits which are paid from the workplaces' current income, however, and are not funded by insurance or reserves. Benefits are usually equal to about 75 percent of the retiree's final base salary, but benefits do not include bonuses and subsidies (which make up about 35 percent of pay while working) and are not adjusted for inflation. Therefore, those who retired years ago when wage levels were much lower and prices were stable are often in dire straits. Retired rural residents, prior to the widespread use of the contract responsibility system, received daily necessities from their collectives, some of which also provided medical care, and they were guaranteed clothing, housing, and burial expenses. Retirees' connections with local government are much less direct under rural reform and their care is reportedly haphazard in some places.

Today, the pension burden on long-established enterprises is such that there are 1.5 times as many pensioners as workers in some cases, while new plants have virtually no pensioners, leaving the new enterprises in a stronger competitive position and threatening not only old enterprises but their retirees as well.

AGRICULTURAL COOPERATIVES   When land reform during 1951–1952 eliminated landlords' holdings and gave "land to the tiller," in accordance with the revolutionary slogan, peasants began forming mutual aid teams among families to use for each other's benefit such implements and expertise as each had. These arrangements were followed in a year or two by small units known as "agricultural producers' cooperatives." Both mutual aid and APCs were encouraged by the state with a view to increasing the degree of collectivization slowly and voluntarily as peasants experienced the benefits of the new form of organization.

In the simple cooperatives of the early fifties, land, equipment, and labor were pooled (with members retaining ownership of physical resources) and members were compensated from profits in proportion to their own labor and contributions of land and equipment. Groups were small enough so that problems of management and motivation to be encountered later on in the communes did not arise, and the simple co-ops thrived.

Their success caused their downfall, however, for it generated the all-too-human feeling that if small-scale cooperation was good, large-scale cooperation would certainly be better. The early ideas of gradualism and voluntarism were lost sight of by eager cadres, who often coerced peasants and small co-ops to band together in larger, or "advanced," co-ops in which land was no longer privately held. (The full name for these units was "advanced agricultural producers' cooperatives.")

In early 1955 only about 15 percent of peasant households belonged to small co-ops and the remainder farmed independently. By the end of the year, however, virtually 100 percent belonged to *advanced* co-ops. In another two years or so, still larger units, the famous communes, were formed with even greater speed. (See separate entry under "People's Communes.")

AGRICULTURAL PRODUCERS' COOPERATIVES   See AGRICULTURAL COOPERATIVES.

ANTI-RIGHTIST CAMPAIGN   See HUNDRED FLOWERS POLICY.

ARMED POLICE OFFICERS   During the Pro-Democracy Movement news reports often referred somewhat confusingly to "security forces" and "armed police officers." In China, unlike most western countries, forces engaged in such ordinary duties as directing traffic, patrolling, etc. are not armed; it is these unarmed police that are called the security forces.

AUTOMOBILES   A sure sign that China is modernizing is the increasing concern over automobiles and the problems they bring, such as traffic jams in streets and lanes never intended for automobiles and increasing numbers of traffic accidents. Before 1978, there were no private trucks or cars, but changes in regulations and new prosperity have led to private ownership of 3.5 million vehicles, of which a large percentage are trucks. Government-owned vehicles have also increased rapidly, imported cars being one of the favorite items on shopping lists for bureaucratic buying binges the government is struggling to control.

Even now, however, automobile ownership is rare among Chinese citizens and not at all common among foreign residents. China manufactures few automobiles (1988 production was variously reported at from 33,000 to 140,000), and imported ones are extremely expensive by the time import taxes and fees exceeding the cost of the car itself are added; in addition, there are monthly operating taxes and other costs. Nevertheless, there are several million trucks, passenger cars, and taxis, to say nothing of millions of transport tractors and tens of millions of bicycles competing for road space—and, now, increasing numbers of motorcycles, as well.

Traffic fatalities are not reported in the western fashion, in terms of so many millions of miles driven or some other relative measure, but the raw statistics are frightening. With probably not even 10 percent of the United States' 180 million vehicles, China had more than 54,000 people killed in traffic accidents in 1988, a per-million-vehicle rate about ten times that of the United States. About 50 percent of mishaps are vehicle-bicycle accidents, and 70 percent of accidents occur in rural areas.

It is understandable that there are frequent safety campaigns. Signs are commonly seen cautioning against running into other vehicles, illustrated by vivid drawings of such accidents. Printed materials posted on streets sometimes show closeups of corpses at the scene of accidents.

Traffic offenses are dealt with on the spot (including collection of fines) unless serious, there is no set scale of fines, and traffic officers' bonuses increase with the amount of fines they collect.

BACK DOOR   See *GUANXI.*

BASIC ACCOUNTING UNIT   See "Production teams" under PEOPLE'S COMMUNES.

BIAOTAI (Bough-tie)   As explained by Richard Bernstein in the *New York Times*, *biaotai* is "a standard technique of Chinese Communism revived by the recent antigovernment upheaval and its suppression. The word means 'to express an attitude.' " What is expressed is not necessarily the speaker's true opinion, however, but may be a restatement, or even just a rote recital, of the government's position on a certain matter. "Everyone knows what to say, which is currently something like this: 'I resolutely support the quelling of the counterrevolutionary rebellion, which was created by a very small number of ruffians whose ultimate goal was the overthrow of socialism and the creation of a capitalist republic for China. China needs above all stability and unity so that it can modernize. . . .'

"The practice of *biaotai* . . . has given rise to a different, bittersweet term, *shuo wei xin hua*, which means 'to speak against your heart.' The point is that one must *biaotai* when called upon to do so but that, as one Chinese put it, 'there is a big difference between what must come out of your mouth and what you feel in your heart.' "

BIG LIE   The Chinese have attempted to deal with the severe damage done to their world reputation by the June Fourth Massacre by implying that videotapes showing military actions are the result of "modern technology"; by using casualty figures that careful estimates by diplomats and journalists show are unlikely to be correct and failing to recognize the differences; by claiming the massacre was necessary because a "counterrevolutionary rebellion" was occurring but without producing any evidence whatever; and so on.

In so doing, they are resorting to a technique used with great success, for a time, by Adolf Hitler which quickly came to be known as "The Big Lie." Hitler believed (and there is some psychological evidence for it) that an enormous falsehood can be counted on to influence many people, and to be actually believed by some, even if most people see it as untrue. He wrote in *Mein Kampf:* "The enormity of the lie is a definite factor in causing it to be believed, for the vast masses of a nation are in the depths of their hearts more easily deceived than they are consciously and intentionally bad. The savage-like simplicity of their minds renders them an easier prey to a big lie than a small one. . . . Something therefore always remains and sticks from the most impudent lies, a fact which all bodies and individuals concerned with the art of lying know only too well, and hence they stop at nothing to achieve this end."

BLACK HAND(S)   A person or persons working behind the scenes to achieve a wicked, villainous, or iniquitous objective. Used in the aftermath of the Pro-Democracy Movement to refer to persons who were allegedly secret organizers of the movement.

BOTH ENDS OUTSIDE THE COUNTRY   A development technique in which capital, raw materials, and technology (one end) come into the country from outside, companies subsidized by the government run processing or assembly operations within China (the middle), and goods are sent to market outside the country (the other end). Also called "Three 'come ins' and one subsidy."

BOURGEOIS LIBERALIZATION   A revival of the label used in an earlier, and less successful, campaign in 1980–81, "bourgeois liberalization" was applied to the alleged counterrevolutionary beliefs of student protesters and some prominent liberals in the 1986–87 unrest which brought down Party Secretary Hu Yaobang, though it was otherwise not vigorously pressed as a political sin and quickly lost currency. The events are discussed in "Student Protests..." in chapter 2.

The concept assumed major importance, however, during and after the Pro-Democracy Movement in 1989, which was seen as evidence of continuing deterioration of ideological commitment and penetration of western ideas in economics, education, government, art, literature, etc., ideas which are thought to subvert Chinese values and corrode Chinese virtues. To the need to oppose bourgeois liberalization, the Party in 1989 also added the need to reinstitute class struggle (see separate entry).

The essence of bourgeois liberalization is questioning the correctness of, or departing from, Party practices, principles, or leadership, although the Party expresses it somewhat differently.

"What do we mean by bourgeois liberalization?" asked *People's Daily* in a 1987 editorial. It went on to quote a 1986 Central Committee resolution on construction of a socialist spiritual civilization as follows: "To carry out bourgeois liberalization is to negate the socialist system and to advocate the capitalist system. ... At present there most certainly are a small number of people who are promoting the thought current of bourgeois liberalization. They want to adopt capitalism completely and apply it to everything. When we talk about reform of the economic system, they want to go down the road of capitalism. When we talk about a reform of the political system, they want to switch to doing things the way they are done under western capitalism. . . .

"There are some of our fellow comrades who regard the 'left' with utter loathing and the utmost hostility. In this regard they show keen sensitivity and intense desire to struggle. This is because the mistakes of the 'left' have actually brought terrible calamities and suffering upon our Party and our people.

"But when it is a question of [struggling against] bourgeois liberalization these comrades let their ardor grow lukewarm and their indignation turn numb. This is the time to wake up and see things clearly. Bourgeois liberalization is definitely an ideological current. It is already poisoning our youth, endangering the stability and solidarity of society, interfering with our program of reform and our policy of opening up to the outside world, and blocking the advance and development of the Four Modernizations. Can we still go on acting as if nothing is wrong?"

Bourgeois liberalization is to be countered by emphasizing the Four Cardinal Principles of Socialism (see separate entry) and stepping up indoctrination in socialism and penalizing in various ways departures from the official line. In a post-crackdown editorial, *People's Daily* denounced western influences and strongly criticized by implication such countries as the Soviet Union, Poland, Hungary, and Bulgaria which are adopting the same kinds of economic and market concepts the current Chinese leadership is fighting to reject. The paper claimed (ignoring open election landslides for reform in the Soviet Union and Poland, for example) that these countries were virtually being forced by unnamed powers to make traitorous changes and said "We must fight against this trend. Otherwise, socialist China will be turned into a vassal of international capitalism."

The concept of bourgeois liberalization is so broad and vague that it can be applied to virtually anything the Party finds distasteful at any time, and recently hard-liners have been finding a great deal in reform that is offensive. Throughout the reform period, advocates of change have attempted to fit reform strategies into a socialist framework, arguing that Marxism is not immutable, for example, and that some practices, such as using market forces rather than attempting to regulate the entire economy, are not in themselves capitalistic but merely rational utilization of historic human experience. (See, for example, the two opening sections of chapter 4, and "Socialism with Chinese Characteristics.")

This attempt was mostly successful, but hard-liners are challenging nearly all reforms as being simply wrong and contrary to socialist principles. In effect, they attack the pragmatism of Deng Xiaoping by insisting that if it isn't a purebred *Red* cat it is not a good cat.

BRIEFCASE COMPANIES   An unexpected and unwelcome phenomenon connected with the new freedom to establish small businesses, a briefcase company has few or no assets, no fixed place of business, and, usually, no particular expertise. It hopes to profit through *guanxi* (see separate entry) or fortuitous transactions, or to become established while learning by doing. (See also "Companies.")

BRIGADE   See PEOPLE'S COMMUNES.

BUILDING SOCIALISM WITH CHINESE CHARACTERISTICS   See SOCIALISM WITH. . . .

BUREAUCRATIC CAPITALISM   Corruption under the Nationalist Kuomintang was so great that bureaucrats and their cronies were able to manipulate the operations of the entire government to their financial benefit, and many came to own large enterprises through their corruption. This condition is referred to by the Chinese today as "bureaucratic capitalism."

CADRES   Used broadly to refer to Chinese government officials and employees at any level, rather than in the more common sense of a nucleus of key, experienced persons. There are about 20 million cadres in China. "Leading cadres" (officials and executives) are found in all government organizations; "cadres" (also known as "staff members") are employees at any level in government offices and cultural, educational, and scientific institutions. (Lower-level employees in state-owned commercial and industrial enterprises, as well as self-employed workers, employees in collective and private enterprises, etc., are known as "workers.")

Formerly, it was customary for a cadre of whatever rank to occupy his post for the remainder of his life, unless promoted—in which case he had the same lifetime tenure in the new job. Competence or productivity was not much regarded, so risk-taking and innovation were rare. Incompetence, short of a major political blunder, was not a reason for dismissal. Many units found it impossible to produce good results because of lack of competent leadership, and capable people were frustrated because their promotion was blocked.

By the late seventies, hundreds of thousands of cadres were elderly and no longer vigorous, and other hundreds of thousands were not competent to meet the demands of the new reform environment. A large majority of such cadres were retired during the early eighties. The government is working toward a thorough overhaul of the cadre system which abolishes life tenure by fixing terms of office (usually three or four years), sets fixed ages for retirement, and establishes procedures for reviewing the perform-ance of leading cadres. Younger, more vigorous, better-trained, and better-educated men and women are being promoted to a large majority of the leading positions. Cadres in upper-level positions receive training in about 8,000 special cadre schools.

A Public Servants Law is being drafted for dealing with cadre selection, performance evaluation, promotion, and demotion. The law is aimed not only at providing standard procedures but also at preventing favoritism, nepotism, the use of political power for personal gain, and other abuses of office, which became especially serious (or began receiving increased attention) in the early eight-ies. Already, a number of provinces and cities have held public examinations; in one province there were twelve applicants for each position.

CAMPAIGN AGAINST SPIRITUAL POLLUTION   In 1983 increasing eco-nomic crime, materialism, and interest in western entertainment and ideas aroused concern among some leaders that internal changes resulting from reforms and from increasing exposure to foreign culture and ideas were damaging Chinese society and were causing "spiritual pollution." (The same condition attributed to the same causes was called "bourgeois liberalization" in campaigns in 1981–82 and 1986–87; see separate entry.) Deng Xiaoping called for "force-ful criticism" of ideological deviations and for restraints against cultural contamination, leading to the Campaign Against Spiritual Pollution. The campaign was pressed with unexpected vigor by leftists but it met with uncustomary resistance from the people, who saw overtones of the Cultural Revolution in it; produced uneasiness among prospective foreign investors; and had negative effects on intellectuals and entrepreneurs, whose contributions were essen-tial to the success of reform. The campaign lost momentum and was essentially ended in December 1983.

CERAMIC RICE BOWL   See IRON RICE BOWL.

CHINESE PEOPLE'S POLITICAL CONSULTATIVE CONFERENCE   The CPPCC was formed by the Communist Party of China in early 1949, with delegates from more than twenty organizations and groups, to serve as a united front legislative body for the reorganization of the country. One of its assignments was to prepare for the establishment of the National People's Congress, which replaced the CPPCC as the highest organ of state power after election of the first NPC in 1954. Since that time, the CPPCC "has helped to implement the policy of 'long-term coexistence and mutual supervision' between the Communist Party of China and the patriotic democratic parties" as a consultative and advisory organ on political and social questions. (See separate entry under "Political Parties.")

The most visible unit of the CPPCC is the National Committee, which meets frequently, usually annually. Like other bodies in China, the membership of the National Committee became quite elderly but about 40 percent of its 2,000 members were replaced before the 1988 session, lowering the average age to under sixty. Delegates are drawn from, in addition to the democratic parties and the CPC, a wide range of groups and personages, including mass organizations, minority nationalities, and outstanding workers, peasants, and intellectuals. A few naturalized foreigners and individual Chinese from Taiwan, Hongkong, Macao, and overseas also serve. About sixty percent of the delegates are members of the democratic parties, with the remaining number mostly Party members, but there are a few unaffiliated members.

There are about 3,000 CPPCC committees at or above the county level, with about 350,000 members.

CLASS STRUGGLE   An academic definition of "class struggle" is: "A Marxist premise is that the history of society is the inexorable 'history of class struggle.' According to this premise, a specific class could rule only so long as it best represented the economically productive forces of society; when it became outmoded it would be destroyed and replaced. From this continuing dynamic process a classless society would eventually emerge.

"In modern capitalist society, the bourgeois (capitalist) class had destroyed and replaced the unproductive feudal nobility and had performed the economically creative task of establishing the new industrial order. The stage was thus set for the final struggle between the bourgeoisie, which had completed its historic role, and the proletariat, composed of the industrial workers, or makers of goods, which had become the true productive class."

"Class struggle" has virtually disappeared from the Chinese vocabulary since its vicious application in the Cultural Revolution. Even in the various periods of agitation against bourgeois liberalization since 1979, class struggle has not been a significant element. The Central Committee at its Third Plenum in 1978 decided that class struggle was not a proper Party activity (see "Ideological Decisions" in chapter 2) and the committee also issued a decision in 1984 saying that "taking class struggle as the key line" in determining party behavior was no longer correct (see "Party Consolidation"). These decisions are apparently another part of the reform the ultraleftists want to overturn; their rhetoric since the June 4 Massacre has included demands for revival of class struggle.

While this concept has been useful in helping oppressed people understand their situation and in inspiring them to take action to remedy it, the idea is also problematic. It has been broadly used by communist governments to justify and encourage a form of institutionalized intolerance which makes it politically permissible for a government to persecute and stigmatize anyone it chooses to label a "class enemy."

COLLECTIVES AND COOPERATIVES   These terms, widely used all-purpose words in Chinese economic discussions, designate a class of undertakings— factories, other enterprises, or, formerly, farms— that are not "state-owned" or not owned "by the whole people," i.e., not owned directly by the national government. "Collectives" applied to enterprises may include not only those owned by groups of workers and family-owned enterprises but, as well, enterprises formerly operated by a commune or brigade in whose profits all now share.

In economic as well as noneconomic contexts, "collectives" may also apply to smaller administrative or governmental groups such as villages and towns.

"Collectives" may be contrasted with "cooperatives"—or the two may also be used synonymously! Collectives and cooperatives are considered to have different forms of ownership, however, as discussed below.

Economic Daily has said that "any economic form that organizes individuals in collective production or commercial business can be called either a collective or a cooperative." *Far Eastern Economic*

Review has used *collective* synonymously with *private:* ". . . growth of the state sector lagged behind that of the private sector. Estimates place state-sector growth at 11 percent, and the collective sector growth at about 22 percent." *China Daily* used the label "Collective Lawyers" for a note about China's first nongovernmental law office, clearly a private enterprise set up with their own funds by three lawyers who quit jobs with state law firms.

The ancestors of today's co-ops were the mutual aid teams and agricultural producers' cooperatives of the early fifties (see "Agricultural Cooperatives"). The later, now-defunct, communes applied the principles of collectivism and were thus the first "collectives" (see "People's Communes"). The historic units offer clues, but clues only, to the status of today's.

Various sources have pointed out the following as some characteristics of the two different forms of organization and ownership:

A Collective—"Collective ownership is a form of socialist public ownership. Its property—land or machines—is owned by all the people who belong to it."

"In a collective, parts of profits are earmarked for further development, for welfare funds, and for bonuses. Thus, the more workers produce the more they contribute to a collective's capital accumulation," and the more they may earn in wages or benefits, depending upon the collective's policies in building its expansion funds, which come largely from the collective's revenues. One writer considers that "a collective unit is directly controlled by its higher administrative authorities," while another speaks of collectives' "independence and flexibility," but perhaps both are sometimes true; it is worth pointing out again that there is a lack of uniformity in many aspects of governmental behavior.

A Cooperative—"The purpose of a co-op is to gather together a group of people who will collaborate in production, selling, or buying. [For expansion funds], in addition to seeking bank loans a co-op collects funds from its members. A unit cannot be called a co-op if it also sells stock to outsiders." Members may be individuals, collective or state-owned enterprises, or others, and may be drawn from throughout the nation if the scope of the undertaking requires it. Admission may be based on a purchase of shares or contributions of technology, physical plant, marketing skill, etc. "Participants in a co-op can freely withdraw from it, transfer investment to others, and share profits" based on their investment or contributions.

Earnings of a co-op are usually fully distributed to its members.

Lines of business in which co-ops are common tend to require much labor and to return relatively small profits. "Workers in these trades are unwilling to have [deductions made from profits for expansion or other purposes], partly because accumulated funds may be embezzled or wasted." A co-op is an independent economic entity not subject to any local or provincial administrative department. It is controlled by state laws and policies and by economic means.

COMMODITY CATEGORIES   References to industries or commodities as being primary, secondary, or tertiary are frequently seen, but often they are not explained. There are, in fact, several interpretations. The Xinhua News Agency has used this definition: *First industry*—Agriculture, forestry, fisheries, livestock production, and mining. *Second industry*—Industry in the usual sense, i.e., manufacturing, construction, and processing. *Third industry*—Public utilities, transportation, finance, insurance, technical services, personal services, etc. Another interpretation is: *Primary commodities*—Products vital to the national economy and the people's livelihood, such as grain, edible oil, cotton, cloth, and coal. *Secondary commodities*—Products of great importance, such as pigs, eggs, sewing machines, and bicycles. *Tertiary commodities*—Everything else.

COMMODITY MARKETS   Until reform began, commercial, or wholesale, purchase and sale of all goods was a highly centralized state monopoly. The system was an allocation system operated in conjunction with state plans, with end users allowed no choices.

Each wholesale agency handled only specific items. Transactions passed through the hands of central, provincial, and county bureaus before reaching consumers, and there was no connection between the distribution of one commodity and another or between suppliers, except at the top. The system was clumsy in the extreme, but it conformed to the administrative system generally and ensured, to a certain extent, that essential and scarce goods reached appropriate users.

The system was being slowly dismantled before the conservatives assumed power in 1989, although shortly before that government had already begun controlling some commodities more closely in its attempts to better control the economy, and it is to be expected that still greater controls are coming. In 1988, less than twenty products were still allocated by the government, and all others were available on the open market. (It should be noted that a statement such as "The state encourages the establishment and development of various markets for production so as to increase channels for circulation of commodities" may refer either to markets in the usual economic sense or to specific points of physical distribution such as those described below.) The government still has considerable control over the distribution process through its sponsorship of some of the major new distribution agencies and its ownership of both principal producers and large distributors. Marketers, however, are no longer (in theory) subordinate to commercial bureaus but are independent entities responsible for their own profits and losses and able to choose both their supplies and their customers. There are several types of entities involved in the distribution system, including:

Trade centers—About 900 of these government-owned centers and related units throughout the country deal in what are called "means of production," including machine tools, heavy industrial products, and major materials. They also sponsor exhibitions and provide other services to participating enterprises.

Single-product markets—There are about 400 of these urban concentrations devoted to a single commodity. For example, China's largest silk market is Shengze, a formerly small town on the Grand Canal which now has 300 dealers and an estimated ten thousand traders daily, and the largest market for small commodities (i.e., goods for personal and household use) is thought to be a 3.5 kilometer long street with about 3,000 small retailers in Wuhan.

Specialized markets—Defined as "big trading markets dealing in single commodities," these 5,500-odd markets are distinguished from the single-product ones above by being largely rural and by dealing primarily in processed goods such as buttons, leather products, and fish nets.

COMMUNE   See PEOPLE'S COMMUNES.

COMMUNIST PARTY OF CHINA   Following organizing activity in several cities, and with financial and policy assistance from the Soviet Union, the First Congress of the Chinese Communist Party was held in Shanghai in July 1921. Mao Zedong was one of less than sixty delegates. Under the advice of the representative from the Soviet Union, the Party consented to work with Dr. Sun Yat-sen in the Kuomintang, and during the next few years came to have considerable influence—a rise that was paralleled by that of Chiang Kai-shek. In April 1927 Chiang and Nationalist Army units suppressed the Party, executed several hundred of its leaders, and forced the Party from its Shanghai headquarters.

This was the first of a series of defeats and retreats that gradually became in 1934 what is now known as "The Long March," although it was never planned as such and there was no particular destination. The trek carried the communist forces over 6,000 miles to Yenan, 200 miles north of Xian in the northwestern province of Shaanxi.

Harrison E. Salisbury says of the heroic journey in *The Long March:* "How many lives it had cost would never be known. There had been 86,000 at the start. There were a scant 4,000 at the finish. But this did not tell the story. The ranks had been recruited and re-recruited along the way. By no means all those 'lost' men had died. Many were dropouts.

"Arithmetic was not the point. This was an epic in blood and courage, in victory and defeat, in despair and hope. Of this sacrifice and bravery would be woven the legend on which China's Revolution would be built. "

Today, the Party is the only political force of any consequence in the nation. Although there are separate, parallel governmental and Party organizational structures, the two are for practical purposes intertwined, with all government officials of any importance also being Party members. In the 1975 and 1978 constitutions it was specifically stated that the nation was under the leadership of the Party; this stipulation is made in a somewhat different form only in the preamble of the 1982 constitution but it can hardly be inferred from this that the Party's power or influence is any the less.

Party decisions on all matters at all levels can be passed on to the related non-Party unit for action without further discussion or review. One objective of political reform before the Pro-Democracy Movement occurred was said to be separation and better definition of the respective functions and interests of the government and the Party, to cut down on day-to-day interference from Party officials and thereby increase the technical and operational efficiency of the government. This is not in keeping with the determination of the new conservative government to reimpose central government authority.

Moreover, the Party has made it clear that there can be no weakening of the Party whatever in this much-discussed but so far little-implemented change. As a recent edition of *Xinhua Digest* expressed it, "the separation of the Party from the government is the first step in ensuring that the Party in control remains in control..."

It might be thought that in a nation dominated by a single evangelistic Party most people would be members of the Party, but that is not the case. Although any citizen over eighteen may apply, the Communist Party of China, like its counterparts throughout the world, bestows the unique prestige of Party membership upon only a select few chosen on the basis of political dedication, reliability, and leadership.

Party membership stood at about five million in 1949, or less than 1 percent of the population. As a result of active recruitment since 1978, 47.8 million people, or roughly 4.5 percent of the population, were enrolled at mid-1989, according to *Party Building*. China's is one of the most restricted parties in the world, ranking twelfth out of fifteen countries in the proportion of the population which belongs. Only about 5 percent of the members are university graduates, and over half have only an elementary school education or are illiterate. It was announced in 1989 that CPC members will hereafter be required to pass an annual examination of their political knowledge to retain membership.

The Party is led by Secretary Jiang Zemin, who was appointed to the post when Zhao Ziyang was dismissed in June 1989. Apparently believing Jiang to be more open to reform than Li Peng and other present top leaders, Deng designated him "core" leader of the Party and his personal successor in November. Given the intransigence and determination of the conservatives, and the narrow power base and limited national experience of Jiang, analysts feel that the designation may be of little importance in averting a power struggle after Deng's death.

The National Congress is in theory the supreme organ of the Party, but since it meets so infrequently the key governing body of the Party is the Standing Committee of its Political Bureau, then the Politburo itself and the Party Central Committee. The Politburo has eighteen members and its Standing Committee, the most powerful body in the country, was enlarged after the June Fourth Massacre from five to six. The Central Committee was reduced in size about 20 percent at the 1987 Thirteenth Congress, and now has 175 members.

The Central Committee, like other Party organs, has undergone radical change in the last few years through supposed retirement of its most aged members—many in their late seventies and early eighties—and the election of more vigorous and better-educated members.

Most retiring Central Committee members have assumed membership on the Central Advisory Commission (about 175 members), established in 1982 specifically to provide continuing official posts for elder members of the committee, who were reluctant to surrender totally their participation in national life. A number of the Party's most important veterans continue to play influential roles from this base, from which many of the group backing Deng in the 1989 crackdown emerged.

The other two key Central Committee units are the Central Commission for Discipline Inspection, which enforces adherence to Party doctrine and regulations, and the Military Commission of the Central Committee (often referred to by the same name as its virtually identical state counterpart, the Central Military Commission). Deng Xiaoping gave up his leadership of the Party commission in 1989 but temporarily remains as chairman of the state body. There have only been four chairmen of this commission in the history of the PRC—Mao, Hua Guofeng, Deng, and since November 1989, Pary Secretary Jiang Zemin. The position's potential was again demonstrated in the 1989 crackdown but, as Hua's record shows and as Jiang may learn, nominal army control does not guarantee political dominance.

The Central Committee secretariat, which is the committee's executive body, oversees the General Office; the United Front Work, Organization, Propaganda, and International Liaison departments; and two national Party newspapers (*People's Daily* and *Guangming Daily*). The widely known Party theoretical journal, *Red Flag*, which had been published for thirty years was replaced in 1988 by *Seeking Truth* (from the slogan, "Seek truth from facts").

The Party constitution requires a national congress every five years, except in extraordinary circumstances. This was not always true, however; there were six congresses during the first seven years of the Party's life, 1921–28, no congress for seventeen years, and irregular meetings thereafter until 1977, when the five-year cycle began.

Meetings of the Central Committee, which has the same

numerical designation as the congress which elects it, normally occur at least once a year, in sessions called *plenums*. Hence, the historic "Third Plenary Session of the Eleventh Central Committee" held in 1978 was the third meeting of the Central Committee elected at the Eleventh National Congress in 1977.

COMMUNIST YOUTH LEAGUE   This organization might be considered the junior section of the Communist Party of China. Despite its semiofficial standing, however, it suffered a loss of prestige and members in the Cultural Revolution, when it was effectively replaced by the notorious Red Guards. (See separate entry under "Cultural Revolution.") Since then, it has regained its status as a desirable affiliation for those who are ambitious to join the Party when they become adults. Students as young as fourteen apply and may be introduced to the league branch by two league members in their class and approved for CYL membership by the School General League Branch. Many also join after entering the work force or college. Leadership in all areas of life—work, academic and political study, and social relations—is the primary qualification for membership.

COMPANIES   "Cleaning up companies" was one of seven goals adopted by the Party and government after the Pro-Democracy Movement's strong protests against official profiteering and corruption in both governmental and private enterprises. What was the significance of "cleaning up companies"?

In China, all economic activity until reform began was carried on by government bureaus, agencies, departments, etc. When private businesses were no longer forbidden, tens of thousands of companies ostensibly not connected to the government sprang up. It quickly became apparent, however, that many were in violation of both governmental regulations and Party standards, but for years no serious regulation was attempted. Therefore, companies (or "business companies"), regardless of their qualifications or assets, are usually suspected of being corrupt and exploitative, and not without reason.

Even before the latest attempt at housecleaning, one of the common economic crimes reported with increasing frequency in the Chinese press was a transaction in which cadres, in violation of numerous edicts and often through fronts known as "briefcase companies" (see separate entry), take advantage of their contacts to make substantial profits on transactions to which they contribute little or nothing. Tens of thousands of firms had been challenged to show that they were legitimate and thousands were reported closed.

In 1988 there were over 290,000 companies in operation (or, equally good sources say, 470,000). Frequent directives notwithstanding, a large proportion of these companies are—or were—run by newly retired government officials with contacts, by working bureaucrats or their families, or by government agencies themselves, anxious to increase their income, bonuses and perquisites. In the absence of political will to support punishment, forcing these companies to comply with regulations is difficult, even for an enforcement bureau that may wish to do so, for someone in a well-connected firm may simply threaten an inspector by saying "You have the power to check up on me, but I have the power to remove you from your job." It remains to be seen if the latest attempts at reforms will be any more meaningful than the previous ones.

A "screening and rectification of business companies," said to be a close examination of all companies in China, began in October 1988 and received increasing publicity as discontent grew. By the fall of 1989 the government reported that about 145,000 companies had been examined; 18,000 companies run by Party and government organs were reportedly closed and 43,000 Party and government officials left either their commercial or official posts. As usual, however, despite this admitted widespread violation of repeated orders, only 800 officials were reported to have been punished, and many of those received only Party or government discipline.

As the examination continued, the government announced that in the last two months of 1989 it would disband "large numbers" of "unnecessary" companies. Closings or mergers will be forced on companies which, in the opinion of a committee headed by a vice-premier, are not meeting social needs; duplicate other services; have poor management; violate laws and regulations; or operate at a loss. The vague nature of some of these criteria, and the fact that the government itself has tens of thousands of large and small state-owned enterprises that have long operated at a loss despite the Enterprise Bankruptcy Law, suggests that not all criteria to be used have been revealed.

COMPETITION   Chinese economic and political theoreticians have worked for years to decide whether competition, the capitalist struggle to derive economic advantage from the sale of goods, also exists in commodity exchange under socialism. Communist theoreticians have held that competition is incompatible with the notion of socialist revolution, and that the apparent contests between socialist producers are really attempts to emulate one another with the objective of mutual help and common benefit. On the other hand, in the context of changes being made to promote the Four Modernizations, the Chinese concluded that since firms in a socialist environment are relatively independent, competition cannot be avoided, although its harmful effects can be. Competition is now regarded as a valuable aspect of the market mechanism which is being depended upon to stimulate and partly regulate China's economy. (Competition was made officially permissible in "Provisional Regulations on Developing and Protecting Socialist Competition," published by the State Council in 1980.)

CONNECTIONS   See *GUANXI*.

CONTRACT SYSTEM (OF EMPLOYMENT)   In reading the discussion of contract workers in the text (chapter 5, "Worker Responsibility Systems") non-socialists may well wonder, "What's so special about the contract system? Sounds just like going out and getting a job to me!" The Chinese, however, see significant *ideological* differences, as expressed in the following discussion based on a *People's Daily* article.

1. Capitalist workers do not own the materials of production, and the union of the workers' labor and the materials of production must be achieved through the selling of the workers' labor. In socialism, materials of production are owned in common. The socialist labor contract system is based on ownership in common of the materials of production, and the workers' union with them is achieved through united decision and arrangement.

2. The capitalist's goal is to use the workers' labor for profit beyond the price of the labor. Socialism's goal is to develop the workers' intelligence and abilities, arouse their positive spirit and creativity, and produce a daily increase in the wealth of society.

3. Under capitalism, the buyer and the bought embody a relation of exploiter to the exploited. Under the labor contract system of socialism, the two parties involved talk things over and sign a contract. They are equal in position. The worker is master in his own household. He must fulfill to the utmost his responsibilities and duties, but at the same time he enjoys the corresponding rights and privileges.

The labor contract system lumps responsibilities, rights, and interests into one package, the workers into a nation, and melts individual and collective labor into one. The system guarantees the worker the protection of equal rights and establishes the right relation between industry and labor and resolves the contradictions between the two parties effectively and in legal form. It helps to strengthen the worker's sense of responsibility as master in his own household and develops his positive attitude and his creativity.

This comparison obviously shows a very vague and abstract understanding of actual conditions in advanced capitalist nations. It is true, for example, that new hirings under capitalism are not necessarily preceded by formal negotiations and signing of individual contracts (and one suspects that isn't really the case in China, either), but in countries with legal systems more fully developed than China's there is already a body of employment law, and perhaps existing union contracts, which are included in the hiring process simply by their existence, even if they are not specifically mentioned.

COOPERATIVES   See COLLECTIVES AND COOPERATIVES; AGRICULTURAL COOPERATIVES; SUPPLY AND MARKETING COOPERATIVES.

COUNTERREVOLUTIONARY REBELLION This is now the government's usual term for referring to the Pro-Democracy Movement of 1989. It labels those people who participated in the movement as naive, villainous, or traitorous. The government claims that nearly all the millions of students, workers, intellectuals, peasants, and unemployed who demonstrated were manipulated by a "very, very few 'black hands'" (persons who worked behind the scenes) in an attempt to overthrow the government. *Counterrevolutionary* in Chinese code implies foreign involvement, and the government asserts that the movement was financed and directed by the United States, Hongkong, Taiwan, and others.

Among the many reports, analyses, and descriptions that have come from the government in its efforts to control Chinese and international perceptions of the bloody crackdown, one of the most concise and colorful characterizations of the movement is found in Deng Xiaoping's now-famous speech of June 9 to martial law commanders. He said that the problem began with "turmoil," and went on to say: "It was also inevitable that the turmoil would develop into a counterrevolutionary rebellion.... Actually, what we faced was not just some ordinary people who were misguided, but also a rebellious clique and a large quantity of the dregs of society. The key point is that they wanted to overthrow our state and the Party. Failing to understand this means failing to understand the nature of the matter."

CROWDED HOUSEHOLDS   Officially defined as households with less than four square meters (an area about 6.5 feet on a side) of living space per person.

CROWN PRINCES   Slang term referring to children of leading cadres who exploit their family connections in extravagant living, business activities, etc., and in general behave in a royal manner. Also has implications of possible succession to political power; many children of officials are in high positions, another object of severe public criticism.

CULTURAL REVOLUTION   John K. Fairbank, renowned China scholar and author of the standard history, *The United States and China*, opens his chapter on the period largely taken up by the Cultural Revolution this way: "The fifteen years from 1962 until Mao's death in September 1976 are the era in China's modern history that we can least understand, not only because it is too soon for definitive studies but also because the events seem so bizarre and confusing to us outside observers. (They confused people in China too.)"

As Fairbank indicates, ideas and concerns "that were to become the stuff of the Cultural Revolution" began appearing several years before the campaign was actually launched in 1966, though there is no indication that they were planned at the time to develop as they did.

During and immediately after the Great Leap period, Mao was opposed, sometimes almost unanimously, by Party leaders and long-term associates in his more xenophobic, anarchistic, anti-intellectual attitudes and formulations of problems. (Mao's judgment, and his contribution to the revolution, are considered to have begun their decline shortly before the Great Leap. According to the Party, his actions between liberation and his death were 70 percent good and 30 percent bad. Some feel the percentages should be reversed, but, until recently, official and public opinion have been fairly tolerant. In the year or two before the Pro-Democracy Movement there were books and articles, with official backing, strongly criticizing Mao, and there was even one suggestion that his portrait should be removed from Tiananmen Square in the center of the city. Mao's standing with the leadership which came to power during the crisis in 1989 can be inferred from the punishments given three men accused of throwing paint and eggs on the chairman's portrait during demonstrations: life imprisonment, twenty years, and sixteen years.)

Mao began to feel that the Party was losing its revolutionary zeal; that the older leaders, the senior bureaucrats, and leading intellectuals in science, culture, and education were becoming a privileged class; and that there was a threat that substantial elements of capitalism would return to Chinese life (as he felt had already occurred in the Soviet Union).

Most people believed that the need for class struggle (see separate entry) had essentially passed with the completion of land reform and socialist transformation of private enterprise in the fifties. However, Mao continued to see (as he had for years) a constant need for permanent, unrelenting, widespread—and sometimes violent—class struggle to combat the rise of a new bourgeoisie. A so-far milder version of this view has surfaced in the ultraleft rhetoric following the June Fourth Massacre.

He encouraged such class struggle in the Socialist Education Movement (see separate entry), which began in 1962 and was merged with the Cultural Revolution in 1966. During the same period, Mao's status as a demi-god was enhanced by the compilation of the "Little Red Book" containing hundreds of quotations from his speeches and writings. The book was an immediate sensation and strengthened the personality cult that was to make Mao even more formidable in days to come.

"The Great Proletarian Cultural Revolution," as the movement was called officially, was launched in a speech by Zhou Enlai at a huge May Day celebration in Beijing in 1966.

(*Cultural* in the name of the movement is an instance of the unfortunate translations sometimes encountered. The Chinese name of the movement includes the words *wen hua*, which have the connotation of culture in the very broadest sense, as when one speaks of Chinese *civilization*. The revolution was never thought of as being limited, as the English translation implies, to art, literature, music, etc.; the broader meaning is confirmed by the fact that the revolutionaries' demand for destruction of the "four olds" referred to old ideas, customs, and habits, as well as to old culture.)

The manifesto appeared a few days later in the "May 16

Circular," in which Mao set out his fears concerning a trend toward revisionism, the return of the bourgeoisie, the revival of the old feudalism and its values, and the other conditions he felt threatened the new socialism. The manifesto demanded that the country "expose our dark aspect openly, in an all-round way from below," proclaimed that "To rebel is justified!" and urged that the "four olds"—old ideas, old culture, old customs, and old habits—be destroyed.

Although commonly considered to have lasted for the ten years from May 1966 through October 1976 (ending with the death of Mao), the Cultural Revolution was not, in fact, carried out in the same manner and with the same intensity and turmoil throughout the entire ten years.

The period from May 1966 through the Ninth National Congress of the Communist Party of China in April 1969 was the most chaotic and saw the greatest damage and suffering. The Ninth Congress declared the revolution ended, but persecution, harassment, torture, unjust imprisonment, and murder continued throughout 1969–76. (It was again declared ended by the Eleventh Congress in August 1977.)

The 1966–69 period was the time when, according to a 1981 Party document, the people who later were called the "Gang of Four" exhorted the masses to "overthrow everything and wage full-scale civil war"; when "almost all leading Party and government departments . . . were stripped of their power or reorganized"; and when millions of murderous Red Guards aged from early teens to early twenties roamed the country ransacking, burning, and smashing everything intellectual, alien, official, or old they could find anywhere, from scholars' libraries to the foreign ministry.

Mao did not attempt to use the army to restore order until the fall of 1968. The Ninth Congress officially approved both the theories and practices of the Cultural Revolution, as did the Tenth Congress five years later. (The ultraleftists were still strong enough just six months before the revitalizing Third Plenum in 1978 to include a reference to "the triumphant conclusion of the First Great Proletarian Cultural Revolution" in the new national constitution. Even so, it probably would not have been credited at the time had anyone predicted the ultraleft had sufficient residual power—or even desire—to jump-start another era of repression as they did in 1989.)

The official verdict on Mao, and particularly his part in the Cultural Revolution, is given in the 1981 document quoted above, the "Resolution on Certain Questions in the History of Our Party since the Founding of the People's Republic of China," adopted by the Eleventh Central Committee in 1981. While it recognized Mao's contributions to the liberation of China and the People's Republic, which contributions were undoubtedly prodigious and unique, the resolution says: "The Cultural Revolution . . . was responsible for the most severe setbacks and the heaviest losses suffered by the Party, the state, and the people since the founding of the People's Republic. It was initiated and led by Comrade Mao Zedong. . . . Chief responsibility for the grave 'Left' error of the Cultural Revolution—an error comprehensive in magnitude and protracted in duration—does indeed lie with Comrade Mao Zedong. But, after all, it was the error of a great proletarian revolutionary . . . . In his later years, however, far from making a correct analysis of many problems, he confused right and wrong and the people with the enemy during the Cultural Revolution. . . . [He] imagined that his theory and practice were Marxist and that they were essential for the consolidation of the dictatorship of the proletariat. Herein lies his tragedy."

That is the political interpretation of the Cultural Revolution. And it reads well, seems to make sense, in political terms, given Mao's philosophy and fears.

But the Cultural Revolution was not a political movement—or not only a political movement: it was just what its name describes, a revolution. Among the activists, there were millions of people involved, ordinary people vilifying other ordinary people, one-time friends betraying each other, Chinese humiliating, wounding, and killing other Chinese.

And why? "How could this have happened?" those same millions of Chinese have asked. They know the political explanation, but what is the human explanation?

Years before his *Death of a Salesman* became a hit in Beijing, Arthur Miller traveled extensively in China. In 1979, he reported in the *Atlantic Monthly* a conversation with William Hinton, an agriculturist and noted author on Chinese topics who has worked in China for extended periods. One thing they talked about was the Cultural Revolution.

"It often happened, you know," Hinton said, "that they'd

suddenly come out of the hills. . . . "

"Who?"

"People. Thousands of them around a leader. A leader nobody's heard of before. A new warlord, young, sassy, who [didn't care] for anything or anybody—right out of some commune somewhere, and behind him his own staff, runners, arms, even concubines. Right out of the tenth century, including the contempt for the peasant, the kick in the teeth. . . . The worst of it was to see how quick they were to tear at each other, to humiliate anyone handy. . . .

"I did a study, *The Hundred Day War,* about the Cultural Revolution in one university, Qinghua. . . . What I found was that after the first weeks of struggle all questions of political principle really collapsed. What you finally had was simply a power fight between leaders. There was no moral or political content anymore, simply the egos. . . . "

Asked whether he thought he understood what had happened in China during the Cultural Revolution, Hinton simply said, "I do not. And I doubt anybody else does."

Most Chinese seem to feel the same way, and, strangely, even those who suffered severely are often unwilling to be very critical of Mao's role, or the government's or the Party's. Astonishing. As Lucian W. Pye put it in *The Mandarin and the Cadre,* "If people who were unjustly jailed for two decades will not criticize what was done to them, why should the authorities worry about the future? Truly it has been said that "Why?" is not a Chinese question."

As the tenth anniversary of Mao's death in 1976 and of the (second) official end of the Cultural Revolution in 1977 approached, a number of Chinese studies of the period were published, along with a number of foreign studies. Some writers were less tolerant of Mao than the Party resolution had been (and what was thought to be the best of the studies was suppressed) but even so more than one raised such questions about personal culpability as, "Shouldn't we take some of the responsibility also? Why did some of us care less about the fate of the country and its people than about our own personal gains and losses?" And another said, "Young people in West Germany in the 1960s once asked their parents: 'What were you doing during the Nazi years?' We who experienced the 'cultural revolution' may well ask ourselves: 'What were we doing then?' "

Of course, there is no one answer as to "Why?" there was a Cultural Revolution, but it seems certain Mao's fears and machinations were central to the whole drama. "How?" it could have happened is speculated on by ex-Red Guardsman Liang Heng in *After the Nightmare:* "To my mind, there was a long list of complex contributing factors: thousands of years of feudal tradition of obedience to authority; the Communist Party's tight control of us; the many years of emphasis on political movements, which made us well-practiced machines for criticism/self-criticism; the special privileges and abuses of power by the new Party elite, which elicited our envy and thirst for revenge; the lack of routes for expressing discontent and appealing injustices, which made us feel so bottled up inside; Mao's taste for categorizing people as members of ranked classes, exacerbating tensions . . . [and] of course, the struggles within the Party leadership over which road to socialism China should follow contributed to Mao's own paranoiac and desperate acts. But no matter which of these factors was most important, it seemed clear to me that as they flowed together tragedy was inevitable."

DANWEI   See UNIT.

DEMOCRACY   See SOCIALIST DEMOCRACY.

DEMOCRACY WALL   With the death of Mao and arrest of the Gang of Four in 1976 and subsequent events indicating that the long repression was lifting, there began to grow throughout China an increasingly outspoken concern with injustices of the past and with destroying bureaucracy and democratizing the government in the future. The discussions were particularly intense in the larger cities, most of all in Beijing.

Along with lectures, discussion groups, mimeographed magazines, and other means of spreading ideas, "big character" wall posters appeared. The best-known location was a highly visible wall on Changan Avenue slightly west of Tiananmen Square that came to be known as "Democracy Wall" and became the symbol of the entire movement.

By late 1978, however, the ferment was becoming troublesome to the authorities and various steps were taken to discourage meetings and attendance at the wall. In March 1979 Deng Xiaoping stated that the quest for democracy was being used to obscure counterrevolutionary intentions. He enunciated the Four Cardinal Principles of Socialism (see separate entry), which principles he insisted must govern any change whatsoever.

Several key figures in Beijing and elsewhere were arrested and imprisoned. Wei Jingsheng, an electrician who was a leader of the movement and author of the eloquent poster titled "The Fifth Modernization: Democracy," was sentenced to fifteen years in 1979, and numerous others are still in custody. Posters were limited to a single inconspicuous location controlled by police, and by late April the movement was essentially stopped.

DEMOCRATIC CENTRALISM   The principle upon which the Communist Party of China is organized. According to its constitution, the Party "practices a high degree of centralism on the basis of a high degree of democracy." The basic principles of democratic centralism as described by the constitution are:

1. Individual Party members are subordinate to the Party organization, the minority is subordinate to the majority, the lower Party organizations are subordinate to the higher Party organizations, and *all the constituent organizations and members of the Party are subordinate to the National Congress and the Central Committee of the Party* [emphasis supplied].

2. The Party's leading bodies at all levels are elected.

3. The highest leading body of the Party is the National Congress and the Central Committee elected by it.

4. Higher Party organizations shall pay constant attention to the views of the lower organizations and the rank-and-file Party members, and solve in good time the problems they raise. The same responsibilities devolve upon lower Party organizations. Higher and lower units exchange information with and supervise each other.

5. Party committees at all levels function on the principle of combining collective leadership with individual responsibility based on division of labor. All major issues shall be decided upon by the Party committees after democratic discussion.

6. The Party shall forbid all forms of personality cult.

DEMOCRATIC PARTIES   See POLITICAL PARTIES.

DICTATORSHIP OF THE PROLETARIAT   See PEOPLE'S DEMOCRATIC DICTATORSHIP.

DOUBLE HUNDRED POLICY   See HUNDRED FLOWERS POLICY.

ENEMIES OF THE PEOPLE   Intellectuals, being given to independent thinking, had a particularly difficult time in China under Mao and continue to be viewed with suspicion or downright enmity even to the present day. (See "Hundred Flowers Policy" and "Bourgeois

Liberalization.") The pervasive denigration was typified by their treatment during the Cultural Revolution, when they were called "the stinking number nine" category among enemies of the people. The other eight were landlords, rich peasants, counterrevolutionaries, bad elements, rightists, renegades, enemy agents, and capitalist roaders.

FAST FOODS   Currently, the Chinese use this term differently from the west. It is applied to "fast-to-serve" prepared foods such as pastries, instant noodles, and precooked meats which can be put on the table quickly at home.

An example of the western meaning reached China in 1987, however, when America's Kentucky Fried Chicken (a subsidiary of PepsiCo Inc.) opened a three-story, 500-seat restaurant costing US$1 million south of Tiananmen Square. It is said to be the largest fast food restaurant in the world. Eight more KFCs are planned by 1990 (and other foreign firms are reportedly making China plans too). A meal consisting of two pieces of chicken, cole slaw, mashed potatoes, bread, and drink costs about thirteen yuan (US$3.00, around 10 percent of an average month's pay). The new spirit shown by some in China was displayed by one young customer who said, "It's only too expensive if you don't like it." Enough people liked it to make the Beijing KFC outlet the leader in 1988 sales among all the chain's 7,700 stores.

An agreement was announced in 1989 with another American fast food operator, New York Pizza Corporation, to open a joint venture New York City Pizza restaurant in early 1990. Like KFC, it will be unusually large for a fast food restaurant, seating about 600, and will be in the center of the downtown business district. There's some question, however, about how far franchised western fast food stores will go—or be permitted. Like KFC and New York Pizza, any future investors are likely to want a joint venture with the Chinese, requiring Chinese capital, producing no foreign exchange, and contributing nothing in the way of advanced technology that would be useful in China's modernization.

FECs   See FOREIGN EXCHANGE CERTIFICATES.

FIVE GOODS FAMILY   The five "goods" required of a family are diligent work and study; consideration for the family members as well as neighbors; careful family planning and attention to children's education; observance of law and discipline; and courteous public behavior.

FIVE GUARANTEES SYSTEM   Elderly people who have no children to support them (a constitutional obligation of living children) are assured that their collective or the state will provide five necessities—food, clothing, medical care, housing, and burial expenses.

FIVE STRESSES   Personal qualities stressed are decorum, manners, good hygiene, individual discipline, and high morals.

FIVE-YEAR PLANS   Like other socialist countries—and nearly all large corporations—China makes five-year plans to summarize its goals and guide its actions. Five years being a long time, whether for a government or a business, plans done so far in advance are subject to changes or outright calamities that work against their achievement in the original form, especially in such a volatile environment as China. The first plan, 1953–57, and the sixth, 1981–85, were generally successful, and are the only ones that have been of much significance.

The second, 1958–62, was in effect for only about a year before it was rendered inoperative by the Great Leap Forward (see separate entry). The years between the Great Leap and the Cultural Revolution, 1963–65, are called a period of economic readjustment, and there was no plan. The third, 1966–70, was aborted by the Cultural Revolution (see separate entry). The fourth, 1971–75, contained elements ideologically offensive to the Gang of Four (see separate entry), who essentially derailed it.

The seventh, 1986–90, focuses on continuation or consolidation of all reforms, technological improvement of existing facilities, strengthening of education, and improvement of the quality of people's lives. Overall growth of the gross national product was expected to be about 7.5 percent, a little less than in recent years. Three years into the current plan the growth target was being exceeded by over 30 percent and threatening to engulf the entire reform movement before cutbacks began late in 1988.

FOREIGN EXCHANGE CERTIFICATES (FECs)   The government announced in April 1986 that FECs, a special currency put into circulation in 1980 to combat a currency black market, would no longer be used, effective at some uncertain date in the future. FECs are issued in the same denominations as the domestic currency, *renminbi* (or "street money," as foreigners often call it). Foreigners receive only FECs when converting currency or travelers checks, and are expected to pay for airplane tickets, hotels, taxis, and virtually everything else with them. Since December 1989 only half of a departing traveler's unused FECs are reconvertible into foreign currency; *renminbi* have never been convertible.

The black market in convertible foreign currencies (primarily Hongkong and US dollars) was never very much affected by the FECs, and in recent years there has been a growing black market for the FECs themselves.

Also, the original rules have been changed to allow Chinese to spend FECs (which means they can buy scarce imported and luxury goods available only with FECs), on the theory that the FECs have been secured legally as a result of gifts of foreign currencies from relatives abroad or in other limited ways. The advantages of FECs mean that they can be sold to furtive money changers on the street for 30 to 40 percent above face value—and often for more. (Today, the increasingly sophisticated money changers will deal in US dollar currency and yen notes, too.) As in all countries with currency controls, however, succumbing to the muttered "Change money?" is illegal and perhaps dangerous.

Not much can be done with *renminbi*, however. Even foreign experts working for Chinese organizations, who are paid in *renminbi* and provided with "white cards" authorizing them to spend *renminbi* as they would FECs, have frequent difficulties with hotels, cabs, restaurants, and stores, which are just as anxious to get FECs as the money changers.

The Chinese feel the situation is detrimental to the country's sovereignty and prestige and decided in mid-1986 to end the two-currency system before the end of the year, but there was no further announcement and no change. In mid-1987 a vice-premier said, "The projected abolishment was postponed because many at home and abroad believed that it would give rise to new problems. The future of the FEC is still under study."

FOUR BIG FREEDOMS   More popularly known just as the "Four Bigs," these freedoms are the right to speak out freely, air views freely, hold big debates, and write big-character posters (for public display). They first came into existence during the Anti-Rightist Campaign in the late 1950s (see "Hundred Flowers Policy"), and were made by the Red Guards into a political slogan of nationwide power during the Cultural Revolution (see separate entry). As supposed unrestrained "rights," the Four Bigs were abused by both the Red Guards and ultraleftists during that period to such an extent that they became one of the major underlying theoretical premises supporting the personal slandering and defamation of the time. Following the Cultural Revolution the Chinese constitution was revised to include the Four Bigs. Deng Xiaoping argued in late 1979 that these rights were being abused in such a way as to "hamper the Four Modernizations, democracy, and the legal system." They were abolished at the 1980 National People's Congress and omitted from the 1982 constitution.

FOUR BIGS   See FOUR BIG FREEDOMS; THREE BIGS.

FOUR CARDINAL PRINCIPLES OF SOCIALISM   Also called the "Four Upholds," the principles are: Adherence to 1) the socialist road, 2) the people's democratic dictatorship (i.e., the dictatorship of the proletariat), 3) the leadership of the Communist Party, and 4) Marxism-Leninism and Mao Zedong Thought. The principles were first enunciated by Deng Xiaoping in 1979 in the aftermath of the Democracy Wall movement and were based on similar historic ideas; they were quickly added to the constitution in June 1979. They assumed fresh importance when broadly used in 1987 in the campaign to oppose bourgeois liberalization (see separate entry) and in 1989 as a key element in the justification for the repression of the Pro-Democracy Movement.

FOUR OLDS   See CULTURAL REVOLUTION.

FOUR POINTS OF BEAUTY   Beauty rests on beautification of mind, language, behavior, and environment.

FOUR UPHOLDS   See FOUR CARDINAL PRINCIPLES OF SOCIALISM.

FREE MARKETS   After being closed during the Cultural Revolution in 1979, retail markets variously called *free markets, rural fairs,* etc., were re-established both in the countryside and in the cities, where peasants came to sell produce from their private plots and other local products and handicrafts (see "Household Sidelines"). Prices higher than those at state shops ("negotiated prices") could be charged if conditions warranted. This gave peasants greater incentive to produce needed supplies. Today, under the policies that allow peasants to sell above-contract (still sometimes called "above-quota") agricultural products and to engage in other forms of private business, more than 70,000 free markets (only about 10,000 of them in cities) attract dealers in consumer goods of all kinds. Prices are higher in free markets than in state shops—sometimes considerably higher—but the quality of agricultural products is better and the attitude toward customers among independent stall keepers is infinitely more friendly. Also, free markets may have products state shops do not, partly because peasants sometimes refuse to honor contracts they have made with the state earlier in the season if they can sell their products at higher prices in the markets, and because entrepreneurs search out new products and small supplies of scarce ones. It is understandable that urban free markets now sell more agricultural and handicraft products than state-owned shops.

No less a voice than *Economic Daily* has suggested that *flea markets* should be added to commodity circulation channels, predicting that there would be a ready supply of second-hand goods offered by those who are becoming richer, and a ready market among those not yet quite so rich who could nevertheless afford second-hand items they could not buy new.

FROM THE MASSES, TO THE MASSES   Slogan describing the method for "following the mass line," the theoretical method of implementing the people's democratic dictatorship. "From the masses" refers to taking rudimentary, unformulated ideas from the masses for consideration by the Party; "to the masses" means concentrating and systematizing these ideas and then, as Mao put it, to "go to the masses and propagate and explain these ideas until the masses embrace them as their own."

GANG OF FOUR   Closely linked with the Cultural Revolution (see separate entry) is the notorious "Gang of Four," which was considered responsible for many of China's problems in the late sixties and early seventies. The four were Jiang Qing (Mao's wife), Zhang Chunqiao, Wang Hongwen, and Yao Wenyuan. Due to her special relationship with Mao, Jiang Qing was elevated to high Party status at the start of the Cultural Revolution. The other three rose under her patronage. About a month after Mao's death in 1976, the four, along with six associates, were arrested.

At their trial beginning late in 1980, the group was charged with committing a wide variety of crimes from 1966 until shortly before their arrest. The indictment charged that "The Lin Biao and Jiang Qing Counterrevolutionary Cliques committed the following crimes:

"1. Frame-up and persecution of Party and state leaders and plotting to overthrow the political power of the dictatorship of the proletariat.

"2. The persecution and suppression of large numbers of cadres and masses.

"3. Plotting to assassinate Chairman Mao Zedong and engineer an armed counterrevolutionary *coup d'état.*

"4. Plotting armed rebellion in Shanghai."

These and other actions are seen as prolonging the damaging unrest and strife of the early Cultural Revolution, and thereby damaging China in a multitude of ways.

Early in 1981, Jiang and Zhang were sentenced to death with a two-year reprieve, upon the expiration of which the sentences of both were changed to life imprisonment. The other two received lengthy sentences, along with the six associates. One died of illness in 1983. In recent years, rumors have circulated that some of the group have committed suicide, that Jiang Qing was living in poor health in a Beijing villa, and that others would soon be released. The government denied them all.

GREAT LEAP FORWARD   By mid-1957, shortly before the Great Leap Forward began, land reform and socialist transformation of most private enterprises had been accomplished. The First Five-Year Plan had been completed with satisfactory success. Continued steady, if not spectacular, progress seemed entirely possible.

For some reason not entirely clear, however, the government (and apparently Mao in particular) felt some compulsion to achieve a dramatic advance in economic development at that time. Specialists in Chinese affairs themselves differ in their perspectives on the forces behind the Great Leap Forward.

One good source says that agricultural stagnation had prevented government grain collection from keeping pace with the rapidly growing population, and fast economic growth was essential. Another says that the amount of food available in 1957 was about 15 percent per person above the 1950 level, and gives no role to agricultural problems in stimulating the Great Leap. A third source, by a Chinese author, points out that Party policy before the beginning of the Leap was "guarding against both conservatism and rash advance," and opines that the Great Leap occurred simply because Mao and other Party leaders "thought that since they had defeated the powerful Kuomintang by mobilizing the masses they could build socialism by simply using the same method." Some think Mao wished to work more rapidly toward extreme collectivization and be able to thumb his nose more convincingly at foreigners by achieving industrial self-sufficiency.

For whatever reason, the Party, beginning early in 1958, launched the heady, radical, inspiring, and catastrophic Great Leap Forward, a movement calculated, to cite one slogan of the time, to "Overtake and surpass Britain within fifteen years in the output of steel and other important products!" Other slogans were more memorable and emotional, such as "Dare to storm the heavens!"

There are indications in Mao's speeches and writings that his original intentions may not have been so grandiose, or at least that he had expected they would be rationalized by his planners and administrators. Instead, he felt, the bureaucrats had disapproved of and feared the scope of the changes he sought and allowed the campaign to get out of hand and fail. His dissatisfaction with their conservatism was later to be reflected in his attempts to shake up the country through the Cultural Revolution.

Whatever Mao's intentions, however, in John K. Fairbank's words the result "was a mighty paroxysm of round-the-clock labor. The face of the country was changed with new roads, factories, cities, dikes, dams, lakes, afforestation, and new cultivation, for which 650 millions of Chinese had been mobilized in nationwide efforts of unparalleled intensity and magnitude." In the single year of 1959, to celebrate the tenth anniversary of the founding of the republic, the citizens of Beijing built the enormous Great Hall of the People—and nine other buildings nearly as large.

But, just as there was great progress there was also great waste, great expense, and near exhaustion. Crops failed because of weather and for other reasons, and problems in the countryside multiplied because of the unwieldy, huge communes formed throughout the country with little forethought in just a few months in 1958–59. (See separate entry under "People's Communes.") Egalitarianism was the order of the day, and incentive was a dirty word. The steel that was made in hundreds of thousands of makeshift furnaces was useless, and much new construction was of poor quality. Government administration was in chaos, and statistics were falsified wildly (see Appendix I). Tens of thousands of "schools" begun with mostly wretched facilities and incompetent teachers were abandoned. By the end of 1959, what Frank K. M. Su has called "a romantic period in China's socialist construction" was over. Its wisdom and consequences are still debated.

GREAT PROLETARIAN CULTURAL REVOLUTION   See CULTURAL REVOLUTION.

GREAT WALL   Ever since China opened to tourism, the Great Wall has been a major attraction. For most of this period, visits to the wall have been concentrated on a single restored section at Badaling, about 50 kilometers from Beijing. A 1984 announcement had 1.3 million people visiting the wall that year and another announcement claimed 5 million in 1985, an unlikely increase but suggestive of the large crowds that undoubtedly do visit. Anyone who has been there can almost believe that at peak times there are four tourists per square meter of wall and that the brick pavement must be replaced in some areas every three years!

The crowds at Badaling are not so great now, however, though certainly large; additional sections of the wall are being restored, partly through a fund-raising campaign called "Love the Motherland and Repair the Great Wall," and several new sites are now open.

There are enough descriptions of this monument to human effort and endurance so that the usual details need not be repeated here. There is one commonly mentioned "fact" that does need correction, however—the oft-heard statement that "The Great Wall of China is the only man-made object visible from the moon." China has enough distinctions that it can get along without this one, which, contrary to the official Trivial Pursuit answer and some other statements, simply isn't true. (The assertion apparently stems from a remark by US President Richard Nixon during his 1972 visit.)

American astronaut Alan Bean wrote to a newspaper columnist who raised the question, saying that "The only thing you can see from the moon is a beautiful sphere—mostly white (clouds), some blue (ocean), patches of yellow (deserts), and every once in a while some green vegetation. No man-made object is visible on this scale. In fact, when first leaving earth's orbit and only a few thousands miles away, no man-made object is visible at that point, either."

GUANXI (*Gwan-shee*) The embodiment of the great importance of personal and family relationships in China, this term translates as "a relationship or connection" but in practice the meaning is much broader. It might be described as a "network of personal relationships based on kinship, loyalty, and mutual obligation"; there may be an element of shared experience or hardship—or an element of bribery.

A great deal is accomplished in China through *guanxi*. It is the embodiment of "who one knows" (sometimes, "who one knows who knows someone," etc., etc.) or the Asian equivalent of the west's "old-boy network," but in some ways it is stronger than either. When one hears of accomplishing something through the "back door," it is often something done through *guanxi*, even if gifts are also involved.

HOUSEHOLD SIDELINES   Rural families are extensively engaged in the spare time farming of private plots, land assigned to grow products for their own use or for sale at rural markets. Depending on circumstances, they may also raise chickens or pigs, tend orchards, do weaving or tailoring, produce handicrafts, etc. Private plots were formerly limited to five percent of the arable land in a unit, but the limit (not usually reached) has been raised in recent years to about fifteen percent, and private plots provide a significant proportion of the agricultural products available to consumers.

HUKOU   See RESIDENCE REGISTRATION.

HUNDRED FLOWERS POLICY   The name comes from a slogan of May 1956, "Let one hundred flowers bloom, let one hundred schools of thought contend"—in other words, let there be a free discussion of many points of view. (The Chinese also refer to this as the "Double Hundred" policy.) It is not, however, by any means, a policy allowing freedom of speech in the western sense.

The abridged history of the policy is this: Never having received the esteem of the government or the Party, by 1956 China's intellectuals (academics, scientists, professionals, artists, writers, etc.) were estranged even more because of 1954–55 ideological campaigns in which tens of thousands of their number had been jailed for suspected counterrevolutionary tendencies and tens of thousands of others had been stripped of their rights. It was necessary for the government to find a way to allow some venting of the discontent and to attempt to bring the special skills of intellectuals into the socialist construction effort.

In a series of speeches and papers by Mao and others, beginning in February 1956, the Hundred Flowers slogan was used repeatedly, and was given its most complete elaboration in May, now regarded as its birthmonth. On countless occasions thereafter intellectuals were urged to speak their minds without fear. As might be expected, most intellectuals were extremely wary of such a change in attitude, and the policy evoked only a limited response for a number of months.

In late April 1957, however, there began a Party rectification campaign, in which frank public comment was again urged, to improve the Party's practices and manner of working. This time the public took quite seriously the invitation to comment. It appears either that no one, least of all Mao, was prepared for the storm of criticism that outside scholars believe broke, or that, as the "Resolution on Party History" of 1981 maintains, only a few people made strong criticisms but that Mao saw those few as members of a vast conspiracy of "bourgeois rightists" who had to be put down.

In any case, the period of actively letting a hundred schools of thought contend lasted only about five weeks. On June 8 *People's Daily* ran an editorial titled "Why All This?" The slogan "Let a Hundred Flowers Bloom" was replaced by "Without the Communist Party There Would Be No People's Republic!" The Double Hundred was dead.

To deal with the supposed threat, an Anti-Rightist Campaign was launched in 1957 which is now considered by the Chinese to be infamous. According to a 1989 issue of *Newspaper and Journal Digest*, more than 550,000 alleged enemies of the Party were stigmatized; thousands were executed and hundreds of thousands sent to the countryside to do manual labor. Many were not rehabilitated (see separate entry) or allowed to hold jobs for as long as twenty-two years, until after the Third Plenum. As of 1989, however, all except 95 had been rehabilitated, causing a pro-Beijing Hongkong paper to comment, "The tiny percentage of 'survivals' (less than 0.00018 percent) is certainly proof of the gross injustice of the 1957 trauma."

As might be expected, the events of 1956–57 "seriously dampened the enthusiasm of the intellectuals," as the Chinese say, and, more importantly, basically closed all channels of constructive criticism from outside the Party. A *Beijing Review* writer said in 1986 that "The vigor that prevailed in China's scientific circles in 1956 has never resurfaced." Some analysts believe Mao's experiences with intellectuals in 1956 forever set his existing prejudices against them and were responsible in part for the Great Leap Forward and the Cultural Revolution.

May 1986 was the thirtieth anniversary of the Hundred Flowers policy. As in 1956, it was urgent to inspire more energetic participation in national life and work by intellectuals, whose enthusiasm is seen to be still dampened by earlier persecutions. The anniversary was observed with meetings, articles, interviews, reminiscences, speeches—in many cases sounding as though the Hundred Flowers policy has been in effect all along even if, most unfortunately, it was sometimes clumsily applied or sabotaged by enemies of the intellectuals. Everyone proclaimed the need to renew the Double Hundred and all offered firm assurances—even extravagant assurances, in the light of history and later events—that things would be different from then on.

Hu Yaobang, then Party secretary, defended on a number of occasions the right to divergent views. *Guangming Daily*, the Party cultural publication, carried an article asserting that "Participants in a debate should bow only to the truth and not blindly follow an 'authoritarian view,' " and maintaining that "a leader's opinion is just one of many." A rising young minister encouraged academics in Shanghai to become the "think tank of the Party."

Others tried to deal with the obviously difficult question of how broadly the Double Hundred principle can be applied. For example, Lu Dingyi, a major proponent of the policy in 1956, wrote in *People's Daily* in 1986 that he believes the principle applies in art and science, but should not be applied in politics. Another *People's Daily* writer disagreed, saying that in the social sciences one can hardly draw a line between academic and political questions, and if there were to be such a line then it would be the end of political science.

However, stressing the importance of freedom of speech, *Worker's Daily* made the really crucial point that in any area whatever "No one will speak his mind if errors in speech or writings are considered unpardonable." Unfortunately for the Hundred Flowers and for the country, China's intellectuals (no matter which way the political winds are blowing) have far less assurance than do their counterparts in most other countries of protection against vicious partisan persecution if offense is given by an honest opinion.

An intellectual who has suffered in the frequent shifts in official attitudes said in *Asiaweek* that " . . . the [Hundred Flowers] policy has been put into action and discarded so many times that few are interested any more. It remains a policy of the Communist Party. The Party can grant it today and withdraw it tomorrow." Su Shaozhi, himself punished in the 1987 campaign by dismissal from his post as director of the Institute of Marxism-Leninism (and who escaped from China after being placed on the government's most-wanted list in June 1989), has pointed out the hypocrisy of the Double Hundred policy, citing thirty-four different mass criticisms, i.e., general Party condemnations of differing views, that have been carried out in natural science since 1949 and many more in social science.

Needless to say, there has been no discussion of letting even two schools of thought contend since May 19, 1989, when the conservatives again shut down debate, this time by imposing martial law. The Hundred Flowers concept can never again be a credible basis for intellectuals' cooperation under any of the present government or Party leaders, severely damaging though this well-earned distrust will be.

IDEOLOGICAL AND POLITICAL WORK   In the wake of the conservative takeover there have been numerous charges that reformers have "neglected ideological and political work" and exhortations that "ideological and political work must be improved." What does this obviously important phrase mean?

In 1982 Hu Yaobang made a speech titled "Problems Relating to Ideological and Political Work." The late Hu, of course, fell from favor partly because he failed in the eyes of the elders to pay proper attention to ideological and political work, but what he had to say still seems to be a good summary of the concept: "Our expertise in doing good ideological and political work is an important distinguishing characteristic between ours and other political parties; it is an extremely important precondition for winning victory in revolution and construction. . . .

"The targets of ideological and political work are people, they are people's thinking, viewpoints, and standpoints. Its objective is to solve problems connected to people's thinking, viewpoints, and political standpoints, to mobilize the cadres and the broad masses to struggle and strive to carry out the present and long-term goal of revolution. . . . The most fundamental task of ideological and political work is, in one sentence, to heighten people's understanding of the world and their ability to improve it."

Put another way, it might be said that ideological and political work involves using reasoning and rhetoric—rather than coercion and force—to persuade the population to support the Party's vision of socialism and to generate enthusiasm for Party programs and policies.

INCONVENIENT HOUSEHOLDS   Defined as households with all members of the family living in one room, especially a married couple living with parents and/or adult children, although living conditions may not be officially crowded. (See separate entry under "Crowded Households.")

IRON RICE BOWL   Jobs in state enterprises, offices, and institutions have long been preferred over jobs with collectives or private enterprises. This is true not only because of the prestige and better benefits but because, until economic reform began, every worker in a state-owned enterprise had job security for life, regardless of how well he or she did the job. (State jobs are now less attractive, because state workers and cadres are falling behind in wages and new employees no longer have job security.) Therefore, the worker was said to have an "iron rice bowl," an indestructible source of livelihood. (Also see entry on "Replacement System.")

The corollary to the worker's attitude was the feeling of managers of state-owned enterprises that the enterprise itself had an "iron rice bowl," that the state would take full responsibility for the debts of the enterprise, and thus that financial failure was impossible. Under economic reform, even state enterprises will take increasing responsibility for their profits and losses. A similar concept is the "ceramic rice bowl," which refers to the financial responsibility local authorities formerly had for enterprises owned by the collective.

JOINT STATE-PRIVATE OWNERSHIP   See SOCIALIST TRANSFORMATION.

LABOR POINTS   See WORK POINTS.

LABOR TRADE   China has a thriving export market in labor. In 115 countries, primarily in Asia, Africa, and the Middle East, China provides about 60,000 engineers, technicians, and manual laborers to build railways, bridges, dams, power stations, etc. It also sends nurses, chefs, drivers, sailors, sports coaches, agricultural experts, and other workers for service trades overseas. Its international China State Construction and Engineering Corporation is the world's sixtieth largest contractor. Much of the foreign construction by Chinese is in the nature of foreign aid financed by China. (China's workers are only a small portion of total workers in the worldwide labor trade.)

LAND REFORM   One of the major goals of the revolution was freeing the Chinese peasant from the domination of feudal landlords by taking land from the landlord and giving it to the peasant. The Communists began implementing the policy of "land to the tiller" in mid-1946 throughout individual areas as they won control of them, at one stroke freeing the peasants and gaining enthusiastic supporters in both liberated and unliberated areas. The Land Reform Law was proclaimed in June 1950 and was essentially completed by late 1952. In total, more than 300 million peasants received over 700 million *mu* (about 120 million acres) of land.

LANE COMMITTEES   See RESIDENTS' COMMITTEES.

LAW OF VALUE   This term is frequently encountered, but rarely in a context that enables it to be understood. *China's Economic Reforms* gives this definition: "The law of value means that the value of a commodity is determined by the socially necessary labor time required to produce it and that the exchange of commodities must be based on an exchange of equal amounts of value. Socially necessary labor time refers to the labor time needed to produce a certain kind of use value under the normal conditions of social production at a given time, at an average degree of labor skill and intensity." No one seems to know whether this formulation allows for assigning value to any component of production other than labor.

Knowledgeable people have said that what the Chinese translate as *law of value* is another term for what the west calls the *law of supply and demand*. This seems to be confirmed by uncommon statements such as the following, which uses the term in relation to concrete circumstances: Reviewing a period when farming supplies were short and their prices soared, and how prices for vegetables rose when they became scarce because of freeze losses, an official said, "Understanding of the law of value is important in both cities and countryside. [All need to understand] that prices can rise as well as fall. All this rising and falling is just the movement of the law of value."

LEFT/RIGHT   The definition of *left* and *right* in China is probably even fuzzier than elsewhere. China-watcher David Bonavia wrote that "both these terms have been virtually stripped of their meaning by their indiscriminate application in the interests of factionalism." Certainly, the meanings are now scrambled; for example, the leftists of yesterday who favored bold, dramatic moves are the conservatives of today who complain that reform is going too far, too fast. Leftists favored extreme decentralization in the Great Leap period, but today, as conservatives, oppose the extent to which central authority has been relaxed and are attempting to reassert it.

However, since the terms are so common in Chinese life and literature it might be worthwhile to list some of the characteristics, tendencies, preferences, etc., that are, or have been, attributed to the two sides, factions, points of view, or whatever they are.

Many characteristics of "right" and "left" are relative, ambiguous, or merely epithetical, and their evaluation is often a subjective matter, but these purported tendencies are suggestive. ("Right" and "Left" are themselves considered simplistic by some. There is further discussion of factions and points of view in "Who's Wearing the White Hat?" in chapter 2.)

Leftists

. . . Are devoted to orthodox Marxism, Leninism, and Mao Zedong Thought

. . . Are revolutionary

. . . Believe perpetual class struggle is a necessity until the final stage of revolution (i.e., communism) is achieved

. . . Place strong political control ahead of all other considerations, including modernization and growth

. . . Claim to rely on wisdom of the masses

. . . Emphasize practical education, with stress on ideology

. . . Favor putting all social and economic activity on a collective basis

. . . Believe the only function of press, television, and other media is to support Party doctrine and programs

Rightists

. . . Consider Marxism and other orthodoxies to be subject to revision or correction in the light of experience and practicalities

. . . Make revolution subordinate, after socialism is achieved, to material growth and modernization

. . . Recognize that Chinese socialism did not develop from a capitalist society, as Marx had envisioned, and therefore believe China is in the primary stage of socialism and needs to incorporate useful economic elements of capitalism; this was adopted as Party doctrine in 1987 but never fully embraced by leftists

. . . Believe the need for class struggle essentially ends with the achievement of socialism

. . . Emphasize academic education, with politics in secondary role

. . . Permit individualism within collectivization for mutual benefit of individual and society

. . . Are willing to accept some "supervision" (see index) of Party and government by mass media as long as it does not threaten Party supremacy

LEGAL SYSTEM   China, ruled for millennia by emperors, warlords, and exploiting politicians, has no tradition of rule by law rather than by men, and her future growth and stability are to a considerable extent dependent on the development of such a tradition. Party and government leaders have on many occasions recognized the importance of the rule of law and the need to observe it. The Party's disregard of the rule of law in its maneuvering to crush the students in 1989 inflicted grave damage on China's attempts to conduct its national life by laws rather than the whims or ukases of authoritarian leaders. It also contributed to its foreign image as a sometimes unpredictable and willful partner.

There is no need here to go into how the Chinese legal system differs from that of many western countries. The extent of the difference can be indicated by the fact that, for example, there is no presumption of innocence at a trial (just the opposite, in fact, because preliminary investigation is supposed to have already established the need for having a trial); there are no rules of evidence; there is no independent judiciary; and there is no expectation that a judicial decision will necessarily be made according to precedents offered by similar cases.

China did not get around to a formal criminal code of any kind until 1979, expressed in the Criminal Procedure Law and the Criminal Law. As will be seen, no one has the power—or even the responsibility—to really enforce it, and it is therefore not very carefully observed. Further, within three or four years, the laws were so altered by "special provisions" and amendments for "serious situations" that the state is virtually unhampered in what it can do while still claiming to observe the law.

China has about 30,000 lawyers (about 1 per 300,000 persons, as disproportionate as the US's 1 per 500), and the number continues to grow rapidly. Lawyers are relied on increasingly by businesses which never gave a thought to legal representation in the past, and previously unrepresented criminal defendants are claimed to now have lawyers, for what they may be worth, in perhaps three out of four cases.

Having a lawyer is perhaps better than not having one, but all lawyers are government cadres, "state legal workers," who are expected to serve the state, the Party, and "the people" rather than their clients, and are not expected or allowed to assert their clients' interests through an adversarial or advocatory presentation.

There is a presumption throughout the whole system that legal officials will be honest, thorough, impartial, and fair, but there are no controls over judges or prosecutors to prevent them from being politically manipulated, and it is acknowledged that there is political interference in judicial decisions. For political or other reasons, "It is not unique for a court verdict to be already bound into the file before a lawyer even makes a defense," according to a leading lawyer quoted in *China Daily*. This was confirmed by a recent article by a judge in *Democracy and Law* magazine in which he said that "The practice of conviction before trial still exists in China. It makes no sense, has no legal basis, and should be ended."

It has been next to impossible for a citizen, or another government body, to get a governmental unit into court. "Their refusal to appear in court and defiance of court rulings that are not in their favor are not unusual." This situation is changing, however. A special administrative division has been set up in people's courts to try to deal with lawsuits against government departments, and the 1989 National People's Congress passed an Administrative Litigation Law under which "common people can accuse officials." What the people can accuse them of is rather closely limited by the law, however, and they cannot challenge even outrageous decisions that are not clearly illegal. Also, though the law states that the government may not interfere with the courts, it does not prohibit or even discourage interference with the court by the Communist Party, despite attempts by some to secure such a provision. A Beijing University law professor said in the outspoken (and now muzzled) *World Economic Herald:* "The reason [China should have] such a law is not because government organs need protection but because it is just the reality of daily life that administrative organs do violate the rights of citizens." Whether government organs can or will be forced to obey the law remains to be seen.

It was only at the 1986 National People's Congress that what is considered the nation's legal "framework" was completed. How bare the structure still is, however, can be judged from the fact that in 1988 a government official pointed out that among many laws still missing were a private enterprise law, a maritime law, an investment law, a company law, a labor law, a law on rural enterprises, laws governing administrative proceedings and public servants, and laws underpinning an appeal system to protect citizens' legal rights and freedoms."

Chinese laws and regulations are shorter, less detailed and specific, and give wider latitude for interpretation and enforcement than in most other countries. A Chinese lawyer's library of national laws, if he has one, consists of two recently published 400-page volumes containing, in addition to other material, all laws and amendments, and all resolutions concerning law-making, approved by the National People's Congress from 1979–86. If he used a new English-language database covering all laws, decrees, and provisions now in force that have been issued by the National People's Congress and the State Council since the founding of the republic in 1949 he would find a total of 1,268 items. There are, however, untold numbers of rules and regulations the people are expected to observe—though many of them are "secret," known only to those who administer them.

Having learned the perils of rule by a few unrestrained men through its experience with the Cultural Revolution and Great Leap Forward (see separate entries), China had, prior to the student crackdown, been attempting a transition to a rule of law. This movement has had as perhaps its leading exponent Deng Xiaoping, who nevertheless gravely damaged it by attempting to whitewash destruction of the Pro-Democracy Movement and, afterwards, by the mass arrests and short, fast, and mostly closed trials.

Leading officials now make frequent reference to the need for expanding the coverage of legislation to provide a common frame of reference for administrators, legal officials, and the public, and to reassure foreign investors. The government attempts to convince an understandably wary public that everyone is equal before the law and that no one is above the law, even important officials.

However, as *Beijing Review* put it in a surprisingly frank article after the conservatives took over: "Not many people say outright that power is bigger than the law. But actually nowhere in the country has a mechanism yet been established capable of restricting power abuse in the true sense of the word. There are no hard and fast rules which can subject power-holders to legal restrictions or bring power-abusers to justice. Some power-wielders, who think themselves superior, always take it for granted that laws are something designed for other people, the rank-and-filers, while they themselves stand high above the law, far out of its reach, and do not need to be limited by it."

The people are equally unaccustomed to thinking in terms of legal rights and responsibilities. There are frequent references in speeches and the press to the need to educate people in the principles of law and to familiarize them with the provisions of some of the basic laws—the marriage law, the law of inheritance, etc. In *China Daily's* words, "The nation is still at a stage of learning—from learning respect for other individuals and their privacy to treating each other really as equal before the law."

Government and Party officials are attending special schools and classes, and mid- and upper-level government, Party, and army officials are expected to become familiar with "the essence of the constitution, the criminal and criminal procedure codes, contract law, army service law, and other important laws, within two years."

Public education is being carried out in a number of ways, from pamphlets to public events. One such event, a "Legal Day" held in a large workers' park in the center of Beijing, featured electronic quizzes, movies and video tape shows, theatrical performances, exhibitions, and a book shop with popular legal reading matter. A group of legal personnel answering questions was kept busy. One of the sponsors was the publisher of a monthly magazine for the public, *Law and Life*, which has a circulation of 300,000.

Despite all the efforts to date, however, the hard questions of assuring objectivity and accountability under the law are not being dealt with. *Wenhui Daily* quoted one commentator on the legal situation this way: "Although the constitution stipulates that the National People's Congress has the right to interpret the constitution and . . . to cancel all decisions and orders that are in violation of the constitution, still, who has the responsibility to punish unconstitutional acts? . . . No one."

LIBERATION   As referred to in China, "liberation" is the victory won by the People's Liberation Army under the leadership of the Communist Party of China which overthrew the Chiang Kai-shek government and made possible the founding of the People's Republic of China in 1949.

There is also a phrase, "The Second-Time Liberation," referring to the defeat in 1976 of the Gang of Four, who were responsible for much of the severity of the Cultural Revolution.

LINE   A "line," as in "party line" or "bourgeois line," is the general line of argument or thought, or the position, of the group or persuasion indicated. (See also "From the Masses, to the Masses.")

LITTLE RED BOOK   Lin Biao, minister of defense and for a time Mao's designated successor, compiled this famous little 3x5 inch volume in the early sixties. Titled *Quotations from Chairman Mao Tsetung*, it was originally intended for indoctrination of young recruits to the

People's Liberation Army, but achieved its greatest fame as the bible of the Cultural Revolution.

LONG MARCH   See COMMUNIST PARTY OF CHINA.

MANAGEMENT BY ADMINISTRATIVE MEANS   See MEANS OF MANAGEMENT.

MANAGEMENT BY ECONOMIC MEANS   See MEANS OF MANAGEMENT.

MARKETS   See COMMODITY MARKETS; FREE MARKETS.

MASS LINE   See LINE.

MASS ORGANIZATIONS   Usually refers to trade unions, women's organizations, and the Communist Youth League.

MAY FOURTH MOVEMENT   The May Fourth Movement, of which the seventieth anniversary was observed during the height of 1989's Pro-Democracy Movement, has many uncanny parallels with the Pro-Democracy Movement. They both were student movements that later attracted great popular support; they both began in protest against governments they saw as uncaring, conservative, and out-of-touch; they both began without the support of an established political apparatus; they both came at a time of intense national self-examination; the Pro-Democracy Movement almost certainly established, as the May Fourth Movement did, a focus that had not existed before for new social and intellectual forces; their demonstrations caused martial law to be declared in Beijing on both occasions; and both movements had impact far beyond anything their leaders could have imagined.

The May Fourth Movement takes its name from May 4, 1919, the day on which, to mention another similarity, a few thousand students marched to Tian An Men (the Gate of Heavenly Peace to the Forbidden City, without the adjoining square, at the time) to protest the government's acquiescence in the terms of the Treaty of Versaille. The treaty favored Japan over China and ignored China's claims to former German possessions in China and in several other matters.

Hostility toward Japan had been building for years, particularly since 1915 when China's weakness forced it to accept the humiliation of Japan's Twenty-one Demands. It exploded after May 4 in marches, attacks on pro-Japanese officials, student strikes through the country, a nationwide boycott of Japanese goods, workers' strikes (especially in Shanghai), and a severe clampdown on the movement by the police and the military. In a few weeks the government was forced by popular sentiment to release arrested students, dismiss the ministers responsible for China's representation at Versailles, and notify the peace conference that it refused to sign the treaty.

But spontaneous fusion of the people also involved strong forces in numerous areas—ideology, economics, politics, literature, science—that were not limited in their objectives to the single cause for which they had come together. The popular fusion produced efforts to have the nation call upon for its development "those western gentlemen 'Mr. Science' and 'Mr. Democracy,' " as someone has expressed the interest in modernization; led to the founding of the Communist Party in China in 1921, and, in many people's opinions, the Kuomintang as well; it inspired for the first time widespread use of *baihua*, the language of the common people, in a flood of popular recreational and instructional literature; and it reinforced a major cultural upsurge and a desire for national freedom and development that has not yet really come to an end. (The beginning of the movement is generally regarded by historians as the divider between modern and contemporary Chinese history.) It is to this broader aspect of the movement and its implications (with a far wider meaning than can be described here) that "May Fourth Movement" usually refers.

MEANS OF MANAGEMENT   These are of two types, administrative and economic. *Administrative means*, which exert direct control, involve strong leadership by a central authority, mandatory plans, monopoly purchasing, etc.; the central authority is responsible for production, pricing, and distribution, and, therefore, for profits and losses. *Economic means*, which exert indirect control, require a market economy, with production and distribution decisions and profit and loss responsibilities in the hands of enterprise managers; if the state wishes to encourage a given line of activity or the production of a given product, it may do so by means of loans, subsidies, tax decreases, permission for bonuses, etc., or it may discourage enterprises in negative ways. Prior to the new conservative surge in 1989, government was attempting to make economic means of management more prevalent in China, but it is the announced intention of the conservatives to restore, at least to a considerable extent, the influence of central authority.

MEANS OF PRODUCTION   A key concept in socialist theory, this term refers to all components required to produce a given article, other than labor. It includes land, tools and other equipment and machinery, buildings, materials, etc.

MEANS OF SUBSISTENCE   These are essentially consumer goods—clothing, food, and other essentials.

MIDDLE PEASANTS   See PEASANTS.

MU   (Sometimes, *mou*) This ancient measure equals about 0.07 hectare or 0.17 acre, and is still widely used. Officially, however, the government abandoned the *mu* in 1988, because it is not an international unit. And anyway, the size of the measure itself varies from place to place, being more than twice as large in some places as in others. Abandoning it leaves the country without an equivalent modern measure; square meters (of which a *mu* equals 666.66) were expected to be used for the time being, but have not caught on at all.

NAP   Latin American citizens who take a siesta in the afternoon are observing an old tradition, but Chinese who formerly took a *xiu-xi*, an afternoon snooze, were availing themselves of a constitutional privilege. The 1982 constitution says in Article 43 that "Working people in the People's Republic of China have the right to rest." (In somewhat different language, earlier constitutions had the same provision, which can be read as a commentary on conditions before liberation.)

But the constitution doesn't say *when* the people shall rest. Chinese offices have traditionally closed for lunch and a nap for two hours during the summer and an hour and a half during the winter, but business people, shoppers, tourists, and others who didn't nap complained that napping created great inconvenience for them. Government officials felt that it was inefficient and caused the work day to be longer than necessary. So, in 1985 the government more or less said, "Sorry, you will have to rest on your own time." Lunch time was reduced to one hour, which meant that most workers could no longer go home for lunch or give their children lunch at home, or do some of the shopping that consumes so much of the people's day.

It is certain that, one way or another, many people continue to have an extended lunch hour—and many no doubt still nap. Nevertheless, restraints on the nap have had a ripple effect into many areas, including school administration and the restaurant business—and into family life, too, since many offices now close earlier.

NATIONAL PEOPLE'S CONGRESS   The first NPC met in 1954, replacing the Chinese People's Political Consultative Conference (see separate entry) as the highest organ of state power. The emphasis in this phrase is on *state*, however; there has never been any doubt in China concerning the actual supremacy of the Party in all matters, and, in fact, since 1975 the constitution has included references to this understanding. (See "Communist Party of China.") A vice-chairman of the NPC recently, according to *China Daily*, made the paradoxical statement that "In fulfilling [its] function of legal supervision [over the government], the People's Congress must consciously subject itself to the Party's leadership. . . . "

A new NPC is elected by provincial people's congresses every five years, and meetings are held each spring. In electing the NPC which began its term in 1988, voters for the first time had a limited but real choice of delegates, selecting from slates which included slightly more candidates than there were seats to be filled. This reflects a new national policy adopted to make the minor elections to county and municipal congresses more meaningful.

It appears, however, that the people do not trust the sincerity of this gesture; despite the interest in change shown by the Pro-Democracy Movement, there have been only about 5 percent more candidates than offices in recent balloting, although the government policy allows two candidates for each office. National delegates are not chosen directly by the people they represent, but by indirect elections at the lower-level congresses.

Currently, workers and farmers, intellectuals, and officials each hold about 25 percent of NPC seats, the army has about 10 percent, and ethnic minority representatives have 13.5 percent; 1.5 percent are returned overseas Chinese. More than 65 percent of all delegates are Party members (who make up only 4.5 percent of the total population), and virtually all members of the powerful 150-odd-member Standing Committee are also high Party leaders. As the conservatives consolidated their gains begun at the October 1987 plenum, the Standing Committee gained broad new powers under a new Rules of Procedures Law which increased the influence of the Party in the government rather than decreasing it, as the Party and government have said was a goal of reform.

The average age of current delegates is considerably lower than a few years ago, and the level of education significantly higher.

The full NPC has about 3,000 members, obviously far too many for legislative debate, and the annual meetings are essentially ceremonial occasions at which speeches from leading government and Party figures are heard and formal approval is given to new legislation. The term "rubber stamp" which is often applied to the NPC with reference to its handling of legislation is not entirely accurate, since there are numerous committees drawn from the membership which do in fact have some role in preparing legislation, or at least in reviewing it prior to presentation to the congress.

The last two congresses have been noteworthy for blocking, or achieving change in, several government proposals after they had already been announced, although the conservative's increasing influence was shown in the more tightly controlled 1989 sessions, which were, said one observer, "merely a party with three thousand guests."

The 1989 NPC was instrumental, however, in delaying indefinitely the Three Gorges project, a gigantic hydroelectric plant backed by Premier Li Peng, and nearly half the congress cast negative votes or abstained on a government proposal to grant the Shenzen Special Economic Zone special powers.

Also, delegates were increasingly critical of the congress' failure to exercise its supposed supervisory role over the government, saying, according to Xinhua News Agency, that NPC Standing Committee posts were awarded to elderly officials merely as "an honor and a comfort." Delegates also said that the NPC's failure to take an active role in dealing with inflation, corruption, and inadequate education "shows that the NPC has no authority over the government," even though it is supposed to be the highest organ of state power. *World Economic Herald*, in an unusually frank comment even for this liberal publication, said that "the government can only hear the echoes of its own voice" in the NPC.

It is to be noted that as many as forty NPC delegates are currently being investigated by the congress for possible counter-revolutionary activity, because when martial law was declared they signed a petition asking to have a special session of the NPC called so that it, as presumably the highest governing body in the nation, could consider the question.

The NPC elects the state president, the chairman of the state's

Central Military Commission, the president of the Supreme People's Court, and the procurator-general of the Supreme People's Procurate. It approves the state president's nomination for premier of the State Council, and the premier's nominations for State Council members.

The day-to-day work of the NPC is carried on through its Standing Committee, consisting of a chairman, 20 vice-chairmen, a secretary-general, and about 130 members.

NEIGHBORHOOD COMMITTEES   See RESIDENTS' COMMITTEES.

NUMBERS IN SLOGANS AND NAMES   The Seventh Five-Year Plan includes as one of its articles the statement that "We shall constantly broaden the campaign to promote the 'five things to emphasize, the four things to beautify, and the three things to love. . . . ' " This typifies the ancient Chinese fondness for slogans and labels utilizing numbers, in matters both minor (the "Three Bigs" for a family are a television set, a washing machine, and a refrigerator) and major (the feudal society demanded a decent woman show three kinds of obedience: before marriage, obedience to parents; after marriage, obedience to husband; when a widow, obedience to her sons). In their current attempts to achieve a beginning relationship with Taiwan, the mainland Chinese have their "three exchanges policy" (exchanges of trade, mail, and transport), and Taiwan officials have their "three noes" (no contact, no negotiations, and no compromises, although the no contact rule has recently been modified a bit by permitting indirect travel from Taiwan to China, indirect exchange of mail, and indirect investment).

There are large numbers of such slogans, sometimes expressing the same ideas under a different label. The "five things to emphasize" mentioned above, for example, are more commonly called "The Five Stresses" (see separate entry), and the "four things to beautify" are usually called the "Four Points of Beauty" (see separate entry). (See also "Three Things to Love.")

There are frequent references to businesses as "Number One Department Store" or "Number One Motor Vehicle Plant" in a city. The numeric designation is part of the Chinese name, and has nothing to do with leadership. It is equivalent to America's "First National Bank" in a specific city—the first of its kind in a particular place. Beijing, for example, has the Beijing No. 1 Daily Use Chemicals Factory, producing toothpaste and soap, and No. 2, 3, 4, and 5, producing respectively cosmetics for women, shampoo, a skin cream, and cosmetics for men.

OFFICIAL PROFITEERS (*Guan dao*)   Term for bureaucrats who take advantage of official positions to make profits from buying and selling various commodities, especially scarce commodities. The practice has been banned for years, but the various orders of the Supreme People's Court, the Party, and the government are somehow not enforced.

Official corruption, long condemned by the public with increasing vehemence, was a primary target of Pro-Democracy Movement protesters, and it is no wonder: Of 1988's 60,000 major cases of profiteering (cases involving 10,000 yuan or more in illegal profit), more than half according to the government's own figures involved state-owned or Party-owned enterprises, collective enterprises (controlled by governments below the national level), government institutions, and social organizations.

The number of individual cadres, active and retired officials, and workers involved was nearly 12,000, up 65 percent over 1987.

These figures fit into the broader profiteering picture thus: The State Administration for Industry and Commerce reported that in 1988 government administrations at all levels dealt with almost 950,000 profiteering cases involving speculating in state monopoly goods, selling fake goods, driving up prices, etc. The government collected more than 600 million yuan in fines. The 950,000 cases were reportedly 22 percent less than in 1987.

However, large cases involving illegal profits of 10,000 yuan or more increased in 1988 nearly 60 percent, because profiteers formerly concentrated on consumer goods, such as color TV sets and refrigerators, where profit possibilities are relatively small. They have now begun to handle much more expensive products, such as steel, vehicles, cement, and chemical fertilizers.

Since Party offices have a reputation for taking care of their own people, it is likely that a large percentage of cases go unreported. There are no published summaries of punishments, but Party members involved in crimes receive notoriously light sentences. (See "Official Corruption Menaces Government's Legitimacy" in chapter 4.)

ONE CENTER AND TWO BASIC POINTS   "One Center" refers to focusing on economic construction, "Two Basic Points" to upholding the Four Cardinal Principles and to economic revamping and opening to economic revamping and the outside world.

ONE COUNTRY, TWO SYSTEMS   After the west began commercializing and exploiting China, The Heavenly Kingdom was forced by means of unequal treaties to hand over part of its territory to foreign powers—Hongkong to Great Britain (1842) and Macao to Portugal (1887). In 1949, the Kuomintang occupied the province of Taiwan after being driven from the mainland by communist forces. China wants these three territories back.

One major problem, among others, is that these territories are far wealthier, on a per capita basis, than mainland China, and their people would be strongly opposed to the government ownership of most property and the egalitarian incomes that still exist in China. Furthermore, it is as important to China as it is to the Hongkong and Taiwan people that these economies remain strong and healthy.

Therefore, in 1981 China offered to negotiate the return of Taiwan to mainland control on the basis of the "one country, two systems" concept, under which Taiwan would retain its capitalist system (and, not incidentally, its own armed forces) after returning to mainland control. Taiwan was not responsive to this proposal.

As Britain's long-term lease on the New Territories (on the Chinese mainland north of Hongkong) was to expire in a few years and China had no intention of renewing it, Britain agreed to consider returning Hongkong Island to China as well. An agreement was signed in 1984 under which China guarantees that Hongkong will retain its capitalist system, within the Chinese socialist system, for fifty years from the expiration of the New Territories lease in 1997, but will again be a part of China. Nearby Macao signed a similar agreement in 1987.

For three or four years after China and Britain reached agreement Hongkong was quite bullish on the future, as indicated by real estate prices and the Hong Kong Stock Exchange index. Hongkong has been increasingly restless, however, as China has been less than straightforward in negotiating the Basic Law Agreement under which Hongkong will be governed and as Britain has essentially abandoned any effort to secure some democratic guarantees for its colony. Hongkong, a generally apolitical and never very democratic place, awoke in an unheard of fashion to mount demonstrations of 500,000 or more during the Pro-Democracy Movement in China, and responded equally forcefully to the repression by driving the stock index down in three weeks about 30 percent (from which it recovered very little in the following weeks) and beginning to withdraw large sums from the local economy.

OWNERSHIP   Though some Chinese feel reform of "ownership" of state enterprises (now considered to be owned "by the whole people") is central to successful economic reform, the meaning of "ownership" remains murky, and no very rigorous discussion has been seen. For example, a cover story, "China's First Share Success," in a 1989 *Beijing Review* says this about "the reform of state ownership of enterprises": "One of the major defects with state ownership is that property rights are unclearly defined. Superficially they rest with the state—the representative of the whole people. But in practice, as the state is responsible for managing all aspects of society, it cannot fulfill its specific functions as the owner of any particular enterprise. Consequently, no one is genuinely responsible for ensuring that enterprises continue to develop and add value to their property." This short statement raises, or begs, questions—such as "Why *can't* the state manage enterprises if it is capable of managing all other aspects of society?"—that interfere with understanding the importance the Chinese place upon the concept.

Nevertheless, changing the ownership of state-owned firms is considered by some to be the first requirement for economic reform, even though the larger firms, at least, will certainly continue to be "owned" by the state, in the sense that the state will maintain controlling interest, just as blocs of a few major shareholders control a corporation in capitalist economies. This seems to be clear from this discussion in the *Beijing Review* article of share sales by a certain company: "Some people have voiced fears that the introduction of stocks would force state-owned enterprises to change their nature. But as Tianqiao's history reveals, such worries are groundless: *public ownership remains dominant.* [Emphasis added] Although the state only owns 24 percent of the stock issued, it is the biggest single shareholder." Some theorists insist that the state should always hold 51 percent of outstanding stock to assure public control.

A puzzling aspect of the Tianqiao stock sale was that the state apparently actually made an additional investment to obtain the shares it holds in the enterprise, which it presumably already owned *in toto*. The article states, "The shares were sold to the state, the public, and other companies. . . . " Thus, at present, stock sales in state enterprises appear to transfer to specific parties interests which by definition formerly belonged to all the nation, without proper compensation to the state or its citizens, reminiscent of what was happening until recently in the sale of land rights. (See "The Land Question" in chapter 6.)

The Chinese meaning of ownership appears to refer not so much to the capitalist sense as to "responsibility for profits and losses" or "financial responsibility."

For example: There are several points of view as to which should come first in the sequence of reforms. The official line has long been that price reform is paramount. A discussion in the *Bulletin of Theoretical Studies* said, however, that "those who prefer ownership reform consider [emphasizing price reform] as somewhat utopian, as fair prices can only be brought about in competition. Yet, if enterprises continue . . . as state-owned enterprises [whose losses are made up by the state], no one can drive them into competition in a real sense." (On the other hand, until the state is able to face up to forcing loss-making units to go out of business—something it has not done thus far because of unemployment and other sociopolitical considerations—it does not make much difference who the theoretical owner is.)

Another clue to the interpretation of "ownership" comes from the fact that discussions emphasize the importance of selling shares in companies as a means of shifting ownership, and refer to the growing number of companies (about 6,000) which have sold shares, most of which are collectives rather than state-owned firms. In fact, however, none of the "shares" sold to date apparently transfer any equity to the share buyer. They are primarily interest-bearing securities which would be known in capitalist countries as "bonds," although some also pay dividends if there are profits.

Selling shares is a subject which has intermittent vogue. These are the latest switches: in December 1988 the People's Bank of China said it was preparing regulations on the sale of shares; in February 1989 the government said shareholding for state firms would be held up for two years or more; in mid-March Premier Li Peng told the National People's Congress that "We shall gradually introduce the shareholding system based on public ownership." The *Beijing Review* cover story referred to above came a few weeks later.

PARTY CONSOLIDATION   "Consolidation" (in the sense of strengthening) was the term applied to an effort to achieve overall rejuvenation of the Party that began after the Second Plenary Session of the Twelfth Central Committee held in October 1984. The Decision of the Central Committee on Party Consolidation lists four tasks, namely, to unify the thinking, rectify the style, strengthen the discipline, and purify the organization of the Party. "Unifying the thinking" covers many objectives, but the most important is described as arousing the sense of historical responsibility among the 47 million Party members, enabling them to rid themselves of the influence of "taking class struggle as the key link," and to shift to the general task of making the country and the people prosperous.

A "Party rectification campaign" concurrent with the consolidation effort focused on a single one of the consolidation objectives, to "rectify the style" of the Party—that is, to correct shortcomings in ideological approach, attitude, and behavior that result in public criticism and cynicism. (There were two major earlier rectification movements—in Yenan, 1941–42, and in 1956.) In this subsidiary campaign, cadres were urged to mend their ways—to avoid the use of power for personal gain, avoid favoritism, and avoid improprieties; to perform rather than to indulge in empty rhetoric; and to get out of their offices and find out what is really going on.

As planned, both campaigns were brought to an end in 1987. *Beijing Review* reported that "Many Party members have deepened their understanding of the Party's political line of building socialism with Chinese characteristics. Factionalism and the pernicious influence of 'leftist' thinking that was divorced from China's reality, both left over from the Cultural Revolution, have been liquidated. The sense of serving the people has been strengthened. Malpractice by Party and government cadres engaging in trade and operating enterprises has been checked and dealt with." (This was highly optimistic, as shown by the corruption reported daily in increasing volume before the Party crackdown on the Pro-Democracy Movement.)

During the campaigns, the Party claimed, about 5,500 members who committed serious ideological or criminal offenses during the Cultural Revolution were "cleaned up"; 43,000 "who made serious mistakes were dealt with"; 34,000 unqualified members were expelled; all members were required to apply for reregistration and 90,000 were refused; 145,000 reregistrations were deferred; and 184,000 were placed on probation or otherwise disciplined. The story recognized, however, that "when the old problems are solved, new ones will crop up."

Apparently, however, not even the old problems were solved. *Workers' Daily* reported in late 1988 that "Between 1983 [shortly before rectification began] and 1988 [a year after it ended], the State Council and the Party Central Committee issued no less than *twenty-four* documents, using very stern words, to forbid Party and government officials from becoming involved in commercial business." The stern words continued nearly every day until the conservatives clamped down on publications, but it is just this offense that is at the root of some of China's worst corruption today. (See "Official Corruption Menaces Government's Legitimacy" in chapter 4.)

PARTY RECTIFICATION   See PARTY CONSOLIDATION.

PEASANTS   In old China, the social structure in the countryside consisted essentially of peasants, who farmed the land, and landowners, who rented land to the peasants. The peasants, however, recognized three further divisions: *poor peasants*, who owned no land or tools and had to rent both from the landlord, and who sometimes worked as laborers for others; *middle peasants*, who owned some land and tools; and *rich peasants*, who were essentially small landowners who farmed with the labor of others.

These divisions became a matter of considerable importance to the country at the time of land reform (see separate entry), when the differing interests of the three groups had to be reconciled. (*Fanshen*, by William Hinton, is a fascinating, classic account of how the complex problems of land reform were handled in a single small village, and conveys the essential feeling of the times in a unique way.)

Today, *peasant* is still the word most often used for all those who live in rural areas. Recently, *farmer* has begun appearing in a few English-language publications, but it refers broadly to those formerly called *peasants*. So far, there is no distinctive term for those who live in the countryside but no longer work on the land—the workers in rural industry, for example, or workers in rural distribution and service trades. Writers have so far tried to avoid the problem by using such terms as "farmer-run factories."

PEOPLE'S COMMUNES   People's communes were the highest form of collective ownership from 1958 until the early eighties, and perhaps the aspect of China best known to foreigners (partly because Chinese communes were one inspiration for communal living in western countries during the sixties). (The name is said to have been created in Qiliying village, Henan province, in 1958. It was inspired by the proletarian, if urban, nature of the Paris Commune of the French Revolution.) As discussed below and in the chapter on "The Changing Countryside," communes have been phased out. However, because communes have had a commanding role in the life of the country, they deserve a brief historical survey.

Some 26,000 communes were organized from 740,000 advanced co-ops (see separate entry under "Agricultural Cooperatives") during 1958–59 in the frenzy of the Great Leap Forward (see separate entry). They were very large compared to co-ops, ranging in size from 15,000 persons to perhaps 30,000 or more in metropolitan suburbs and very productive areas. Creation of the communes from advanced co-ops involved drastic, indiscriminate transfer of the assets of the former co-ops to the commune without compensation to co-op members, who had owned their assets, and without consideration of fairness. It also involved the abolition of private property. In size, power, and relationship to its members, the commune was much more a state agency than a community organization, as the co-ops had been.

Egalitarianism prevailed in all areas of life, theoretically (although favoritism was rife), and the socialist principle of "To each according to his work" was ignored. Family life was severely disrupted by communal nurseries which cared for children day and night throughout the week and by communal dining halls. (The dining halls, however, were reportedly so welcomed by some women that they threw their pots out the window!) Household sidelines (see separate entry), including cultivation of private plots, were forbidden.

By 1960, peasant morale had been driven very low, farmers' productivity had plummeted, and drastic changes were made. The sprawling communes were reduced in size (resulting in about 56,000 units), and reorganized into a three-level ownership and management system. The unit at each level had ownership of and responsibility for equipment and facilities appropriate to its level, and the right to manage its own production.

These were the new units at the three levels:

People's commune—Communes were the grassroots level governmental administrative units (next below the county level), and also had ideological responsibilities as well as jurisdiction over economic and agricultural matters, but had less direct control over day-to-day activities than formerly. They directed implementation of state plans; provided unified local planning; managed the larger and more important public services, such as hospitals, power plants, and upper-level schools; oversaw major agricultural and conservation projects; and directed farming as well as commune-run workshops and factories.

Production brigade—Brigades were the middle unit in the system, and had responsibility for brigade quotas and for brigade-level construction, supply procurement, marketing, and sideline enterprises.

Production team—Production teams are usually referred to in translations from the Chinese as the commune's "basic accounting unit," which they were, in a way, but it is perhaps more understandable to think of them as the "basic unit of accountability" or the "basic accountable unit." The production team assigned work, handled distribution of income according to work points (see separate entry), and managed its land, equipment, and personnel.

There was an improvement in agricultural output in the early sixties following changes in commune organization, but during the decade-long Cultural Revolution starting in 1966, farm output and the peasants' standard of living declined severely. Over the roughly twenty years between the beginning of commune formation and the end of the Cultural Revolution in 1976, the peasants gained only about 13 kilograms in their annual grain allowance and 23 yuan in their annual cash income. Even in the more successful communes, the peasants' return from each yuan of investment was 30 percent less in 1980 than in 1957.

The commune as described above existed from the early sixties until after the Cultural Revolution. Later developments are discussed in chapter 6 in the section "New Economic Relationships in the Countryside."

PEOPLE'S DEMOCRATIC DICTATORSHIP   The traditional communist expression of this idea has been "Dictatorship of the Proletariat," conveying that "the interests of the working people and of socialism are guaranteed by the socialist state until a communist society replaces it and the state withers away."

The discussion of the draft of the 1982 PRC constitution includes this comment on the meaning and use by the Chinese of the alternative expression, "people's democratic dictatorship": "The dictatorship of the proletariat takes different forms in different countries, and the people's democratic dictatorship is a form created by the Chinese people under the leadership of the Chinese Communist Party that suits the conditions and revolutionary traditions of our country. . . . The people's democratic dictatorship is a formulation which accurately states the present condition of the classes in China and the broad basis of our political power, and it clearly shows the democratic nature of our state power."

The Party's Shanghai newspaper, *Wenhui Daily*, has described the following characteristics of the people's democratic dictatorship: 1) An alliance between the industrial and agricultural classes as well as between the working classes and the bourgeois classes of the ethnic groups. 2) Existence of various democratic groups and their participation in the nation's political life. 3) In the period of the socialist revolution, all classes and groups approving of, protecting, and participating in socialist construction fall within the scope of "the people." In this sense, the people is a broad entity, accounting for 97 percent or more of the population. 4) The democratic dictatorship of the people for a certain period of time must perform the task of completing democratic revolution, strengthening and developing the historical destiny of socialism.

POLITICAL PARTIES   Political parties as known in the west do not exist in China. In addition to the Communist Party of China, the country has eight small groups, known as "democratic parties," which are actually more patriotic than political in nature and which receive attention seemingly out of proportion to their size or influence, including a prominent role in the Chinese People's Political Consultative Conference (see separate entry). They have a combined membership of about 300,000, up from 80,000 ten years ago.

All have histories going back to preliberation days and most were organized to resist the Kuomintang or Japan. They are: The China Revolutionary Committee of the Kuomintang; China Democratic League; China Democratic National Construction Association; China Association for Promoting Democracy; China Zhi Gong Dang (overseas Chinese now living in China); Jiu San Society; Taiwan Democratic Self-Government League.

Beginning late in 1988, the democratic parties have received increasing attention from the Communist Party as talk of increased political reform grew. First came comments in Communist Party publications by leaders of the democratic parties on the need for "all" political parties to work together, etc., then by a response from the Party secretariat that "close cooperation between the Communist Party of China and other democratic parties is important for us to overcome difficulties and achieve victories." The democratic parties are always reliable echoes of the Communist Party's views, and predictably approved the military crackdown on the students.

The government suggested that it might open a third of the ministerial level seats in the State Council to noncommunists. (But only two non-Party persons were given seats—relatively minor ones— during the 1989 National People's Congress session, when the suggested changes were expected to occur). When the Party first came to power in 1949 noncommunists did in fact hold a third of top government posts, but the proportion quickly declined; before the two additions just mentioned, the democratic parties had only a single token representative, a deputy minister; representation of those with no affiliations whatever is unknown.During this period, Fei Xiaotong, chairman of the Democratic Alliance (the umbrella organization of the eight parties), made clear that he did not believe adversarial political parties in the mold of those in the west were practical, the position held by the Party.

POOR PEASANTS   See PEASANTS.

PRIVATE PLOTS   See HOUSEHOLD SIDELINES.

PROCUREMENT QUOTA SYSTEM   See PURCHASING POLICIES.

PRODUCTION BRIGADE   See "Production brigade" under PEOPLE'S COMMUNES.

PRODUCTION TEAM   See "Production team"under PEOPLE'S COMMUNES.

PURCHASING POLICIES   Readers of older material about China will find several terms related to agricultural purchases from peasants by the state before 1985 which have apparently similar meanings, but whose exact meanings are seldom clear. (These are of historic importance only, since sales to the state are no longer mandatory as of 1985, except as agreed under production contracts.) Here are explanations of commonly used terms:

Prescribed purchases—Grain, for example, was purchased on this basis. Through administrative channels beginning at the province level, the state *fixed the amount* of grain to be purchased from each peasant, specialized household, etc. If the producing unit had surplus grain, it could sell it to the state at a premium price, or sell it at free markets.

Unified purchases—Cotton was purchased on this basis. *All* cotton was sold to the state, except for a specified amount kept for individual use, or, if preferred, for sale at free markets. Until recently, cotton goods were rationed.

Procurement quota system—Pigs and eggs were purchased on this basis. The state purchased a *certain portion or percentage*, which varied by locality, while the rest could be used or sold.

Purchasing policies, together with pricing policies, were basic parts of the sensitive system through which production and distribution of essential products were maintained when supplies were limited and before reform brought market forces into play. It was necessary to plan policies carefully because, as one statement put it, "when the amount of prescribed purchases and the procurement quotas are too high, the peasants who grow the crops cannot eat their fill and those who raise pigs do not have pork on their tables." On occasion, peasants have felt that the quotas were unfair, and "their flagging enthusiasm for production impaired the growth of agricultural production, which in turn made the shortage of supplies in the cities even more acute."

QINGMING (Ching-ming)   The Qingming Festival (or the Ghost Festival, April 5), now has double significance because it was also the occasion on which tens of thousands of people gathered in Tiananmen Square in 1976 to honor recently deceased Zhou Enlai, only to be forcibly dispersed by police under orders of the Gang of Four. Resentment of the repression was instrumental in the fall of the Gang after Mao's death later in the year. Traditionally, Qingming is a key date for farmers, marking the date on which it was safe to begin planting, a day for sweeping the graves of ancestors, and, by extension, a day for honoring martyrs and heroes. In many areas, visiting and sweeping graves are combined with family picnics, although the egg shells and other foods sometimes found near graves after Qingming are not litter but symbolic gifts. Taking walks in the awakening countryside and flying kites are other customs.

QUOTATIONS FROM CHAIRMAN MAO TSETUNG   See LITTLE RED BOOK.

RED ENVELOPE   To give a "red envelope" is to give a bonus or extra payment for some special work. The practice is sometimes abused by giving bribes under the pretext of giving such gifts. Gifts of money, as to children on special occasions or to newlyweds, are also customarily given in red envelopes.

RED EYE   Chinese term for envy.

RED GUARDS   See CULTURAL REVOLUTION.

REGISTERED HOUSEHOLDS   A term used earlier for households registered with the government as proprietors of small, privately owned industrial and commercial businesses (a type of "specialized household"). Now the usual, and somewhat broader, term is simply "individual businesses." (See "Private Business" in chapter 5.)

REHABILITATION   Used in a phrase such as "During the three years of rehabilitation . . . ," *rehabilitation* refers to the period from the founding of the People's Republic in October 1949 through the end of 1952 during which the country's attention was primarily devoted to normalizing national life after years of war and turmoil. This period, also often called the period of "economic reconstruction," was part of the program set forth in the Common Program recommended by the Chinese People's Political Consultative Conference in September 1949.

Used in a phrase concerning a person—"He was rehabilitated in 1979"—the word refers to the restoration of reputation, post, privileges, etc., to someone unfairly deprived of them through being wrongly labeled a rightist, capitalist, landlord, deviationist, etc., during various periods of class struggle (see separate entry) or in the Cultural Revolution. It was not until 1986 that the government felt it appropriate to rule that all persons—and their descendants—labeled "landlords," "rich peasants," and "capitalists" in the fifties could be considered to be rehabilitated.

REPLACEMENT SYSTEM   Not only did the worker formerly have an iron rice bowl (see separate entry), but so did his children. It has long been customary for a son or a daughter to take over a worker's job when the father—or mother—retires, which means that many inexperienced and unsuitable young people get jobs for which they are not qualified. Except in industries that employ artisans (where apparently it is assumed parents pass on their skills to children), the replacement system was forbidden by the 1986 labor regulations providing for public recruitment and employment based on examinations. But a mere decree has not been enough to end this system, as there is still considerable abuse in this area.

RESIDENCE REGISTRATION   One's *hukou* (*hoo-ko*), or residence registration, is even more basic than one's affiliation with a work unit.

Each person has a rural registration or an urban registration; changing from urban to rural is no problem, but it is almost impossible for a rural resident to obtain an urban *hukou*. The government allows two rural-to-urban changes per 10,000 people each year. Changes from one urban area to another are equally difficult, which results in situations where, for example, husbands and wives may be separated for many years when one is transferred by a work unit to another city. Labor mobility is impossible, and numerous other problems are created by the system. The government has shown no inclination to modify the system, however, because doing so could create more problems than it solved.

After liberation, there were no restrictions on freedom of movement, and in fact the first constitution specified that citizens had that right, but as centralized planning increased people were frozen into their current places of residence. When rural reforms began, however, people in the countryside were no longer forced to farm, and as peasants began to work in local industries they tended to migrate to the smaller towns. As time passed and commerce grew, both peasants and urban residents found ways to move more freely, with the result that already crowded major cities now also have large unregistered populations. (See "The Growth of Small Towns" in the section "Peasants Become Workers" in chapter 6.) Strong measures are now being taken, however, to force unregistered persons to return to their official homes.

RESIDENTS' (or NEIGHBORHOOD) COMMITTEES   (See "Villagers' Committees" for the equivalent rural organization.) In 1954 the National People's Congress promulgated the "Organic Regulations of the Urban Neighborhood Committees." Today, there are about 70,000 such locally elected but unofficial committees with over 465,000 cadres. A committee serves perhaps 10,000–12,000 persons.

According to the Organic Regulations and the nation's constitution, the neighborhood committee "should be a self-governing organization of the masses." Committees deal with "matters pertaining to the public welfare of residents, mediate disputes between them, lead them in maintaining public order, and canvass their opinions and convey their suggestions to the local government," and hold the secret personal files of individuals not affiliated with a work unit. They also keep a very sharp eye out for infractions of rules, strangers, and suspicious behavior by residents, particularly in tense periods.

Committees have been crucial in some of China's notable achievements, such as improving public health and increasing literacy. Starting from scratch, neighborhood committees established cooperatives which have now developed into sizable collective enterprises. A majority of workers are women, and many find the work rewarding. Some housewives who once could neither read nor write are now shop managers or factory directors. Increasing numbers of retired persons are now serving on neighborhood committees.

Neighborhood committee work has been expanded since 1979, and now includes population control; providing clothing, food, housing, and medical care for childless elderly people and the handicapped; finding work for the handicapped; organizing nurseries and kindergartens and after-school guidance centers; setting up small companies to employ young people who have completed their schooling; and other projects.

RICH PEASANTS   See PEASANTS.

RIGHT   See LEFT/RIGHT [FACTIONS].

SECOND-TIME LIBERATION   See SOCIALIST TRANSFORMATION.

SHAREHOLDING   See OWNERSHIP.

SINGLE-PRODUCT MARKETS   See COMMODITY MARKETS.

SOCIAL SECURITY   See AGING.

SOCIALISM WITH CHINESE CHARACTERISTICS   Lenin said in 1918 that "We cannot give a description of socialism; what socialism will be like when its completed forms are arrived at—this we do not know, we cannot tell." Just what Chinese socialism is remains vague over seventy years later, and the ambiguity of the basic idea extends to "Socialism with Chinese characteristics," a phrase first used by Deng Xiaoping in 1982 but never adequately defined by him or anyone else.

In the crises of earlier days the Party strove to find socialist revolutionary paths suited to China's conditions by refining and reinterpreting socialist principles in the light of those conditions, and the process continues today—both assisted and impeded by divergences of opinion as to the meaning of socialism itself.

A resolution of the Twelfth Central Committee at the session proclaiming urban reform in 1984 described characteristics of socialism. The list included some "Chinese characteristics" but did not specifically limit the discussion to Chinese socialism. The characteristics of classical socialism included:

1. Abolition of systems of exploitation.
2. Public ownership of the means of production.
3. Remuneration according to work.
4. A planned commodity economy. (The classic socialist economy would not include a commodity aspect, nor would it allow the competition implicit in the idea of the commodity economy. See "Commodity Economy" and "Competition.")
5. Political power in the hands of the working class and other laboring people.
6. Highly developed productive forces and labor productivity which will eventually be higher than in capitalist countries.
7. Socialist ethics cultivated under the guidance of Marxism.

It has long been asserted that socialism was the only form of government that could have saved China, and *People's Daily* stated recently that "Only socialism can develop China because it is an objective law of social development." Socialism is not only supreme in China but, said *People's Daily*, "It is an objective reality independent of man's will that socialism will replace capitalism in the world."

Adaptations of classical theory made in recent years by reformers are now being strongly challenged by conservatives (see "Bourgeois Liberalization"). Before the conservative takeover, however, Chinese theoreticians offered analyses of traditional concepts that were considered "breakthroughs" in "forbidden areas" of socialist economic theory. No doubt the most basic breakthrough is the assertion that China is in a primary stage of socialism. A second important point is that a socialist economy is no longer seen as monolithic but as highly diversified.

It will be left to others to analyze what these new formulations owe to theoretical insight and what to pragmatism, and the extent to which they are indebted to the experience of other controlled economies such as Hungary and South Korea. (It is interesting to see, however, that development and expansion of "Marxism" has continued, despite the intermittent pressures toward orthodoxy.) The following summary highlights the Chinese point of view on breakthroughs, given in articles by and published interviews (before the Pro-Democracy Movement began) with Liu Guoguang, a vice-president of the Chinese Academy of Social Sciences.

□ Economists have discarded the traditional idea that only an economic system built on the imaginary social model conceived by Marx is socialism and that only the Soviet model of forty or fifty years ago is out-and-out socialistic. There might be many economic models leading to socialism, and a socialist economic system should not be one that defies all changes.

□ It has been emphasized that China is still in the primary stage of socialism. (From 1956 until fairly recently, it was believed that China had reached an advanced stage.) This recognizes, for example, that production is undeveloped and that total central planning or distribution according to need rather than according to work is not possible. Guidance planning should be used with mandatory planning, and it is permissible for some to get rich before others. (See discussion of later developments of this breakthrough below.)

□ At present, so long as the public sector predominates, it may be supplemented by collective, private, foreign, and other sectors, with companies under the same or different types of ownership allying themselves with or even merging with one another. It is erroneous to believe that at this stage China will be more socialist if the size of production units is larger or the degree of public ownership is greater. (See "Ownership.")

□ Because increasing productivity is a goal of socialism, it is not only permissible, but often desirable, to contract or lease state enterprises to motivated entrepreneurial managers while the state retains actual ownership. The theory that ownership and management must be combined shackles productivity.

□ It is necessary to combine planning with a commodity economy incorporating market mechanisms. It has been realized that a planned economy with an excessively high degree of centralization is not the only form of socialist economy.

As mentioned in "The Big Thirteenth" in chapter 2, the theory that China is in the primary stage of socialism was proposed by Zhao Ziyang and accepted by congress delegates. In a little more detail, this is the background and significance of that theory, as described in a *China Daily* interview with a leading economist, Xue Muqiao.

Zhao's statement that China will remain in the primary stage until about 2050 is based upon the fact that the basic goal of socialism is the advancement of productivity to and beyond the level of capitalist countries. Marxist theory, however, saw the advance as starting after socialism had taken over a developed capitalist society. (For example, the communist rallying cry has always been, "Workers of the world! Unite!" not "Peasants of the world. . . !") China was capitalist in 1949, but far from developed. (The strength and speed of reform has led Chinese citizens to feel that their country is a rapidly developing country, even if it may not rank with the "developed" countries of the west. An implication of the "primary stage" theory that has not escaped the people's notice is that it can be used by the government to excuse lack of change and improvement for a great many years.)

Therefore, to lay the base for development China must "go through a very long primary stage to accomplish industrialization, commercialization, and modernization of production which many other countries have achieved under capitalist conditions."

In the primary stage, the theory goes, it is understandable and inevitable that within the developing socialist economy there should be an element of capitalism. Such elements of capitalism as there may be in China's reforms are not subject to criticism as being counterrevolutionary but are in fact desirable and necessary for achieving the socialist goal of enhancing productivity.

Furthermore, the two can cooperate within the socialist economy, just as in other countries workers and capitalists often cooperate for mutual advantage.

SOCIALIST DEMOCRACY   In discussions of political reform, there have often been assertions that, "of course," socialist democracy is superior to nonsocialist forms, but there is a scarcity of detail. The Chinese view on this superiority is given in the following excerpts from a 1986 Xinhua News Agency dispatch reporting on a speech by Peng Zhen, an aggressive old revolutionary who was then president of the National People's Congress: "Our democracy is the broadest kind of democracy, the democracy of the overwhelming majority. [Citizens are limited by only one condition, they] must not impair the interests of the nation or of society or of collectives or the legal rights and freedoms of their fellow citizens. The breadth and scope of this democracy of ours is beyond comparison with the democracy of capitalism.

"Our democracy is a democracy of all the people of our entire country whatever their race. It is a democracy of the workers. . . . Capitalist democracy is a democracy of the capitalist class.

"Our system of democracy is different from the capitalist system of democracy. . . . [The nation] is a socialist country with a people's democratic dictatorship based on an alliance of workers and peasants. . . . Leading organs are produced through elections.

"What principles are followed in the discussion of problems? All men are equal before the truth. We follow whatever ideas are correct. . . .The minority submits to the majority. . . , the individual submits to the organization. . ., the entire country submits to the central government. . . . All must submit to the law. This is the essential content of our system of collective democracy."

SOCIALIST EDUCATION MOVEMENT   As economic conditions improved after the Great Leap Forward, Mao in 1962 again became concerned over the appearance of what he considered capitalist and counterrevolutionary tendencies, particularly in the countryside.

In launching the Socialist Education Movement in 1963, Mao intended to emphasize ideological education, strengthen the collective economy by countering recent capitalistic changes in the communes, mobilize those formerly classed as poor and middle peasants to oppose the developing tendencies, and ferret out cadres in key positions who had become lax or corrupt. His plan was twice revised by others and changed basically in method and tone, and the sharpening struggle between left and right spilled over into other economic areas and into art, culture, education, etc., with inconclusive results. The movement was redefined once more in early 1965 in Mao's "Twenty-three Points," a strong challenge to his opponents. It contained many of the objectives and concepts to be found in the Cultural Revolution (see separate entry), with which the movement was finally merged in December 1966.

SOCIALIST TRANSFORMATION   Refers to the process and the period (1953–55) following rehabilitation (see separate entry) during which industry, agriculture, and handicrafts and other small businesses became cooperatives, collectives, or state-owned enterprises. During this period even the smallest private stalls or workshops entered neighborhood cooperatives. In agriculture, the peasants who had only just become private, independent landowners nearly all joined agricultural producers' cooperatives. The first stage of transformation in industry was usually for the government to buy part-interests in enterprises; this was done mostly on a case-by-case basis until 1955, when it began to proceed on an industry-by-industry basis. In the next stage many capitalist enterprises and joint state-private ventures became entirely state-owned through agreements by the state to pay private owners for their assets over a period of seven years, an agreement that was honored. By 1956, socialist transformation was considered to be essentially completed.

SPECIALIZED MARKETS   See COMMODITY MARKETS.

SPIRITUAL POLLUTION   See CAMPAIGN AGAINST SPIRITUAL POLLUTION.

SPITTING   Expectorating on the streets and elsewhere is a bad habit the government is attempting to change. There are signs everywhere in public areas, even in toilets, prohibiting spitting, and there are periodic enforcement attempts. Recently, an anti-spitting campaign employed inspection squads roaming the streets with microscopes through which offenders could be shown a close-up view of their spittle, after which they were fined on the spot. *Beijing Daily* even published the names and addresses of some cyclists apprehended after spitting who had counted on not being chased.

STOCKS AND BONDS   See OWNERSHIP.

SUGAR-COATED BULLETS   Bribes made acceptable to the receiver by flattery, etc.

SUPPLY AND MARKETING COOPERATIVES   These rural organizations date from before the founding of the People's Republic, having been founded as cooperatives by pooling funds of rural households as liberation progressed. They are sometimes called the mainstay of rural commerce, and engage in virtually all lines of business in rural areas from farming through processing of agricultural products and operation of wholesale and retail enterprises. Their net turnover is now almost equal to total rural sales of state-owned enterprises.

As an example of the large scale of co-op activity in one area, *China Daily* reported that 820 such co-ops around Beijing and Tianjin supplied the two municipalities with 200 million kilograms of vegetables; 60 million of fruit; 20 million of pork, poultry, and eggs; and 160 million of grain and edible oil in 1986. At the same time, they purchased 246 million yuan worth (about US$66.5 million) of industrial goods from the municipalities for rural areas. Co-ops also make loans to farmers and provide technical training and scientific and marketing information to members.

Supply and marketing co-ops increased rapidly after liberation but were sucked into the state apparatus during the Great Leap Forward and communization periods, and became state-owned in name as well as in fact in 1977; the change back to cooperative ownership began in 1982, with original investments being credited to the proper families.

Today, more than 85 percent of all rural families are shareholders. There are 32,000 independent units in the countryside, 2,100 more at the county level, and over half a million marketing and sales centers throughout 85 percent of the country, all formed voluntarily by individuals and small businesses to provide needed services or facilities for themselves.

The co-ops comprise the All-China Federation of Supply and Marketing Cooperatives, the largest such organization in the world, with about four million workers.

TAKE GRAIN AS THE KEY LINK   This Mao Zedong slogan has guided the development of agriculture since the Great Leap Forward, but has guided it somewhat erratically at times. Mao's complete instruction to agriculture was not only to take grain as the key link but also to develop other crops, forestry, animal husbandry, fisheries, and sidelines. The full slogan tended to be shortened in the mind of the bureaucracy, with the result that, for example, at some periods orchards were uprooted to use the land for grain, even though it was totally unsuited to the purpose.

TAXES   A taxation system called "substitution of taxes for profits" has been developed in the past few years under which enterprises pay a part of their profits in taxes and keep the rest, instead of paying over all profits to the bureau or agency responsible for the enterprise.

The change is regarded as important, but its significance is usually not made clear. It is simply this: From the reformers' point of view, the advantage is that financial authority and resources—and rewards—are unequivocally moved past supervisory agencies to the enterprise level. This makes it more practical to begin requiring all enterprises to be responsible for their own financial health—"to be responsible for their own profits and losses," in the current phrase.

From the enterprises' point of view, even though they wind up keeping less than 40 percent of profits before local taxes and levies, there is the advantage that they do keep at least a small portion and it is theirs; they do not have to negotiate with their superior agency for a share.

Taxes of all kinds now account for over 80 percent of the

government's income; the proportion was 46 percent in 1978. It has been said elsewhere that "cadres hold only a threadbare concept of laws and legality," and apparently this is especially true of the tax laws; the State Taxation Bureau estimated in 1988 that more than half of China's enterprises were evading taxes. Officials attempting to collect taxes are often beaten and occasionally killed.

Taxation in China is not yet as complicated as in most large countries, but there are already many refinements and exceptions in tax laws and a wide variety of national, provincial, and local taxes. These include not only income taxes but a tax on total sales and a regulatory tax intended to soak up windfall profits from the vagaries of state-set prices. The following will give an indication of the general level and scope of taxation.

State-owned enterprises pay a 55 percent income tax on profits, plus a 5 percent industrial tax and a 5 percent commercial tax. There is a further regulatory tax on excess profits. (State-owned enterprises willing to operate under a contract system are able to negotiate in advance a flat amount of taxes they must pay regardless of losses or whether they earn large profits. This will probably be switched to a fixed percentage of all profits in 1989.) Collective enterprises pay a progressive rate of from 20 to 40 percent on profits, plus a local tax of 10 percent of the national tax.

Both state and collective enterprises pay capital use fees (essentially interest) on funds obtained from the state, an energy and communications development tax, and a variety of provincial and local levies.

Joint Sino-foreign enterprises pay a 30 percent tax on profits, plus 10 percent of the national tax to local tax bureaus. Independent foreign businesses pay 20 to 40 percent on profits, plus the local tax.

Privately owned businesses pay no taxes until after they have been profitable for three to five years. Thereafter, businesses with more than eight employees pay income taxes at ten progressive rates, from 7 percent on income below 1,000 yuan, 15 percent on the amount between 1,000 and 2,000 yuan, through 60 percent on the amount above 30,000 yuan. Smaller businesses pay 52 percent in taxes on profits, and are supposed to reinvest 30 percent of profits and pay no more than 18 percent in salary and bonuses to the owner. (See new restrictions in "Private Business," chapter 5.) The new government claims that tax evasion is widespread among small businesses, and this is one basis for a strong crackdown on the operation and even the number of private businesses. As of mid-1988, personal income derived from private businesses is taxed at a beginning rate of 40 percent, about double the ordinary income tax rates mentioned below.

A sure sign that things are improving is the1988 imposition of a monthly *Personal* Income Adjusting Tax, to avoid too great an imbalance between incomes of individual citizens. It applies on virtually all income above 400 yuan per month at the rate of 20 to 60 percent on the amount above 400 yuan, and at present payment is on the honor system. An experimental income-reporting system is going into effect in 1989 for the first time, in just a few cities, covering state employees and owners of registered private businesses. There are no estimates on the number of potential taxpayers— but there have already been stories about evasion attempts in which it is estimated that 80 percent of self-employed individuals evade taxes. Enforcement publicity cites names of some famous people who have been caught evading income taxes, and, curiously, also mentions some who have paid voluntarily.

TEAM   See "Production team" under PEOPLE'S COMMUNES.

TELEVISION   As everywhere else in the world, television is an extremely popular pastime in China and has an important role in formal education. (See "Television and radio colleges" under "Adult Education" in chapter 7.) Also, as the use of TV in attempting to control the effects of the June Fourth Massacre shows, it is highly regarded by the government as a propaganda tool.

From the first TV broadcasts in 1958, Xinhua reports that today 90 percent of urban residents and 75 percent of rural residents—totaling 700 million—have access to television programs through some 75 million sets. There are now 202 TV broadcasting stations and over 2,000 relay stations as well as two telecommunications satellites used in part for television. Service to the entire country will require, however, the construction of about 8,000 more relay stations.

TEST-TUBE BABIES   Interestingly, even though China's population is growing faster than desired, the country's scientists are nevertheless pursuing research on infertility. Its first test-tube baby was born in the spring of 1988. It was reported that "Different opinions on whether a country with a population of over 1 billion needed to do research into test-tube births kept China from the work until six years after the world's first test-tube baby was born," but that the interests of basic research into reproduction, genetics, embryology, and other subjects tipped the scales.

THREE BIG MOUNTAINS   Metaphorical phrase for imperialism, feudalism, and bureaucratic capitalism (see separate entry), which are considered to have weighed like mountains on the backs of the Chinese people before liberation.

THREE BIGS   When reform began, the "three bigs" for consumers were a bicycle, a wristwatch, and a sewing machine. Today, they are a refrigerator, a washing machine, and a television set. For many people, there are now "four bigs," with a video cassette recorder added.

THREE COME INS AND ONE SUBSIDY   See BOTH ENDS OUTSIDE THE COUNTRY.

THREE EXCHANGES POLICY   See NUMBERS IN SLOGANS AND NAMES.

THREE-STEP DEVELOPMENT PLAN   This plan was referred to by Deng Xiaoping in his talk of June 9, 1989, to martial law commanders in Beijing. It is not new, but a restatement of general objectives for China's long-term development as set by the Twelfth National Congress of the CPC in 1982. (Deng refers to the objectives in connection with the Third Plenum of 1978, but it was not until 1982 that the goals were set. See "The Goal of Reform" in chapter 4.) Deng's formulation is: 1) Double the gross national product (which has already been achieved); 2) double the GNP again before the year 2000; 3) [this step is only implicit in the 1982 statement] reach the level of a "moderately developed" country, i.e., a country with average annual growth of 2 percent or more, within 50 years.

THREE THINGS TO LOVE   The motherland, socialism, and the Communist Party of China.

THREE WORLDS   This is a concept developed in the fifties by others (primarily French social scientists) used in analyses of the world situation in the 1970s by Mao Zedong and Deng Xiaoping. In their view, the nations of the world are classified into three categories, which they called "three worlds." The Soviet Union and the United States, the two super-powers, make up the First World. The western European countries and Japan belong to the Second World. The rest—developing countries throughout the world—make up the now well-known Third World, in which China classifies itself and to which it sends substantial economic aid.

TRADE CENTERS   See COMMODITY MARKETS.

TWO WHATEVERS   After Mao's death, his followers attempted to uphold a "two whatevers" policy—"We will resolutely uphold whatever policy decisions Chairman Mao made and unswervingly follow whatever instructions Chairman Mao gave." (See "Ideological Decisions," chapter 2.) In a satellite speech to the World Economic Forum in 1988, Zhao Ziyang set forth China's new "two whatevers"—"Whatever is beneficial to the growth of China's productivity should be allowed and encouraged; and whatever is necessary for promoting the market economy should not be rejected."

UNHEALTHY TENDENCIES   Shortly after the reform movement began, various kinds of corrupt and disreputable behavior began to come to light among government cadre and Party members, which was most often referred to under the label "unhealthy tendencies." This term covers such things as using power for personal gain, yielding to the temptation to think of everything in terms of money, clinging to one's post even if no longer competent or behaving as though one is indispensable, seeking personal profit or currying favor at the expense of the state, and performing duties carelessly or shirking them entirely.

UNIFIED PURCHASES   See PURCHASING POLICIES.

UNIT   In China, one's unit *(danwei [don-way])* is the factory, office, store, etc., where one works, but it is a great deal more. Virtually all housing is assigned through work units as are places in nurseries and some schools; units provide medical insurance and pensions; permission to have a child is secured through work units (and sometimes even permission to marry); and the work unit's recommendation is critical if one wishes to secure permission for studying abroad or other special privileges. It is at or through the work unit that political study and teaching is carried on, and the principal place where political dedication is judged. The work unit may be brought into cases of criminal or anti-social behavior.

Reviewing this explanation, a Chinese friend said, "Your unit also recommends you to book hotel and plane tickets, to do divorce or population registration, to visit any government official on any matter—in a word, without a work unit recommendation a Chinese won't be able to do *anything.*"

The insidious possibilities of the system are apparent in this story in the *South China Morning Post* on the problems of workers who wish to study abroad: "While often overstaffed offices have no particular interest in holding back employees who arrange and pay for their own studies abroad, they do have an interest in making it costly. Individuals must have written permission from their units in order to get a passport, an open invitation for blackmail.

"One friend recently paid 2,000 yuan in cash and another 1,000 yuan in gifts and banquets before her boss would sign a release form. . . .

"Some people simply quit their units and apply for passports through their local police stations, where they may have bribable acquaintances. So some clever bureaucrat created another hurdle: in order to take the university-required (in English-speaking countries) TO E F L (Test of English as a Foreign Language) examination, applicants [must now] secure a letter of permission from their work place. If they are unemployed, tough luck."

UNITED FRONT   Originally, United Front was the Party name for the alliance between the Party and the Kuomintang during the war against Japan; today, it refers to the department of the Central Committee through which the Party maintains relations with people of all nationalities, democratic parties, and social strata, and persons without party affiliations in China.

VILLAGERS' COMMITTEES   (See "Residents' Committees" for the equivalent urban organization.) Villagers' committees, now numbering 950,000, came into existence in 1982 with the replacement of communes by township governments. The committees assumed the economic and social (but not governmental) functions of the old brigades. On the average, a committee represents about 250 households or 1,000 persons.

Responsibilities of villagers' committees cover approximately the same wide range as residents' committees (see separate entry) in urban areas but also include organizing production and supervising public utilities.

Despite such broad powers and despite being constitutionally mandated elected bodies, villagers' committees are considered unofficial groups, not subject to the leadership of township governments (the lowest level of state power).

An attempt at the 1987 National People's Congress to recognize the unofficial status of villagers' committees and at the same time protect them from impositions by township governments sparked one of the most spirited discussions in NPC history, and made it necessary to extend the session by one day. Opponents of the resolution maintained that committees should be made official bodies because of their many responsibilities and importance in local life. Delegates voted to adopt only a draft version of law, to be implemented on a trial basis.

WALKING ON TWO LEGS   One of the most famous of modern Chinese metaphors, it is best known for its application to agriculture and industry, a way of pointing out that both are important. It may also be used in other contexts where ideas of balance, mutuality, coordination, etc., are involved.

WHOLESALE MARKETS   See COMMODITY MARKETS.

WORK POINTS   In people's communes, the work point was a numerical value which rated a person's basic daily work capacity, his or her assumed contribution to the total output of a production team. The work point value for a given worker was based on the team's group assessment of the person's health, age, skill, and involvement in household work. The maximum daily credit for a man was usually ten points, and eight for a woman. Distribution of annual crops and cash income was then made on the basis of individual totals for the year.

Today, the term is still sometimes encountered, often in an ambiguous context. For example, in some localities the work point rating is taken into account in determining the amount of land to be allotted under the responsibility system. There is apparently no longer any basis for its use in determining compensation simply because communal work teams no longer exist, but one does find puzzling references, such as that in one largely rural province "An only child is entitled to five work points a month as a health subsidy."

WORK UNIT   See UNIT.

XIU-XI   See NAP.

YOUNG PIONEERS   Distinguished by their red neckerchiefs sizable groups of primary school Young Pioneers of both sexes are often encountered in China at various kinds of events or at cultural institutions. Membership in the organization is not automatic, but while it is based on success at school and on good citizenship, most children do belong. Promotion of extra-curricular activities is the objective of the organization, and, unlike the Communist Youth League (see separate entry), membership has no political significance.

Appendix Three

Chronology of Economic, Social, and Political Events in China, 1949–1989

1949

Beijing liberated peacefully (January).

Nanjing, capital of "Nationalist regime," liberated; Chiang Kai-shek and Kuomintang government retreat to Taiwan (April).

People's Republic of China founded (October 1). Some fighting continues in the south and southwest and in east coast areas until well into the first half of 1950.

1950

Marriage Law becomes effective; stipulates free choice of mates instead of arranged marriages, equal rights for both sexes, and protection of rights of women and children.

Sino-Soviet Treaty signed (February).

Land Reform Law proclaimed. (June; see also 1952).

Korean War begins (June); China enters conflict in support of North Korea, and Chinese troops cross Yalu River (October).

1951

Resist America, Aid Korea campaign begins, the first nationwide mass campaign.

United States enacts a trade embargo against China which continues until 1972.

Missionaries leave China.

Movement Against the Three Evils (namely, corruption, waste, and bureaucracy) begins, aimed against corrupt officials of the Party, government, army, and mass organizations; it is the first large-scale postliberation political movement in China (December).

1952

Land reform essentially completed; over 700 million *mu* of land (about 120 million acres) and large amounts of farm implements redistributed to peasants; extortionate annual payments to landlords are eliminated.

Most sectors of agriculture and industry greatly exceed highest preliberation production levels.

Movement Against the Five Evils (namely, bribery, tax evasion, theft of state property, cheating on government contracts, and stealing of economic information) begins, aimed against actions of private commercial and industrial enterprises. Both Three Evils (1951) and Five Evils movements are concluded in midyear after numerous punishments and several executions.

General Line for Transition to Socialism adopted; calls for socialist ownership of agriculture, industry, commerce, and handicrafts (December).

1953

Constitution Drafting Committee established, headed by Mao.

Election Law passed.

First Five-Year Plan (1953–57) begins.

Agricultural producers' mutual aid groups popularized nationwide. (See "Agricultural Cooperatives" in the Mini-Encyclopedia.)

State begins planned purchase and supply of grain products.

Korean War ends (July).

1954

Beginning of rural collectivization marked by promulgation of Central Committee decision on the development of agricultural producers' cooperatives. (See "Agricultural Cooperatives" and "People's Communes" in the Mini-Encyclopedia.)

First National People's Congress held in Beijing.

First constitution adopted by the congress.

China's foreign policy, contained in its treaty with India, is summarized for first time in the Five Principles of Peaceful Coexistence: mutual respect for territorial integrity and sovereignty; mutual nonaggression; noninterference in each other's internal affairs; equality; and mutual coexistence.

About 2,000 state-owned enterprises placed under central ministries.

1955

State expands its monopoly in the purchase and supply of agricultural produce.

Graded wage system, which also provides for monetary wages, adopted for all state employees, replacing the system of payment in kind that had prevailed since before liberation.

Central Committee passes resolution on socialist transformation to effect joint state-private ownership of capitalist industry and commerce.

1956

"Hundred Flowers" or "Double Hundred" policy adopted (May); the slogan is drawn from the name of a policy which, in full, advocates "letting a hundred flowers blossom and letting a hundred schools of thought contend," in questions of art, literature, and science. (See "Hundred Flowers Policy" in Mini-Encyclopedia.)

Eighth National Congress of the Communist Party of China held

(September), first congress since liberation. Congress decides that the main contradiction in China is no longer between the working class and the capitalist class, but between people's demand for a better cultural and economic life and the inability of the country to meet the need. Country's main task designated as development of productive forces. Liu Shaoqi, then Mao's designated successor (but demoted and persecuted during Cultural Revolution), proclaims China has reached the "advanced" stage of socialism, and congress backs agricultural collectivization. Congress also emphasizes the need for democratic centralism (on the basis of democracy and democracy under centralized guidance), collective leadership, and fighting against a personality cult in inner Party life.

Joint state-private ownership established in almost all capitalist industrial and commercial enterprises by the first half of the year; socialist transformation of agriculture and handicrafts and the last stage of change to state-private ownership completed by end of year.

1957

Anti-Rightist Campaign, a major post-1949 political movement, is launched (April), aimed at subjectivism, factionalism, and bureaucracy within the Party. (See "Hundred Flowers Policy" in Mini-Encyclopedia.)

More than 9,300 state-owned enterprises under central management, compared with 2,800 in 1953–54; 530 kinds of products and supplies under central management, compared with 220 in 1953.

Collectivization under advanced agricultural producers' cooperatives, begun in 1955 as an extension of the successful and smaller agricultural producers' cooperatives, is completed by end of year, one year ahead of schedule set by National Agricultural Development Program.

1958

Great Leap Forward and establishment of people's communes begin late in the year. (See "Great Leap Forward" and "People's Communes" in Mini-Encyclopedia.)

Chinese troops begin to withdraw from Korea in March, complete withdrawal in October.

In last nine months of year, the control pendulum again swings dramatically, shifting managerial control of more than 8,000 enterprises to local authorities. In many respects, however, enterprises continue to be merely extensions of their administering authorities. Beginning this year, enterprises are permitted to keep a portion of their profits to cover bonuses, collective welfare, etc.

1959

By the end of the year, it is obvious that the Great Leap Forward is an economic and political catastrophe, despite some notable accomplishments achieved at extremely high overall cost. Severe economic hardships persist for about three years, during which millions die of starvation.

1960

Second Five-Year Plan fulfilled three years ahead of schedule (January).

Soviet Union abruptly cancels its aid commitments to China as a result of long-standing ideological and political frictions (July) and withdraws its experts with all their plans and equipment. Move leaves 250 major projects at a virtual standstill.

1961

Attempting to recover from the Great Leap Forward, China starts its first period of economic readjustment. The policy of the period is to "readjust, consolidate, fill in, and develop." Central ministries reassume control over most enterprises, as well as over planning authority and other management powers transferred earlier to lower echelons. By the end of 1962 central ministries control 10,000 enterprises, even more than before the Great Leap, and most supplies are again allocated centrally.

1962

Central Committee holds its famous 7,000-person "enlarged meeting" (January) to sum up Party's positive and negative experiences since liberation and during the Great Leap. Mao makes a self-criticism concerning the Great Leap, and deputies analyze their own work. They conclude that the Party has made errors because, in addition to a lack of experience in socialist construction, some leading members have become conceited, violated the long tradition of seeking truth from facts and the mass line, and weakened the practice of democratic centralism.

Meeting is credited with a major role in success of economic readjustment.

Tenth Plenum of the Eighth Communist Party of China Central Committee holds a three-day conference (September). Mao develops his theory that the main social contradiction is the conflict between the working class and the capitalist class, and says that the struggle between the two must continue through the socialist period until communism arrives. Thus class struggle should always be the Party's paramount task. In accepting this formulation, the conference contributes to later upheavals.

1963

Socialist Education Movement begins officially in May, although it has been underway experimentally since late 1962, and continues until it is officially merged with the Cultural Revolution in December 1966. (See "Socialist Education Movement" in the Mini-Encyclopedia.)

Zhou Enlai proposes worldwide nuclear disarmament (September).

China becomes self-sufficient in oil and petroleum products.

1964

As the turmoil of the Great Leap Forward passes, the shortcomings of extreme centralization again become evident, and decentralization begins once more.

China explodes its first atomic bomb, and pledges no first use of the weapon.

Four Modernizations (modernization in agriculture, industry, science and technology, and national defense), the first mention of the concept under this name, urged by Zhou Enlai.

1965

Tibet Autonomous Region established.

Mao's continuing exaggerated concern with eliminating elitism and privilege is typified by eliminating the system of rank in the People's Liberation Army (May).

1966

Cultural Revolution begins (May), commencing a three-year period considered the most violent and vicious stage of the campaign. (See

"Cultural Revolution" in the Mini-Encyclopedia.)

1967

Deng Xiaoping purged from government as "capitalist roader."

China explodes its first hydrogen bomb (June).

1968

This is a year of "struggle-criticism-transformation," during which an attempt is made to begin recovery from Cultural Revolution damage of the past two years. Many changes are made in all areas of life, most with a strong flavor of egalitarianism and decentralization and all supervised by "revolutionary committees" which appear in virtually every institution and enterprise by the end of the year.

1969

Chinese and Soviet troops clash at Zhenbao Island in Heilongjiang Province (March).

Ninth National Congress of the Chinese Communist Party held (April), first in thirteen years. Approves Cultural Revolution and declares it over (for first time; see also declarations in 1976 and 1977). Approves Mao's theory of continuing revolution.

United States relaxes travel and trade restrictions on citizens dealing with China (July).

1970

Natural population growth rate reaches 26 per thousand.

Nearly all enterprises under central ministries are turned over to local authorities, including some of the very largest (defense-related industries excepted).

China launches its first earth satellite (April), a radio transmitter continuously broadcasting the revolutionary anthem "The East is Red."

1971

Henry Kissinger, Assistant to the President of the United States, makes his first trip to China; Zhou Enlai extends China's official invitation to President Nixon to visit China (July).

Lin Biao, Mao's personally chosen successor and a principal leader of the Cultural Revolution, reported killed in a plane crash while fleeing after alleged coup attempt (September).

People's Republic of China seated in the United Nations, replacing the Kuomintang government of Taiwan (October 25).

1972

President Nixon visits China (February); he and Zhou Enlai issue Shanghai Communiqué, which calls for closer relations between United States and China and includes US acknowledgment that Taiwan is part of China.

Japanese Premier Tanaka visits China; Sino-Japanese diplomatic relations normalized (September).

1973

Deng Xiaoping emerges from limbo as vice-premier, his first appearance in a political role since being purged in 1967.

New birth control campaign announced, after neglect of the subject during earlier period of the Cultural Revolution.

Tenth National Congress of the Communist Party of China convened. At the congress, Wang Hongwen, leader of the Shanghai ultraleftist mass organizations, becomes Party vice-chairman; other ultraleft Politburo members—Jiang Qing, Zhang Chunqiao, and Yao Wenyuan—join with him to form the strong clique within the Party leadership which becomes known as the Gang of Four.

1974

Japan and China conclude a most-favored nation trade agreement (January).

Criticize Lin Biao and Criticize Confucius Campaign begins; ideological criticism in cultural and political matters intensifies (February).

China admitted to International Amateur Athletic Union (August).

1975

Deng Xiaoping becomes vice-chairman of Central Committee (January).

1976

This year—with the Tiananmen Incident (see April), the death of Mao, and the arrest of the Gang of Four—is generally considered the end of the Cultural Revolution. The end was first declared at the Ninth Congress of the Communist Party of China in April 1969; the most violent period was past, but turmoil continued for several years. It was again declared over at the Eleventh Congress in August 1977

Zhou Enlai dies (January 8).

Deng Xiaoping again purged from leadership, after Mao criticizes him on several ideological and political points (February)

Hua Guofeng appointed acting premier (February), premier (April) and, after Mao's death in September, acting chairman of the Party and of the Military Affairs Commission, thus becoming the only person ever to hold these three key positions at one time.

Spontaneous outburst of homage for Zhou Enlai by hundreds of thousands in Tiananmen Square in Beijing and in other major cities during Qingming Festival (April); demonstrations are also in opposition to the Gang of Four and in support of recently purged Deng Xiaoping, whom many Chinese considered Zhou's proper successor; large-scale police actions organized by Gang of Four suppress the demonstrations.

Tangshan suffers earthquake which takes 240,000 lives (July 28).

Mao Zedong dies (September 9).

Gang of Four (Jiang Qing, Mao's widow; Yao Wenyuan; Wang Hungwen; Zhang Chunqiao) arrested (October 6)

Centralization again undertaken, to help cope with the severe problems brought on by the turmoil of the Cultural Revolution.

1977

College entrance examinations restored.

End of Cultural Revolution officially declared at Eleventh National Congress of the Communist Part of China (August); Hua Guofeng appointed Party chairman; the political report to the congress continues to speak approvingly of the theories, policies, and slogans of the Cultural Revolution.

Deng Xiaoping reinstated as Politburo member, deputy premier, and chief of general staff of People's Liberation Army at same congress.

Widespread public discussion and writing on democratization of government begins spontaneously.

1978

Constitution of 1978 promulgated; preamble refers to the "triumphant conclusion of the First Great Proletarian Cultural Revolution;" includes the Cultural Revolution's "Four Bigs"—the right to "speak out freely, air views fully, hold great debates, and write big-character posters," and specifies that citizens should not be subjected to arbitrary search, arrest, or harassment.

Deng Xiaoping elected chairman of the National Committee of the Chinese People's Political Consultative Conference.

Growth targets considered excessively high by many are set for 1978 in Hua Guofeng's report to the First Session of the Fifth National People's Congress (February). Targets include building "10 big oil fields" by the end of the century and realizing agricultural mechanization by 1980. High capital spending in efforts to reach these goals led to the severe economic cutbacks of 1979–80.

Democracy movement muted by official monitoring, some arrests.

Third Plenary Session of the Eleventh Central Committee of the Communist Party of China meets (December), in perhaps the most important session since liberation. The Plenum rules that "practice," rather than writings of Marx and Mao, "is the sole criterion for judging truth," and lays other foundations for reform. Adopts draft of "Decisions on Acceleration of Agricultural Development" which allows compensation linked to production and thus makes responsibility system possible. (See "Background of the New Revolution" in chapter 2 and note on final adoption of "Decisions" under 1979.)

1979

United States and China establish full diplomatic relations (January).

In response to growing democratization movement Deng enunciates Four Cardinal Principles of Socialism, emphasizing supremacy of the Party (March); Democracy Walls in Beijing and elsewhere suppressed and several movement leaders arrested.

Central Committee Work Conference (April) formulates the principle of "readjusting, restructuring, consolidating, and improving" the country's economy, with emphasis on readjustment. Practical results with respect to improving the people's livelihood are to be emphasized. (See "Readjusting, Restructuring, Consolidating, and Improving China's Economy" in chapter 5.)

"Decisions on Some Questions Concerning the Acceleration of Agricultural Development" adopted by the Fourth Plenary Session of the Eleventh Central Committee (September). Major provisions are that prices paid by the state to peasants will be raised substantially and a 50 percent premium paid for above-quota production; peasants have the right to grow crops of their choice, and to be protected from exploitation by higher authorities; collectives may adopt compensation methods based either on quotas or on time worked, and may include performance evaluation in determining payment due; peasants may not be criticized or called "capitalist roaders" for use of private plots, selling in free markets, etc.

1980

"One couple, one child" policy proposed early in year, detailed in open letter to Communist Youth League members in fall. (See "The One-Child Policy"in chapter 3.)

Natural growth rate announced as 10.7 per thousand in 1980, down from 26.0 per thousand in 1970, which meant 68 million fewer births in 10 years.

"Decision on Problems of Making Elementary Education Universal" issued by Central Committee and State Council, requiring that universal elementary education be implemented as far as possible before 1990.

Special economic zones created. (See "Opening to the Outside World" in chapter 5.)

Constitution of 1978 revised (April) to eliminate Article 45 covering the "four bigs" (see 1978), which the government felt had been abused in both the Cultural Revolution and in the Democracy Wall movement.

"Guiding Principles for Inner-Party Life" adopted by Fifth Plenary Session of the Eleventh Central Committee (February) is a twelve-point statement summing up the Party's experience in handling inner-Party relations, with special emphasis on applying lessons learned during the Cultural Revolution. One point requires opposition to "the making of arbitrary decisions by individuals."

Zhao Ziyang replaces Hua Guofeng as premier (September).

1981

System of graduate education inaugurated which makes use of bachelor's, master's, and doctor's degrees, thesis research and defense, etc.; the recognition of completion of the first level of higher education will still be a diploma, but no degree.

Another readjustment (cutback) of the national economy announced (February). The 1979 adjustment did not achieve its objectives, in part because agencies found various means and rationales for continuing their own projects.

"Resolution on Certain Questions in the History of Our Party since the Founding of the People's Republic of China" adopted by Sixth Plenary Session of the Eleventh Central Committee (June). Essentially, the resolution made the first substantial Party criticism of Mao's conduct of the government, but drew a careful distinction between his early contributions and his "mistakes in his later years."

Hu Yaobang succeeds Hua Guofeng as Party chairman; Hua and Zhao Ziyang become vice-chairmen (June).

1982

By the end of the year, 92 percent of production brigades have adopted various forms of responsibility systems linking income with production, of which household contracts account for 87.7 percent. Specialized households account for about 10 percent of the total number of rural households.

Shift of peasants since 1976 from agriculture to fish and poultry breeding, processing industries, transporting farm and sideline products, commerce, service trades, and other nonagricultural occupations passes 100 million.

Central Discipline Inspection Commission of the Communist Party of China begins investigation of officials suspected of economic crimes.

Premier Zhao announces that there will be no further increases in autonomy of enterprises and localities in 1982, and that previous reforms might be rescinded (March).

Third national census taken on July 1 shows that China had 1,008,000,000 people on the mainland, approximately 22 percent of the world's population, an increase of 460,000,000 (85 percent) over 1949, the year of liberation, when the population was about 540,000,000.

Twelfth National Congress of the Communist Party of China (September) adopts new constitution setting stricter standards for behavior and work style of Party members, stressing collective leadership, and forbidding any form of personality cult; eliminates posts of Party chairman and vice-chairman; Hu Yaobang becomes general secretary of Party; adopts proposal for socialist modernization aimed at quadrupling gross annual value of industrial and agricultural production from 710 billion yuan in 1980 to 2,800 billion yuan in 2000.

1983

Employment system reform begins under the new concept of "contract employment" (February).

Central Discipline Inspection Commission reports finding widespread economic crime and corruption in government and the Party (July). There is growing awareness of the problem.

Concern grows among many leaders that reforms and increasing exposure of China's people to foreign culture and ideas are damaging Chinese society. Deng Xiaoping calls for "forceful criticism"of ideological deviations and restraints against cultural contamination, which leads to Campaign against Spiritual Pollution. Campaign frightens many Chinese with its Cultural Revolution overtones, damages China's image abroad, and raises questions in minds of foreign investors about possible change in business climate; campaign loses steam in December.

1984

Vast number of bonuses, loans, and other financial transactions, which are particularly heavy late in year, put record amount of currency into circulation and create serious economic problems.

Communist Party of China membership announced as 40 million; 4.5 million new members since 1979.

Crackdown on violent crime results in thousands of arrests and numerous public executions.

Premier Zhao Ziyang visits the United States (January).

Economic development zones created in 14 cities to encourage foreign investment (April). (See "Opening to the Outside World" in chapter 5.)

"Regulations on Further Extending the Decision-Making Powers of State-Owned Enterprises" adopted by State Council (May). Regulations, which are a basis for Central Committee's economic reform decision in October, give enterprises the right to increase production above the state quota or to request that quota be reviewed in light of market; to set limited floating prices for market sales of above-quota production (quota amounts are sold to state at fixed price); and to make decisions on personnel, bonuses, finances, etc.

Sino-British joint declaration on Hongkong is initialed (September 26), providing for return of Hongkong to Chinese control in 1997 and for continuation of Hongkong's capitalist economy for fifty years thereafter under the "one country, two systems" concept. (See "One Country, Two Systems" in the Mini-Encyclopedia.)

"Decision on Reform of the Economic Structure" adopted at Third Plenary Session of the Twelfth Communist Party of China Central Committee (October); formally announces urban reform campaign which has been partially and experimentally underway for several years. (See chapter 5, "The Six Big Reforms.")

Thirty-fifth anniversary of People's Republic is celebrated (October).

Second stage of Party rectification begins (November). All 40 million members of Communist Party of China must reapply for membership during next two years; those guilty of various forms of wrongdoing will be denied re-entrance.

"Circular on Resolutely Correcting Evil Practices Appearing Under the New Situation," concerned with Party corruption and rectification, issued by Central Discipline Inspection Committee (December).

People's Daily carries a front-page article (December) headlined "Theory Not Enough for Success," a major restatement of the view which first surfaced at the Third Plenum in 1978 that it is not necessary to follow Marx blindly. (See "Are the Chinese Going Capitalist?" in chapter 4.)

1985

Wage and price reforms begin. (See "Price Reform: Making Prices Reflect Realities" and "Smashing Egalitarianism's 'Big Pot' " in chapter 5.) Price controls removed from large number of agricultural and industrial commodities, with prices left free to fluctuate according to the market (February); there is a rapid increase in some prices, especially food.

Mandatory sales quotas ended for purchases from peasants (February).

"Decision on Reform of the Educational System" issued by Central Committee (May). (See "The 1985 Decision on Educational Reform" in chapter 7.)

Government announces plan to reduce size of army by a million men inside of two years (June).

Runaway industrial growth of first half of the year, resulting from excessive currency put into circulation in 1984 and disregard for development plans, said to be under control (November).

1986

Corruption becomes a paramount concern early in year after heavy publicity in government periodicals extending back into 1985. (See "Official Corruption Menaces Government's Legitimacy," chapter 4.)

Compulsory education draft law providing for nine years of schooling adopted by National People's Congress (March). (See "Compulsory Education" in chapter 7.)

Bankruptcy Law in draft form becomes effective in an experimental application (March), is in effect in Shenyang, Chongqing, and Wuhan by midyear, and is passed (December) for trial implementation (but only after Factory Enterprise Law is passed and becomes effective).

Political reform is placed on the nation's agenda by remarks by Zhao and Deng (July) and other events. (See "What About Political Reform?" in chapter 4.)

Negotiable securities trading begins in Shenyang, China's first market of its kind (August).

Foreign investment regulations are revised to counter increasing criticism from foreign investors concerned with bureaucracy, delay, high costs, and unfairness encountered in attempts to establish business ventures in China (October).

New employment regulations for state enterprises make crucial changes in personnel policies (October); require contract form of hiring for all new employees (see "The Workers' Role," chapter 5); outline competitive hiring procedures; prescribe grounds for dismissing employees; establish unemployment insurance system.

China's population estimated at 1,060,000,000 (December); original goal of preventing population from passing 1,200,000,000 by year 2000 no longer can be achieved.

First of student protest marches occurs in Anhui at Hefei Science and

Technology University (December 5) and movement spreads to twenty cities by end of month; students have a wide range of complaints, from poor food and living conditions, bureaucratic job assignment practices, and other personal matters to desires for a different election system, more democracy and freedom of discussion, etc.

1987

Student demonstrations continue into new year and bring increasingly harsh criticisms from Party figures who see in the situation evidence of "bourgeois liberalization" and a threat to the Party and social order.

Party secretary Hu Yaobang, viewed by some as contributing to student unrest and widespread bourgeois liberalization, is severely criticized and resigns (January); retains Politburo post. Zhao Ziyang becomes acting Party secretary. During same period, three leading intellectuals are expelled from Party for bourgeois liberalization.

An insurance-based pension plan is expected to be in effect nationwide by the end of the year, replacing the old practice under which units attempted to pay pensions from current income.

Harbin Industrial University School of Space Flight, China's first school for astronaut training, begins enrolling students.

Factory director responsibility system regulations promulgated (January), placing decision-making authority in hands of director rather than Party secretary, as in past; workers' congresses empowered to review director's decisions on wages and benefits.

Personal Income Regulatory Tax, levying 20 to 60 percent progressive tax on monthly income above 400 yuan, becomes effective (January).

China Reconstructs, popular monthly magazine which has told China's story in several languages since 1952, celebrates thirty-five years of publishing (February).

Third Antarctic exploration team completes its expedition (February).

Students to be required to meet political as well as academic standards before being allowed to sit for university admission examinations (April).

Portugal and China sign agreement (April) returning Macao to Chinese sovereignty by 1999. Like Hongkong, Macao is guaranteed fifty years continuation of its capitalistic system and way of life.

Greater Hinggan Forest, 300 by 500 miles in area and thought to be the world's largest evergreen stand, is swept by a series of fires (May) constituting one of the world's major ecological disasters. The forest included about a third of China's timber. A forest about three times as large is thought to have burned across the border in Russia.

Consolidation and rectification drive begun in 1983 to improve Party style of work, level of ethics, and commitment comes to end (May); more than 500,000 members (of the 40 million members at the start of the drive) were disciplined in some way; 172,000 of those were expelled or denied re-registration.

Party announces (July) that any Party member accepting any bribe whatever will be expelled, regardless of rank.

Daya Bay nuclear power plant begins construction (August).

First commercial satellite launching and recovery completed (August).

Tibet is disturbed by twenty days of sporadic protests against Chinese rule by some persons favoring independence (September-October).

Thirteenth National Congress of Communist Party of China convenes in Beijing (October). These were some of the major events of the congress, considered one of the most important in history: Zhao Ziyang was confirmed as Party secretary; Deng Xiaoping resigned from the Politburo and took with him nearly all the elderly conservatives who have opposed reform (though a rough ideological balance was maintained by selecting new members with similar points of view); the theory that China is in the primary stage of socialism was fully explored authoritatively for the first time, providing ideological basis for several aspects of reform; and economic and political reform processes and goals were broadly reaffirmed. (See "The Big Thirteenth" in chapter 2.)

After forty years of refusing contact of any kind with the People's Republic, Taiwan decides to permit indirect travel to China for reunions with relatives who remained behind on the mainland when the Kuomintang left China at the time of liberation (November).

Li Peng appointed acting premier by the Standing Committee of the National People's Congress (November).

1988

Chiang Ching Kuo, son of Chiang Kai-shek and president of Taiwan since 1975, dies (January). Succeeded by Lee Teng Hui.

Male contraceptive method developed by Chinese physician is announced; it is claimed to be 100 percent effective, reversible, inexpensive, and requires no hospitalization (January). Method involves removable block in sperm duct and has been approved by World Health Organization.

More than 100 prominent intellectuals submit petition (February) for release of Democracy Wall dissident Wei Jingsheng and other political prisoners. Petition is refused, the government saying that it has no political prisoners.

With the launching of the nation's third telecommunications satellite (March), China is less dependent on the use of satellites of other nations.

Seventh National People's Congress opens first session in Beijing (March). During the congress: Li Peng is confirmed as premier; Yang Shangkun is elected President of China; Wan Li is elected chairman of the congress; the long-delayed Enterprise Law governing state-owned enterprises is passed, nominally giving enterprise directors primary control instead of Party secretaries and defining rights and responsibilities of Party secretaries and workers (see "Factory Director Responsibility System" in chapter 5); the constitution is amended to approve private businesses and to allow sale of long-term rights to use land (although technically the state continues to own all land).

US Peace Corps invited to work in China (March); first time corps volunteers have been allowed in a communist country. It is later announced that twenty volunteers will arrive in November to teach English, primarily, at Sichuan Province universities. (Invitation withdrawn; see June 27.)

Li Xiannian, retired President of China, is elected chairman of the Chinese People's Political Consultative Conference (April).

Vegetable prices soar 50 percent in first quarter; state decontrols prices on eggs, vegetables, pork, and sugar, and simultaneously orders 10-yuan monthly subsidy for each worker in state enterprises and collectives (May).

State Family Planning Commission receives 1988 award of International Council on Population Program Management (May).

Climbers from a joint Chinese-Japanese-Nepalese expedition conquer Mt. Qomolangma (Mt. Everest) for the first time from north and south slopes simultaneously (May 6).

Deng Xiaoping, as chairman of the state Central Military Commission, reveals that de facto control of the military now rests with vice-chairman, and Party secretary, Zhao Ziyang (June).

Communist Party of China membership announced as 47.8 million; 8.9 million new members since 1983 (June).

Ninth meeting of the Communist Party of China Political Bureau (May 30-June 1) asserts that reform has reached a critical stage which necessitates immediate attention to the soaring inflation rate and the antiquated and unreasonable wage system. Zhao Ziyang emphasizes the need for increased commodity production and for turning away from the old concept of "product output," which inhibits adjustments for market influences. Groups are formed to formulate plans for the coming five years.

First issue of *Seeking Truth*, the successor to the Party magazine *Red Flag*, is published (July).

Enterprise Law intended to give state-owned enterprises greater managerial autonomy goes into effect (August). (See "Factory Director Responsibility System" in chapter 5.)

China and Japan sign major investment protection agreement which gives Japanese firms in China (unlike other foreign firms) equal rights with Chinese firms in securing raw materials and labor and in some other matters. In return, Japan is to provide credits of several billion dollars (August).

Tenth meeting of the Communist Party of China Political Bureau (August 15-17) at Beidaihe resort announces a "Tentative Plan on Price and Wage Reforms." Ranks and insignia restored to the People's Liberation Army (embracing army, navy, and air force). Formerly, only differences in uniform designated three general grades—enlisted, junior officer (below regimental level), and senior officer (regimental level or above) (August).

China announces that it has been successful in firing missiles from submarines equipped to launch guided nuclear missiles (September).

Chinese and western sources say China explodes a neutron bomb, its first (September).

State Council and Central Disciplinary Inspection Commission of the Communist Party of China separately issue regulations for punishing government and Party functionaries guilty of embezzlement, bribery, violation of Party discipline, etc. No details on how provisions or enforcement differ from those announced numerous times before which have been ineffective (September).

China acknowledges that it is no longer possible to meet its longtime goal of limiting its population to 1.2 billion at the end of the century. Likely total will be 1.25 to 1.28 billion (September).

Zhao Ziyang makes major policy speech to the Third Plenary Session of the Thirteenth Central Committee of the Communist Party of China (September 26–30) presenting the results of several months of top-level meetings concerned with the proliferating problems created by reform. Speech, not released for more than a month, makes proposals that, essentially, are not new, but, as *China Daily* points out, "they have never been implemented in an effective manner."

The Beijing Electron-Positron Collider, China's first high-energy accelerator, goes into operation (October). French physicists collaborated in design and construction.

Taiwan announces that it no longer considers its relationship with the People's Republic of China to be a hostile one.

Bankruptcy Law goes into effect (November 1).

New heavy ion accelerator, one of the world's largest, completed in Lanzhou, a project of more than a hundred institutions and enterprises (December).

Massive twenty-one generator Gezhouba Hydroelectric Power Station on the Changjiang (Yangzte) River, under construction for more than eleven years, is completed (December).

Qian Qichen, Chinese Minister of Foreign Affairs, visits the Soviet Union, the first such visit since 1957 (December).

Rajiv Gandhi, the Prime Minister of India, visits China (December) the first visit of an Indian prime minister since 1954. During the visit, Gandhi reaffirmed "that Tibet is an autonomous region of China and that anti-China political activities by Tibetan elements are not permitted on Indian soil."

Chinese Academy of Aeronautics and Space Flight, the largest such institution in these fields in China, is founded in Beijing (December).

December ends a memorable and painful year of floods, drought, a major earthquake, disappointing crops, the highest inflation in the history of the People's Republic, and broad setbacks in economic reform.

1989

China begins 1989 with a population of 1.096 billion, and will pass the 1.100 billion mark in April. *People's Daily* announces (February) that the likely total by 2000 is more than 1.3 billion, 100 million more than planned.

Heart disease, stroke, and cancer are found to be the three leading causes of death in China in a major eight-year survey of one percent of the population (January).

The Panchen Lama, Tibet's second highest religious leader, dies of a heart attack on January 28. Only four days before, in probably the most frank admission to date of possible Chinese malfeasance in Tibet, the Panchen Lama, who was also a vice-chairman of the Standing Committee of China's National People's Congress, said that the major threat to Tibet is leftism and that it has cost the region dearly in the past thirty years. "The price we have paid for our development outweighs the achievements. The mistake must never be repeated."

Eduard Shevardnadze, Foreign Minister of the Soviet Union, visits China (February). During his visit, arrangements are made for a summit meeting in May between Deng Xiaoping and Mikhail Gorbachev.

China and Indonesia agree to normalize relations after a twenty-two year break (February).

US President George Bush visits Beijing briefly after attending Emperor Hirohito's funeral in Tokyo (February).

State Council and the Central Committee of the Communist Party of China issue a joint circular requiring government and Party officials who are participating in commercial firms to resign their posts by March 31 (February).

Lhasa, Tibetan capital, put under martial law by Chinese government March 7, after three days of riots by pro-independence demonstrators.

Second session of Seventh National People's Congress opens (March 20). The unusually long 17-day session adopts Premier Li Peng's proposals for improving the economic environment and rectifying the economic order, through economic austerity and further attempts at recentralization of power; his position constitutes an unusually strong criticism of the policies of his predecessor as premier, Zhao Ziyang. The conflict, and its tone, foreshadow later attacks on reformers by conservatives during Pro-Democracy Movement.

(*Events from April through July which are connected with student protests, the Pro-Democracy Movement, and the June Fourth Massacre are covered separately in Appendix IV.*)

"1.1 Billion Population Day" observed April 14 (the day China's population is estimated to have exceeded this figure).

Government is failing to control nonproductive expenditures and use of foreign exchange, as it announced it intended to do in imposing austerity plans in recent months. For example, it is revealed (May) that first quarter imports of automobiles rose more than 50 percent compared to first quarter 1988.

Mikhail S. Gorbachev, president of the Presidium of the Supreme Soviet of the Soviet Union and general secretary of the Soviet Communist Party, arrives (May 15) for a long-planned and historic summit meeting with Chinese leaders; he is the first top Soviet official to visit China in thirty years. He meets with Deng Xiaoping, Zhao Ziyang, Li Peng, and other leading officials to discuss Cambodia, economic relations, military contacts, and other issues; talks were cordial but without announced major result. Gorbachev's visit, long savored by Chinese leaders, is overshadowed by continuing public protests and marches.

Gorbachev tells a news conference in Beijing (May 17) that it is not true that political reform was initially emphasized over economic reform in the Soviet Union, as is often asserted by foreigners. (China has chosen to emphasize economic reform first, and has made relatively minor political changes, one complaint of the Pro-Democracy Movement.) *China Daily* reported Gorbachev said economic problems were tackled early, but "... the roots of many economic problems were much deeper than expected and they stemmed from politics. Without political restructuring economic reform could not make headway."

The Nationalist (Kuomintang) government of Taiwan, after forty years, officially acknowledges that it does not control the mainland of China, but refuses to give up its claim to the mainland (June 4).

Zhao Ziyang dismissed as Party General Secretary (June 24) and replaced by Jiang Zemin. (Further details in Appendix IV.).

Because of tensions between the two countries, China withdraws (June 27) invitation extended to US Peace Corps earlier in year.

In choosing future state-supported candidates for study abroad, the State Education Commission announces (July 1), the student's "level of patriotism [i.e., devotion to the four cardinal principles] should be a major criterion in the selection."

Government orders withdrawal from sale or use of all books and journals tending toward bourgeois liberalization (July 3). Ban includes works by such famous persons as Hu Yaobang, Zhao Ziyang, and Fang Lizhi, and intellectual figures Yan Jiaqi and Su Shaozhi.

Sale of foreign periodicals is forbidden (July 15) and all newsstands, including those in hotels and stores for foreigners, are raided by security police. A spokeswoman said, according to *China Daily*, "We do not resist any foreign newspapers and magazines," but "it is only natural that we disallow to prevail on our land newspapers and magazines which interfere with China's internal affairs and hurt the national feelings in China." Ban is later relaxed.

Fourth national census of population will begin July 1, 1990, only three years after the third census (July 19).

Government announces that identification checks can now be made in most places throughout the country because more than 500,000,000 citizens have already received ID cards (July 21). About 200,000,000, 35 percent of the total, remain to be issued, largely in remote areas.

Politburo bars children and spouses of top officials (but only the very top officials) from working in or owning private businesses (July 28). Relatives of officials have for several years been widely believed to be using their political connections to realize enormous profits. (This and other official corruption was one target of the Pro-Democracy Movement.) Politburo also directs that leaders will no longer be provided foods which are unavailable to the public.

Amnesty International charges that the government has ordered secret executions of demonstrators "who have committed the most serious crimes" (August 30).

A United Nations subcommission approves a resolution expressing concern over China's actions in suppressing the Pro-Democracy Movement (August 31).

Wang Meng, an intellectual and victim of the Anti-Rightist Campaign who has been Minister of Culture since 1986, is replaced by He Jinzhi, a major official in the Party propaganda department (September 4).

Li Peng admits in an interview published in France (September 6) that the spring's demonstrators "had good reasons to protest" and that the Party had been "incompetent." He said, however, that the government's actions had been entirely proper and that there would be no amnesty for protesters whom the government considers to have committed serious offenses.

Deng Xiaoping reportedly has designated as his successor the new Party Secretary Jiang Zemin. Deng is thought to consider Jiang dedicated to the policy of economic opening to the world and to furthering economic reform. Observers say that Jiang has too narrow a power base and too little experience to escape a succession struggle upon Deng's death.

Federation for Democracy in China (known as Democratic Front for China during its organizing period) is formed in Paris (September 24) despite efforts by Chinese government to pressure France into preventing the meeting. A representative of Poland's Solidarity Party attended. Founders include Yan Jiaqi, a political scientist and close adviser to Zhao Ziyang (Yan was elected president); Wuer Kaixi, a student leader in the Tiananmen Square demonstrations, vice president; Liu Binyan, famed investigative journalist and writer; Su Shaozhi, former director of the Institute of Marxism-Leninism under the Chinese Academy of Social Sciences; Wan Runnan, ex-chairman of the Stone Corporation, a major computer company outstanding among China's private enterprises; and Chen Yizi, an economist and top aide to Zhao. The group says that it intends to be a nonviolent organization working toward greater democracy in government and improvements in human rights and that its goal is to provide a choice of government, not to overthrow the present regime.

The fortieth anniversary of the founding of the People's Republic of China is celebrated in festivities that were essentially private observances for the leadership (October 1). Military security was extremely tight and the general public was not allowed within about a mile of the historic Tiananmen Rostrum, scene of Mao's announcement in 1949 that the republic had come into being. Many foreign governments were not represented at all, and many others only by low level delegates. Leaders' remarks at events related to the anniversary reaffirm the hardline, orthodox direction taken by the new government.

The Dalai Lama, Tibetan leader-in-exile, is awarded the Nobel Peace Prize for 1989 for his non-violent campaign to return Tibetan rule to Tibetans (October 5). The Chinese government is offended, saying the award interferes in its internal affairs.

Party Secretary Jiang Zemin is designated as the "core" leader of the Party and the third heir-designate to Deng Xiaoping (October 10; confirms September 18 reports).

Former US President Richard M. Nixon visits Beijing from October 30, and tells leaders that "many in the United States, including many friends of China, believe the crackdown was excessive and unjustified. The events of April through June damaged the respect and confidence which most Americans previously had for the leaders of China," but urges attempts to restore good relations between the US and China. Deng Xiaoping says he too hopes for improvements, but maintains that "it is up to the US to take the initiative."

Martial law troops which have remained on duty on overpasses and at crossroads are withdrawn (October 30), and troops at Tiananmen Square are replaced by armed police. Some troops remain in Beijing and suburbs, however.

Fifth Plenum of the Thirteenth Central Committee concludes (November 9) a session intended to chart China's course through 1991. It accepts Deng Xiaoping's resignation from his major remaining official postion, that of chairman of the Central Military Commission, and appoints Party Secretary Jiang Zemin to the postion. However, the session is primarily devoted to attempts to meet the economic crisis facing the country. Five problems are targeted as critical—inflation, money oversupply, budget deficits, overheated growth, and industrial and agricultural maladjustments. Methods to be used to solve problems are vague.

Appendix Four

Special Chronology of Events During the Pro-Democracy Movement, April - July, 1989

(Compiled from newspaper, magazine, and broadcast
sources and translation service accounts)

In early April

The Central Advisory Commission denies a report by a Hongkong magazine that a group of its elderly revolutionaries including Chen Yun, Bo Yibo, (ceremonial) President of China and Central Military Commission Vice Chairman Yang Shangkun, and Wang Zhen, a vice-president, have joined Deng Xiaoping to form "a group to look after affairs of state behind the scenes. . . . "

April 5

Beijing University students defy official ban and hold meeting observing the thirteenth anniversary of the Tiananmen Incident (in which supporters of Deng Xiaoping fought police attempting to halt their observance of Zhou Enlai's death). Meeting is to seek ways for speeding democratic reforms but participants are reported in foreign press as saying they have lost hope. On April 3 Premier Li Peng refused to consider democratic changes, saying that change in the near future would undermine stability.

April 15

Hu Yaobang dies, reportedly of a heart attack suffered April 8 during Politburo meeting. Hu was once heir apparent to Deng Xiaoping, but was ousted in disgrace as general secretary of the Party in 1987. (See January 1987, Appendix III.) A veteran of the Long March, he was especially remembered for his success while Party secretary in reversing more than three million condemnatory verdicts delivered during the Cultural Revolution which destroyed the reputations of more than a hundred million people, and for his support of Deng Xiaoping's reforms.

Upon his death pro-democracy Beijing students disregard their and the Party's former opposition to him. They choose to remember him as a friend of intellectuals and of reform and immediately begin gathering to honor him. They make seven demands: a reevaluation of Hu's dismissal; punishment of official corruption; reappraisal of 1983 and 1987 campaigns against intellectuals; rehabilitation of victims of those campaigns; freedom of speech and press; better treatment for intellectuals; and restoration of the right to hold demonstrations.

Activities center on Tiananmen Square, where mass gatherings, a sit-in, and a hunger strike to press student demands will continue until students are forced out by troops in the June Fourth Massacre.

April 17–21

Concurrently with mourning Hu, students begin (April 17) a series of marches and demonstrations that are to continue in Beijing and many other Chinese cities at moderate to great strength until the movement is crushed on June 4. At various times during this mourning period the students march on Zhongnanhai, the compound near Tiananmen Square where Party leaders live and work—an unheard-of affront. They are resisted by guards and several dozen beaten.

April 18

In the first major event of what is to become the Pro-Democracy Movement, several thousand students hold sit-in and demonstrate in Tiananmen Square, demanding rehabilitation of Hu and various reforms to bring about a more democratic government.

April 19

Students hold huge sit-in outside Great Hall of the People and urge Deng to retire.

April 21

On the evening of this day before Hu's funeral, well over 100,000 people come to Tiananmen Square to mourn him.

April 22

When the government announces that Tiananmen Square will be closed during Hu Yaobang's funeral in the Great Hall, 100,000 students occupy the square and force government to back down.

At the funeral, which is shown on national television, Party leaders lavish praise upon Hu. There is no reference to Hu's having been strongly criticized and dismissed in 1987. But he is lauded (perhaps in the hope of defusing the rapidly growing Pro-Democracy Movement) for developing and supporting modern interpretations of Marxism and for his work for economic reform and opening to the outside world.

April 24

Tens of thousands of Beijing students begin boycott of classes in support of Pro-Democracy Movement and of their demands for a dialogue with the government. Boycotts will spread across the nation until most universities are affected.

April 26

In today's edition, *People's Daily* runs a harsh editorial, "Take a Clear Stand Against the Upheaval!," condemning the student democracy movement and accusing students of a planned conspiracy against the government. It says in part: "All the comrades of the Party and the whole nation must understand clearly that, if we do not resolutely stop this unrest, our state will have no calm days. Our reform and modernization depend on this struggle, and the future of our state and nation depend on it."

Several correspondents report that Deng Xiaoping ordered the editorial and that he has ordered the hard line being followed. He has been widely quoted as saying that "if we have to shed some blood" that would be all right and that the world would not seriously object. His June 9 speech indicates that this attribution is probably correct, but Deng's prediction of the world's reaction was seriously in error—at least in the short run . . .

Also on this day, 20,000 troops are sent to Beijing in the hope of preventing continued growth of the democracy movement. Since Hu's death, there have been demonstrations similar to Beijing's in numerous other Chinese cities, including Shanghai and nearby cities, some involving more than 50,000 students, workers, and others; with very few exceptions, all the demonstrations are peaceful and orderly.

April 27

Students (who were intimidated by similar threats and criticisms during the unrest of 1987) defy the implied threats in the *People's Daily* April 26 editorial by holding a fourteen-hour march for democracy and against corruption. Troops and security forces are overwhelmed. Students ask again for a re-evaluation of Hu's dismissal and for a larger education budget and for more factual and complete media coverage of the student movement.

The protest involves about 150,000 students, workers, and others, plus hundreds of thousands of spectators, and reveals the development of a political awareness among the populace as a whole which had not manifested itself before. The demonstration is probably the largest, and surely the most humiliating, protest ever (to that date—but see May 17) against the government. National television does not mention the event. The government continues to speak of the protests as the work of "a very, very few people who want to spread chaos."

To the general surprise of students and public alike, in what is seen as a retreat the government agrees to the students' demands for discussions. Officials insist, however, that the government must choose student representatives, demonstrators must return to their campuses and be "reasonable," and that all talks must be conducted "through appropriate channels. . . ." Conditions are unacceptable to students.

April 28

There is an even bigger march today, involving about 200,000 people.

April 29

Tens of millions of Chinese watch as Yuan Mu, a spokesman for the

State Council, and He Dongchang, vice-chairman of the National Education Committee, meet with forty student representatives from sixteen universities in Beijing in a "dialogue," one of the demands students have been pressing for several days. The officials were relatively low-ranking, however—not at the vice-premier or Politburo level as the students demanded, and the students participating were selected by the government. (See April 27.) Also, the broadcast was not live, as the students wanted, and there were complaints later that the government showed only an edited version of the meeting. (See also reference to meeting between dissidents' leaders and Li Peng on May 18.)

Spokesman Yuan Mu says Premier Li accepted that the demonstrators have the same goals for improvement as the government and the Party—a dramatic reversal of the government's charges in the April 26 *People's Daily* editorial. Yuan said, according to *China Daily*, that "Premier Li Peng had entrusted him to explain [that the editorial] was directed against the unlawful acts of a few people, not at the masses of students"—again a reversal of the editorial's condemnations. The spokesmen's answers were mostly innocuous or repeated information already known. Class boycott continues.

April 30

Student talks with officials continue, today with government representatives Beijing Mayor Chen Xitong and Beijing Party Secretary Li Ximing.

May 1

Country is quiet on this national holiday, although student talks with Beijing officials continue through their second and final day.

May 2

Disappointed with the results of talks with officials, students submit new list of ten demands to National People's Congress Standing Committee outlining the conditions under which the students believe talks should be conducted. They continue to ask for student-selected representatives; for government representatives who have decision-making powers; and for live television coverage and attendance of Chinese and foreign reporters.

May 3

The government expresses willingness to continue talks with students, but rejects their conditions as "unreasonable, emotionally impulsive, and menacing to the government." The government spokesman claimed, according to *China Daily*, that the conditions "showed that a small minority of people were inciting the students behind the scenes."

May 4

Mass protest observes the seventieth anniversary of May Fourth Movement, the first protest in modern history by Chinese intellectuals (see "May Fourth Movement" in the Mini-Encyclopedia). Crowds exceed 100,000 in Beijing and 20,000 in Shanghai, with smaller crowds in many other cities. Demonstrations create another serious embarrassment for the government, since they coincide with first-ever meeting in China of the Asian Development Bank.

At ADB meeting, Zhao's speech includes passages on reform intended primarily for students' ears, including indications that the leadership (which is known to have approved his speech) now accepts that protest doesn't automatically generate instability; praise for the students' "rational" demands; and recognition that students are not opposing the present system but seek only to improve it. The speech is of a tone quite opposite to the April 26 editorial so resented by the students.

May 5

Inexplicably, student leaders call off class boycott, although official newspapers for first time have given extensive coverage to demonstrations in Beijing and throughout China. (Boycott is reinstated a few days later.)

May 9

More than 1,000 journalists from about thirty newspapers and press services petition All-China Journalists Association for right to report accurately. (Association is a government organization which grants journalist status.)

May 11

5,000 bicycling students parade in support of journalists' petition presented yesterday.

May 13

Pro-Democracy Movement is electrified when students occupy Tiananmen Square and about 1,000 begin hunger strikes; they protest "false charges against student demonstrations" and support movement demands. Strikers swell to 3,000 in twenty-four hours and there is great outpouring of support and sympathy from the people.

May 14

Lengthy talks between about fifty students and three ministerial level officials held, without agreement.

May 15

Mikhail S. Gorbachev, president of the Presidium of the Supreme Soviet of the Soviet Union and general secretary of the Soviet Communist Party, arrives for a long-planned and historic summit meeting with Chinese leaders. Gorbachev is welcomed enthusiastically because of his political reforms in the Soviet Union; one poster says, "Russia Has Gorbachev—Who Does China Have?" Embarrassed officials must repeatedly change schedules and itineraries to avoid 150,000 students and workers outside the Great Hall of the People, site of the summit, and other tens of thousands along the original route.

May 16

Hundreds of thousands again march to Tiananmen Square; they are joined by many staff members of *People's Daily* and intellectuals from research institutes, universities, and government offices.

May 17

Zhao makes early morning visit to square and says April 26 editorial was too harsh. He asks students to leave.

The motivation, determination, and example of 3,000 students in their fifth day of hunger strikes for democracy inspire the people of Beijing to make May 17 a historic day for China. Waves of Beijingers—more than a million—peacefully march for basic reforms in their government and essential changes in their lives. Similar, if smaller, demonstrations are reported from more than twenty other cities. Most factories, stores, and offices are empty, in what is essentially a general strike, and most of the thousands of marching groups carry banners boldly identifying their work units. Clearly, the Pro-Democracy Movement has now reached far beyond intellectual, theoretical circles, presenting the government with a united front of citizens seeking change that it has never encountered before.

May 18

Crowds even larger than yesterday pour from homes, offices, and factories to support hunger strikers and the Pro-Democracy Movement in drenching rain. By today, over 2,000 hunger strikers had fainted and been revived in aid stations and hospitals; most returned to Tiananmen Square and continued fasting.

About 1,000 people from China Central Television are among today's marchers. Later, CCTV broadcasts extensive and unusually frank coverage of the day's march and other events in the Pro-Democracy Movement.

One program segment covers the first meeting between Li Peng and the dissidents' leaders, held earlier today, in which he reveals anger at and lack of understanding of the strikers and the movement. He opens by saying, "Today, we will talk only about one thing: how to get the fasting students out of their present plight." He grants that questions raised by students are legitimate and many of their actions are correct, but lectures them peevishly on their behavior and the damage he feels they are causing. Students try to press him, but he refuses to discuss any of their demands.

May 17 and 18 saw demonstrations reported from twenty other cities. The number of hunger strikers in Shanghai grew to 300 and the crowd there reached 400,000. Crowds of over 100,000 marched in Hangzhou, where hundreds of students were fasting, and in Xian.

May 19

Zhao Ziyang visits hunger strikers in Tiananmen Square before dawn, where he makes his later much-quoted statement, "I came too late, too late. We deserve your criticism and we are not here to ask for your forgiveness." According to Xinhua, he also said "You have good intentions. You want our country to become better. The problems you have raised will eventually be resolved. But things are complicated, and there must be a process to resolve those problems." He begs them to end hunger strike, saying "You should live to see the realization of the four modernizations in China." Li Peng comes close behind Zhao, but says nothing and remains only a few minutes.

Crowds today are somewhat smaller than yesterday and the day before, but still number in the hundreds of thousands.

Hunger strike ends in evening.

Politburo meets. Without explaining why Zhao Ziyang is not present or speaking, Li Peng makes angry midnight speech to senior cadres, which is televised to the nation and the world, demanding that students end their protests and occupation of Tiananmen Square and claiming that the hunger strikers are being used as "hostages" by a "handful of persons" who wish to overthrow the government and "totally negate the people's democratic dictatorship"; he states the charges of subversion and treason in several different ways. He grants that students' motives are sincere, but says the government will deal with their concerns later, that stability and end of turmoil are paramount. It is reported later that Zhao refused to make the speech, or even to attend. The speech is widely resented.

May 20

Government imposes martial law on some areas of Beijing during morning and students resume hunger strike. (The first troops move into television and newspaper offices to "protect" them, as government begins the propaganda effort that will continue to grow after June 4.) Martial law cannot be enforced, however. Crowds estimated to be the largest ever block routes with their bodies and primitive barricades, a tactic that will be used repeatedly in the coming days. Troops refuse to move against the people and remain stationary or retreat. Tear gas and water cannon equipment is in evidence but is not used.

Half a million protesters are reported in Shanghai, 300,000 in Xian.

There is no word from the government except constant repetition on TV of Li Peng's speech of last night, and it becomes more and more apparent that a power struggle is occurring at the highest levels. Involved Party members report privately to journalists that Deng, though he has no official standing in the Party hierarchy, has essentially taken over and forbidden Zhao to exercise any of his powers as Party secretary, and the Central Military Commission is reported to have stripped Zhao of his power to control troops. Zhao retains his titles, however.

May 21–24

Military stalemate and political struggle reportedly become more intense, but country receives no official information or reassurance of any kind and no senior official is seen in public. However, Li Peng on May 22 takes personal charge of propaganda and dismisses all leaders of the propaganda apparatus, replacing them with hard-liners. Delay and silence emphasize the seriousness of the problems that are keeping the factions apart. Clues rather than specific information indicate that hard-liners may be gaining upper hand.

Demonstrations also continue, but, for the most part, at a much lower pitch, although a crowd thought to be something less than a million marched in defiance of martial law on May 24.

Daily life, though hardly normal, is reported to be less disturbed.

May 25

Li Peng returns to public view in a showpiece televised meeting with several minor and previously credentialed new ambassadors and asserts that the Chinese government is stable, capable, and in control. The meeting is seen as a sign that Li is winning in the hidden power struggle still going on; students continue to support Zhao. Li tells diplomats that troops have not forced an advance "because the government is the people's government and the People's Liberation Army is the people's own army."

Beijing newspapers carry a letter from top echelons of the People's Liberation Army stating that troops came to Beijing "in accordance with the strong wishes of the masses," though it gives no explanation of why the masses are preventing troops from carrying out their assignment. It also claims that the turmoil is becoming more serious.

May 26

Chen Yun, chair of a meeting of the Central Advisory Commission (a body of retired leaders, mostly hard-liners), says that "At such a critical time we old comrades must stand up and, along with the entire Party, boldly expose the conspiracy of the very, very small number of people who want chaos and . . . fight against them without making concessions." Meeting blames unrest in part on a failure to stress Marxist ideological education. (See also first item under April, concerning Chen Yun and an advisory group of elders.)

May 27

Student leaders propose end to occupation of Tiananmen Square by May 30. They cite exhaustion after six weeks of protest, wretched sanitary and living conditions, and the fact that Party and government leaders are so engrossed in a power struggle that no progress is likely. A vote on withdrawal is called for, but some students begin leaving immediately.

May 29

Only about 10,000 students remain in Tiananmen Square, most of them from other cities, and railroad officials say that the number of students leaving now exceeds the number arriving. Those remaining, however, reject their leaders' recommendation of two days ago that they end occupation of the square. They plan to remain until at least June 20, when a session of the Standing Committee of the National People's Congress is scheduled.

Students unveil a statue called the Goddess of Democracy in Tiananmen Square. National television calls it "an insult to our national dignity" because of its resemblance to the Statue of Liberty.

June 1

The six weeks of demonstrations and sit-ins appear to be winding down. It is already clear that the Pro-Democracy Movement, though short-lived, will be long remembered as a spontaneous people's campaign, without a prominent leader, of a kind not seen in China since the May Fourth Movement (see Mini-Encyclopedia) and perhaps stronger than any other such movement in history.

The government will in days to come attempt to portray the movement as a "counterrevolutionary rebellion" led by a very few people who tricked naive students. However, this effort cannot obscure the fact that, misled or not, the students never advocated overthrow of the government or abandonment of socialism and that the government several times expressed agreement with their aims.

Demonstrations ranging in size from tens to hundreds of thousands are reported over time in more than eighty large to medium-sized cities throughout China, including Shanghai and several surrounding cities, Tianjin, Wuhan, Chengdu, Kunming, and others, plus the special economic zones, Macao, and Hongkong. Most demonstrations were without incident, but there was some rioting and looting in Shanghai, Xian (where martial law was declared for twenty-four hours), Chengdu, and Changsha. Chinese news agency reports generally emphasized that students were not involved in violence.

China Daily reports that: "Since mid-April, most of the undergraduate and graduate students in China's more than 1,000 institutions of higher learning have boycotted classes in support of the demonstrations and the hunger strike staged by students in Beijing [confirming a far wider impact of the strike than had been announced previously].... According to incomplete statistics from the Beijing Railway Station, more than 300,000 college students from other provinces dropped their studies to come to Beijing since the beginning of May."

The turnout of the general public in support of the students and contributions of money, food, and supplies have decreased markedly in recent days, as the government has made strenuous efforts in factories and offices to assure that people observe the prohibitions against demonstrating.

The remaining students are determined to make the government take a stand, however. If the government compromises, the Pro-Democracy Movement will gain. If the government represses the students, it will be saying not only to the students but to the millions of citizens who sympathize with them that the government and Party are contemptuous of the people's opinions and difficulties, and this will lend further support to reform demands.

June 3

The government chooses repression. Showing by their remarks and reactions that they are humiliated, angered, frustrated—and frightened—by the persistence and force of the Pro-Democracy Movement, and disregarding that the problem is even now solving itself as the movement rapidly disintegrates, hard-liners continue to insist on imposing their will on demonstrators and finally prevail after a weeks-long struggle among the national leadership. Orders are given that the student movement be ended, Tiananmen Square be cleared, and martial law be made effective in those areas of Beijing where it has been declared.

Two thousand unarmed troops from various locations about the city try to reach Tiananmen Square in the afternoon and evening of June 3. Some tear gas and clubs are used, but although they beat many protesters the troops are routed by a quickly formed crowd of tens of thousands of students and citizens, the largest turnout for several days. Late in the evening, tanks and heavily armed troops in armored personnel carriers begin arriving, setting the stage for the June Fourth Massacre.

June 4

Large numbers of troops move from positions around the city toward Tiananmen Square, beginning in the early hours. They are no longer deterred by the large but unarmed crowds on the street; instead, in the face of token resistance from the unarmed crowds, troops disperse them with live ammunition fired overhead or, frequently, directly into the crowds. No attempt is made to use tear gas, water cannon, or other forms of crowd control, nor are people specifically warned that troops will use deadly force. The horrified and infuriated crowds resist with rocks, Molotov cocktails, and any other weapons that come to hand. Troops reach Tiananmen Square about 4:30 in the morning, and students remaining there leave without further resistance.

In the next few hours a large but still unknown number of people, mostly students and other civilians, are killed by gunfire and, as some maintain, by tanks which deliberately ran victims down. The government forbids hospitals and crematoriums to give death figures. (See notes on casualties under June 6–8 and June 30.)

As the day wears on, more troops move into the center of Beijing and strengthen their control, patrolling on foot and in armored vehicles and sometimes firing at crowds or at random. There are many burned-out vehicles on main roads, evidence of the people's determined resistance last night, which continues at a much lower level.

When news of the Beijing crackdown spreads, so do protests. Demonstrations come to a head on June 4 and 5 in Chengdu, capital of Sichuan Province, where the situation had been tense for weeks. Perhaps 50 people are killed and 100 or more seriously injured.

June 5

The Party and the government issue a joint statement about yesterday's events that borders on the hysterical in view of the quarter-million troops holding the armed and unresisting city in their grip, but it is calculated to serve as a basis for the propaganda defense being launched. As reported in *People's Daily*, the statement claims that Beijing is now in

a "critical state" as a result of the "shocking counterrevolutionary riot
. . . [instigated by a handful of people with ulterior motives and aimed
at] negating the leadership of the Communist Party, denouncing the
socialist system, and overthrowing the People's Republic." No remorse
and no regrets are expressed.

June 6–8

Tension increases as secrecy continues concerning the leadership of the
country. Growing rumors that deep divisions have spread to the army
lead to rumors of military clashes between hard-liners and moderates,
and of possible civil war. Troops and vehicles still travel in groups and
fire on remaining protesters, but citizen resistance has ebbed.

Other countries are unanimous in their condemnation of China's leaders' bloodthirstiness. Restrictions of varying severity are imposed by
nearly all non-communist countries on economic, diplomatic, and
cultural relations with China. China reminds the world that it has never
been, and is not now, concerned with the opinion of foreigners.

Thousands of foreign tourists, workers, and diplomats are fleeing
China, particularly Beijing.

Yuan Mu, a frequent government spokesman, estimates on television
that only 300 were killed and 6,000 wounded on June 3–4, with more
than 5,000 of the wounded being soldiers; he does not specify the
number of military deaths, but implies large military casualties in saying
that only 23 students died. (An official later gave revised figures which
reduced the number of civilian deaths, increased the number of wounded
to about 9,000; he also appeared to reduce the number of military deaths
claimed, saying that "dozens" of soldiers died, but increased military
injuries to more than 6,000. See June 30.)

When spokesman Yuan Mu is interviewed by NBC anchorman Tom
Brokaw some days later, Brokaw says that he finds astonishing Yuan's
statements claiming a lack of violence in clearing Tiananmen Square,
citing thousands of feet of videotape showing otherwise. Yuan implies
that the video pictures are false, saying "The development of modern
technology has provided this possibility for some persons. They can
record longer videotapes than you just mentioned to distort the real
situation."

Independent casualty estimates reported several weeks later, based on
compilations by diplomats, news services, and others, place the probable number of deaths at 400–600, including no more than about a dozen

soldiers and police. It is noteworthy that in the intense propaganda campaign supporting the government crackdown a large number of military deaths continue to be claimed, but the human interest stories concerning bereaved families, etc., always focus on the same six or eight soldiers.

On June 8 Li Peng appears on television, the first time a Chinese leader has spoken since May 25. Li congratulates the military on its crackdown on students and civilians, and demands that leaders of independent student and worker unions turn themselves in to police. Mass arrests are expected soon.

June 9

With a group of elderly colleagues, Deng Xiaoping appears on television for the first time since Gorbachev's visit, ending the many rumors concerning his death or critical illness. The appearance of these figures on this occasion, to congratulate martial law commanders on putting down what is now labeled a "counterrevolutionary rebellion," indicates that they are now the de facto power center in China; *Far Eastern Economic Review* headlines its cover story on the occasion "The Triumph of Senility." (See notes at beginning of this appendix and at May 26 concerning the working of elders behind the scenes.)

The group of elders is a rump group, demonstrating the strength of personal relationships in Chinese affairs and that Deng's often–asserted dedication to the rule of law, not men, is as pragmatic as his devotion to reforms. He apparently was forced to bypass existing bodies and procedures to get the crackdown he wanted, and could call only on the old comrades to get some kind of legitimacy for his actions. The group includes the three men still in conservative favor who are on the Standing Committee of the Politburo, but few of the others are even on the Central Committee; they are retired from all posts and have no right to active participation in Party or government affairs. Except for the three now in official leadership positions, their average age is 82.

Deng's speech to the troop commanders—not televised and, in fact, kept mostly secret for about two weeks—is unrepentant, mirroring the same resentment, lack of understanding, and extreme apprehension shown in the *People's Daily* April 26 editorial, which he is said to have ordered. He expresses several times his gratitude to his "senior comrades," who, he says, understood what others did not, that "Actually, what we faced was not just some ordinary people who were misguided, but also a rebellious clique and a large quantity of the dregs of society [who] wanted to overthrow our state and Party."

The speech has become a major tool in apparent attempts to create around Deng the sort of personality cult that surrounded Mao and everyone from senior officials to the lowest workers is being ordered to study it.

In Shanghai, tens of thousands of citizens led by students mourn those killed in the June Fourth Massacre, defying auxiliary police intent on curbing the observance.

June 10

Government begins nationwide crackdown on dissenters with 400 arrests of those referred to continuously in a new propaganda campaign as thugs, ruffians, hooligans, counterrevolutionaries, people with a deep-seated hatred of the Communist Party, troublemakers, scoundrels, bad elements. . . . (See later arrest estimates under July 16.)

China is attempting to rewrite history on a scale that recalls the Hitlerian Big Lie of World War II (see term in the Mini-Encyclopedia). The government claims, for example, that military force was necessary because there was a "counterrevolutionary rebellion" going on, although it presents no evidence; this theme was established in Li Peng's speech on May 19 before martial law was declared, when he repeatedly charged that overthrow of the government was the true intent of the student movement. Government also claims there were not many casualties and most of those were soldiers, but cites no names or figures, although this information should be readily available from military records. There are constant television pictures of students attacking tanks but none showing the carnage wrought by the troops and soundtracks have been edited to eliminate sounds of troops firing. Soldiers are shown driving through the city with loudspeakers on trucks blaring, "We love the people, we love the capital"—all the while keeping their assault rifles aimed at the sidewalks.

June 12

Government bans unofficial pro-democracy organizations and gives police the right to shoot persons they believe to be rioters.

June 13

Television displays names, pictures, and personal details concerning twenty-one student leaders police are seeking who are said to be members of the illegal Autonomous Students Union of Beijing Universities and are accused of "inciting and organizing counterrevolutionary rebellion in Beijing."

June 14

The propaganda department of the Beijing Communist Party issues an official account of the "counterrevolutionary rebellion," and the events of June 4 and 5. The account claims: a "certain small group of people didn't stop their efforts to create unrest even for a single day, nor did they swerve in the slightest from their aim of overturning the leadership of the Communist Party"; only four people participated in the Tiananmen Square hunger strike; the troops used utmost restraint and showed superhuman patience; "there is no truth to the so-called 'Tiananmen bloodbath' "; the total civilian casualties amounted to 100 deaths and nearly 1,000 injuries, while 100 soldiers and police were killed and thousands were injured.

The *New York Times* correspondent Nicholas D. Kristof writes that the official account, "while it is sure to be widely circulated in China in the coming weeks... bears little relationship to the scenes that actually took place on the Avenue of Eternal Peace ... and in other parts of Beijing, as witnessed by this reporter and other correspondents." And, he might have added, by viewers and readers all over the world.

June 21

Three men, all workers, are publicly executed in Shanghai for allegedly helping set fire to a train on June 6. Show trials attended by thousands are being held, the first use of such public intimidation since the death of Mao.

Reportedly on orders from Deng, who is said to be concerned with increasing international revulsion, arrests and sentences are rarely reported beyond this week. (See later estimates under July 16.) Arrests are said to be proceeding, work units have reinstated mandatory "political study sessions," persons not associated with demonstrations are detained on other political allegations, and, in general, ideological orthodoxy is being imposed to an extent not seen since the Cultural Revolution.

June 22

State Security Ministry arrests ten "Kuomintang secret agents" who "had a hand in" turmoil, according to *China Daily*.

June 23

Seven men described as "rioters" executed in Beijing.

June 24

As expected for weeks, Zhao Ziyang is "dismissed" from post of Party General Secretary and all other Party posts, indicating that he refused to admit mistakes and resign. However, he continues to be a member of the Party, leaving him subject to further discipline later if the Party wishes. (He was also removed on June 30 from his post of vice-chairman of the State Central Military Commission.) The Party announcement says that he "made the mistake of supporting the turmoils [the student demonstrations] and splitting the Party, and he had unshirkable responsibilities for the shaping-up of the turmoils. . . . He took a passive approach to the adherence to the four cardinal principles and opposition to bourgeois liberalization, and gravely neglected Party building, cultural and ethical development, and ideological and political work. . . ."

Zhao is replaced by Jiang Zemin, former mayor and Party leader in Shanghai. Hu Qili, the former propaganda chief and a Zhao associate, is dismissed from the Standing Committee and his other posts; his status with respect to Party membership is not clear. Two other Zhao associates in the Party secretariat are purged. At the same time, the Standing Committee is enlarged from five to six; there are now no active reformists among the members—Jiang Zemin (new), Li Peng, Song Ping (new), Li Ruihuan (new), Qiao Shi, and Yao Yilin.

June 25

Party's Central Commission for Discipline Inspection calls for a purge of Party members who did not oppose the student movement. Criminal penalties are called for.

June 26

Consideration of a law expanding press freedoms, in preparation for two years or more, is indefinitely postponed.

June 29

Postponed meeting of the Standing Committee of the National People's

Congress convenes and approves military crackdown on student movement.

June 30

The most extensive report to date on the "counterrevolutionary rebellion" is authorized by the State Council and delivered by Chen Xitong, mayor of Beijing, to the Standing Committee of the National People's Congress. He presents revised casualty figures, claiming that only about 200 civilians were killed, including 36 students, and more than 3,000 were injured. "Dozens" of police and soldiers were killed, and more than 6,000 were injured. (See earlier government and independent estimates under June 6–8.)

His report is the major attempt to defend the government's claims that force was necessary because there was a "counterrevolutionary rebellion" but it presents no evidence. Neither does it contain any support for the claim that "A tiny handful of people both inside and outside the Party . . . echoing the strategy of western countries . . . colluded with foreign forces, ganged up themselves at home and made ideological, public opinion, and organizational preparation for years to stir up turmoils in China, overthrow the leadership by the Communist Party, and subvert the social People's Republic. . . . The entire course of brewing, premeditating, and launching the turmoil . . . bore the salient feature of mutual support and coordination between a handful of people at home and abroad."

July 1

Nation observes the sixty-eighth anniversary of founding of Communist Party of China and wreaths are laid for soldiers killed during the June Fourth Massacre. Yesterday, Beijing's Mayor Chen Xitong said that civilians killed "deserved the punishment," commenting on the verdict of national leaders that civilian victims cannot be remembered in traditional mourning by their families.

July 3

Li Peng claims in visit with Chinese-American visitor that the government did not use crowd control measures instead of live ammunition in the June Fourth Massacre because China does not have enough suitable equipment and supplies; his statement is immediately disputed. The visitor said Li told him soldiers wished to avoid bloodshed because "they wanted peace and they knew the students' intentions were good."

July 11

End of martial law not foreseen at present, State Council spokesman says; implies it will continue until "rebels" who allegedly took soldiers' weapons are rounded up.

July 16

Arrest and execution information is vague. Chinese and foreign observers say that arrests, executions, and widespread purges are continuing, but are no longer being announced, an indication of sensitivity to foreign opinion even though government denies any concern. There are continuing announcements or indications that officials are being replaced. A *Beijing Evening News* story today includes discrete statistics through June which, when compiled, indicate that about 3,600 persons have actually been sentenced in the continuing roundups, but it is unclear whether this is a national total. The latest official figures—more than two weeks old—show over 2,000 persons arrested; twenty-nine executions have been announced since June 4, but it is not known whether all have involved people from the Pro-Democracy Movement. A dissident who escaped to France says a cooperating Chinese official reports that arrests of intellectuals are widespread and growing, having reached about 10,000 in Beijing and 120,000 nationwide.

July 28

More than 1,100 Chinese students from over two hundred American universities meet in Chicago at the first Congress of Chinese Students in the United States to consider ways to keep the Pro-Democracy Movement alive. The group forms the Federation of the Independent Chinese Student Unions in the United States; Liu Yong Chuan, a doctoral student at Stanford University, is elected president.

(Events related to the Pro-Democracy movement which occured after July 28 are included in the general chronology in Appendix Three.)

Appendix Five

Ten Books for Understanding China Better

(Not necessarily "The Ten Best Books About China," but certainly ten outstanding and mostly recent titles that readers would find very useful in satisfying their curiosity about China.)

Barmé, Geremie, and John Minford. *Seeds of Fire: Chinese Voices of Conscience*. Hill and Wang, 1988, 491 pages. A collection of intellectuals' and dissidents' essays, prison diaries, cartoons, stories, poems, and miscellany, some informative, many quite powerful. Incredibly, it has no index, not even an index of persons whose work is represented, but it is a source for rich browsing.

Bonavia, David. *The Chinese—A Portrait by David Bonavia*. Penguin Books, 1982, 317 pages; the 1989 "revised" edition is apparently changed only by an epilogue dated several months before Bonavia's death in 1988, but at least the book is available again. Bonavia, a fluent, observant, and very rewarding writer, captures the character and personality of China and the Chinese. He was Beijing correspondent for *The Times* and on the *Far Eastern Economic*

Review staff in China and Hongkong.

Harding, Harry. *China's Second Revolution: Reform after Mao*. Brookings Institution, 1987, 369 pages. Largely straightforward, factual reporting on economic and political reform; with copious interpretative and source notes.

Hinton, William. *Fanshen: A Documentary of Revolution in a Chinese Village*. Monthly Review Press, 1966, 637 pages. Hinton first went to China in 1937, and has visited and worked there numerous times since. He worked as a tractor technician for six years in Long Bow, the village followed in *Fanshen*. In an introductory note Hinton wrote: "Every revolution creates new words. The Chinese revolution created a whole new vocabulary. A most important word in this vocabulary was *fanshen*. Literally, it means 'to turn the body,' or 'to turn over.' To China's hundreds of millions of landless and land-poor peasants it meant to stand up, to throw off the landlord yoke, to gain land, stock, implements, and houses. But it meant much more than this. It meant to throw off superstition and study science, to abolish 'word blindness' and learn to read, to cease considering women as chattels and establish equality between the sexes, to do away with appointed village magistrates and replace them with elected councils. It meant to enter a new world. That is why this book is called *Fanshen*. It is the story of how the peasants of Long Bow Village built a new world."

   Fanshen has been called an epic, a classic, an extraordinary book—and it is all of these. Dense with beautifully written impressions, details, conversations, reflections, explanations, descriptions, history, folklore, and more. It is a gratifying read and an ideal introduction to the peasant mentality and to the complex problems of the shift to communism in rural post-liberation China.

Hinton, William. *Shenfan: The Continuing Revolution in a Chinese Village*. Random House, 1983, 785 pages. In *Shenfan* Hinton returns to Long Bow in 1971 after 20 years, to renew his friendships with Long Bow peasants and to hear from them the peasants' view of life after liberation, including their experiences in the Great Leap Forward and the Cultural Revolution.

Hsu, Immanuel C. Y. *The Rise of Modern China*. Oxford University Press, third edition, 1983, 934 pages. A well-written, well-arranged, and well-indexed reference for answering a variety of questions, with emphasis on the period 1800–1982.

Leys, Simon. Leys, a lover of China and a passionate, vitriolic, and effective critic of its present political system, has written four books on contemporary Chinese culture and politics—*The Burning Forest, The Chairman's New Clothes: Mao and the Cultural Revolution, Chinese Shadows,* and *Broken Images.* They are each worth reading for themselves, but any one will give a spine-tingling commentary on the government that Leys says is "cretinizing the most intelligent people on earth."

Pan, Lynn. *The New Chinese Revolution.* Contemporary Books, 1988, 248 pages. This Chinese-born, British-educated writer covers many of the same topics as *China's Unfinished Revolution,* but in both a more rounded and a more personal way. A first choice for a lay reader's survey of contemporary China.

Rodzinski, Witold. *The People's Republic of China: A Concise Political History.* The Free Press, 1988, 304 pages. A lively, unusually readable account of China's political development after 1949, and related social and economic matters; by a political historian who is also a former Polish ambassador to China.

Zhang Xinxin and Sang Ye. *Chinese Lives: An Oral History of Contemporary China.* Pantheon Books, 1987, 368 pages. (Translated from sketches first published in Chinese periodicals, where they created a sensation.) A collection of informal interviews with ordinary, anonymous Chinese of all ages and conditions—a prison warden, a beautiful woman, a steel mill worker, shop managers, peasants, newlyweds. Translations sometimes jar with British and American slang, but the sketches are both pertinent and impertinent, and full of glimpses into everyday concerns.

Index

TEACHING CHINA'S LOST GENERATION:
Foreign Experts in the PRC
by Tani Barlow and Donald M. Lowe

". . . a colorful and unusual. . . portrait of students at Shanghai Teachers' College who are trying to come to terms with America." **—Los Angeles Times**

"A perceptive book, which shows two 'foreign experts' striving to come to terms with China." **—Jonathan Spence, Professor of History, Yale University**

"In this lucid, honest and human book we are asked to share what might be called the post modern condition. If the modernists thought you couldn't go home again; Barlow and Lowe show that the invention of the world is an ongoing process of juxtaposing values, experiences, languages. Partially opaque, local and global, the task is to invent a new language to understand and form this cosmopolitan reality. TEACHING CHINA'S LOST GENERATION is an illuminating step forward."
—Paul Rabinow, Professor of Anthropology, U.C. Berkeley

"The best I have read anywhere on Asian youth." **—Jerome Ch'en, Professor of History, York University**

Tani Barlow and Donald Lowe spent 1981-82 teaching American literature and society at Shanghai Teachers' College. Perceptive observers, their lively account supplies us with a thoughtful, informative look at the views and attitudes of a generation that will be leading China in the future. Many of their students were members of China's "lost generation" who came of age during the Cultural Revolution. This new edition follows their student's progress through the past half decade.
China Books, 1987, 288 pp..$9.95